Why Buy This Book?

"Education would be so much more effective if its purpose were to ensure that by the time they leave school every boy and girl should know how much they don't know, and be imbued with a life long desire to know it."

—Sir William Haley
Chairman of the BBC, Editor of *The Times* of London

FAQs about *The Lazy Man's Way to Riches*

Q. "I've read the other Self-Help/Business books—Why should I read *The Lazy Man's Way to Riches* also?"

A. It picks up where the others leave off—we don't just tell you what to do and leave you there like other books—we show you, help you, and guide you so you <u>finally</u> achieve your life long goals.

Q. "How do you do that?"

A. You get an Internet workbook free with this book—that takes you, step by step, from where you are to where you want to go—both personally and professionally. And, it is interactive. Just Imagine—now you can learn on-line and be connected to the author and other experts. Finally you can get all the help you need to become the success you deserve!

Q. "I'm not lazy—or a man, what's in it for me?"

A. The title refers to Joe Karbo. This is his story—how he overcame a debilitating illness that sapped his physical energy to become a multi-millionaire. He developed simple techniques to work smarter because he couldn't work hard. The techniques work equally well for women.

Q. "Is there a philosophy behind the Lazy Man that's different from other books?"

A. Yes. We believe that adults need to <u>learn how to learn</u> again. We show you exactly how to do that—and then we teach you about new success tools and we show you how to use them.

Q. "Sounds exciting, why hasn't anyone done this before?"

A. It's taken us 10 years to bring this dream to reality. The technology just wasn't perfected until recently.

Q. "Is there a theme to the book?"

A. Yes, the theme is *"personal growth always precedes business or professional growth."* So if you want more you must first become more.

Q. "Who is this book written for?"

A. Those who are already successful but want to go to a higher plateau. It's written for those who work harder and now realize that they can't work any harder—so they want to work smarter. That's how you get Rich—in every way.

Q. "I don't have a computer, will this work for me?"

A. Without a computer to access the interactive workbook you will miss most of this program. Your public library has computers and great on-line access. Use theirs until you get your own computer.

Q. "Why do you call this a <u>program</u> rather than a book? Looks like a book to me."

A. The program includes the book you hold in your hand. And, it also includes a workbook, a newsletter, a readers forum, and more. And all of it linked to our "Lazy Man" Web site. It's a new way of learning.

Q. **"Tell me about the workbook—why would I want it?"**

A. The workbook is your key to success. It gives you forms, tools, tips, tests, and resources to learn the skills and techniques we teach you in the book. The workbook separates this program from all other books because it provides you with <u>everything</u> you need, now and for at least another year, to grow and prosper then grow some more. It's like having a personal success coach.

Q. **"How much extra does the workbook cost?"**

A. The *Roadmap to Riches* workbook is included in the price of this book. There is <u>no</u> extra cost.

Q. **"How do I get the Roadmap to Riches workbook?"**

A. You register on-line at: <u>http://www.thelazymansway.com</u>. Registration is quick and easy. As soon as you register, we will assign you a password to a private membership Web site where you will have access to the workbook.

Q. **"Tell me about the newsletter? What is it and how do I get it?"**

A. The newsletter is *The Game Plan for Success*™. It's published monthly and is considered a post-graduate course to take you to higher levels of success once you finish the Lazy Man program. We e-mail it to you monthly and/or you can read it on the Web site. We archive the old issues, which you are welcome to read any time. You get a 1-year subscription when you register your copy of *The Lazy Man's Way to Riches*. The newsletter *(The Game Plan for Success)* contains articles on the subjects in the Lazy Man program, new resources for you, interviews with top business and personal coaches, links to additional information you can use, and my editorials and essays.

Q. **"What is the readers forum and where is it?"**

A. The *Lazy Man's Readers Forum* is on the members' private Web site. The Forum is where you can log on and ask (or answer) questions of any subject in the Lazy Man's program. It is a place where you can have discussions with me or moderators who monitor the forum. We monitor the forum so it remains a place of value for everyone around the world who is in the program and on the same success journey we are all on.

ReCap—What's in it for you?

You will get the entire "Lazy Man" program when you buy this book.
"What does the entire program contain?" It contains all of the following:

1. You get *The Lazy Man's Way to Riches* book.	$19.95 Value
2. You also get the *Roadmap to Riches* E-Book.	$19.95 Value
3. You also get 1-year access to the confidential Membership Web site.	Annual $120.00 Value
4. You get a 1-year subscription to *The Game Plan for Success*™ Newsletter.	$120.00 Value
5. You also get membership in the "Lazy Man Forum" online.	$49.95 Value
6. You get 1-year subscription to Mr. Nixon's personal *Internet Success Encyclopedia*.	$29.95 Value
7. You also get two other <u>bonus</u> books for your success library.	$25.00 Value
	$384.80 Value

Why do we give you all this for only $19.95—the price of *The Lazy Man's Way to Riches* book? Because I want you to buy the program—it can't work for you if you don't have it. So buy this program and change your life!

The Lazy Man's Way to Riches

Version 3.0

Completely Revised, Updated, and Expanded by

Richard Gilly Nixon, Ph.D.

Based on the book by Joe Karbo
The Original "Lazy Man"

WILEY

John Wiley & Sons, Inc.

Published by John Wiley & Sons, Inc., Hoboken, New Jersey
Published simultaneously in Canada

For general information about our other products and services, please contact our Customer Care Department within the United States at 800-762-2974, outside the United States at 317-572-3993 or fax 317-572-4002.

Wiley also publishes its books in a variety of electronic formats. Some content that appears in print may not be available in electronic books. For more information about Wiley products, visit our web site at www.wiley.com.

ISBN: 0-471-68368-X

Printed in the United States of America

10 9 8 7 6 5 4 3 2 1

CONTENTS

The Secret of Success

You are about to read an updated, expanded and revised classic—a book that has sold over four million copies and was only in a bookstore one year out of the 30 years it's been published. The original author, Joe Karbo, sold this book from 1973 until his death in 1980 through the most powerful channels of sales in existence—Direct Response marketing and word of mouth.

JOE KARBO

Joe Karbo was a uniquely amazing man and both he and this remarkable book were the subjects of articles and stories in *Time, Money, Changing Times, Forbes,* and even *Consumer Reports.* Newspapers too numerous to mention also chronicled the story of Joe Karbo and the book that was changing the lives of those who utilized its secrets.

Joe was most probably the very first, and possibly the only author of a book of this type, to write in the first person. Others tell you "how" to do what they themselves haven't done successfully based on some theory or principle, but Joe wrote from personal, practical experience. Joe was a self-made man—a lazy man by his own admission—and a rich man.

Some people thought Joe made his fortune from the enormous sales of this book, but he had made millions prior to even thinking about writing a book. *The Lazy Man's Way to Riches*™ is Joe's philosophy on life and how to live it richly, successfully, lovingly, joyously and lazily.

It is also a detailed report on *exactly* how he made millions of dollars and in it he reveals those secrets to you. In his masterful simplicity, Joe Karbo records some of the most dynamic principles ever penned regarding what it means to be truly rich and how to get there.

TRUE WEALTH

The valuable and lasting lessons you will receive from this book will bring you the freedom to be, to do, and to have what you want. It will also bring you financial freedom, but more importantly will bring you your idea of true success—*true wealth.* Success is best defined by one's own achievements which may include excellent mental health, physical health, loving relationships—with both family members and friends—spiritual fulfillment, self-actualization, material wealth and a rarely achieved peace of mind

Bottom line? This book can help you attain all that's important to you, to become all that you were created to be and to do—become that uniquely wonderful person that is hiding down deep inside—the real you.

That is a good book which is opened with expectation and closed in profit.

AMOS BRONSON ALCOTT
(1799–1888)
American author, educator, mystic

The man who writes about himself and his own time is the only man who writes about all people and about all time.

GEORGE BERNARD SHAW
(1856–1950)
Irish playwright, critic, social reformer

Books give not wisdom where none was before. But where some is, there reading makes it more.

JOHN HARINGTON
(1516–1617)
English satirist, writer

No mind ever receives the truth until it's prepared to receive it. Remember the old adage, "When the student is ready, the teacher will appear." You're obviously ready to receive this new truth. Congratulations as you enter the world of freedom, success, and true wealth. So, let's get started now!

THE BEST OF YOUR LIFE

Welcome to the first day of the *Best* of your life. We are going to take you step by step down the road to Riches, success and happiness. I'm Richard Gilly Nixon, and it is my pleasure to be your guide on your exciting journey to everything you have ever wanted. I am going to bring you Joe Karbo's personal advice, and together with some wonderful people who helped me on this project, I will tell you how to find within yourself the talents and resources to get everything you want out of life . . . The Lazy Man's Way.

In order to bring you this exciting new book, we have spent countless hours revising, expanding and editing Joe's original book. We have added the lessons learned from the business and psychological communities, in the past thirty years since its original printing, and our own experience learned from *The Lazy Man's Way to Riches*.

I first became aware of Joe Karbo in September of 1973, while I was running a successful television promotion company. A bright employee named Linda brought in an ad written for *The Lazy Man's Way to Riches*. She was so impressed with the ad that she sent for the book. When the book arrived, she read it over and over again, carefully highlighting key thoughts and ideas on each page, in a different color with each new reading. By the fifth reading, she had a virtual rainbow of colors throughout her treasured new book. She didn't simply read it; she studied, visualized, and consumed it.

Instead of sharing her copy of *The Lazy Man's Way to Riches* with me, she bought me a copy of my own. Upon studying the book, Linda's self-esteem dramatically improved and her performance at the office sky-rocketed. It was astonishing! She credited *The Lazy Man's Way to Riches* for it all.

Linda went on to become successful and rich beyond her dreams, in the medical supply business and as an entrepreneur. Linda bought many copies of *The Lazy Man's Way to Riches* as gifts for her friends. She became a disciple of Joe Karbo and the lessons that brought her true Riches.

I read the book for myself and found, much to my delight that it lived up to its promises as expressed by Linda. Unfortunately, as a student, I wasn't ready for it yet. I was impressed because it rang true to my own life experiences, but because I was already successful beyond my limited dreams, I didn't pay much attention to it then.

After leaving the television promotion company, I helped establish a company that manufactured medical X-ray equipment. This company became enormously successful, through internal growth and the purchase of other companies, and was quickly listed on the stock exchange. Because of this success at that point in my life, no self-help book mattered to me. What more could there be for me to know? I felt there wasn't much more for me to know.

At age 40, I retired. I felt I had worked long enough and had achieved all my goals. I decided I had enough money to last for the rest of my life; I could finally relax

---

No man is great enough or wise enough for any of us to surrender our destiny to. The only way in which anyone can lead us is to restore to us the belief in our own guidance.

HENRY MILLER
(1891–1980)
American writer

The books that help you most are those which make you think the most.

THEODORE PARKER
(1810–1860)
Unitarian theologian, publicist

and play. But in my "success," I managed to destroy everything over the next four years—a lifetime of money went down the proverbial drain. This self-destruction culminated in a divorce and a bankruptcy.

I was living proof that this book works—by diligently applying everything *backwards*—I went from wealth to poverty; from physical health to sickness; from mental health to stressed-out; from loving relationships to wrecked relationships—and certainly there was no inner peace.

When you hit bottom, there's no place to go but up. But because the human mind works in wonderful ways, I remembered *The Lazy Man's Way to Riches*. I dug it out. I read it for the second time—but studied it for the first time. The student was finally ready; I was prepared to learn.

Having applied the principles of *The Lazy Man's Way to Riches*, I have successfully rebuilt my life based upon what I really want to do with my life. I can personally testify that these principles work—often in spite of me. That's how powerful this book is. It helped me deactivate the self-destructive and self-limiting mechanisms and begin to rebuild my positive self-images and my self-esteem. I now enjoy the Riches that have blossomed from the most revolutionary life-principles.

My success story is a direct application of the powerful principles in *The Lazy Man's Way to Riches*. These principles have given me a way to effect long lasting results and have put me on the road to permanent change.

THE POWER OF BELIEF—FOR YOU

The power of belief can be a destructive force or a dynamic, positive force for you. You decide which it will be.

It has been said that "When one person believes he can and another person believes he can't, they are both right." The power of believing in your purpose or vision is at the core of all performance, achievement and Riches.

Your beliefs create your reality. This book, its interactive workbook, and its website will show you a way to transform your belief system from a passive, destructive force into a positive, dynamic force.

> One day Mara, the Buddhist god of ignorance and evil, was traveling through a village in India with his attendant. He saw a man doing meditation whose face was lit up in wonder. The man had just discovered something on the ground in front of him. The attendant asked Mara what the man had found, and Mara replied, "A small piece of truth."
>
> "Doesn't this bother you O Evil One, when someone finds a piece of truth?" asked the attendant.
>
> "No" replied Mara, "because right afterwards they usually make a belief out of it."

Be careful of what you believe—especially that which you accepted as truth before you learned to reason, discern and question. The lessons and concepts that follow will not work for you if you hold steadfast to some of your old limiting beliefs. So I ask that you suspend dis-belief and accept that what we tell you will work for you until you have some new successes under your belt.

I suggest that the only books that influence us are those for which we are ready, and which have gone a little further down our particular path than we have yet got ourselves.

E. M. FORSTER
(1879–1970)
English novelist, short-story writer, essayist

How many a man has dated a new era in his life from reading a book?

HENRY DAVID THOREAU
(1817–1862)
American essayist, naturalist, poet

When one person believes he can and another person believes he can't, they are both right.

HENRY FORD
(1863–1947)
American industrialist

One must live the way one thinks or end up thinking the way one has lived.

PAUL BOURGET
(1852–1935)
French novelist, critic, poet

A man only learns in two ways, one by reading, and the other by association with smarter people.

WILL ROGERS
(1879–1935)
American actor and humorist

Insanity is doing the same thing in the same way and expecting a different outcome.

LESLIE CALVIN BROWN
(b. 1945)
Lecturer, speaker, motivator, author

Some of the statements and lessons in this book may be argued; but everyday these same principles are working for us as well as millions of others, and they will work for you, too. So, here is what I ask of you to insure that you get the Riches you want from this program:

- **TRY TO PROVE IT RIGHT.**
- **DO IT.**
- **DO IT NOW.**
- **DO IT FOR YOU.**

With this program you <u>can</u> have *everything* you want.

Yes, I said everything. There is probably a good chance that you were drawn to this program primarily for the reason of improving your life financially and that you relate to everything in terms of what only having more money can provide for you.

I promise you that as you travel the road to success with *The Lazy Man's Way to Riches* you will discover that you can have *everything* in <u>all</u> areas of your life so that your life will be balanced; the stimulation of having a clear mind, the joy of feeling good about yourself, the satisfaction of relating effectively with your fellow man, the thrill of loving your vocational endeavor, the exhilaration of feeling physically fit and the comfort of finding your place in the universe and with the beliefs you hold dear. True Riches. Everything!

You may say there has to be a limit to what you could be and do and have; but no one, not even you, knows what that limit is. So, break through the barriers. Remember, one person's floor is another person's ceiling. Break through that ceiling.

It's time to educate yourself beyond your current education, because your current education only got you where you are now. To grow and prosper you will need new tools and skills.

Get yourself a "Ph.D." in who you can be, what you can have, what you can do, and how to get your success—your Riches. Just remember . . .

"IF YOU KEEP DOING WHAT YOU'RE DOING YOU'LL JUST KEEP GETTING WHAT YOU'RE GETTING."

Once you begin applying the Dyna/Psyc™ principles of *The Lazy Man's Way to Riches*, program you'll make more progress in a very few months or even weeks than in all the preceding years of your life.

Now turn to Step #1 "The Secret of Success" in your *Roadmap to Riches* workbook. Your personal edition of the *Roadmap to Riches* E-book workbook is included free with your purchase of this book. To download Step #1 go to http:www.thelazymansway.com and follow the simple instruction labeled: *Roadmap to Riches* v.3 your personal workbook.

2

The Keys to Success and Riches

So, how has this book become one of the biggest international best sellers of all time? Simple. It works.

This book will not only show you how to have *anything* you want, but *everything* you want.

I wish it were possible for you to read the thousands of letters written to us in praise of this book. They are such dramatic testimonials to the worth of a single book. For some people, it meant a drastic change of direction in their lives.

For some, it meant a subtle fine-tuning of their thinking that opened new worlds. For others, it meant a new flow of wellness—including personal, mental, emotional, relational, and *financial wealth*. For most the story was pretty much the same—it was positively life changing.

There is one thing these letters have in common. They are all "thank you" letters to Joe and me for writing this book. You may want to write us such a letter yourself after you achieve your Riches. There is no magic, no hocus pocus, no mumbo jumbo here; it's just uncommon thought presented in a common way. It's common sense and, it works!

TRUE RICHES

Joe's insight into how life works brought him true Riches in addition to the millions of dollars he earned: joy, love, fulfillment, satisfaction and freedom in all its forms.

He was free to do *what* he wanted to do, *how* he wanted to do it, *where* he wanted to do it, *when* he wanted to do it and *with whom*.

It also brought him the Riches of *"freedom from:"* freedom from want, *freedom from* fear, *freedom from* jealousy, *freedom from* envy and *freedom from* worry. Joe's insights can do the same for you.

All you have to do is follow along and do the steps in the *Roadmap to Riches* workbook that will lead you to your life of Riches.

YOUR RICHES?

Different Riches await you—*your* Riches—when you dig into this book/program and find the treasures for yourself. It's knowing what courses to take in the "school of life" and having a teacher who cares. All of us who are enjoying a heartbeat right now are enrolled in this universal school.

What a sense of security in an old book which time has criticized for us.

JAMES RUSSELL LOWELL
(1819–1891)
American poet, critic, editor, diplomat

The secret point of money and power in America is neither the thing that money can buy nor power for power's sake . . . but absolute personal freedom, mobility, privacy. It is the instinct, which drove Americans to the Pacific.

JOAN DIDION
(b. 1934)
American writer

The question is: What classes must you attend? What courses must you take in order to graduate to your Riches, to experience and enjoy life to its fullest? Here are just a few of the "courses" we are offering in this book:

PURPOSE 101

Purpose is the primary "course" necessary for growth and progress throughout your life. It's the answer to the question, Why am I here? And without the answer to that question, no amount of money will ever satisfy you.

Each of us has been uniquely created to be and do certain things—our purpose. It's a sense of destiny. This is the life course that drives all of the others.

If you feel your purpose is to be a teacher or coach, then stop kidding yourself about buying expensive new sports cars, a multi-million dollar oceanfront home or anything else that demands big bucks. Follow your purpose and be that teacher or coach. You'll never be happy or find that inner peace and joy of life, until you find and follow your own powerful purpose.

It's been said, "If you do what you love—the money will follow." (Note the order: Do what you love, and then the money will follow.) Following your purpose assures you the Riches you seek.

SUCCESS 101

Some say the real answer to enjoying life to its fullest is to have P.M.A. (Positive Mental Attitude): positive expectations, motivation, desire, and commitment to go along with the dynamic principles available through the "self-help" movement. But there are "missing links" that are most often overlooked.

You need someone to walk you through the application of the great truths of life. You need a mentor, a teacher, a tutor or an assistant to help you process what you know to be true and incorporate that truth into your entire lifestyle—your purpose statement.

Your mentor is exactly what this book is. Use it that way. When you purchased this book, you enrolled in one of the most exciting classes of your life... SUCCESS 101.

SELF-LOVE 101

A third course, which shows you how to experience and enjoy life to its fullest, is SELF-LOVE. One of the keys to self-loving is to permit yourself to *be* and *do* what you really love to be and to do. Being and doing what you love is vital to a highly successful life. There is an epidemic of toxic thought in our world today that goes like this:

"I MUST KEEP DOING ALL THE THINGS THAT I HATE DOING IN ORDER TO GET AHEAD IN LIFE."

I don't believe that and I'll show you why you shouldn't either.

It is true that you must learn to discipline yourself to things that you don't necessarily love; but when you see that these things are going to give you what you want, you begin to see them as friends, not enemies. The best-selling author, Dr. M. Scott Peck, defines discipline as "love translated into action."

Existence is a strange bargain. Life owes us little; we owe it everything. The only true happiness comes from squandering ourselves for a purpose.

WILLIAM COWPER
(1731–1800)
English poet

There is only one success—to be able to live your life in your own way.

CHRISTOPHER MORLEY
(1890–1957)
American novelist,
 journalist, essayist

To love oneself is the beginning of a life-long romance.

OSCAR WILDE
(1854–1900)
Irish-born English poet,
playwright, novelist

Some of us have easily become our own worst enemies. It's so easy to become toxic—poisonous to ourselves. Many of us learn to sabotage our lives by listening to the many "expert" voices out there rather than looking within ourselves; therefore, the masses of people just like us are living our lives to please everyone else in order to simply get by. How sad. What a miserable existence that is. It is so important to trust your own inner voice, your own integrity, to be dependent upon only yourself and to be honest with yourself.

Be careful of the toxic people in your world. They are like weeds in your garden. They will inevitably choke the very life out of you. Toxic people are everywhere, you just can't help but encounter them. They are at work, in the clubs you belong to, at the restaurants, in the stores, and even in your family.

Because toxic people are so damaging in every way, I want to give you an effective and simple way to determine who among the many people you encounter every day are toxic to you. Ask your self these questions about the people in your life.

1. **Who am I around?** (Who do I spend time with?)

2. **What have they got me becoming?** (Are they nudging me toward—or away from becoming the better, more successful, nicer, Richer person I want to become? Be honest here, this is important because there is no greater pressure than peer pressure.)

3. **Is that OK with me?** (If not, then by all means limit your exposure to those people so that you can replace them with people who are beneficial to you.)

You want someone in your life who is your best friend. Someone who will hang in there with you and support you no matter what. Someone who is always on your side, good times and bad, aware of your needs, willing to encourage you and to challenge you to do your best. Someone who is considerate, dependable, honest and loving. Someone you can trust. Someone who really gives a rip whether you live or die. Who is that someone? It's *you*.

When Jesus was asked to summarize the Law of Moses He said, "Love God with all your heart, soul, and mind. And love your neighbor as yourself." In other words, if you don't love yourself, your neighbor is in a heap of trouble. In this book, SELF-LOVE teaches you how to love yourself most effectively. The first act of self love is to replace toxic people with people who are examples of the person you want to become.

PERSONAL RIGHTS 101

You have the right to be happy. You have the right to be prosperous. You have the right to be productive. You have the right to be healthy in body, mind and spirit. You have the right to be who you want to be. You have the right to be Rich and successful.

The Constitution of the United States of America is set up to protect the rights of its citizens. Those who attack those rights within its borders are brought to justice by the constituted authorities. Those outside the borders who attack the rights of U.S. citizens are repelled by its armed forces.

What I must do is all that concerns me, not what the people think.

RALPH WALDO EMERSON (1803–1882) American poet, essayist, philosopher; "Self Reliance" Essays First Series (1841)

They have rights who dare to maintain them.

JAMES RUSSELL LOWELL (1819–1891) American poet, critic, editor, diplomat

When our bodies are attacked by various diseases, our immune system fights back to keep us healthy. Most people are in the same way affected by "viruses" outside the body causing a "dis-ease" in financial, mental, career, physical, social, family and spiritual areas of their lives. You have the right to fight that dis-ease. You can do that by learning WHO YOU REALLY ARE, WHAT YOU WANT IN LIFE AND HOW TO GET IT. This book/program helps you do just that.

GROWTH 101

Although change is constantly happening, it's natural to try to avoid it. People just don't like change; it's too uncomfortable. But, in order to get what you want in life, it will require some changes. If you are not truly happy where you are, a lack of change will surely keep you where you are—dissatisfied and stuck.

Master Motivator Les Brown says that, "Insanity is doing the same thing in the same way and expecting a different result." So let's grow.

- **YOU HAVE THE RIGHT TO GROW.**
- **YOU HAVE THE OPTION TO GROW.**
- **YOU CAN ALLOW YOURSELF TO GROW.**
- **YOU CAN ENCOURAGE YOURSELF TO GROW.**

Growth comes in three opportunity packages:

First, growth comes by *stopping* something you are presently doing that isn't working or is getting in your way. Remember, if you keep doing what you're doing, you will just keep getting what you're getting.

Growth sometimes is easiest to affect by simply stopping the doing of that which isn't working for you. (Growth doesn't have to mean doing something.) If it isn't working for you, it can't propel you toward your personal Riches. It follows then that it would be wise to learn how to stop doing what you're doing that's getting in your way.

So, stop kidding yourself. Stop lying to yourself. Stop hanging around with toxic people. Stop blaming others. Stop drinking, drugging, overeating, procrastinating or whatever it is that gets in your way. Stop doing those things that are not working for you and your life will instantly and dramatically improve. You may be thinking, "Easy for you to say" and it is. With Dyna/Psyc and the other principles you will learn in this book you can stop putting speed bumps roadblocks on your way to your Riches.

Second, growth can come by learning something new. New Mentors and coaches are a good place to start because they can teach you the new skills and tools you will need to grow. As you read this book you will be motivated and challenged to make several decisions. It's your choice. You are in the driver's seat. You can choose to do new things and try new approaches. Let the Lazy Man program show you the way to a new life of success and Riches.

Third, growth through the mistakes we make. Mistakes offer you a major opportunity for personal growth, if you take advantage of them. Mistakes can be encouraged, even welcomed. That's how we learn and grow. They are course corrections in your life, *if* you know where you are headed. So, welcome your mis-

---

The strongest principle of growth lies in human choice.

GEORGE ELIOT
pen name of Mary Ann Evans
(1819–1880)
English novelist

At the end of the next 20 years you can have 20 years experience—or you can have one year's experience 20 times. It's a matter of choice.

RICHARD GILLY NIXON
(b. 1940)
American entrepreneur, publisher, author, speaker, seminar leader

takes as friends that provide stepping-stones and course corrections on your journey to your personal successes and Riches.

In the motion picture business when a scene is not done properly they re-take it. They may retake it many times until they get it the way it works. These mis-takes are just a part of the process. If you make a mis-take, simply start over. Practice until you get it right. And here is a nugget that can help—forget the old notion that "Practice makes perfect"—it doesn't. In our house we were taught, "*perfect* practice makes perfect. That's a subtle but important distinction for achieving the success and Riches you want.

THE GIFT OF TRIAL AND ERROR
by Buckminster Fuller

"We are deliberately designed to learn by trial and error. We're brought up to think that nobody should make mistakes. Most children get "degeniused" by the love and fear of their parents—that they might make a mistake. But all of my advances were made by mistakes. You uncover what is, then you discover what isn't."

GROWTH REQUIRES MAKING CHOICES

We live the way we have chosen to live, but seldom is it the way we want to live. Our choices are driven by our purpose (or our lack of a clear purpose) and emerge out of our, beliefs, preferences, habits, tastes, and behaviors. What we want can only come to us through *positive* change. First we stop doing what *doesn't* work for us, and then we start doing what *does* work for us.

What if someone else were to take your liberty from you? The authorities would arrest and punish that person. But aren't *you* the one who has taken away your liberty? And haven't you punished yourself by being unwilling to grow so that you can change those things that don't work for you?

Do you like where your life has been? Do you like where it is now? And where it's probably headed if you continue without change? Are you involved in worthwhile and meaningful pursuits of your own choosing? Are you satisfied with your job, your career? Do you like how you're living—your home, your neighborhood, your clothes, your furniture, your cars, vacations and recreation? Are you happy with your relationships and friends? If not then it's time to make some new choices. You can answer "Yes" to all of these questions with the lessons you will learn in Growth 101. GROWTH IN ALL AREAS WILL BE YOURS!

ABOUT THIS PROGRAM

This program is organized in a special way for you to maximize your efforts learning everything you possibly can for yourself. **There are four important components that make up the program:**

1. THE BOOK *The Lazy Man's Way to Riches*

The book is made up of 6 parts:

Your Itinerary. In this part of the book (Chapters 1–11) you begin your journey on the road to Riches by looking at yourself and the tools necessary for the trip— putting things into perspective.

The man who makes no mistakes does not usually make anything.

EDWARD J. PHELPS
(1822–1900)
Lawyer, diplomat

As a man thinketh so is he, and as a man chooseth so is he.

RALPH WALDO EMERSON
(1803–1882)
American poet, essayist, philosopher

When it is dark enough, you can see the stars.

CHARLES AUSTIN BEARD
(1874–1948)
American historian

On The Road. You're on your way, and in this part (Chapters 12–24) you learn to deal with what you will find on your journey, as you choose the right paths to your destination—success and your Riches.

The Destination—Your Way! This part of the book (Chapters 25–34) moves you along the road to your personal Riches by showing you the application of the principles you have learned and how to take control of your life. It's a game plan for living your life on purpose.

Turning Dyna/Psyc Into Dollars. In this part of the book (Chapters 35–43), we tell you all of the secrets that will enable you to make lots of money just as Joe Karbo and I have done. We actually spell out the success formula for what many people call, "the most exciting business in the world." This may be why you bought the book, but please read the chapters in order—that is the only way to maximize the program's benefits.

The Internet. The last several chapters (Chapters 44–54) are about the Internet and are as new and as up to date as it gets. They are designed to get you up and running on the internet quickly, inexpensively and effectively.

The Quotes

As an added bonus throughout the book, we bring you over 400 quotations from all of recorded human history on the subjects we are discussing. The quotes serve to reinforce and amplify the text, with the wisdom of the ages. You'll see that the ideas we present are solid, time-tested, accepted, and valued by scholars, writers, religious leaders, politicians, thinkers and just plain folks from all corners of the world, for over 2,500 years.

It is one thing for me or Joe to say something profound, but it is quite another thing to see that Socrates, Napoleon Hill, Plato, Gandhi, Henry Ford, Thoreau, Jesus, and so many others agree with us and said so in their own unique and memorable way.

Quotes are mankind's way of "snapshoting" the truths of the ages. We use them to provide you with food for thought as you ponder the concepts we are presenting that may be foreign or new to you. There is not a right way or wrong way to read these quotes. If you find it too distracting to read them as you are reading the text, then don't read them at that time. It may work better for you to come back and read the quotes separately. Some people have read the quotes along with text and have enjoyed the experience as a nice set up for the material. You may find that you want to review the quotes as you finish reading each chapter. Experiment. See what works for you.

2. THE E-WORKBOOK *The Roadmap to Riches; Your Personal Guidebook*

This is a special free on-line book that is available *only* on our website to readers of *The Lazy Man's Way to Riches*, designed to work in conjunction with *The Lazy Man's Way to Riches*. The *Roadmap to Riches* Guidebook is available free to you by logging on to our website at http://www.thelazymansway.com. It is an easy to use

---

A fine quotation is a diamond in the hand of a man of wit and a pebble in the hand of a fool.

JOSEPH ROUX
(1834–1905)
French priest, writer

In the case of good books, the point is not how many of them you can get through, but rather how many can get through to you.

MORTIMER JEROME ADLER
(b. 1902)
American author, philosopher

E-book of exercises, tools, and resources that help take you step-by-step on an exciting life-changing journey to Riches, The Lazy Man's Way.

The workbook is what separates this program from all other programs because it helps you learn how to use the tools and the skills that will propel you toward the success and Riches you want. I am certain you will find—as so many others have found—that the Guidebook is vital in facilitating the changes you choose to make in your life.

I've designed the *Roadmap to Riches* workbook as an online book for several reasons. Most importantly, as you change and grow with the Lazy Man program, you can return to the website and get fresh new pages of the guidebook to re-do exercises. Then you will continue to grow to new and higher levels of learning and accomplishment.

Why didn't we just add a CD Rom to *The Lazy Man's Way to Riches* like some other books have done?

Because CD's become outdated almost immediately, and—they can never be updated. We can keep the *Roadmap to Riches* workbook constantly up-to-date online, and we can assure you that the links will always work. Also, by having it on our website, we can update the latest technology as it becomes available. But, most importantly, the *Roadmap to Riches* workbook is interactive, so that tests and quizzes can be scored immediately. That way you can monitor your own progress instantly—another first in publishing.

The purpose of this great companion workbook is to take you by the hand from where you are, to where you want to be. There is no other program like this on the planet—yet. Someday all books will have an on-line component. But this is the first of its kind.

The *Roadmap to Riches Guidebook*, then, acts as your personal tutor. Taking you by the hand, guiding you, as a friend would guide you, through each of the steps along the way. It's a vital ingredient that will assist in the application of all that you are about to learn. It is an ingredient that must be included if you are to receive the full benefit of *The Lazy Man's Way to Riches*.

3. THE WEBSITE (http://www.thelazymansway.com)

Here is where this program really shines! Because of the Lazy Man website we can now bring you what no book in history could ever bring you before. Communication with the author and other experts, and even a community of readers who are on the same path you have chosen to take. (We call it a forum—you'll love it as soon you use it!) We can now bring you resources—and tools that would have taken an entire encyclopedia before now.

Imagine what awaits you with this program because of the Internet and our website. You can hear audio clips, view video clips, take Interactive tests, and view materials we could never fit into a mere book before—now with just a mouse click a new learning experience awaits you. With our website you will see exactly how to do everything we discuss in the book in detail as never before.

4. THE NEWSLETTERS

We publish two newsletters for readers of *The Lazy Man's Way to Riches*. Both are delivered to you via E-mail or you can view them on our website where you will find the current issue of each as well as archived copies of back issues.

Why would you want our newsletter? Learning never stops for the self actualized person. Physicians, lawers, realtors, teachers, C.P.A.'s, policemen, pilots—practically everyone who needs to keep sharp, stay up, pull ahead, grow, and do better gets continuing education in as many ways as possible.

Why two newsletters? Because *The Lazy Man's Way to Riches* is really two books in one.

The first part of the Lazy Man's program is all about becoming more, learning more, acquiring new tools and new skills. It's about getting personal success—personal growth.

The second part of the book is really about business success and money Riches. Here is how my Grandma Rose said it: **"To have more—to achieve more—one must first become more."** In TEC, I teach CEO's that your business won't grow until you do.

That's why we publish two newsletters for you.

The Game Plan for Living™ newsletter is all about personal success and growth so that you can continue to grow and improve long after your first reading of the Lazy Man. It continues where the Lazy Man left off, giving you guidance, mentoring and so much more. It's insight. Awareness. A resource. A microscope and a telescope. I believe as the farmers say "when you're green you're growing; when you're ripe you're rotten." Stay green—read *The Game Plan for Living*.

The Game Plan for Success™ newsletter is all about Riches and the business that will supply your Riches now and for the rest of your life—and beyond—for your family. Here the focus is on business success as we teach it in TEC—the largest CEO membership organization in the world, "Dedicated to Increasing the Effectiveness and Enhancing the Lives of CEOs." Look at *The Game Plan for Success* as a graduate school for those who want to progress beyond the heights that the Lazy Man will take you to. It is a graduate school for making money in business.

One final thing. *The Lazy Man's Way to Riches*, with its accompanying workbook, is not an ordinary program. It's an **extra**-ordinary program. It will tell you all you need to know to have everything you want. So it should not be read like a novel or story. It should be read with thought about what you have just read, then digested, mulled over, and questioned (What does this mean? What does this mean to me? How can I apply this to my life? Could this possibly be true?). Read it chapter-by-chapter, concept-by-concept; then read it again and again. The exercises in the *Roadmap to Riches* workbook are the action steps necessary to form new success habits. Do them and do them right—remember, only <u>perfect</u> practice makes perfect.

HOW TO READ THIS BOOK

Of course you know how to read—but if you merely read this book as you have read other books, you are going to cheat yourself out of one of life's great experiences. So, let us help you—please.

As you read this book imagine that you are at a buffet. Take only those ideas that appeal to you now and use them only if they make sense to you. If something doesn't appeal to you skip it.

From my experience, I find that a book of this type is most beneficial when I withhold my natural or fear-driven skepticism.

Read the following pages with an open mind. If something makes sense to you, try it. If it doesn't make sense to you or your feel it doesn't apply to you at this point in your life, feel free to discard it. In whatever you do, be a student, not merely a follower.

Joe Karbo's suggestion to **R.S.V.P.** (**R**ead it, **S**tudy it, **V**isualize it, **P**erform it) was most beneficial in making me a more effective student.

WRITE IN YOUR BOOK

Write in the margins of your book. Yes, write in it. Why not? It's yours. Make notes about those things that you feel are most important to you. Underline in pencil or ink. Use a highlighter—whatever; use something, even a crayon will work.

The first time I read the original *The Lazy Man's Way to Riches* I used a yellow highlighter. The second time, I used a pink highlighter and found I had highlighted passages and thoughts I had missed my first time through. The third time I read the book, I used a blue highlighter. This time I discovered new insights and principles that just didn't seem so important the first two times.

Just as Linda had done years before, I was creating my own rainbow. I was highlighting ideas I repeatedly viewed as important, each time I reviewed the book, it took much less time, because I simply reviewed the highlighted passages.

With each successive review, I began to learn more about me, what I wanted, and how I could and would possess my Riches. The fourth time I used orange to highlight those parts that now jumped out at me. They were becoming keys to my success. The last color I used, on my fifth journey through *The Lazy Man's Way to Riches*, was red; it was too dark to read through with all the other colors layered under it. So then I bracketed the sentences or paragraphs (even whole pages) that now reinforce the way to my Riches.

On subsequent re-readings you could even use arrows or exclamation points in the margins to draw your attention. You do what you want with your book. After all, it's your life we are talking about, and it deserves to be understood, highlighted, underlined, and punctuated.

FINDING RICHES IN THE PAGES OF THIS BOOK

Imagine how different your life is from your parents' lives when they were the age you are now. Then consider how different your life is from your grandparents when they were the age you are now. Everything is different in the world today

> You can't expect to hit the jackpot if you don't put a few nickels in the machine.
>
> FLIP (CLEROW) WILSON
> (1933–1998)
> American actor, comedian

There are two kinds of success. One is the very rare kind that comes to the man who has the power to do what no one else has the power to do. That is genius. But the average man who wins what we call success is not a genius. He is a man who has merely the ordinary qualities that he shares with his fellows, but who has developed those ordinary qualities to a more than ordinary degree.

THEODORE ROOSEVELT (1858–1919)
26th President of the United States

Your life is an expression of all your thoughts.

MARCUS AURELIUS ANTONINUS (121–180)
Roman emperor, stoic philosopher

because of someone's thoughts resulting from their desires and beliefs. Absolutely everything has changed.

Thoughts created all of the inanimate things you see. Some human being thought of it, worked to bring it into existence; and we enjoy it today. Houses, X-rays, cars, airplanes, vaccines, appliances, televisions, contact lenses, computers, the internet, jet planes, skyscrapers, frozen food, plastic, running water, supermarkets, wristwatches, tampons, pantyhose, email, cell phones, DVDs, I-Pods—everything is either new or radically different from your parents or grandparents.

Imagine that! Everything was first just a thought that someone made up to improve something, solve a problem or simply because of the joy they received by bringing something that they loved into existence. Our modern buildings are just an improvement on the cave of ancient man. All of our modern appliances are nothing more than thoughts on how to solve various problems of performing some task in an easier manner.

Some of what we enjoy is the result of pure creative thought for no purpose except the love of it: music, poetry, dance and most of the arts. No one really "needs" the arts; they are pure manifestations of the love of their creators. Mozart created his music because he loved it. Picasso created his paintings because he loved to paint. Fred Astaire loved to dance. Walt Disney created several characters all for the sheer love of doing it and for the potential entertainment value they might offer.

The United States of America was created from a vision (a thought) of the love of freedom backed by a burning desire and a belief that it could be created. Your thoughts create your reality and your thoughts will create your future—*Change your thoughts and you change your life now and for the Best of your life.*

GETTING EVERYTHING YOU WANT

That's what this program is all about—thoughts, self-love, and creating your life the way you want it. That's part of what Riches are. This is not just another self-help book on the latest fad out of pop psychology.

This book contains the proven best thinking from over 3,500 years of human civilization upon which to build the foundation for your life. It is from this foundation that you can get *everything* you want out of your life.

In "computerese" the saying goes, "Garbage in; garbage out." Most of us are where we are now because of input fed to us—and accepted by us during the course of growing up. This input was from our role models: parents, teachers, playmates, friends, and the myriad of other people, who formed and guided our lives; who were probably not highly trained, well educated, super intelligent or enormously successful. They were just average people.

If you are looking today for your version of success as you know it to be in your heart, then you need to reprogram yourself using different input from an entirely different set of people. Would Bill Gates or Donald Trump use your old role models as a way to further their success today? Probably not. Then why should you?

It is now up to you to accept responsibility for erasing inadequate and incorrect old data, and inserting new data that is being offered to you in this program. It is our job to supply that new quality input—but it's your job to determine how it can best serve you—and then apply it to your life.

Many of the thoughts that we will expose you to may be new to you, but they are not necessarily original. They are simply presented in new and easy ways so that you can apply them to your life.

This book was written for average people who are reasonably healthy in spirit, mind and body. (If you are suffering from some addiction, abuse, or emotional handicap, you may need to seek out professional assistance.) If you are the average person who is dissatisfied with where you are and where you are going, this is the right program for you. This program will help you get total control over your life and your destiny.

No matter what your definition of Riches is, this book shows you how to get them. Is there a limit to what you can have? Perhaps—but we don't know what that limit is for you—and neither do you. So, why not make it your goal to find out how high "up" is for you . . . The Lazy Man's Way?

So cozy up and get comfortable because you are about to launch yourself on a major trip—an exciting adventure. The destination? Your success—your new life of Riches!

CAN YOU REALLY EXPECT TO FIND RICHES IN THE PAGES OF THIS BOOK? YOU BET YOU CAN!

IF RICHES MEAN HEALTH, YOU CAN IMPROVE YOUR HEALTH WITH THE TEACHINGS OF THIS BOOK.

IF RICHES MEAN HAVING BETTER RELATIONSHIPS, THIS BOOK CAN BRING YOU THOSE RICHES.

IF YOUR IDEA OF RICHES IS GETTING OUT OF POVERTY, THIS BOOK CAN SHOW YOU HOW TO ATTAIN THE WEALTH YOU WANT.

IF RICHES MEAN JOY AND HAPPINESS, THIS BOOK CAN EASILY SHOW YOU HOW TO ACHIEVE THOSE RICHES.

Read on.

A thought is often original, though you have uttered it a hundred times. It has come to you over a new route, by a new and express train of associations.

OLIVER WENDALL HOLMES
(1809–1894)
American physician, professor, man of letters

Climb high. Climb far.
Your goal the sky,
your aim the star.

Inscription

Knowledge of what is possible is the beginning of happiness.

GEORGE SANTAYANA
(1863–1952)
Spanish-born American philosopher, poet, novelist, critic

Now turn to Step #2 "The Keys to Success and Riches" in your *Roadmap to Riches* workbook.

CHAPTER
3
Do You Have What It Takes?

Is The Lazy Man's Way really the best way? All of our lives we have been warned of the destructive results that will surely come our way if we are lazy. Maybe what we need is the "committed man's way" or the "disciplined man's way" or "work-til-you-are-exhausted man's way."

The primary difficulty with these and countless other, well-intended "ways" is that, for the most part, none of these "ways" work. The secondary difficulty with all other "ways" is that they are the "ways" of "experts"—the "ways" of "others!" They are not *your* way. Rather than living life your natural way, you are asked to "adopt" someone else's "way." *The Lazy Man's Way is living your life your way.*

I truly believe that our discontent and "dis-ease" is our true self—our nature, our inner vision of our self—trying to get out; not only do we not act upon it, we don't seem to know that it even exists. When we learn to allow our inner visions to become the embodiment of all of our actions, we achieve a remarkable balance, a contentment which, in turn, frees us up to a full expression of what is really inside us—and it is beautiful. You can see this emergence of true self most clearly in people in the arts: writers, dancers, painters, singers, poets, sculptors and composers. But the potential exists in all of us.

An inner vision allows you to be who you were meant to be.

It is not just problem solving.

It is not just "fixing" your life.

It is not just "relief."

It is not just programming your sub-conscious.

It is not just changing your view or attitude.

It is the answer to the questions that all people ultimately ask themselves: Why am I here? and, What does my life stand for? IT'S YOUR PURPOSE IN LIFE. Purpose gives meaning, power, focus and direction to your goals and therefore to your life. We will talk about purpose a great deal in later chapters.

EXPERTS—WHAT DO THEY KNOW ABOUT YOU?

All of the "experts" in the world are more than willing to show you "how," offer you "the" solutions, and guide you through the obstacles of life; there is no lack of advice for living out your life. The "experts" are everywhere. There are medical "experts," legal "experts," political "experts," economic "experts," psychological "experts," religious "experts," scientific "experts." They are most eager to squeeze you into their molds for working, parenting, marrying, dating, buying, selling, managing, dieting, exercising, feeling, being, doing and just plain living.

> It is our less conscious thoughts and our less-conscious actions which mainly mould our lives and the lives of those who spring from us.
>
> SAMUEL BUTLER (1835–1902)
> English novelist, scholar, translator

> There is only one meaning of life; the act of living itself.
>
> ERIC FROMM (1900–1980)
> German-born American psychoanalyst, philosopher

> An expert is one who knows more and more about less and less.
>
> NICOLAS MURRAY BUTLER (1862–1948)
> President of Columbia University

Some of these "experts" have Ph.D's or other prestigious degrees that move you to awe and respect. Others have positions of power that impress you. Still others have unusual testimonials that dazzle you. All of these experts want you to follow their advice for how you ought to live your life—their way—the way they think is best.

These "experts," for the most part, know plenty about their field of endeavor and definitely can be helpful—to a *point*. They can offer you helpful facts which can be verified. They can give you several helpful principles and observations related to their particular field. They can present to you the history of what does and doesn't generally work in a given area. But they don't know what *you* want. And they don't know your way of doing things. You see, your way is the best way for you. *You are the best and only expert on you that exists.*

WANTED—MY OWN PERSONAL EXPERT

You can take in all the rent-an-expert advice that you want; but let's face it; you are the captain of your ship. Even if you work for someone else, you are actually self-employed. You go out into the marketplace and sell your services, whatever they may be, to the highest bidder, but you always work for the same boss—you. You are the Chief Executive Officer of your personal corporation, the President of your personal country, and the Emperor of your world.

In other words, you must call the shots about your life at every turn. We seem to jump on every opportunity to be responsible for everyone else. The fact is we are only responsible for ourselves, and we are the only ones who know our own truths. It has been said that the true start of maturity is the realization that no one else is coming to our rescue. With *The Lazy Man's Way to Riches*, you will want to take responsibility for you.

Now let's get you started along the road to your Riches. Each chapter is a new idea right out of Joe's success story and the success stories of the many others who have followed his method to attain the Riches they desire. Each chapter brings a new message, or an expansion of a message, which you can use to develop attitudes and habits that guarantee success. *Your success.*

I'm going to ask you to do something—something simple and easy to do, (after all this is The Lazy Man's Way) but nonetheless something very important. Just to make sure you don't forget what you're supposed to do, your separate guidebook called *The Roadmap to Riches* (get it free at http://www.thelazymansway.com) contains a step-by-step program that reinforces each message in the book. I'm asking that you not skip any of the steps, even if they seem trivial to you. Each and every step is important and part of the total picture; miss one or two and you won't get the best results. I'll do everything I can to encourage you to do all that we ask of you. Once you have gone through all of the chapters, you can go back and use the individual steps in the Roadmap whenever you run into a particular roadblock on the way to your personal Riches.

The Lazy Man's Way to Riches is built around the development of success habits. About 90 percent—no, I believe its closer to 99 percent—of what you do every day is habitual behavior. The difference between being successful and not being successful really depends on those habits. We have to change our failure habits into

---

An expert is a man who has made all the mistakes which can be made in a very narrow field.

NIELS BOHR
(1885–1962)
Danish physicist

Every man is the architect of his own future.

SALLUST
(86–35 BC)
Roman historian

success habits and that takes time and constant reinforcement. Psychiatrists tell us it takes the average person about 30 repetitions of an activity to turn it into a habit. And the more you are involved, the quicker you will develop the new habit. That's why I'll ask you to write some things down. So take it from me, don't try to rush things, be patient, do your part in every chapter and step. Let The Lazy Man's Way do the rest.

WRITING IS FOCUSED THINKING

By the way, *don't even think about skipping the writing.* There is no better way to "think" than to write things down. If you are serious about getting the Riches you have not yet been able to attain, you must do things you are not used to doing. If writing is one of those things you never do, or haven't done for a long time, or have been afraid to do, relax. It's just talking on paper. But the impact on your thinking process is dynamic and, in some cases, it is the only way to reach the parts of the mind you haven't been exercising lately. To that end . . . .

KEEP A JOURNAL

Here is something that I learned from our readers. Keep a Journal. The benefit of keeping a journal is so much more than I ever imagined that I want to recommend it to you as a daily activity as you start on this journey with the The Lazy Man. Keeping a journal involves regularly taking solitary time to reflect and record in written form your thoughts on your day and your life. The act of keeping a journal, coupled with solitude, can be a wonderful tool in the discovery of your true self. Here are just some of the benefits of keeping a journal.

- Self-discovery. Writing consistently in a journal will give you a deeper connection with your inner self.
- Less Stress. Releasing all your inner thoughts and anxieties through writing can help release unwanted stress.
- Gives you courage. Knowing what you want to do with your life is the first step in making it happen.
- Understanding the past. Journaling can bring up many issues in life that are still unresolved. Writing about them helps take you to a place of forgiveness and healing.
- Greater sense of peace. Listening to your inner thoughts through writing gives you a greater sense of peace and a more positive outlook on your experiences in life.
- Awareness. Get to know what really brings you joy in life.
- Uncovering. Uncover your inner spirituality.
- Healing. Mobilize your healing system to help you fight off illness and process painful emotions before they make you ill.

In case you have never journaled before and don't know how, or are afraid to try it for some reason, or perhaps you feel you just don't have time to journal . . . let us help you get started in the *Roadmap to Riches* workbook.

To learn new habits is everything, for it is to reach the substance of life. Life is but a tissue of habits.

HENRI FREDERIC AMIEL
(1821–1881)
Swiss philosopher, poet

How can I know what I think till I see what I say?

E. M. FORSTER
(1879–1970)
English novelist, short-story writer, essayist

THE LAZY MAN'S WAY—EASY AS 1.2.3

At this point I would like to give you a general idea of what we are going to do together. It's my intention to help you answer the three most fundamental questions in your life.

1. Who am I?
2. Where am I going?
3. How am I going to get there?

I know that when you possess clearly defined answers to these three questions, nothing can stop you from attaining all the Riches you desire. I'm not talking just about money, although that is an important part, I'm talking fulfillment in every aspect of your life. After all, when you have all the money you want, you will find there are other facets that add Riches to your life.

Since the way to Riches is what we are after, maybe we should start by asking what kind of qualities you actually need to be a candidate for a successful journey on this road. What is really necessary for success?

Before we answer that, let's look at some things that are **not** necessary—a college degree, for instance. Many people think a college degree is essential for success, and some even go farther and believe that it must be from a particular school. Interestingly enough, it's usually people without a college degree who feel that way. Most of the people with a college degree know better. All a college degree does is train you to work for someone else, and nowadays, it doesn't even guarantee you a decent job, let alone success.

Or maybe you're one of those who think it takes money to make money. Obviously it doesn't hurt to have some capital. But for every person who started out with money and made a lot more, there are two who managed to lose what they started with and several more that started with nothing or—as in Joe Karbo's case—less than nothing and made it big.

And it's not brains, either (if by brains you mean the kind of intelligence that is indicated by getting good grades in school). The ranks of successful people are full of people whose report cards had more D's and C's than A's. Some of the most brilliant people are failures at almost every area of life, because they never learned that in this life **you get paid for what you *do*, not what you know!**

And it's not good looks, or where you live, or how old or young you are, or who your parents were, or who your contacts are. I could go on and on listing all the alibis, rationalizations, justifications and excuses people give for not getting out of life all the happiness and success they desire.

Recognize any excuses that you have used? You are not alone. All of us find ways to excuse our lack of success. The thing is, we can't go any farther until we realize the painful truth: The lack of education, contacts, money, brains or luck are the most common excuses that people give for not getting what they want out of life.

You should have heard Joe Karbo back in the days before he found out the truth. Since he was then focused on what he didn't have, he was fighting a constant, exhausting battle to overcome his limitations—a battle he could never win because his problem was with his own *attitudes* about himself, not his so-called limitations. Most of his time and energy went into trying to climb over and break down barriers, which existed mostly in his own mind. It wasn't until he started building on what he had, instead of worrying about what he didn't have, that he was able to find *The Lazy Man's Way to Riches*. And that's where you are going to begin—by finding out just who and what you are, and what you have to offer. Are you ready for the first step?

In a minute I'm going to ask you to turn to the third step in your *Roadmap to Riches* workbook titled, My Success Assets. This is not an examination of your physical assets. It's a look at your personal qualities and abilities, and, most importantly, your attitudes that will be helpful in building your success.

We are interested in your honesty, the quality of your family life, your outlook on life and your flexibility. You'll see as you go through the questions that you are measuring your skills and talents also. Can you communicate with others, either verbally or in writing? Do you enjoy responsibility? What have you done in the past that shows determination, ambition and persistence? Be truly honest with yourself in this step; but don't fall into the trap of giving away all your talents, while you cling to your problems. Most people have the attitude, "If I can do it, anyone can." That's not exactly the truth. The easier something is for us, the more likely we are to assume that it is easy for everyone.

Dick Johnson, an associate of Joe's, tells the following story that illustrates the point.

Since Joe started me on The Lazy Man's Way to Riches, *I've taught many seminars on personal development. To break the ice in my classes I usually have the students stand, introduce themselves and tell the class one interesting thing about themselves. One student, we'll call her Fritzi, introduced herself and said, "I can't think of one interesting thing about myself" and quickly sat down. Her friend Pat, who was sitting next to her, was astonished. "That's the most ridiculous thing I've ever heard," Pat said, and proceeded to list some of Fritzi's talents and accomplishments. These included skydiving, dancing (well enough to win contests), and a job as a fashion buyer at a large department store chain. "As I came to know Fritzi I realized she had many personal qualities as well, but she just couldn't see them in herself."*

ACTION!

Take consistent, persistent and SMART action

Taking action is what moves you forward and propels you to your dreams and goals. Taking action requires discipline to create new behaviors. Because we are creatures of habit, we feel a natural tendency to slip back to old and established habit patterns. One way to break old habits and move into action is to make your goals SMART goals.

Specific

Measurable

Achievable

Realistic

Time-Based

> All glory comes from daring to begin.
>
> ANONYMOUS

A journey of a thousand miles must begin with a single step.

CHINESE PROVERB

Now, please turn to your *Roadmap to Riches* workbook where you will find all the steps on the journey to whatever Riches you want. See if you can "see in yourself" all of your success assets. Keep this in mind: the longest, hardest journey is nothing more than a series of small manageable steps.

PLEASE NOTE!

To help you understand and appreciate the exciting metamorphosis of this book, we have set off all of Joe Karbo's original book, from the expanded revision, with a faint gray line running alongside Joe's text (illustrated next to this paragraph) so you will be able to identify and taste the unique flavor of Joe Karbo. When a black line is present, you are reading new, expanded and revised text of *The Lazy Man's Way to Riches*. We have taken the liberty of updating some of the figures in Joe's portions so that they might be more easily understood in relation to today's economy and have made some minor changes to better fit the times.

Now turn to Step #3 "Do You Have What It Takes?"
in your *Roadmap to Riches* workbook.

4

Yes, You Can Have Everything You Want!

Y ou are now on your way to having everything in the world you really want! Notice I say *"everything"* not *"anything."* There is an important difference!

If someone were to give you "anything" in the world for which you might wish, the gift would automatically be *limited.* And far more would be withheld than would be given. "Anything" really means "any **one** thing." If the world were someone's to give, you'd get a tiny fraction of it, and the giver would keep the rest.

But to have "everything" is a promise without limitation! And an important part of Dyna/Psyc practice is the need to detect and be free of *any limitation.* When you read the first sentence above, you may already have started to limit what this book can give you. It is important that you do not let this happen.

Let's look at that first sentence again!

YOU ARE NOW ON YOUR WAY TO HAVING EVERYTHING IN THE WORLD YOU WANT!

What was your reaction when you read it? Did you start to reject the *possibility* of truth in that simple statement? Did your habit-conditioned mind automatically say, "Not me, no way," "Is, he kidding?" The strong possibility that you did *just that is* the reason we're dwelling on this statement at length.

Only a fool would accept such a statement on absolute faith, without any evidence whatsoever. But, a wise man, free of deadly self-limitation, would merely ask, "How?"

Don't be guilty of self-limitation. Don't reject the Riches which can be yours by "knowing" or "fearing" you can't have them. Ask only, "How?"

How can you have everything in the world you really want? Go with me through these pages, step by step, and you will KNOW! Can you forget self-limitation for the moment? Can you cast aside failure-oriented doubt long enough to try to *learn how?*

This is all that is required of you at this step. You don't have to believe anything, yet. But you must not *disbelieve* the possibility that Dyna/Psyc, *The Lazy Man's Way to Riches,* just might work for you.

WHAT IS DYNA/PSYC?

What is Dyna/Psyc? It is the "code word" I have found most fitting to use when referring to that collection of natural laws or truths which make up this fantastic success formula. **Dyna**, because it is indeed a dynamic concept, one which moves you

As long as I have a want, I have a reason for living. Satisfaction is death.

GEORGE BERNARD SHAW
(1856–1950)
Irish playwright, critic, social reformer

Men are not troubled by things themselves, but by their thoughts about them.

EPICTETUS
(c. 55–c. 135)
Greek Stoic philosopher

forward with great energy to the achievement of any goal. It is a source of great power, like some giant dynamo creating endless energy. And **Psyc**, because of two sciences fundamental to the method...Psychology, about which we have learned so much in the last seventy-five years, and Psychic Research, those far-less understood natural laws we are barely beginning to understand.

Dyna/Psyc: the programmed study and practice of achieving success by the planned application of important, but little understood, natural laws.

There may be certain fundamental truths in this approach to Dyna/Psyc, which you have heard before, but now you will see even these familiar facts in a new light and you will learn how to apply them to your problems. (You knew there were automobiles long before you were old enough or skilled enough to drive or repair them.)

Most of the things you will be learning, however, will be new and perhaps even a little strange to you. To help you rid yourself of disbelief, let me remind you of what Dyna/Psyc has done for me. To put this in its proper perspective, you have to be aware of my situation 11 years ago.

I was out of a job. My wife and I and our eight children were renting a ramshackle house in a deteriorating neighborhood. We were driving an old Falcon we'd had to refinance. We were $50,000 in debt. Under those circumstances, can you imagine how I felt when I was told that with Dyna/Psyc I could have "everything I really wanted?" I didn't believe it, but I had to admit that I had very little to lose. And maybe that's what saved me; I was desperate enough to try anything, even if it seemed foolish and ridiculously easy.

So they were saying that I could have "everything I really wanted"...well, I'd put that theory to the test. I'd set goals that were beyond my wildest dreams.

As God is my witness, these are the goals I wrote out during those black days—and this is what happened:

Goal: "I own a house on the water."

Fact: Three years later I bought a home in a marina community. With the improvements we added, it's now worth over $1,000,000. I know, because I turned down an offer for that much.

Goal: "I drive a brand new, black Thunderbird."

Fact: Within 30 days, I'd picked up an advertising account. It was a Ford agency. The manager said the Falcon I was driving was an embarrassment to the agency. He gave me a brand new, black Thunderbird to drive. A few months later I bought it.

Goal: "I earn $100,000 a year."

Fact: The next year I made $216,000 and haven't made less than that since.

Goal: "I own several small successful businesses. I leave the actual management to other capable people."

Fact: I do.

Goal: "I own a boat just like my neighbor Steve's!"

Fact: For a couple of years, I'd admired a boat that belonged to a friend of ours. Within 30 days, he phoned and told me he'd decided to sell it for a fraction of what he'd paid for it—and I could pay for it any way I wanted. It was so spooky that I accepted his offer. Now we have two boats—and we paid cash for them.

Goal: "My bills are paid."

Fact: That was really a tough one to say without feeling like an idiot. But, contrary to my lawyer's advice (who thought I should declare bankruptcy), I had a meeting with my creditors. I told them that I wanted to pay them back, but I couldn't concentrate on the effort with the fear that they'd attach my bank account every time I made a few bucks. They agreed to a repayment program that I felt I could live with. I never missed a payment and a few years later I paid off the balance in a lump sum.

Now, in case you are afraid the truths of Dyna/Psyc are somehow personal ones, producing rules that will work only for me, consider this:

Seven years ago I told a young man who sold me a boat dock about Dyna/Psyc. I did so because we had become friends, and he told me that the company he was working for was going broke and he'd be out of a job. His total assets were a half-interest in a motorcycle. He owed the bank for a loan. He'd never earned more than $10,000 a year.

He dropped by my office the other day, showed me his original goals and told me about his progress—every bit of which he credits to Dyna/Psyc. He not only reached but also surpassed every one of his goals and has set new ones.

Original goal:	A salary of $18,000 a year.
Fact:	He earns $60,000 a year and has stock options in the New York Stock Exchange listed company he works for.
Original goal:	Ownership of a vacation hideaway.
Fact:	He owns a half-interest in a $200,000 ranch.
Original goal:	To quit drinking.
Fact:	He did.
Original goal:	To own income property.
Fact:	He does. Two duplexes.
Original goal:	To own speculative and growth stocks.
Fact:	He does—$60,000 worth.

And there are lots of other people who have rebuilt their lives with the information I'm going to give you here.

There's a widow in Chicago who's earned $25,000 a year for the past five years, using my methods. The 70-year-old woman who has traveled all over the world is making all the money she needs, doing only what I taught her. Another man who works a lot harder than I'm willing to do, who is using these same principles, made 11 million dollars in eight years.

> Give me a stock clerk with a goal, and I will give you a man who will make history. Give me a man without a goal and I'll give you a stock clerk.
>
> JAMES CASH PENNEY
> (1875–1971)
> Founder JC Penney Co.

> **Fact:** It's worked, without exception, for everyone who's tried it! I'll admit, 'til now, I haven't shared the secret of Dyna/Psyc with too many people. Because most of the time, my only reward would be a patronizing smile. "After all," I can see them saying to themselves, "it couldn't be that easy."

But it is.

IT'S THAT EASY—IF YOU KNOW HOW

Perhaps you are wondering how so many people came to know of these natural laws and learned to take advantage of them. As long ago as the 1950's, key executives of highly successful, really big corporations, began to be "turned-on" to the very same truths you are to receive. No one knows, or at least I have been unable to determine with accuracy, the names of the very first researchers into what might be called the Scientific Basis of Success. But soon a number of costly but highly effective classes, seminars and private sessions were being carried on by the various practitioners.

The price for such services was high. But the thousands of dollars that were paid by the blue-chip executives was a paltry fee for the immediate and spectacular success stories that resulted from the application of the secrets they had learned.

Needless to say, as is always the secret with power, the men who were fortunate enough to have gained it were in no hurry to broadcast the news of it. They wanted to keep the powerful advantage they had received.

So great was the desire for secrecy that most of these power sessions were carried on away from the executive towers of the corporate giants. Small groups journeyed to mountain or desert retreats for the closed meetings. The fees were so high that, attendance was already limited to these top executives but, beyond that, only key people were even informed of the opportunity.

Since those early days, research has continued. The truths which evolved were the result of putting together facts from every, phase of human development. And as the findings of this research were assembled, certain well-defined *patterns of power*, making for *certain success*, became evident.

Those patterns explain why "some must win, some must lose." More importantly, the rules evolved from those patterns eliminate losing for those who follow them.

YOU CAN WIN TOO!

Can you learn how to apply Dyna/Psyc to your life? Indeed you can.

In the chapters that follow, you will learn things about yourself, which you never knew 'til now! You are going to learn why you have not been more successful than you have (and, incidentally, learn why you did things which you later called yourself a fool for doing). Just as importantly, you are going to learn how to have other people striving to give you what you want.

Never again will you look at a particularly successful person and sigh, "How lucky he is." Because you will know **that "luck" or "fate" has absolutely nothing**

To be conscious that you are ignorant is a great step to knowledge.

BENJAMIN DISRAELI
(1804–1881)
English statesman, writer

Success is the progressive realization of a worthy idea.

EARL NIGHTINGALE
(1921–1989)
Speaker, motivator

Luck is a matter of preparation meeting opportunity.

OPRAH WINFREY (b. 1954)
African-American television talk show host, actress

to do with success or failure. What we call "luck" is, in fact, a direct result of the correct or incorrect application of natural laws anyone can use effectively *if he/she knows how.*

Remember, the power to make things happen the way you want them to happen has always been available. You aren't going to have to create some new source of power within yourself. You are merely going to "plug-in" to the existing power.

The forces of Dyna/Psyc are very much like electricity. No one invented electricity; it existed in nature. But, until man learned how to make use of the already existing natural phenomenon, he had no electric lights to turn night into day. Now anyone can perform that miracle with the flick of a switch. He knows how to "plug in" to the electricity. You are going to learn to do this same thing with yet another natural power source.

Just as electricity can serve man when handled properly and injure him if mishandled, the forces of Dyna/Psyc are raw power and can work for your good— or your ill—depending on how they are utilized. There is every chance that you will learn, as you study, that you have been causing your failures through misuse of powers you did not even know you had.

But you have taken the important first step to undoing past mistakes and *creating* a whole new life for yourself—The Lazy Man's Way.

HOW DO YOU SPELL SUCCESS?

What represents success to you? Your answer would probably be similar to someone else's, but surely not identical. It should cover all the things which you feel make for success in your life: money, work, health, possessions, and love and for some, tranquility; for others, excitement. It isn't important how your view of success differs. What is important, according to scientific evaluation and research, is **for you to know what you really want out of life**.

Part of the work ahead of you will concern itself with an exact answer to that question of your desires. Why? Why do you have to have a specific inventory of what you want? Because surveys show that less than two people out of a thousand know what they want from life or have definite plans for achieving their desires.

And the same surveys show that people who do have such plans are able to make life payoff on their own terms. You will learn why this is an important factor, and how to effectively create a plan.

A specific plan is only one of the factors in the success of truly successful people. Here's a list of some of the other things that come to mind when we think of a person's success. From the list, select what you feel is the other quality all *real* successes have in common.

1. Luck, the "breaks"

2. Family background

3. Social achievement

4. Basic intelligence

> Men habitually use only a small part of the powers which they possess and which they might use under appropriate circumstances.
>
> WILLIAM JAMES
> (1842–1910)
> American philosopher, physiologist, psychologist, teacher

> There is only one success— to be able to spend your life in your own way.
>
> CHRISTOPHER MORLEY
> (1890–1957)
> American novelist, journalist, essayist

> The gent who wakes up and finds himself a success hasn't been asleep.
>
> WILSON MIZNER
> (1876–1933)
> American author

5. Education advantage

6. Good health

7. Enthusiasm

8. Winning personality

9. Real determination

10. Plenty of financing

**TAKE TIME TO EXAMINE THE CHOICES CAREFULLY
BEFORE YOU TURN TO THE NEXT PAGE!**

You're wrong!

For the sake of helping you learn a truth, which is essential to your acceptance of the natural laws that lie ahead, you've been tricked.

The correct answer, the other quality which all successful people have in common, was not listed. Think of that for a moment. Doesn't the list include every factor we're accustomed to thinking of when we think of success? Isn't the essential quality there?

No. Many people have had combinations of the qualities listed above and have failed miserably. Yet, people suffering severe handicaps of bad luck, poor beginnings, little formal education, ill health, shyness, and only a "shoestring" on which to begin have been preeminently successful.

What is that second quality common to all really successful people? The second step after knowing what you want and having a concrete plan for getting it? It is ***the ability to use effectively whatever asset you have.***

Every successful person has overcome his drawbacks by making effective use of whatever time, energy, money, ideas, etc., he possessed. They knew it wasn't what you had that counted…but how effectively you used it.

A learned man once wrote that there were really only three kinds of failures:

FAILURE TYPE 1: WELL DEFINED GOALS—INEFFECTIVE PURSUIT OF THEM.

This is the man who knows where he wants to go, but never quite gets there.

FAILURE TYPE 2: PUSHES HARD, USES EVERY ASSET—NO WELL DEFINED GOALS.

This man is like a powerful ship…without a rudder. He always seems to be making great headway but never arrives.

FAILURE TYPE 3 IS THE SADDEST OF THE LOT: HE HAS NEITHER WELL DEFINED GOALS, NOR IS HE EFFECTIVE.

Whatever your pattern has been in the past, whatever has caused your drives for success to fall short of your desires, your answer lies within these pages.

Think of your position at this time as though you were the owner of a palatial ocean-going yacht. I am the captain you have hired. The ship is yours; the choice of where you go is *yours*. My job is first to suggest the possible destinations, then, when you have made your choice, to layout a course that will take you there. That course must steer clear of any hazard that might prevent our safe and speedy arrival.

Since you will want to sail your own ship as soon as possible, we will see to it that you learn everything you need to know on this voyage. You will be your own captain long before we finish.

In other words, Dyna/Psyc promises to assist you in finding your purpose in life and in selecting important specific goals which support that purpose. Dyna/Psyc will provide you with all the effective tools you will need on your voyage toward your purpose—to success!

Everyone has a talent. What is rare is the courage to follow the talent to the dark places where it leads.
ERICA JONG (b. 1942)
American author

A teacher can only lead you to the threshold of your own mind.
KAHLIL GIBRAN
(1883–1931)
Syrian-American mystic, poet, painter

What is expected of you? What must you do in order to make the transition to the successful person you could be? Very little—when you measure the reward against the effort required attaining it. That's why I call this The Lazy Man's Way.

However, because so little is required of you, it does not follow that you can be lazy or haphazard in doing what is required. Quite the opposite. It is important that you *perform* in order to have all the benefits that Dyna/Psyc can bring you.

But the tasks are not numerous or difficult. You have only to R.S.V.P. to this invitation to wealth, success, and satisfaction!

R.S.V.P.: READ STUDY VISUALIZE PERFORM

As you go forward in the program, think of R.S.V.P. in these terms:

READ I must read in order to learn the secrets which will make my life easier, my success in every field of endeavor certain. How else but by reading, can I receive the truths, which come from the natural laws expressed by Dyna/Psyc?

But, if I *only* read, I cannot really learn. I did not learn my lessons in school by merely reading them in the same way that I read the daily paper.

Therefore, I must. . . .

STUDY I must study the things I read. I must do more than merely apply my eyes to the printed page. I must apply myself, mind, ideas, and thoughts to the substance of the words I read. By doing this, I will begin to make the power of Dyna/Psyc grow within me. That power comes from understanding; and to understand anything more than the simplest things, one must study.

Once I am building that power, I will need to apply it to my life situations. I will need clear outlines or blueprints of when, where, and how to apply the new-found power.

For this I will have to. . . .

VISUALIZE I must cultivate the capacity to visualize, in concrete form, everything I read and study. I must learn to take a mental or written suggestion and be able to project it like a motion picture on the hidden screen of my mind's eye. I must really see those suggestions, those plans, and those goals, in solid form in my mind's eye. Then they can be mine, in fact, through Dyna/Psyc.

Visualization is far more than mere imagination. It is always more complete, more detailed. In short, it has the effect of adding the potential of reality to the unsatisfying dream that is imagination.

The man who creates a new and important invention often starts with mere imagination—a dream. But, as his mind ponders the idea, he begins to visualize with ever-increasing exactness of detail. He begins to "see" his invention almost as though it were physically present in front of him. This I must do. It is not easy at first. But the unfolding of the program contained in these pages will provide many ways to help me visualize—and turn dreams into reality.

Visualization of your goals allows your subconscious mind to work for you, behind the scenes, to manifest the situations that will ultimately enable your goals

The man who does not read books has no advantage over the man who can't read them.

MARK TWAIN
(1835–1910)
Pen name of Samuel Langhorne Clemens
American writer and humorist

Vision is the art of seeing things invisible.

JONATHAN SWIFT
(1667–1745)
English satirist;
Thoughts on Various Subjects
(1711)

To accomplish great things, we must not only act but also dream, not only dream, but also believe.

ANATOLE FRANCE
(1844–1924)
French novelist, poet, critic

and dreams to come true. The process of achieving your goals through the application of positive mental images (visualizations) will empower you to create reality from your desires.

I can reach that plateau of ability if I....

PERFORM The manner in which I perform is all outlined in great detail in the chapters and steps which lie ahead. I have only to promise myself that I will try the outlined steps. The success factor is already built into each step.

This means the scientific basis of achievement have been studied and analyzed for me in order to create Dyna/Psyc.

I have only to perform the basic, simple steps outlined by reading, studying, visualizing and then performing.

When this R.S.V.P. is complete—success must be mine!

Men are all alike in their promises. It is only in their deeds that they differ.

MOLIERE
(1622–1673)
French comic playwright;
The Miser (1668)

Now turn to Step #4 "Yes, You Can Have Everything You Want!"
in your *Roadmap to Riches* workbook.

5

A Successful Journey—Onward!

Let's look at your success-asset score. Were you surprised at the way we determined your success-ability? How often did you think to yourself, "How could that be important? What's that got to do with success?" Did you complete the step by figuring your success score? If not, then PLEASE go back to those pages now and do that before reading any further.

Do you feel like a valuable person? Are you a little concerned that your success-ability score is low? Don't be. Remember we are measuring your attitudes not what you really are. It's pretty obvious from the scoring that we consider certain personality traits far more important than the skills you have developed. We are much more interested in your attitudes about yourself than we are in your accomplishments at this point. If someone had rated Joe's chances at becoming a millionaire based on his accomplishments before he started on The Lazy Man's Way, he'd have been considered a very long shot. His greatest accomplishments, at least financially, had been to get himself deeply into debt. He often said that was a blessing in disguise, because it forced him to pay attention to the principles that now form the core of *The Lazy Man's Way to Riches*.

If your success-asset score is low does that mean you can't make progress on The Lazy Man's Way? No. What it really means is that you can't see what you really are. You'll have to pay extra attention to Chapter 22, which covers your self-images and self-esteem. It's obvious from the way we scored the success asset quiz that the first answer to each question is the one that shows the highest success-asset. You may disagree with our choices; that's fine but look at each question to try to see why we think those qualities are important.

Regardless of your success-asset score you can still make rapid progress on The Lazy Man's Way. It's a fundamental part of this program that you are not stuck with what you said you think you are or were in the past. Take charge of your life and make a change for the better—Now!

WE BEGIN

You and I have now examined together some important concepts which you must have before we commence the actual work of improvement. We are now ready for your first positive action.

It is an action that sounds easy. But don't be fooled; it is going to take you quite a lot of time to complete. And I promise you it is going to produce some truths about yourself that you never really knew until now.

There's only one corner of the universe you can be certain of improving and that's your own self.

ALDOUS HUXLEY
(1894–1963)
English novelist, essayist, satirist

Convictions are more dangerous enemies of truth than lies.

FRIEDRICH NIETZSCHE
(1844–1900)
German philosopher

Understanding human
needs is half the job of
meeting them.

ADLAI STEVENSON
(1900–1965)
American statesman,
politician

Your first positive action is to answer this short question:

"WHAT DO YOU WANT?"

The work of it begins when I tell you that you must answer that question, *fully and completely* in black and white! Right now you may begin a complete list of what you want.

Why such a detailed list? Because that is the first step to getting them. This list becomes a list of your goals, your destinations.

Tell me this. Can you imagine a man going to the nearest airport to catch a plane with only the vaguest idea of where he wanted to go? If you were the ticket seller, what would you do to help him? Can you visualize what would happen?

Man: I'd like a ticket, please.

You: Certainly, sir, where to?

Man: Oh . . . uh . . . some place nice.

You: I don't understand.

Man: Well, it's important I get someplace, I don't want to just waste time. I want to really get someplace.

You: Someplace like where?

Man: Oh, someplace where I can be happy. Where I can have a good income. Get a new car, maybe. Perhaps become an executive with a good company or even have my own business of some sort. Be able take care of my family. You know, I'd like to get someplace where things are really great for me and my family, just give me a ticket, I'll pay for it.

You: But, sir, I can't sell you a ticket until you know exactly where you want to go.

Wouldn't that be your reaction? You would have no way to help that man until he could tell you where he wanted to go.

And isn't that what you've been saying to life? "I want to get someplace" covers everything and yet nothing! One thinks he has a goal because he wants to "be somebody." But until there is a very clear picture of that position, one cannot hope to achieve it.

Looking at your life in this way, it isn't surprising that you have not already reached the height of success you might desire—on the contrary, it is remarkable that you have achieved any success at all.

Goals are not only
absolutely necessary to
motivate us. They are
essential to really keep
us alive.

REV. ROBERT SCHULLER
(b. 1926)
Minister, author, social leader

Without clear, well-defined goals, success is impossible. We are now going to establish those goals. We are going to first put them into the simplest practical terms. We will be exact, for simplicity requires exactness. To make it easy for you to list your wants, I have broken the task down into three parts and included a few typical suggestions to illustrate which "want" fits each category in Step 5, in your *Roadmap to Riches* workbook.

LIST 1—THINGS I FEEL I NEED RIGHT NOW.

LIST 2—THINGS I WANT.

LIST 3—PERSONAL QUALITIES I NEED OR WANT.

List 1 and 2 will probably be easy for you because they deal with tangible things, but List 3 may be more difficult because it deals with intangible things, personal qualities. Don't worry about how to get the newer and better qualities any more than you worried about the "things" you need and want; just list them as they occur to you.

The Journey Has Just Begun

　　by Francis X. Maguire

Perfection is being right.
　　Excellence is willing to be wrong.

Perfection is fear.
　　Excellence is taking a risk.

Perfection is anger and frustration.
　　Excellence is powerful.

Perfection is control.
　　Excellence is spontaneous.

Perfection is judgment.
　　Excellence is accepting.

Perfection is taking.
　　Excellence is giving.

Perfection is doubt
　　Excellence is confidence.

Perfection is pressure.
　　Excellence is natural.

Perfection is the destination.
　　Excellence is the journey.

The keener the want the lustier the growth.

WENDELL PHILLIPS
(1811–1884)
American abolitionist, orator

Now turn to Step #5 "A Successful Journey—Onward!"
in your *Roadmap to Riches* workbook.

6

Tools You Need to Get What You Want

Welcome to the first day of the **Best** of your life. I said that in the first chapter, didn't I? But it's true today as well as every day if you stick to The Lazy Man's Way. Every page is a step in the right direction.

How many people do you know who think the best is behind them? People who think they have missed the boat and are now content to sit on the shore and just watch the water flow by?

A lot of people are washed up at 25 or 30, 35 or 40, because they think they are. But many others didn't get started on the road to success until they were in their 60's, 70's or even 80's. Ronald Reagan was the oldest man ever elected President of the United States at the age of 69. Colonel Sanders started his fried chicken empire at an age when most people are thinking of retiring. Dr. Forest Shacklee started his $500 million marketing and manufacturing company when he was 62. Carman K. Jones founded Kids Korner Fresh Pizza in Wausau, Wisconsin at age 61, and Tom Duck founded Ugly Duckling Rent-A-Car in Tuscon, Arizona at age 63. I read in the *Wall Street Journal* just the other day about a man who enjoys a six-figure income from a business he started when he was 86. I suspect you are probably younger than 86, but if you're not, don't let that stop you, the best is yet to come if you want it that way.

Using the *Roadmap to Riches Guidebook* you have put down in black and white what you want for yourself and have evaluated your success-ability. Let's look at the assets necessary to achieve those goals. Joe began addressing the subject by stating two assets absolutely necessary as:

1. Having a defined plan and

2. The ability to use effectively whatever assets you have.

Let's further identify, and focus on, which qualities are essential for success.

BELIEF AND DESIRE

Many years ago, Andrew Carnegie, an uneducated immigrant who started with nothing and built an enormous business empire, decided to find out just what made successful people successful. He knew from his own experience it wasn't family background, or education, or having money to start with; rather, it was certain universal principles or assets that any person could apply to become successful.

He commissioned a young and talented writer, Napoleon Hill, to interview the most successful men of the times. Using the magic of the Carnegie name, Mr. Hill was able to speak to several hundred outstanding business and political leaders and presented his results in his famous book, *Think and Grow Rich*. (Available for purchase on our website; http://www.thelazymans_way.com/)

He who has patience may accomplish anything.

RABELAIS
(1494–1553)
French scholar, humorist

Man is what he believes.

ANTON CHEKHOV
(1860–1904)
Russian writer

People who are unable to motivate themselves must be content with mediocrity; no matter how impressive their other talents.

ANDREW CARNEGIE
(1835–1918)
American industrialist, philanthropist

Mr. Hill found thirteen magic assets for finding and guiding personal success that appeared time and time again in his interviews. Of course not everyone had all thirteen assets; in fact, most people had only five or six. But there were two assets that every single person absolutely possessed, and if someone had only these assets to begin with, he or she quickly and easily acquired the others that were needed.

These are the two assets I believe you are going to have to acquire before you'll ever achieve the Riches that The Lazy Man's Way has in store for you. Fortunately, if you don't already possess these assets, I am going to show you how to develop them. What are these two magical qualities that absolutely guarantee success?

The first is a **burning desire**. I can hear you saying "Oh come on—quit kidding around. I've had a burning desire for a million dollars for years and I'm not even close." Let's look a little closer at your burning desire. Is what you want really important to you? I mean really important—or is it just what I call a "wouldn't it be nice if" desire. Wouldn't it be nice if I had a million dollars, or wouldn't it be nice if we had a home on the beach? Everybody has those kinds of desires; in fact, lots of them. But they come and go, and, more importantly, most people never allow those desires to interfere with the pleasures of the moment. In other words, "Sure I'd like to have a million dollars, but you don't expect me to give up watching Monday night football on television to get it, do you?"

I don't expect you to give up anything that is important to you because I believe you can have everything in the world that is truly important to you. It's an essential part of The Lazy Man's Way that you don't have to make sacrifices; but if everything in your life now is more important than what you think you desire, maybe you really don't have a burning desire after all. There is nothing wrong if this is the case. Perhaps you're happy, just as you are, and that's great. But if you do see some important things as lacking in your life, then you'll have to find room for the things that you need to achieve—the things your heart desires.

What do I mean when I talk about burning desire? A true burning desire is that honest "knowing" that resides in your core being or "soul" that is undeniable and honest and when clearly defined and allowed to be brought into the light, will grow into a powerful force that will propel you forward over seemingly insurmountable obstacles. Your true burning desires are undeniable, true, absolute and powerful. Acknowledging a burning desire is the key that can open any door to a life filled with reward, joy and satisfaction. Recognizing a true burning desire is what gives you the confidence and therefore the power to act decisively and effectively to overcome all obstacles that stand in your way.

THE "GNAW" FACTOR

A true burning desire gnaws at you from the inside. It claws at your inner self trying to get out. It is something that you probably have always "known" was there because you could feel it. Well, now is the time to let it out. Stop kidding yourself that your burning desires don't exist. Stop hiding it because you are not sure you could ever have them or that you don't deserve them or that "they" (whoever they are) won't approve. Attainment of your burning desire has little to do with age, race, gender, background, education, experience; geographic location,

I have a dream.

MARTIN LUTHER KING, JR.
(1924–1968)
American clergyman and civil-rights leader

Hold fast to your dreams, for if dreams die, then life is like a broken winged bird that cannot fly

LANGSTON HUGHES
(1902–1967)
American poet

You're not free until you've been made captive by supreme belief.

MARIANNE MOORE
(1887–1972)
American poet

the weather, the IRS, the government... The only thing that matters is whether or not it's something that you truly want—something you honestly desire in your heart of hearts.

When he was asked during an interview how he managed to reach the top as a professional bodybuilder, become one of the worlds most famous movie stars, and Governor of California, Arnold Schwarzenegger replied with a single word, "Drive!" All great success ultimately begins with an idea, but what makes ideas become reality is the fuel of human desire. An idea by itself can give you a temporary feeling of inspiration, but a burning desire is what gets you through all the perspiration necessary to overcome the inevitable obstacles along the way.

One way to determine whether your burning desires are valid and not just "wants" or "shoulds" or "ought to's," is to check where they are coming from. True burning desires come from your inner self and will elicit feelings and emotions in you that may expresses itself with words of; "Yes, that's it. That's what I want!" You may find yourself smiling or on the verge of tears or your pulse may quicken. You may simply feel yourself overwhelmed. Whatever you feel, you'll recognize the truth and honesty of the feeling as you admit your true burning desires to yourself. You'll see the significance of burning desires throughout this program.

But for now let's discuss this second vital asset; it can be called various things, but I call it **belief.** The belief that you actually can have the object or condition you desire. If you actually have a burning desire for something and you are not making progress toward it, it's a sure thing that the lack of this second asset is where the problem lies. You really doubt you can have it. There is a simple test to see if you believe or not.

> Man is a credulous animal, and must believe something; in the absence of good grounds for belief—he will be satisfied with bad ones.
>
> BERTRAND RUSSELL
> (1872–1970)
> English philosopher, mathematician, and social reformer

Let's say you have a burning desire to be a millionaire—or maybe it's just to have all your debts paid and $10,000 in the bank. Say firmly to yourself, "Within the very near future I am a millionaire." Or, "Within the very near future I have paid all my debts and have $10,000 in the bank." Now quickly, focus on the immediate thought that floods your mind. Do you have doubts about your statements? Make the statement again and this time really get in touch with how you feel.

Are you filled with a feeling of confidence that you're actually going to succeed, or are your thoughts primarily negative? The more doubts, the harder it will be for you. The less doubts, the easier.

DOUBTS—GET RID OF THEM!

When you eliminate all the doubts, your goal is accomplished almost without effort. This is why we call it The Lazy Man's Way.

So, how do you get rid of doubts? First, you've got to identify the sources of those doubts and eliminate them. I want you to do two things: Write down one thing you really want (something that is important enough to you to be a burning desire) from each of the seven categories listed. They are: Financial, Mental, Emotional, Social, Vocational, Physical and Spiritual. These seven categories are the areas that can help you achieve balance in your life, if you pay attention to each and every one of them. Some people seem to focus on the financial; and that's OK, as long as you don't do so to the exclusion of the others.

Look hard for what you really want and don't worry about locking yourself into your current desires and if you can't find something right away, don't worry. Later on I'll tell you three things that are probably blocking your desires (You may just need permission to have a desire.) By the time you are through reading this book and having used the Guidebook; doing all of the exercise steps, I'll be very surprised if you haven't revised your goals several times. But for now, get something started and write it down in your Guidebook.

Once you have done this, look at the pros, obstacles and evaluations of your desires, in order to analyze why you are not getting the things that you really want. What has stopped you? What's holding you down? What are the obstacles or circumstances or handicaps that have held you back? The pro's—Why do you want them? What's the payoff for you? Be specific, spell it out. And the cons—What's standing in your way? Why haven't you done more? Gone on further? Made it happen? Get it *all* down on paper, every problem that stands between you and what you want. List every link in the chain that is holding you back.

Take a moment to think about the goals you've set for yourself. How committed are you to achieving these goals? Under what conditions would you give up? What if you could significantly increase your desire to achieve these goals? What if you wanted them so badly that you knew with total and absolute certainty that you would absolutely, positively never ever give up? When you are truly 100 percent committed to reaching your goals, you move from "hope" to "know". If you want something badly enough, then quitting is simply not an option. You either find a way or make one. You pay the price, whatever it takes.

People with an intense, burning desire to achieve their goals are referred to as "driven." Is this special quality reserved only for a privileged few? I think not because below I am giving you seven steps to cultivate the fertile ground on which to grow your burning desires. With the right approach, anyone can cultivate a deep, burning desire within them and move to a state of total commitment, knowing with certainty that success is as inevitable as the sunrise.

So, how do you reveal, or discover, and finally admit your burning desires so that you can then nurture and cultivate a burning desire? You begin with an outside-in approach, altering your environment in ways that will strengthen your resolve while eliminating doubt. If you take the time to do it right, you'll establish a positive feedback cycle, such that your desire will continue to increase on a daily basis and become a success habit.

Here are seven steps you can take to cultivate burning desire to achieve any goal or desire you set for yourself:

1. Burn your ships.

This can't be stressed enough. If your goals are really important enough to you, then you can start by burning the proverbial ships, so that you have no choice but to press on. That's exactly what the ancient Greeks used to do. For example, if you want to launch your own business, you can begin by making the commitment to quit your job. Write a letter of resignation, and put it in an envelope with a date on it when you hand it in. I'd make the date short term, and then cut that frame in half.

My life is one long obstacle course—with me being the chief obstacle.

JACK PAAR
(b. 1918)
American author and television show host

In the classic book *The Art of War*, Sun Tzu notes that soldiers fight the most ferociously when they believe they're fighting to the death. A good general knows that when attacking an opposing force, it's important to create the illusion of a potential escape route for the enemy, so they won't fight as hard. What escape routes are you keeping open that are causing you not to fight as hard?

If you don't burn those ships, you have just sent another message to your subconscious mind that it's OK to quit. And when the going gets tough, as it inevitably does for any worthwhile goal, you will quit once again. If you really want to achieve your goals, then you've got to burn those ships to the ground, and scatter the ashes. If you're thinking that the average person won't do this, you're right . . . *that's why they're average.*

2. Fill your environment with desire boosters.

Let's say one of your important goals is to lose weight. Get some easel paper, and make your own posters that say, "I weigh X pounds," where X is your goal weight, and put them up around your house or office. Change your screensaver to a text message that says the same thing (or to some equally motivational imagery). Cut pictures out of magazines of people who have bodies similar to what you'd like to have, and put them up around your house. Cut out pictures of healthy food that look good to you, and post those on your refrigerator. If you work in an office, then alter your office in the same manner. Don't worry about what your coworkers will think, and just do it! They may poke a little fun at you at first, but they'll also begin to see how committed you are.

3. Surround yourself with positive people.

Seek out and make friends with people who will encourage you on the path to your goals, and find ways to spend more time with them. Share your goals only with people who will support you, not those who will respond with cynicism or indifference. If you want to lose weight, for instance, get yourself into a gym, and start befriending those who are already in great shape. You'll find that their attitudes become infectious, and you'll start believing that you can do it too. Meeting peple who've lost one hundred pounds or more can be extremely motivating. If you want to start a new business, join the local chamber of commerce or a trade association. If you want to take your present business to the next level, join TEC (The Executive Committee http://teconline.com). Do whatever it takes to make new friends who will help you keep your commitments to yourself. Don't have time to make those positive new friends? Sure you do, just replace some of the toxic and negative people in your life.

Although this can be difficult for some people, you also need to fire the toxic and negative people from your life. It's been said that you can see your future just by looking at the six people with whom you spend the most time. If you don't like what you see, then change those people. There's no honor in remaining loyal to people who expect you to fail.

One of the reasons people fail to start their own businesses, for instance, is that they spend most of their time associating with other employees. The way out of this trap is to start spending a lot more time associating with business owners and entrepreneurs, such as by joining a trade association. Mindsets are contagious. So spend your time with people whose mindsets are worth catching.

4. Feed your mind with empowering information on a daily basis.

Motivational, inspirational, personal growth books and audio CD programs are one of the best sources for cultivating desire and building confidence. Nightingale Conant has some of the best. If you want to quit smoking, read a dozen books written by ex-smokers on how to quit the habit. If you want to start a business, then start devouring business books.

Go to seminars on occasion. I advise that you feed your mind with some form of motivational, inspirational or personal growth material (books, articles, and audio programs) for at least fifteen minutes a day…(listen to an audio CD while at the health club, or in the car while driving to work, to start your day off right). This will continually recharge your batteries and keep your dreams and desire strong.

5. Replace negative energy with positive energy.

Take an inventory of all the sensory inputs into your life that affect your attitude—what you read, what you watch on TV, the newspapers and magazines you read. Note which inputs influence you negatively, and strive to replace them with positive inputs.

Here are some good places to start. First, avoid watching TV news—it's overwhelmingly negative. Do you really need to hear another "victim" crying about how unfair this or that is? Fill that time with positive inputs instead, like inspirational and motivational tapes and CDs. If you like to watch movies, watch movies that are full of positive energy and stories of triumph over adversity. Read biographies of people who have done what you aspire to do. Spend more time laughing and less time worrying. If you have a hard time motivating yourself, chances are that your life is overflowing with too many sources of negativity. It's far better to happily achieve than it is to feel you must achieve in order to be happy.

6. Dress for success.

As you pass by mirrors you get an instant dose of image reinforcement. What image are you currently reinforcing? How is your posture? How differently will you dress when you are the successful person you want to become? Would you dress any differently if your goals were already achieved? Would you wear a different hairstyle? Shine your shoes? Remove some tattoos?

For years I enjoyed the faded jeans and polo shirt look. I noted that when I visualized myself in the future, having achieved certain goals, I was dressed a lot more nicely. Like many in the speaking and consulting industry, I'm almost allergic to suits now because I only wore suits and a tie for years. I still own several for the necessary business functions and weddings and funerals.

However, I was able to find a style of nicer-looking clothing that is also very comfortable for me. So I gradually donated my old clothes to charity and replaced my wardrobe with clothes that fit the new identity I was growing into. I call it a casual business look—my wife calls it a blazer with turtle neck look. I learned this idea from a retired-CEO, who stressed to me the importance of taking pride in my appearance, and I can say with certainty that it makes a noticeable difference. So make sure the clothes you wear each day are consistent with your new self-image.

7. Take immediate action.

Once you set a goal for yourself, act immediately. As you begin working on a fresh new goal, don't worry so much about making detailed long-term plans. Too often people get stuck in the state of analysis paralysis and never reach the action stage. You can fully develop your plan later, but get moving first. Just identify the very first physical action you need to take, and then do it. For instance, if you've decided to get in better shape, put on your exercise clothes right now (this book will be here when you finish) and do some exercises. Don't think about it. Don't ponder the consequences. Just do it immediately.

One of the secrets to success is recognizing that motivation follows action. The momentum of continuous action fuels motivation, while procrastination kills motivation. So act boldly, act as if it's impossible to fail. If you keep adding fuel to your desire, you will reach the point of knowing that you'll never quit, and ultimate success will be nothing more than a matter of time.

If you apply these seven strategies, you'll add so much fuel to your burning desire that the fire will continue to burn brightly as you accomplish your goals, dreams, ambitions and your destiny. You'll move towards your goals like a homing pigeon to its nest, and you'll enjoy the process because you'll be focused on the positive rewards you want instead of the difficulty of the tasks. If you get enough positive energy flowing into you, you'll soon have positive results flowing from you and you'll quickly become the kind of person that others refer to as truly "driven."

This may not be easy because you'll really have to be honest; but do it. When you have all of your pro's and con's on paper, do one more thing: decide whether each obstacle you face is a problem with your attitude or your environment. In other words, is the obstacle in your mind or is it something outside you that stands in your way? Be honest with yourself. This is a very important step in *The Lazy Man's Way to Riches*.

Now turn to Step #6 "Tools You Need to Get What You Want" in your *Roadmap to Riches* workbook.

7

Turning Your Desires into Goals

Now you have completed the first step in arriving at the blueprint for the future—which is the prime requisite to using Dyna/Psyc to attain Riches. You have made lists of those things you need and want, tangible and intangible, which make up your desires; and you have evaluated them carefully.

The next step is laying out those *listed* items in a manner that lends itself to the constant "use" which your success will require. In short, we must turn loose "lists" into concrete goals. This must be done by applying certain qualities or points of reference to the lists, in order to make them entirely consistent with you, your purpose and goals, your life, and with each other.

A bit further on is a checklist consisting of nine questions, for goal development. Take each one of the "burning desires" you have listed; and using these questions, examine each one carefully. The desire may have to be altered slightly to meet all tests below, but it can be done. Once the desire in a form that will meet each test below— I want you to *write it down* in your workbook. These writings are your GOALS.

Remember, this is one of the most important steps in your progress; it you do not write your goals, you cannot use them as set forth in later chapters. If they are not made to conform to the following checklist, you will find you cannot use them properly and they will be far less effective.

WHAT COMES FIRST? THE HEAD OF THE LIST GOALS

In addition to the desires you have listed as needs and wants, and now are converting to positive goals, there are a few goals/declarations that are included on your list.

I ask that you include them because it has been my experience and the experience of many others, that they do much to guarantee the fulfillment of your own unique desires.

When you read them, you will see that they are all positive in nature, I have come to call them the "head of the list" goals. This is because they are already in a form you can use—they start you on the task of writing goals instead of just "thinking about them;" and they are the basics which underlie all that you will add after them.

So, start your list of goals with the following "Head of the List Goals":

1. Each and every day I follow these procedures set out for my improvement. I become more effective, better able to function without limitation.

2. I pursue my goals free of any feelings of ill will or animosity toward others. I am a warm, friendly, well-liked person. My success is assured and does

He has half the deed done who has made a beginning.

HORACE
(65–8 BC)
Roman poet and satirist

Until you write down your dream it is just a dream. Writing it makes it a goal.

JOHN GODDARD
(b. Witheld upon request)
Anthropologist, explorer, adventurer, speaker, author

not require me to take advantage of any other person.

Rather, it obliges me to help others, without telling anyone about my "good deeds."

3. I see myself with the success-eye of NOW. I have discarded the failure-eye of my infancy. I am free at last of failure or limitations.

Now, add your own goals. Add *every* goal you require to fill your needs and wants and to acquire the necessary personality factors from your early lists. Put them into your own words, being careful only that they be stated as positive, already accomplished, and set forth in great detail.

Now please turn to *Step 4*, of your Guidebook, *Turning Burning Desires into Goals.* Use the checklist below to start writing your desires as stated goals. You will probably restate these *goals* several times, so I have provided you with lots of room so get started; and don't worry if they're not exactly "right" at this point.

9 CHECKLIST QUESTIONS FOR YOUR GOALS

1. **Do you really want this?**
   (Or will it just "sound good" if someone else reads it? Or is it so small a goal you think you have a good chance of getting it? This must be something you really want—the ultimate!)

2. **Does this goal contradict any other goal you are setting?**
   (Such as wanting a $500,000 house with a $20,000/year income?)
   Solution: Raise your salary or income goal.

3. **Any problems with goal cooperation?**
   (Would your family be against your achieving these new goals? Talk it over and adjust your goals only if necessary.)

4. **Is your goal stated as positive rather than negative?**
   (As we said before—it's what you want, not what you want to get rid of.)

5. **Is your goal expressed in total detail?**
   (Not a big new car; not a big, new $65,000 car; not a big, fancy BMW; instead: a brand new, black BMW 745 IL, with . . . GPS, XM Satellite Radio, etc. . . . listing every detail as though you had to depend on this description alone after giving the company your cash!) No matter what it is, make it exact in the same degree of detail.

6. **Is it realistic?**
   (And here I mean only—is it possible for some human beings to achieve it? I do not mean is it realistic for the "you of today" to have it?) The realism to which I have reference is shown by contrast:

   Unrealistic: I want to fly through the air without a plane or any other appliance of flight.

   Realistic: I want to pilot my own private $1,250,000 aircraft. (If it's a goal *someone* could attain, it's a realistic enough goal.) Let's face it, we are all created equal. If he/she can do something, we all can do that thing also. If you can learn to walk, I can learn to walk. If you can learn to read. I can learn

---

A strong passion for any object will ensure success, for the desire of the end will point out the means.

WILLIAM HAZLITT
(1778–1830)
English essayist and critic

to read. If you can learn to drive, I can learn to drive. If you can learn to operate a computer, I can learn to operate a computer. If you can learn to run a company, I can learn to run a company. Where does it end? It doesn't—until you quit.

7. Is this goal high enough?

(Because this factor is so important, and so often misunderstood, I want to tell you about it before we go any further.)

Number seven is the most serious checkpoint for turning your lists into goals, because it is the last chance I have to persuade you to *stop limiting yourself.*

If you have asked for an income (a paltry two or three thousand dollars more than what you are making), if you've asked for a position which is up the ladder only a rung or two from where you now stand—you are asking not to succeed!

More than that, you are guaranteeing you will not succeed!

You're using what should be a FLOOR for a CEILING! Don't use the goal method as a system of limitation. Reach out! Set the goal limit in every area of your life at the very peak of what you'd like to have—not at what you think doesn't sound too "greedy" or "unreal."

Be sure your goals are set high enough! I cannot emphasize this too much. There is no goal which is so high that it is not realistic if some human being can make or has made it!

(Take a look at number six on our checklist again.)

Nothing should enter your mind, at this point in time, as to how you are going to achieve these goals! That's not your problem; that's my problem. I've made you a promise—"everything in the world you really want." All I'm asking you to do now is make up a **full** and complete list; your task is not to decide for yourself whether or not you could achieve a certain goal.

I'll show you the "how you get" after you've established the "what you want."

8. Am I including the personality factors necessary for goal achievement?

(If you are going to have changed circumstances, you will need the perseverance, determination, self-confidence, and other traits which you know are requisites. Don't worry about how to get the newer and better qualities any more than you worried about the "things" which are your goals. Just list them with the other goals.)

9. Is each goal stated as though already accomplished?

(That is, are the things you want worded on the goal list expressed as though you already had them? They must be!)

Don't write: "I want . . . I wish . . . I need . . ."

Do write: "I have . . . I am . . . I own . . . ."

It is always too soon to quit.

REV. DAVID T. SCOATES
(1934–2000)
Minister, author, counselor

I will go anywhere, as long as it is forward.

DAVID LIVINGSTONE
(1813–1873)
Scottish missionary, explorer

Ah, but a man's reach should exceed his grasp, or what's a heaven for?

ROBERT BROWNING
(1812–1889)
English poet

The world is moving so fast these days that the man who says it can't be done is generally interrupted by someone doing it.

ELBERT HUBBARD
(1856–1915)
American businessman, writer, printer

EXAMPLES OF HOW TO STATE YOUR GOALS

I own a brand new, black BMW 745 IL automobile, equipped with GPS, XM Satellite Radio, etc.

I am an effective person who always follows through on things I start. . . etc.

Note: This form is essential to the psychological and psychic effectiveness of the declarations, which are to come. Be certain you use this form in writing up your goals.

WHAT COMES SECOND? THE POWER OF CLARITY

Nelson Bunker Hunt, a man who rose from being a bankrupt farmer in the 1930s to a multi-billionaire oil man when he died in the 1970s, was once asked during a TV interview what advice he could give to others who wanted to be financially successful. He responded by saying that it's not terribly difficult to be successful and that only two things are required. First, you must decide exactly what it is you want to accomplish. Most people never do that in their entire lives. And secondly, you must determine what price you'll have to pay to get it, and then resolve to pay that price.

Study after study has shown how essential clear goals and objectives are to the success of any business. If you do not take the time to get really clear about exactly what it is you're trying to accomplish, then you are forever doomed to spend your life achieving the goals of those who do.

"University of Illinois football coach Bob Zuppke was renowned for the fire and flavor of his half-time pep talks. One afternoon, his team hit the locker room after the first half well behind in both points and enthusiasm. Zuppke began talking to the team and the more he talked the louder and more dramatic his voice became. The momentum built in the players. Then coach pointed to the door at the far end of the locker room and said, "Now go out there and win the game." Filled with emotion the players got off the bench, ran towards the door and charged through it. But it was the wrong door, and one by one they fell into the swimming pool." It is one thing to be all charged up—it's another to be headed in the right direction.

—As related by Rev. David Tyler Scoates of
The Crystal Cathedral in Garden Grove, CA

In the absence of a clear direction, you will either meander aimlessly or you will go where you don't really feel good about being. You may make some progress and even some money, but the end result will not resemble anything you ever made a conscious decision to be or have and ultimately you will be left with the sinking feeling that maybe you took a wrong turn somewhere along the way. Do you ever look at yourself and think, "How on earth did I wind up here?"

If setting goals is so critically important, then why is it that so few people take the time to define exactly where they want to go? Part of the reason is a lack of knowledge about how to set clear goals. You can go through years of schooling and never receive any instruction on goal setting at all. A failure to understand the immense importance of establishing clear goals is all too common.

WHAT THEY FOUND AT YALE

In 1954 Yale University did a study that found that only 3 percent of the graduating seniors had clear written goals. Twenty years later, in 1973, the surviving members of that class were interviewed, and it was found that the 3 percent with clear written goals was worth more in financial terms than the other 97 percent combined. Those who truly know what they want commonly outperform everyone else by an enormous degree. Let that sink in.

A frequent deterrent to goal setting is the fear of making a mistake. President Franklin Delano Roosevelt said that "the best thing you can do is the right thing, and the worst thing you can do is nothing." The best way I know to guarantee failure is to avoid making clear, committed decisions. Every day starts as a mistake if you don't know where you're going.

Many people assume that because they have a direction, they must therefore have goals, but this is not the case and merely creates the illusion of progress. "Making more money" and "building a business" are not goals. A goal is a specific, clearly defined, measurable state. An example of the difference between a direction and a goal is the difference between the compass direction of West and the entrance to the West rim of the Grand Canyon. One is merely a direction; the other is a definite location.

One critical aspect of goals is that they must be defined in absolute terms. At any point in time, if you were asked if you had achieved your goal yet, you must be able to give a definitive "yes" or "no" answer; "maybe" is not an option. You cannot say with absolute certainty if you have achieved the outcome of "making more money," but you can give a definitive answer as to whether or not you are currently standing at the entrance to the West rim of the Grand Canyon. That is the level of clarity you need in order to form a goal that your mind can lock onto and move towards rapidly.

Be as detailed as possible when setting goals. Give specific numbers, dates, and times. Make sure that each of your goals is measurable. Either you achieved it, or you didn't. Define your goals as if you already know what's going to happen. It's been said that the best way to predict the future is to create it.

Setting **clear** goals requires a positive **action**. It can only happen deliberately. You must take direct conscious action in order to make it so. Everything counts, and nothing is neutral. You are either moving towards your goals, or you're moving away from them. If you do nothing or if you act without clarity, then you are almost certainly a victim of "being outgoaled." In other words you are spending your time working on other people's goals without even knowing it. Then you are happily working to satisfy your father, mother, teachers, coaches, or someone else's goals for you. Or, you are doing it to enrich your landlord, other businesses, advertisers, your boss, etc.

Each day you spend working without a sense of clarity about exactly where you're headed is a step backwards for you. If you don't actively tend your garden, then weeds will grow. Weeds don't need to be watered or fertilized. They just grow by themselves in the absence of an attentive gardener. Similarly, in the absence of conscious and directed action on your part, your personal and your business life will automatically become full of weeds.

Reading this will do absolutely nothing for you unless you turn it into some form of physical action. Even the best thinking without action always gives you zero results. You only get results from the physical actions you take, never for the ideas you have. In order to get any kind of tangible results at all, you must act on an idea. Grandma Rose always said to me "Always remember, GOAL begins with GO."

Clarity is a choice, not an accident or a gift. Clarity doesn't come to you—you have to go to it. Not setting goals is the same thing as deciding to be a slave to the goals of others. Failing to plan is actually planning to fail.

Your reality will not match your vision exactly. That's not the point. The point is for your vision to allow you to make clear daily decisions that keep you moving in the direction of your goals. When a commercial airliner flies from one city to another, it is off course over 90 percent of the time, but it keeps measuring its progress and adjusting its heading again and again. Goal setting works the same way. I maintain a vision for the end of the year because that's where I want to end up, it also allows me to see with tremendous certainty what I need to do today, and every day, in order to keep myself moving in that direction. If I'm presented with an "opportunity" out of the blue, I know instantly whether it's a real opportunity for me or a waste of time based on my priorities. The long view sharpens the short view.

I was told by someone that I should end each day by crossing it off my calendar and saying out loud, "There goes another day of my life, never to return again." Try this for yourself, and notice how much it sharpens your focus. When you end a day with the feeling that you would have lived it the same if you had the chance to re-peat it then you gain a sense of well-being and power that helps you focus on what's really important to you.

So, if there's such a thing as a silver bullet in business and life, this is it. You will see a **measurable difference** the very first day you establish clear, committed goals, even if your first few attempts aren't perfect. You'll be able to make decisions much more rapidly because you'll see how they'll either move you towards or away from your goals. When Disney World finally opened, a reporter commented to Walt Disney's brother, Roy, "It's too bad Walt did not live to see this." Roy replied, "Walt saw it first. That's why we are seeing it now."

Clear goals allow you to achieve the first half of Nelson Bunker Hunt's success formula. By deciding exactly what it is you want to accomplish, committing it to writing, and reviewing it on a daily basis, you bring your goals to reality with the power of your focus.

A WORD OF CAUTION

Don't tell anyone about your program, your new goals, and your hopes for the future except someone taking the steps with you! This is of the utmost importance as you begin. Your frame of mind at this critical point can easily be infected with doubt, just as a tiny, newborn infant could fall prey to disease.

Give yourself a chance by giving no one the opportunity to keep you from the wealth and success which can be yours.

After you have started to achieve that success—they will be asking for your secret. Now, they have to deny it, or admit their own lack of qualifications. Take no chances!

Now turn to Step #7 "Turning Your Desires into Goals"
in your *Roadmap to Riches* workbook.

Turning Goals into Reality

As set forth in Step 4, the form of your goals has been determined as positive, already accomplished, complete.

They have been written in the proper form and include everything in the world you really want together with every personal quality you might need to acquire. Enjoy them and keep them as a part of your life as long as you live.

Now the process of actually acquiring all these things you want begins, and it begins with a **Daily Declaration**; the first of three very important tools you will be introduced to in the Dyna/Psyc process.

Here is an example of a Daily Declaration:

"I *(Space for your name)* accept that everything changes including me. I am free of all past limiting attitudes."

That statement is what we call a Daily Declaration. It is a statement of belief even though when you first wrote the statement you might not have completely believed it. By constantly repeating that statement, you are planting that message in your subconscious. And there it will begin to overcome your previous training, mindsets, and beliefs which reinforced the negative attitudes such as: "That's the way I am and I can't change," "I can't do that," or "I can't afford to do that."

Think of your subconscious as a plot of fertile ground in which all kinds of seeds have been allowed to take root. You can imagine what such a plot would look like. There might be a lot of beneficial plants there, but there will also be a lot of weeds, and the weeds tend to grow faster and be the most obvious plants. Negative limiting attitudes are like weeds. They tend to multiply rapidly. They have deep roots and, given half a chance, will take over.

PLANT PLENTY OF FLOWERS IN YOUR GARDEN

The Daily Declaration process is just a way of planting the right kinds of seeds and planting them in such large quantities that they eventually overwhelm the weeds and slowly replace it with a confidence building power set of new productive and helpful attitudes.

Making Daily Declarations is basically very simple, but there are some important rules to follow. Your declaration must state the attitude you are trying to develop within your subconscious in positive terms as though it were already true for you. Of course when you begin working with a declaration it will not be your current

> Life consists in what a man is thinking of all day.
>
> RALPH WALDO EMERSON
> (1803–1882)
> American poet, essayist, philosopher

> Believe that life is worth living and your belief will help create the fact.
>
> WILLIAM JAMES
> (1842–1910)
> American philosopher, physiologist, psychologist, teacher

attitude, otherwise you wouldn't have to work to develop it. Your whole purpose is to build your belief as the foundation for what you want to become.

THE DAILY DECLARATION PROCEDURE

Here is how they are undertaken:

Each Morning

1. Immediately upon awakening, read your list of goals as you have prepared them in their positive, already accomplished form.

   Read every one of them. Read aloud if at all possible. If this cannot be done, then move your lips and form the words silently as you read. (This adds another physical dimension to the intellectual declaration.) Some people tape them so they can be played in the car.

2. After you have read each declaration . . . pause . . . visualize it completely. In your mind's eye, see the car, the home, the office with your name on the door. Touch the steering wheel, walk through the door. Feel the money from that first paycheck in your hands in cash, count it, see each bill and know its denomination.

Each Evening

Just before you retire . . . no matter how late it is, no matter how tired you are, repeat the morning process.

Because it is *essential* that the Daily Declarations be carried out completely and in the most effective manner, let me give you an example of just two properly worded goals and the proper way of declaring them. As you will see, one is a declaration concerning a physical property, the other a personality quality.

We start with the need for $850 to pay an overdue debt and the desire (want) for greater confidence.

Correctly stated those listed "burning desires" became the following goals:

1. The $850 bill from Smith & Company is paid in full within 60 days.

2. I face each day supremely confident in my ability to handle every detail of my thoughts and activities. I am certain of my capacity to perform in a superior manner.

When making the Daily Declarations, the first one will be read aloud. Then the declarant will *visualize* the bill in question with "Paid in Full" stamped across it. Or, if the bill itself is in the possession of the declarant, it is taken in hand . . . examined . . . the declaration is stated again, and the bill is turned face down. Again the declaration is stated aloud.

In the personality quality declaration, it is first read aloud, giving thought to the exact meaning of each. Then the declarant visualizes a situation in which that quality—self-confidence perhaps—would be important. (Attempting a sale, trying to convince a superior, for example.) Now, visualize the situation, as the declarant would like it to occur. The declarant shows great self-confidence; this confidence is sufficient to bring a desired result. The visualization has produced a *correct* image in the subconscious. Then, when you are faced with the real situation, you will have this positive material to draw on rather than the "failures" that were the only information available before.

This process is to be carried on for every single goal on your lists.

This process of Daily Declarations is *absolutely essential* to your successful practice of Dyna/Psyc. It is not necessary that you understand completely WHY it works. It is only important that you practice it long enough to learn (as thousands of others have learned) that it does work! For now, merely accept that fact as you would accept an antibiotic from your doctor without a detailed understanding of the scientific reasons for its effectiveness.

A NOTE TO SKEPTICS

Generally, at this point, in the examination of Dyna/Psyc, a handful of would-be practitioners begin to grumble things like: "mumbo-jumbo," "daydreams," "sounds ridiculous" or words to that effect.

If you are in that number, let me suggest this—*suspend your skepticism and give yourself a chance.* Notice I said "give *yourself* a chance." I am not concerned for Dyna/Psyc. Your doubts cannot harm it one iota. It works; the wealth that I, and others have achieved using the method has proven time and time again that it works! But your skeptical refusal to at least TRY will once again *deprive* you of the success and the Riches that come with the success you want so badly but which continues to elude you.

Look at it this way. You have nothing to *lose* but a little time, and you have a world of wealth and happiness to gain. Surely, with the odds so overwhelming—nothing vs. EVERYTHING—it's worth trying.

To be unwilling to try is to cut yourself off from at least the possibility of success for the dubious pleasure of *never knowing* what might have happened.

For your convenience and in order to help you with your Daily Declarations we have included the morning and evening process in your *Roadmap to Riches* workbook, Step 8. You might want to turn there now, and familiarize yourself with the morning and evening process and use it to guide you each time you make your Daily Declarations until the process becomes as familiar to you as your address and phone number and you no longer need this guide.

The second part of the process is to restate your goals as a Daily Declaration. Step 8 shows you how.

> Being a skeptic is like playing defense—you never get to score.
>
> RICHARD GILLY NIXON
> (b. 1940)
> American entrepreneur, publisher, speaker, author, seminar leader

> You may be disappointed if you fail, but you are doomed if you do not try.
>
> BEVERLY SILLS
> (b. 1929)
> American opera singer, double Emmy winner, Medal of Freedom winner

Now turn to Step #8 "Turning Goals into Reality" in your *Roadmap to Riches* workbook.

9

How Long Will It Take?

The answer to that question lies in assessing the following factors:

- How long did it take you to build your present Inadequate Self-images?
- How bad a self-image do you have, and how longwill it take to change it to positive?
- Are you secretly afraid of success? (are you sure?)
- How burdened are you with guilt from past failures?
- Will you consistently make your Daily Declarations?
- Will you really see when you attempt to visualize?
- Are you prepared to leave yesterday behind and live TODAY with your Daily Declarations?
- How much time and effort are you willing to give to your progress?

CAN YOU SPEED UP THE PROGRESS?

Yes! There is a method to bring about the wanted changes to your life at an even faster rate than you can achieve through your Daily Declarations alone.

While it is similar in nature to the use of Daily Declarations, it is somewhat different in use and application and totally different in the *degree of power* generated.

You might think of the comparison between the two by thinking of the Daily Declarations as the ordinary 110-volt current, which is used to power electric lights and small appliances in your home. The power of Super Suggestion, which we are going to discuss, is then like the 220-volt current which is used to power heavy machinery or bigger home appliances which require far more energy.

Super Suggestion carries a far greater charge of power. For that reason it is capable of moving your progress forward at a *more accelerated* rate than the Daily Declarations alone. Used *together;* the two kinds of motivating power, Daily Declarations and Super Suggestion, assure the most rapid results possible.

Before outlining the use of Super Suggestion and showing how it works, it is well to consider its limitations.

Super Suggestion can only be used on the intangible goals you are seeking. You can use it to build yourself, bring about in yourself the personality factors that make for success. But, you must *not* use it for acquisition of *things.* The realities which Super Suggestion creates in your subconscious mind must be limited to intangibles or you can do great harm to your ability to reach chosen goals.

Lord give me patience—
and give it to me now.
ANONYMOUS

Here's why: Super Suggestion creates full-belief even before the subject goal has been achieved. This is fine with the mental, emotional, and behavioral patterns you are seeking. Once you behave as though these intangible changes have already occurred, they dictate your behavior and you reap the benefits.

But, if the subconscious is assured (through Super Suggestion) that you already have the salary, the house, the car you are seeking, your entire subconscious mental levels cease to help you acquire them.

> Our unconscious is like a vast subterranean factory with intricate machinery that is never idle, where work goes on day and night from the time we are born until the moment of our death.
>
> MILTON R. SAPIRSTEIN
> (b. 1914)
> American psychiatrist
> and writer
> *Paradoxes of Everyday Life*

Remember, we said that the subconscious works without logic; it is an uncritical force. When we declare in our fully conscious state that we have things we are seeking, our conscious mind knows of their future state and "edits" the information it passes on to the lower levels of our consciousness. Then all systems will work to help us acquire them.

HOW TO DEEP CONDITION AND USE SUPER SUGGESTION

In order to understand the necessary steps you must take so that you can use Super Suggestion, it is necessary that we examine *how* and *why it works*. To help you do this I have made the following graph. It attempts to demonstrate the levels of consciousness which all of us may experience at one time or another.

- **100% Consciousness**   **Wide Awake**—*alert, some muscular tension* (participation at top level of efficiency in some sportinvolving quick reaction, muscular force, i.e. tennis)

- **65% Consciousness**   **Awake**—*not especially alert or tense* (preoccupied)

- **45% Consciousness**   **Half Asleep**—*vaguely aware of what is going on about you*

- **20% Consciousness**   **Light Sleep**

- **10% Consciousness**   **Deep Sleep**

- **0% Consciousness**   **Coma**—*impossible to awaken*

As you can see, at one end of the scale is 100 percent consciousness—a wide-awake, alert condition in which there would also be some degree of muscular tension.

One of the best examples of this condition of *full* consciousness might be at the moment of participation at top level of efficiency in some sport involving careful attention, speedy reactions, muscular energy, etc.

At the very opposite end of the scale is a deep coma, unconsciousness so complete that the person cannot even be aroused from it medically.

As you examine the various degrees of consciousness, imagine, if you will, how you would react at each stage to *suggestions* from a source outside your own body.

The top-form sports champion, intent and alert, is not swayed from what he is doing even by shouts from spectators. His own mind is in full control of his consciousness. He is not about to take *suggestions* from unskilled members of the watching crowd.

Yet, the same athlete, awakened from a sound sleep, still drowsy, might be fooled into running for an exit with the false suggestion, "GET OUT OF HERE, THE ROOM'S ON FIRE!" Every muscle of his body would then be reacting, *not to his own conscious mind*, but to the suggestion!

These two examples—suggestion rejection on the playing field and suggestion acceptance in the half-awake state—can be very helpful to our effective use of Super Suggestion.

Note that in both cases the same mind was the subject of an outside suggestion. The only differences were the *condition of consciousness* at the moment of suggestion and the power of the suggestion.

In the suggestion rejection case we had a fully conscious, concentrated mind. The suggestion was but one of many shouts, with little chance of penetrating the subject's consciousness.

In the *accepted* suggestion situation, the level of consciousness was far down our scale. Thus, it was more readily accessible to the suggestion. The suggestion itself was clear, urgent, and without outside interference.

Preparing to use Super Suggestion, we set up the suggestion—acceptance conditions which are best for reaching the "open" level of consciousness and presenting the suggestion in the most "powerful" manner.

When you are first learning to use Super Suggestion, it is best to:

1. Condition yourself in a quiet, darkened room.
2. Sit in a comfortable position and relax your muscles.
3. Close your eyes.

Taking these steps, you reduce many of the consciousness factors: folding your hands in your lap or resting them on the chair arms causes you to reduce muscular tension. Closing your eyes, you close off the perception of extraneous matters. The quietness of the room reduces distractions of the noise around you.

This matter of relaxing *muscular* tension is one which some people have considerable trouble achieving. If this is the case, the following procedure is suggested:

As you are sitting in your chair, visualize the various parts of your body. Start with the very tips of your toes. Think of them relaxing...slowly, gradually, relaxing. Proceed up your body, a section at a time, thinking of each specific part and feeling it relax. Don't make it relax, *let* it relax. By the time you have reached the top of your head, you will be in good muscular relaxation.

Muscular relaxation completed, you are already half-way through the mental conditioning which is the balance of the conditioning preparation required for Super Suggestion, because the very suggestion process used to relax those muscles has also been establishing mental relaxation as well.

Now, begin to count, silently, slowly, feeling yourself slip gently downward to a perfect conditioning level of consciousness. You will count from 1 down to 20. At 20, you will be where you need to be.

Once this physical-mental conditioning is completed, you begin to use the Super Suggestion material you already prepared for this session before going into your room and commencing the conditioning.

PREPARE YOUR SUPER SUGGESTION

Unlike your Daily Declarations in which you work on everything on your list of goals, Super Suggestion is used on just one intangible quality at a time.

First, select one of the basic personality or character qualities from your list of intangible goals. Since you must work with only one at a time, making your choice should be based on the most important quality first. You will continue to use only that one quality for Super Suggestion until you have attained it. But, I promise you it will be attained in far less time than you can imagine. Super Suggestion works wonders!

Of course, you have reworded your desire for the quality into a present and positive goal. Now, select from the wording of the goal, two or three key words to act as a sort of "code" for the entire goal. You do this so that you do not have to commit the entire declaration to memory. (Remember, you will use Super Suggestion with your eyes closed.)

You will read the entire declaration each time before you begin the process of "conditioning" down to the lower level of consciousness. Once there, you will repeat the "key" or "code" words and that will be all that is necessary. The speaking of those words, while in the requisite "conditioned state," will implant the entire declaration with a force and power beyond your prior imaginings.

PUTTING IT ALL TOGETHER

Let me now list for clarity the entire procedure for using Super Suggestion:

1. You have prepared a single intangible (character, behavior, or personality) goal, the one quality you feel you need most.

2. You have selected a key word or two to use as a "code" in your lower-level suggestion effort.

3. Now you go into a dimly lit or darkened room, close the door, seat yourself comfortably to relax every muscle.

4. Read the full declaration slowly and carefully. Remember the "key words" from it as you begin to condition yourself into a lower level of consciousness.

5. Go into your lower level of consciousness as outlined previously.

6. Repeat the key words silently to yourself to implant the declaration at the lower level.

7. Return to your fully conscious level, thinking as you do that you are going to feel more alert, more relaxed, more energetic than you ever have before.

That's it! That's all there is to do, and you are putting Super Suggestion to work! The desired effect will come before you know it. How soon? That depends on how well you learn to "count yourself down" into deep relaxation—and the frequency and consistency with which you perform both your Daily Declarations and utilize Super Suggestion.

Note: Do not lie down as you prepare to condition yourself to use Super Suggestion. Since you are moving to a lowered level of consciousness it would be very easy to fall asleep. In fact, I have known many people who use a Super Suggestion of sleeping in order to solve their problem of insomnia.

The only way to know you are effectively using your Daily Declarations is to follow the instructions to *declare them every day . . . at least twice a day*. But, how can you know you are reaching the proper depth of consciousness for effective use of Super Suggestion?

This is difficult to define exactly. For it is a highly personal or subjective "feeling" which, when achieved, is evidence of the proper state. However, it is not a condition similar to the lit or unlit light bulb. It is not a completely "on" or "off" "state.

Therefore, as you approach the essential level, you are "fading in" on it. The deeper you descend, the closer you are to the ultimate level. But Super Suggestion used anyplace along the spectrum will be effective. It will be effective in direct ratio to the degree of conditioning you have reached.

Simply put, you need not worry about your Suggestions "not working" because you have not yet developed the ability to go quickly and surely to the deeper level of consciousness. They will work better as you increase your efficiency in this conditioning, but they will be "working" for you all the time you are improving.

Practice is the secret of more efficient or more effective conditioning for Super Suggestion. Some people will find it easier than others (just as some people take to swimming or golf rapidly and with greater ease than do others). But YOU will develop an ever-increasing facility for rapid and effective descent to the lower level of consciousness as you repeat the experience.

How does it feel? There are as many answers to this question as there are people who have tried it; however, their answers all contain certain elements: relaxed, almost no body-feeling, a little drowsy perhaps, sounds fade away. You will be aware that you are you; you will not be unconscious, but you will be remote from the press of normal everyday sensation and thought.

And it is important for you to know that you will be able to reach this relaxed condition with greater and greater speed and less and less effort, as you practice it. Like the ability we develop to run rapidly along a well-known path where at first we could only inch our way.

One word of caution! Don't try too hard. This defeats the very effort itself. This is a *relaxing* effort—NOT a *concentrating* effort. *Let yourself go*—Don't try to make yourself descend!

> Always think of what you have to do and easy it will be.
>
> EMILE LOUE
> (1857–1926)
> English naturalist

At this point I want to remind you that this conditioning to a lower level of consciousness and using Super Suggestion is ONLY for the intangible goals, for changing qualities of basic character, personality, behavior. You don't use this method to acquire the new car, the larger salary, the new home. These goals all require a certain amount of time. But *personality changes* can be made as rapidly as you can Super Suggest them.

In addition to the basic and lasting personality changes which we can effect through repeated Super Suggestion, you will be able to use this method of conditioning to achieve many short-term advantages.

Temporary uses to which this capacity has been put include:

> As if principle: If you want a quality, act as if you already had it.
>
> WILLIAM JAMES
> (1842–1910)
> Amercian teacher, physiologist, philosopher

- Fear of the Dentist . . . Used before the visit, fear gone!

- Late night, important work to complete, too tired . . . Super Suggestion of alertness and concentration   provides both.

- Long drive, sleepy. . . Two or three minutes of a Super Suggestion of alertness at side of the road. Perfectly able to continue.

- Interview for new job, fright and feeling of panic . . . Brief descent and Super Suggestion of calm and poise. Problem gone for interview.

- Can't sleep at night . . . In bed, a Super Suggestion of sleep, deep and restful. Success!

- Pain (dentist, childbirth, etc.) . . . Used by one proficient in the preparatory conditioning. No pain.

COMING BACK

A plus factor which you can add to your conditioning when you begin to develop some degree of ease in its practice is *enhancement of later consciousness*.

This is a simple process by means of which you will return to the high consciousness level feeling *refreshed*, with new energy, vigor. Your mental outlook will be happier and more confident than it was before you conditioned for Super Suggestion.

Adding this factor is simply a matter of counting backwards as you begin your return from the point of suggestion—20, 19, 18, etc. As you pass 10 and again at 5, tell yourself silently of the conditions that will be yours when you reach zero.

In other words, as you are arising from the lower level of consciousness, you make double use of the trip. Not only do you strongly implant the Super Suggestion, but on the way up, you emphasize the energetic feeling of power and well being which will be yours once you return to full consciousness.

A final point—when and how often do you use Super Suggestion in preparing to achieve a basic "personal quality" goal?

As an aid to reaching the fullest efficiency of self-conditioning at the lower level, you need not limit the number of times you practice it daily, but, as a matter of effectively using a single Super Suggestion, you'll get the maximum benefit from a once-a-day use. However, you can—and should—use the Super Suggestion technique for emergencies (a trip to the dentist, a job interview, etc.).

The best time to use this powerful aid to achieving your intangible goals is when you are not tired and are reasonably alert. Thus, it becomes clear that the first things in the morning, late at night, or just after eating *are not* the times to condition. If possible, perhaps just before your luncheon period, or just after work if you are on a tight working schedule. Otherwise, any period you can set aside while you're wide-awake.

SUMMARY

This now gives you two of the important tools which make Dyna/Psyc effective:

DAILY DECLARATIONS and SUPER SUGGESTION.

As you can see, they work in the conscious and subconscious levels of our mind.

In the next chapter we examine the third and most powerful tool Dyna/Psyc has to offer you.

As we did with Daily Declarations, we have provided you with a guide to help you in becoming familiar with the Super Suggestion procedure. It is Step 9 of your workbook; and I would like you to get acquainted with it now. Please use it as you learn about the power of Super Suggestions.

Let Go and Relax with Super Suggestion

Because of the hundreds of readers who have told us how invaluable Super Suggestion has been to them since Joe first introduced the concept 20 years ago, I would like to expand upon the procedure and the importance of learning to relax to effectively use the most powerful technique ever developed for changing habits and attitudes. This technique is based on ancient knowledge, but we have updated it with a couple of modern wrinkles.

In the Bible, Jesus taught his disciples the same technique as a way to pray; and it is found in the fundamental teachings of many other religions. It has been used by mystics throughout the ages and has been given a great deal of scientific support with the work of modern psychologists beginning as far back as William James. Super Suggestion opens up *direct* communication with the amazing power of your subconscious mind. You bypass the editing function of the conscious mind and go directly to the subconscious with positive suggestions that develop in you the attitudes that you desire to obtain. The process that we will use is a combination of ancient knowledge and the modern scientific principles of biofeedback and conditioned reflex.

Completely Relax to Relieve the Tension

I told you the most important requirement for Super Suggestion to succeed is to quiet the conscious mind and body—to completely relax the mind and body so that you are free of all tensions. This allows you to reach the deeper levels of the mind. For most people it is difficult to completely relax. You may think you are completely relaxed when you are sleeping, but most people are in a state of considerable tension when they are sleeping. To really relax you are going to have to exercise but not the way you think. (This exercise even appealed to Lazy Joe.) The process is basically simple. You start with a mental exercise designed to open up our awareness of the tension in our bodies. Then, you use the same kind of conditioning that Dr. Pavlov used on his dogs; only you are in charge of what is going on. You take control of a process, which has been going on in you for a long time tobuild a conditioned relaxation reflex. Now think for a minute about something that causes you to really get uptight—something that creates a lot of tension in your body. There are lots of examples that could be used.

Relaxing on the Freeway?

The one that used to always bug me before I understood this process was fighting traffic on the freeway. All I had to do was just think about getting on the freeway at rush hour, and I could feel the tension building up in my body. Now even if you haven't experienced freeway traffic, you have had the experience of being late for an appointment, being trapped behind a slow moving car on a narrow road and you reacted with physical tension. You get a knot between your

Believe that life is worth living and your belief will help create that fact.

WILLIAM JAMES
(1842–1910)
American teacher, physiologist, philosopher

shoulder blades, maybe a tension headache. Have you ever asked yourself why? When you think about it there is no more reason for your body to react to such a situation with tension then there was for Dr. Pavlov's dogs to respond to bells by salivating. You have simply been conditioned to react that way. Haven't you ever used the expression, "I get so uptight when" such and such happens, or, "That really bugs me." I used to say those things before I knew what I was doing to myself. I kept reinforcing it. "I get so uptight when I have to fight the freeway traffic," and sure enough I did. And I continued to as long as I kept reinforcing that suggestion. Fortunately for us, the mind can also learn how to relax our body on cue. It's just that very few of us have discovered how to do it, so we never try even though we have all experienced this process. I am sure that you can think of something right now that you find very relaxing. Maybe it is a hot shower or lying on the beach listening to the waves or stretching out in a hammock under whispering pine trees. These are things that can become relaxation keys for you. Unfortunately, you cannot always lie out in a hammock or stretch out on the beach or listen to the waves or climb into a hot shower. But what you can do is condition your body to respond to symbols in your mind just as though you were doing those things. And that is what you are learning about, with the aid of the Super Suggestion. This is an important step along your Way to Riches.

Develop New Habits

Remember, you are working with habits and habits take time to develop (remember—about 30 or more repetitions). Developing your relaxation reflex takes time as well. So plan on using your Super Suggestion exercise daily from now on. After a while with practice you will develop relaxation abilities that you can use in any circumstance. You may worry that you will fall asleep and become completely relaxed in a situation where it would not be appropriate. Your mind will not let that occur. It is possible, with just a little practice, to completely relax your body to the extent that is appropriate for the activity in which you are involved. You will be able to use this while driving, while speaking in front of an audience, while doing just about any activity. You will be able to maintain the relaxation that is so helpful, so important for your body. By the way, if you practice this faithfully, I think you will notice very definite positive side effects as far as your health is concerned. Dr. Hans Selye, in his book *The Stress of Life*, estimates that 95 percent of all disease is either a result of, or severely aggravated by, the kind of tension we are talking about. Just think what an improvement it can be to remove that tension from your life.

Symbols of Relaxation

Just like the bell for Pavlov's dogs or freeway traffic as a tension symbol, you will need a *relaxation symbol*. You don't want to use the word "relax," because many people have been conditioned to respond to that with tension. Have you ever been really tense and when you try to relax have the tension increase? You need a symbol that is either neutral or always has a positive relaxation association for you. One of the things that works for me is sailing. For you it might be a warm bath. For someone else, the bubbling of a mountain stream or the crackle of an open fire.

Search your experience for such a symbol; but since relaxation symbols are not universal, you need something you can use for everyone—one that you hope is neutral. The symbol we have chosen is "LET GO." It is short and, hopefully, no one has any tension associated with that symbol. Initially, you will condition yourself to relax in response to this symbol. As you gain more experience you can substitute your own symbol in the exercise. Step 9 of your Roadmap contains a very important part of this. It is an affirmation of your new relaxation ability. Actually, it is an instruction to your mind, the conscious part, telling it how to behave. During the exercise you will be reinforcing this affirmation several times speaking directly to your subconscious, teaching it how to react.

When you do the exercise, it is important that you are physically comfortable. You may sit or lie down. But if you are sitting, make sure your neck is supported such as in a recliner or in a chair that allows you to lean back. You need to set up a situation where you can have complete quiet. You do not want the telephone ringing and interrupting the exercise. It may be that the only time you can do this is at bedtime, but if you can find some other time you can take 15 or 20 minutes to be completely alone that would be a good time to do it. It is an important little decision for your continued progress on The Lazy Man's Way that you actually find the time to do this exercise every single day. It is excellent for you mentally, emotionally, physically and spiritually. I have provided you with a step-by-step guide for the relaxation declarations as well as the Super Suggestion procedure.

(By the way, we've just produced a most remarkable audio program that takes you through, step-by-step, the Relaxation Declaration and Super Suggestion exercise. It is really quite effective and I urge you to order one. It's available on our website, http://www.thelazymansway. com/ as a CD, or as an MP3 Download.)

> Now turn to Step #9 "How Long Will It Take?"
> in your *Roadmap to Riches* workbook.

10
Discovering Your Subconscious Computer

Decision-making is the most significant work you ever do. That is because it is impossible for the human animal to even exist without a steady stream of decisions.

The decision to eat or drink and the choice of what you will eat or drink is a simplified example of the decision-making process to which we give little or no importance but which is essential to our continued existence.

Other than breathing, the beating of the heart, etc., the bodily functions are generally carried on after making a decision or a series of decisions. Think of the number of decisions, each tiny and insignificant, but each essential in the process of merely scratching your nose.

First, there's the awareness of the itch. Then, the decision: Rub with the back of your hand? Rub with your sleeve? Scratch with your fingers? Which fingers of which hand? How hard, how long? Is the selected hand free to scratch or must some burden in the hand be set down or shifted to the other hand before scratching? These are merely the highlights of the number of decisions that can enter into a simple act.

And that is only part of it. In addition to making the basic decision to scratch, we must make innumerable calculations in order to effectively carry out the decisions; i.e., how far to lift the hand, the planned trajectory which will bring the fingers, flexing and unflexing properly, into just the exact position on the nose we cannot see. From a calculation standpoint, it is something like plotting a rendezvous of two spacecraft.

The hardware which the space agency has developed for such command and guidance is complex almost beyond belief. Yet, a single day's activity of an average, active human body requires that decisions and computations be made which are so numerous and must be made with so much complex input of information and in such short periods of time that no computer in existence could handle it.

Plotting and executing a space voyage is not one bit as complex as your decision and computing problems in driving downtown through busy traffic as you go to work-each day. You make more decisions based on more information inputs and must make more instantaneous calculations of speed, proximity, even potential personality of other drivers ("...that s.o.b. won't let me in here") in a half-hour drive than is required on any flight to the moon.

In short, the message is brief. NO MAN-MADE CALCULATOR OR COMPUTER EVEN BEGINS TO APPROACH THE COMPLEXITY OR EFFICIENCY OF THE HUMAN MIND.

In the creative state a man is taken out of himself. He lets down as it were a bucket into his subconscious, and draws up something which is normally beyond his reach. He mixes this thing with his normal experiences and out of the mixture he makes a work of art.

E. M. FORSTER (1879–1970)
English novelist,
short-story writer,
essayist

The final step in the implementation of Dyna/Psyc—and the changing of your life is the creation of CONSCIOUS ACCESS TO THE COMPUTER OF YOUR SUBCONSCIOUS MIND!

Make no mistake; *ordinary people* never learn to use the great Subconscious Computer. The day they learn to use it, they cease to be *ordinary*.

Searching the writings of famous men, the statements they have made as to their source of creativity (which is essentially a matter of decision-making) and reading everything I could find in this area, I can tell you this:

Edison, Einstein, Mozart, Emerson, Tchaikovsky, Steinmetz, James Watt, and innumerable other inventors, scientists, writers, and composers, all have given evidence of their using the great Subconscious Computer that exists in all of us. Each of them somehow happened upon this great resource. YOU are going to learn how to use it knowingly and at will.

WHAT WILL IT DO FOR YOU?

1. Provide meaningful and productive answers to your problems.

2. Increase the efficiency and well being of your mind itself.

3. Furnish the POWER that turns your Daily Declarations into actual possessions.

1. In the **PROBLEM** area, we all know that the burden of decision-making (which is what problems are—difficult decisions) increases in direct ratio to the complexity of the problem. If the decision is yes or no, stay or go, black or white, it is usually less complex than if there are several possible solutions and you must decide which is the best course of action.

Immediately we are faced with a lot of information of varying degrees of importance, a number of answers of varying worth and, very often, emotional pressures to make one decision or another. In short, a "computer-like" problem.

Using our subconscious power we can have the answer computed and delivered to us!

2. MENTAL WELL-BEING comes into focus when we understand how the Subconscious Computer can be used to reduce stress and tension in the nervous system. Permit me to quote from a work I read some years ago:

"Recent research on sleep has reversed some of the fashionable conceptions which were widely discussed in years past. The fact is that, although the number of hours required varies slightly between individuals and also varies with age, the idea that only four or five hours are actually required is fallacious. New findings point up that your actual requirement conforms more closely to your common practice of sleeping seven, eight, or nine hours than was previously thought. Assuming that your true requirement is eight hours, then the first half or approximately four hours is devoted to your body repairs or the rejuvenation of the tissues that have been worn down during the day. Scientists, in making observations of this period, note that during the first hour sleep is particularly deep and there is an accompanying increase in basal metabolism. There is an extra expenditure of energy involved in the first hurried elimination of the major aspects of purely physical fatigue. The second, third, and fourth hours produce somewhat lighter sleep

The more extensive a man's knowledge of what has been done the greater will be his chance of knowing what to do.

BENJAMIN DISRAELI
(1804–1881)
English statesman, novelist

and require considerably less energy, while the more intricate physical repairs are accomplished— such things as reflexes and various physically derived judgments such as distance, form, and color are thus returned to normal through cell repair and reproduction."

Since this is the case, it is imperative that you have some method of reducing the tension and pressures which modern day living places upon us.

The use of the Subconscious Computer can be put to work to clear your mental system of each day's problems, as you sleep and prepare your mind for the following day's activities.

3. DECLARATION ACHIEVEMENT is accomplished through the use of this same Subconscious Computer.

Here is how that works. As your Daily Declarations are made, the subconscious computer receives that information from you. It becomes the function of this giant calculator to devise the methods that you can use to get those goals!

I will show you how to be able to receive those solutions or answers as they have been calculated.

Every time you had a "hunch" that solved a problem for you, you were using this power. When a name was "on the tip of your tongue" but you couldn't think of it, haven't you often told someone "I'll think of it on the way home." And then, just as you said you would, you remembered it later? That too was an example of the use of this power.

Those people who, when faced with an important decision, decide to "sleep on it" and awaken the next day with the answer, are unconsciously using their computer.

But I want you to be able to use it consciously, not by default. The hardest job I'll have in getting you to put this fabulous power to work is getting you to try. That's because the method of using it is so simple, it seems so easy, that many persons are totally unable to accept it. I hope you don't suffer from that limitation.

PUTTING THE SUBCONSCIOUS COMPUTER TO WORK

The three key words for putting your subconscious to work are:

WRITE—TRY—ASK

WRITE *Write out your problem.* This may sound foolish, but my experience has shown that a great number of problems exist only because they have not been clearly defined or outlined.

Once you actually write out the problem, you are going to find that you will see it in a new light On your paper start with the words, "Shall I do this . . . ?"

Carefully, fully, yet concisely, state the problem to which you are seeking an answer.

TRY *Try to answer it yourself.* On the piece of paper that contains your stated problem, place two columns. In one column put all the reasons for taking the particular step. In the other, all the reasons against.

Put in enough time doing this so that you are relatively certain you cannot solve the problem consciously.

There is no failure except in no longer trying.

ELBERT HUBBARD
(1856–1915)
American businessman,
writer, printer

Ask, and it shall be given.

BIBLE
MATTHEW 7:7

Once you are forced to reach the decision that you cannot solve the problem consciously, go to Step three.

ASK *Ask your Subconscious Computer to solve it for you.* This is the part of the procedure that many people find hard to accept.

They simply cannot believe that any task of such magnitude could be carried on by simply "asking" part of your mind to take care of it.

Yet, these same people drive a car to work every morning, many times becoming so involved in their own conscious thoughts that they are letting their Subconscious Computer do all the driving.

They will suddenly become aware, almost like someone awakening from sleep, that they are ready to turn off the freeway or turnpike. They will be unable to recall clearly the specifics of what occurred, in connection with their winding their way through traffic.

ACCEPT IT! Think of your subconscious as another person, an employee or assistant. Just say to that force: "I want the answer to this problem by tomorrow morning—or four o'clock this afternoon," or, if it is particularly difficult, give the computer more time. Tell it you want the answer by next Saturday or something of the sort.

Then, FORGET IT! Forget the problem completely. Your computer will not work on a problem while you are working on it in your conscious mind. It is as though you had to release all the figures on some job to another person before he could go to work on it.

So, forget it once you have asked the Subconscious Computer to solve it for you. And you *can* forget it because your Subconscious Computer *will* solve it.

Simple as the use of this powerful force is, there are a number of questions which people have asked me concerning it. I have set them forth below, together with my answers, in case you too are wondering the same things.

More men fail through lack of purpose than lack of talent.

(WILLIAM ASHLEY) BILLY SUNDAY (1862–1935) American baseball player, evangelist

Q. **Doesn't someone have to have a really brilliant mind for this to work?**

A. No. It can work for anyone if he/she will merely follow the three steps outlined.

Q. **Are there any limitations on using the Subconscious Computer?**

A. Only those I set forth already. First that the problem must be written out in a clear, complete form. Second, you must go through the steps of *trying consciously* to solve it. You must put on paper the various pros and cons which you can find.

Q. **How do you decide "when" the computer must give you the answer?**

A. Don't put off a decision that really needs to be made. But don't try to fool the computer. If you don't have to make the decision for some time, don't give the computer a false deadline.

"Need" seems to be an important element in the speedy functioning of this power. Also, the "when" is seldom a problem IF you have honestly gone through steps one and two. The dimensions of the problem and the quantity of material for and against the decision will influence your timetable as well as your *need* for the answer at a particular time.

Q. How and Why does it work?

A. There are a number of theories put forth by psychologists, psychiatrists, even mystics and religious teachers. I don't really know. I simply know that it does work. The success this method has given me is the recommendation I offer for your trying it. It does work! That's all I ever really needed to know about it.

Q. Why is it important?

A. Because really effective people cannot afford to go around carrying dozens of unsolved problems in their minds. They need the free use of their consciousness to take care of the matters of the moment. Yet, they also encounter larger problems that they are unable to readily solve for themselves even after defining them, laying them out fully, and going over the pros and cons. Unsolved problems are worries! Worries are destructive.

Q. What is its greatest value?

A. The fact that you are able to use the greatest part of your mind, a secret part, inaccessible to most people . . . at will! There is no question that the subconscious part of our mind (for reasons I still do not completely understand) has a capacity for creativity, problem solving, etc.,—far beyond the other portions of the mental equipment. The Subconscious Computer (S/C) is truly a super power: Its relationship to our conscious mind is like comparing a single man's efforts with those of a computer.

Q. Can it be used only on a basis where the answer will not be forthcoming for some time?

A. No. There is a technique for nearly "instant" application. All you have to do is "condition" yourself as though you were preparing to use Super Suggestion. At that level, ask the Subconscious Computer your question. If, prior to this step you have defined the problem and tried consciously to solve it by weighing the opposing advantages and disadvantages, you will only have to wait a bit in that deeper state of consciousness and the answer will come.

Q. How will I know the answer?

A. First, let me explain you will not begin to hear mysterious "voices." It is just that the solution to the problem will come to you in a form immediately capable of application to your problem. It will "feel" like the right answer. You will also "feel" you want to get right back to the problem and put that answer to work at once. If you have had some mental block that kept you from seeing the solution at an earlier stage, the answer may have to come to you in a "disguise." That is, something may keep coming to your mind, in connection with the problem, which seems to have no application—a snatch of an old song, a childhood game, etc., but then it will suddenly occur to you that *"Bye Bye Blackbird"* may be an unconscious suggestion to get rid of the source of the problem. And that will be one of the two courses between which you had been trying to decide.

Generally, the feeling of "rightness" and the feeling of "eagerness" to carry out the solution are all you will need to identify the correct answer from the Subconscious Computer.

Q. Can I do this right away... or does it take a few tries to get it working?

A. It will respond when you properly prepare and ask. However, as you continue to use it, proficiency will grow as it does with all familiar things.

But, if it doesn't work at all, YOU ARE PREVENTING ITS FUNCTION! It won't work if you consciously KNOW it won't. Accept that it will! And I assure you...it does!

A Word of Warning: Don't fail to act on the answer you are given! Or you will find it is some time before it will function again!

THE SECOND ASPECT OF THE SUBCONSCIOUS COMPUTER

As we noted earlier, there are three ways in which your subconscious can be put to work to great advantage.

We have examined one—the problem-solving capacity. Now, let us consider its use as an aid to mental health and to increasing your general efficiency.

During your hours of sleep, your subconscious works, primarily through the use of dreams, to lower the tensions and pressures that have accumulated during the day.

However, that function is only carried on after the process of *physical* rehabilitation is carried out, during the first four hours or so of your sleep.

If the day's problems, pressures, tensions have been particularly heavy, or if you just didn't get enough sleep during the night, your mental rehabilitation may be incomplete upon awakening. This means you will face the new day with a lowered tolerance for the day's demands on your nervous/mental capacities. Irritability makes itself felt; problems loom larger than life-size.

And, when you are at your lowest ebb the next day (for we all seem to have "cycles" of more energy, less energy, etc., in regular patterns throughout our waking hours), your reserves are shot and you're in trouble.

It is at this point that you can utilize your subconscious computer to give yourself what I call the Silent Treatment. This Silent Treatment is a method of permitting your subconscious computer to "catch up," for a brief time on the chores it was unable to complete thou be doing during those few minutes? Nothing!

SILENT TREATMENTS

Here's how to give yourself this rewarding Silent Treatment:

1. Make a conscious determination that the time has come for a treatment. Don't just let yourself "happen" into it. Tell yourself you are going to turn things over to the Subconscious Computer for a time.

2. Sit down or, if possible, lie down. Close your eyes and step outside of yourself. Lying there with your eyes closed, become as though you were a passive spectator of yourself. Don't try to think of anything—don't try not to think of anything. Relax—just exist for the moment with closed eyes. Think of yourself as having "stepped aside" while some workmen carry on an important task of "cleaning up" the area where you have been working. Just relax while they put everything in order for your return after a while. Sit or lie with eyes closed and—let go!

3. When you feel an almost uncontrollable desire to open your eyes—do so. This will be somewhere from five to twenty minutes later.

Here are the results you can expect from Silent Treatments: You will find increased enthusiasm, energy, and an overall increase in your sense of well-being. Tiredness falls away.

These results will increase in effect after you have been giving yourself a daily treatment for a week or two.

But a warning. Sometimes, just as you open your eyes, it is such a pleasant experience you have just had, you might think of closing them again for a time. *Don't!* A second Silent Treatment, immediately upon the heels of the first, is sure to not only *undo* the benefits of the first, it will leave you feeling terrible. You will probably have a headache. One treatment only. That's the rule.

Remember, the Silent Treatment does not involve *sleep*. It is simply a means of quieting your conscious mind and permitting the unconscious to get terribly busy for a brief time. The results are well worth the trouble it may be to you to find a way to do it each day.

If you have a place at work to do it, fine; if not, perhaps you can go to your car for the few minutes required. At any rate, get comfortable, as comfortable as possible.

Another side benefit of the use of these treatments is the increasing ease with which you are able to reach your Subconscious Computer. This greatly enhances the success of the problem-solving function as well.

THE THIRD ASPECT OF THE SUBCONSCIOUS COMPUTER

This utilization of the great power of the subconscious within you requires no more effort on your part than the continued use of your Daily Declarations.

Just as Super Suggestion *enhances* the speed with which you can acquire a positive trait or quality that you've set up as a goal, the Subconscious Computer also makes important contributions to goal fulfillment. Both the "things" you want and the intangible goals are conditioned into your mental apparatus.

Day by day, you will perform acts that forward you in your pursuit of those goals. Your Subconscious Computer enhances the speed and certainty of your goal attainment with every decision it makes, every calculation you turn over to it. It *includes* your goal needs as one more element in making each decision.

Your Subconscious Computer will *suggest* moves, ideas, strategies to you that will make your declarations realities. New and creative ideas will just seem to "come from nowhere" as you progress in the application of the natural laws of power which have been summed up for you in Dyna/Psyc.

Be responsive to your own ideas! Forget the past when you had a tendency to immediately "put down" an idea that came into your mind as "impractical" or "daydreaming." Be alert and ready to be responsive to the wealth of material that your Subconscious Computer can develop for you. If you turn it down, the spontaneous activity will cease. Accept it, examine it, put it into operation, and the supply will increase!

Men are made stronger on realization that the helping hand they need is at the end of their own right arm.

SIDNEY J. PHILLIPS
Address, July 1953

Now turn to Step #10 "Discovering Your Subconscious Computer" in your *Roadmap To Riches* workbook.

11

Where Are You Now?

If you have read carefully all the material presented thus far, then you are 25% along the way to *The Lazy Man's Way to Riches* I promised you . . . because we have set forth the basic principle of Dyna/Psyc.

As you recall, I mentioned at the beginning that yours must be an **R.S.V.P.** response to this invitation to get "everything in the world you really want." **R**— must READ it all. **S**—more than merely reading, you must STUDY it. **V**—you have to VISUALIZE the steps outlined and the steps within each step. And finally, **P**— you have to PERFORM the works as outlined.

If all you have done so far is READ, you're 25 percent there. To the extent you have been STUDYING what you have read, you are even further along.

Now, let us quickly review all things you have to VISUALIZE and PERFORM.

1. You have DAILY DECLARATIONS. Those positive and present tense statements made up from the lists of things (tangible and intangible), which you want and need. You are prepared to VISUALIZE them as you use them at least twice daily.

2. You have prepared SUPER SUGGESTIONS from the most important intangible goals. You have prepared code words to summon them up for use, as you are in that conditioned state where you can offer suggestions to your subconscious levels.

3. You are prepared to use your SUBCONSCIOUS COMPUTER in three ways:
   - To overcome obstacles you perceive as problems.
   - To give yourself SILENT TREATMENTS.
   - To gain added impetus to your DAILY DECLARATIONS.

Now, you are ready to establish:

4. The daily programming of these elements so that you receive the maximum benefit from Dyna/Psyc. To help you do this, I have provided a chart located in the workbook, on which you can check off the necessary actions each day.

By all means use it. Do not begin your program of goal attainment without a *programmed approach*, which will assist you in making all these things HABITS as soon as possible.

Success is not the result of spontaneous combustion. You must set yourself on fire.

REGGIE (REGINALD JOSEPH) LEACH
(b.1950)
Canadian hockey player
"Rifle"

Great works are performed not by strength, but by perseverance.

DR. SAMUEL JOHNSON
(1709–1784)
English lexicographer, essayist, poet

This is the PERFORMANCE that is the last essential to success. And I assure you that *essential* means just that! There is simply no way to achieve the wealth you want without following through *consistently*.

Because the performing of these daily acts is so easy, and requires so little time or effort, I think you must agree with me that it is indeed a "Lazy Man's Way."

Following are a few questions many people have asked about Dyna/Psyc after they have begun its practice. I have included them in the hope that, as you progress, you may find among them the answers to your questions. They follow the form because you do not have to read them before full participation in the program.

QUESTIONS AND ANSWERS

Q. How many Daily Declarations do most people have?

A. The average seems to be around 20; however, the more you have the better! Just be sure you use them twice daily. If the list can be handled on that basis, the number is unimportant.

Q. Why do you emphasize daily activity? Does missing a day or two hurt?

A. YES! If you are not prepared to *regularly* practice the application of the natural laws of Dyna/Psyc, you reduce its effect dramatically. Only consistent application pays off. But it does payoff big!

Q. Is one's age a handicap in practicing Dyna/Psyc?

A. Not at all. It is equally effective for teenagers or those "four-score" and older. In fact, "keeping young" has been an important goal for many.

Q. In discussing your approach with friends they said they thought I was too tense for such an effort. Isn't everybody tense?

A. More or less; some emotion is felt by everyone at all times. The pleasant emotions make you feel good; unpleasant ones make you feel bad. Repressed emotions create tension. Dyna/Psyc makes it possible to ease the tensions of unexpressed emotions. A simple way to help reduce tension is through Silent Treatments. Suggestions of relaxation and renewed energy and enthusiasm when "coming-up" from Super Suggestions are also beneficial.

Q. What is the greatest enemy of success?

A. Fear—the fear that caused the early negative conditioning, which, in turn, gave us an Inadequate Self-Image to begin with. And fear is the worst of all tensions. It creates anxiety—which creates further tensions. Declarations for courage, confidence, relaxation and effectiveness are all helpful in controlling this threat to success.

Q. Are there any good ways to get rid of the tensions you feel at work so that you don't bring them home to "let loose" on the family?

A. A minute or two of any strenuous physical activity can work like magic. Punch a bag you hang up in the garage for that purpose. Pound a few heavy nails into a piece of timber. Chop a piece of wood. Even "shadowboxing" vigorously will relieve the tensions.

Q. Isn't it shameful for a grown man to cry?

A. Indeed not. I was once told that many psychiatrists believe the acceptance of women's tears, but not of men's, is one of the reasons women outlive men. Human beings should be able to relieve grief by this perfectly natural outlet. It has been said (and I think, truly) that those who are unable to express grief in this manner are also unable to express joy.

A childish outburst is of course inappropriate. But the inability to express emotion in some physical *form* is also a handicap.

Q. Can one person literally give another person a "pain in the neck?"

A. Indeed! There are a number of "sayings" which we hear frequently which show how deeply our emotions affect us in physical ways. "She makes me sick—I can breathe easier, now that the bill is paid—I've got something to get off my chest—I'm boiling mad—He gets me hot under the collar—He gives me a headache—That makes my stomach turn." These are all sayings that actually describe the physical manifestations of various emotional problems. Don't let them get to you. Use Dyna/Psyc to free yourself from the destructive tensions.

Q. How can I use Dyna/Psyc to get the support of other people?

A. You will get it *automatically* when you make your Daily Declaration, "I have a warm regard for others at all times and in all situations." Your success does require the help and cooperation of other people, and a warm regard for others *communicates itself to them.* Feeling it, they must respond. Sometimes you will feel you have met someone who is immune to this treatment. But persevere, you will win! And, remember this: helping others helps you rid yourself of guilt for mistakes or wrongs in your past. Guilt is a great drawback in the search for success. Rid yourself of it by unselfishly giving of yourself without fanfare or reward. It will aid you in many ways.

He who chooses the beginning of a road chooses the place it leads to. It is the means that determine the end.

HARRY EMMERSON FOSDICK
(1878–1969)
American theologian

Q. I had barely started on my Daily Declarations when I began to feel they were not what I had really wanted. Is this wrong?

A. No. You will find your goals change as you progress. Merely revise your goals to conform to your new desires. Word the new ones for Daily Declaration and continue as before.

Q. Should I tell my husband the goals I have set for myself or that I'm changing my personality and character so that things will be more peaceful and happy at home?

A. No! Keep those intangible goals to yourself. As your behavior manifests the new qualities, everyone will be aware of it. But if you talk about it, there is a too-human need to call it to your attention if, as you are beginning to establish the change, you should "slip back" to the old you for even a moment.

Remember, I have cautioned you *not* to discuss *any* of your goals or efforts with others. The main reason for this is the energy you dissipate by telling others of your projected changes or acquisitions. Sometimes it seems that, by telling, a person substitutes the "story" for true achievement.

Keep your own counsel! Follow the plan! Don't waste your thoughts and energies.

Now turn to Step #11 "Where Are You Now?"
in your *Roadmap to Riches* workbook.

12

Focus on Your Destination, Not Your Problem

You have been conditioned to think of situations that are inadequate for the attainment of our desires and aspirations as "problems." Then, you were conditioned to spend your life solving those problems.

When you focus on solving problems, you are spending your life-energy to make something go *away*—to get rid of something. When you are focused on creating your inner vision, you are expending your life-energy toward making something you want *come into being*—your Riches. The basic intentions of these actions are opposite one another.

One creates stress and frustration that can lead to anger and rage (The Los Angeles riots come to mind); the other brings us satisfaction. (The Los Angeles Summer Olympics is a good example). Through The Lazy Man's Way, you will learn to focus on creating your vision of your ideal life—finding your purpose—which brings you a life of fulfillment, satisfaction and Riches.

I think the reason we stay with our problems is that they have become comfortable and familiar. They seem to work for us. They help organize our thoughts, focus our actions, and fill up our time. Our problems relieve us of the need to think. We can just obsess instead. We can dwell on what's wrong. We can go over it in our mind repeatedly. We can worry about it. We can blame our problems for our troubles. We have something to talk about with our friends.

WE ARE MEASURED BY THE SIZE OF OUR ADVERSARIES

Our colleagues will be impressed and attentive. It's us against the problem, and because our victories are measured by the size of our adversaries, the bigger the problem the better. Problem solving inevitably distracts and deceives us by giving us the illusion that we are doing something important and valuable.

When we think to examine our lives in the context of having a purpose, we ask better and more useful questions. Rather than asking, "How can I get this unwanted situation to go away?" We might ask, "What results will my vision create?" "How can I get to where I want to go?" "How can I have the joy I want?" These questions direct us in a positive manner and produce better, more satisfying results than, "How can I get rid of my problems?"

WHICH WILL IT BE? THE FOREST OR THE TREES?

The difference in orientation can change your life and can change your world. Dr. Martin Luther King didn't just solve a problem. He created a vision of a new structure of equality and justice—"I have a dream."

Problems are only opportunities in work clothes.

HENRY J. KAISER
(1882–1967)
American industrialist

Our problems are man made; therefore, they may be solved by man. And man can be as he wants. No problem of human destiny is beyond beings.

JOHN F. KENNEDY
(1917–1963)
35th President of the United States

Happiness is essentially a state of going somewhere wholeheartedly; one-directionally without regret or reservations.

WILLIAM H. SHELDON
(1898–1977)
American physician. psychologist

We grow by dreams. All big men are dreamers, some of us let dreams die, but others nourish and protect them, nurse them through bad days . . . to the sunshine and light, which always come.

WOODROW WILSON
(1856–1924)
28th President of the United States

John F. Kennedy didn't just solve a problem. He created a vision of U.S. leadership in space, education, and social welfare. (We began to dream of Camelot.)

Mahatma Gandhi didn't just solve a problem. He created a vision that dramatically changed India, England and the whole world.

Because a change in structure—from problem solving to creating a vision—changes the way things are accomplished (from a path of least resistance, which takes us all over the place, to a more direct, clearer path) these men, and many others like them, have been able to bring into their lives, and ours, what truly mattered to them.

This book is not just about solving problems or moving away from problems, but about how to create *your* vision of *your* purpose and moving your life forward under your control. As you read this book, and do the steps in the Guidebook, your perspective will be changed forever and lifted to new heights. You will get a "big-picture" look at the forest of your dreams, not a close-up look at the logs and stumps of your problems.

REACTIVE/RESPONSIVE VS. PROACTIVE/CREATIVE

My dissatisfaction and frustrations in any aspect of my life seem to come from a feeling that I'm not in control of whatever situation appears to be affecting me. The situation or circumstance is in control of me, if all I am doing is reacting or responding to it. A friend used to tell me that allowing myself to be in the reactive/responsive mode is living life like a ping-pong ball on a windy day. It is easily blown to and fro, bouncing up and down and off of everything in sight. It reacts and responds to the currents of the winds. It has no real purpose or direction, but goes with the wind (the circumstances) around it.

Circumstances—what are circumstances? I make circumstances.

NAPOLEON BONAPARTE
(1769–1821)
Emperor of France
(1804–1815)

The real problem of the reactive/responsive way of living your life is that it assumes that you are *powerless* over the circumstances of your life. It assumes that your only options are to react or respond to a given situation or circumstance. If you find yourself repeatedly in a reactive/responsive mode, you might then want to ask yourself, (Are you ready for the truth?) "Who has the power here, me or the thing to which I am responding or reacting?" Clearly the power is in the circumstance and not in you, if you are reacting or responding. So you never get anything done. It's like the old saying, "When you are up to your butt in alligators, It's too late to think about draining the swamp."

DON'T DELUDE YOURSELF

There are two ways of meeting difficulties; you alter the difficulties or you alter yourself to meet them.

PHYLISS BOTTOME
pen name MRS. ERNAN
FORBES–DENNIS
(1884–1963)
English author

I feel that power is *always* internal. If you believe, and therefore live your life, as if changing your external circumstances will bring you success, you are deluding yourself . . . ***And you are the last person you ever want to delude***. Understand that nothing external, in and of itself, can bring you genuine success and happiness. If you think that people (a new boss, a different spouse, or better friend), places (a new neighborhood, world travel, or a better location) and things (money or property, a face lift, winning at gambling, a new car, better wardrobe or a new job) will make you happy, you are into a major delusion. You just can't find happiness, security, health, or peace of mind that way. (Although they may be wonderful short term diversions.)

There are many people who have everything you wish you had and lots more. And guess what? They are still miserable, unfulfilled, lonely and dissatisfied. You read about members of the British Royal family who are in one unhappy situation after another—even to the point of trying to commit suicide. I'll bet that in your wildest dreams you never thought of having all they have: castles, world class yachts, a fleet of aircraft, assets all over the world (including billions in cash) and they don't even pay taxes. How lucky can you get?

Changing your circumstances won't change who you are. Only you can do that. CHANGE. Permanent, powerful, lasting change can only come from within. Responding and reacting to what drifts your way on the currents of life, can only sweep you along with the current. If you want to visit certain Riches along the way to your destination, then look at your map, turn on your motor, and grab your rudder.

It's time to stop trying to only solve your problems—responding and reacting to the circumstances of life. It's time to MAKE THINGS HAPPEN—the proactive and creative way—by taking control of your circumstances when you focus on your vision. It's time to *live your life on purpose*—The Lazy Man's Way.

YOUR PERFECT JOURNEY—OR JUST A DULL RIDE?

You have become used to accepting "generic" versions of almost everything. There was a time when you would order your new car direct from the factory just the way you wanted it. You could order exactly the options you wanted—your color, specified interior, your choice of engine size and transmissions were all available to you.

Now, with over half of our cars being built overseas, you probably take what the dealers have in stock, and your choices are most likely now limited to color selection.

You used to be able to build your home to suit your needs and personality. Now, your choice of a new home may be a condo, or a town house, or a tract house with a couple of floor plans from which to choose. But don't expect to choose your room sizes, number of windows, premium fixtures, or even paint color. Now you take what they build, and you take it the way they build it with no changes and certainly no customization,

Weddings now seem to be prepackaged and even wedding gowns mass-produced. Vacations are pre-packaged for us so we buy tours that are some travel agent's idea of an ideal vacation (a five to seven day cruise or a Club Med package). Health care is going the way of the H.M.O. or the P.P.O. where you can't select your own doctor. Any selection is from "their" list of doctors—not yours. It's kind of like your aptitude test in junior high school. It may be a choice, but it's limited to someone else's choices—not yours.

Clothes are now generally "ready to wear" or "one size fits all" or "unisex". Shoes seem to be getting harder to find in correct widths, unless you have a "medium" sized foot. Now, even much of our food is pre-packaged, frozen or "fast." So, even if they tell you that you can "have it your way," you still have only their limited menu choices.

Well, from this moment on I want you to know you have choices—choices to live your life on your own terms. All you need are two documents and you can design them for yourself. They will carry you from where you are right now to anywhere

Destiny is not a matter of chance; it is a matter of choice. It is not a thing to be waited for; it is a thing to be achieved.

WILLIAM JENNINGS BRYAN
(1860–1925)
American political leader and orator

When the fight begins within himself, a man's worth something.

ROBERT BROWNING
(1812–1889)
English poet

The block of granite, which is an obstacle in the pathway of the weak, becomes a stepping-stone in the pathway of the strong.

THOMAS CARLYLE
(1795–1881)
Scottish-born English prose writer

If you don't know where you are going, you might wind up someplace else.

YOGI BERRA
(b. 1925)
American baseball player

We accept the verdict of the past until the need for change cries out loudly enough to force upon us a choice between the comfort of further inertia and the irksomeness of action.

JUDGE LEARNED HAND
(1872–1961)
American jurist

We take our shape, it is true, within and against that cage of reality bequeathed us at our birth, and yet it is precisely through our dependence on this reality that we are most endlessly betrayed.

C. S. LEWIS (1898–1963)
British author

and everywhere you want to go. It's your journey to Riches. It's the journey that is the rest of your life.

YOUR ITINERARY AND TICKET PACKAGE

Your journey to Riches begins with the itinerary and the ticket package. Both must be clearly identified as belonging to you with your name on the line designated as "the traveler."

Now that you have entered your name, it's time to ask yourself an interesting question. "Who is that person I just named on my ticket?" If you can step back from yourself for a moment, I would like to ask you to consider several possibilities. Is it really going to be you on the journey that will be the rest of your life? Or, will it be the person you have come to see yourself as over the years—either from others' view of you or from your own mistaken view of yourself. We tend to see ourselves through the eyes of others—through the massive amount of feedback from others—family, friends, classmates, teachers, and even strangers. We take on an identity. This is a natural process for children as they grow up. But now that you are an adult; it's time for a reality check before you plan the rest of your life. It's possible that the *dissatisfaction* you felt in your life that caused you to buy this book is a red flag. If so, pay careful attention to it.

LIVE YOUR OWN LIFE

You can only be happy living your own life. If the life you are living is the life your parents wanted for you and you're not happy living it, then it's time to start to live your life. If the life you are living is the life of any stereotype you accepted for yourself and it isn't working for you, then now is the time for you to stop living that other life and start living your life. How do you know if you are living a stereotyped life? Look at the images you have of yourself.

Examine carefully the many limits and the qualifiers of these images you have embraced. These will prove to be unnecessary and unwanted baggage on the journey. We deal with your unwanted baggage in Step 33 in your Roadmap workbook.

Some of the images you hold of yourself may be based on facts, yet still may be in subtle conflict with who you really are. My friend, David, who is Jewish, is a New Yorker, the grandson of a Rabbi, the son of a doctor (his mother) and a lawyer (his father). When he thought of the rest of his life, he assumed he would stay in the old neighborhood in New York City, vacation in the Catskills, marry a nice Jewish girl, go to graduate school and become a professional like his parents.

He hated the whole idea yet felt compelled to live out these life-images. This he did until *dissatisfaction* caused him to awaken to the fact he just wasn't happy being or doing any of these things. In his heart he knew what he really wanted for his life, but felt guilty even having those feelings. His parents had been so good to him. They had such hopes for him. They lived their lives for him. How could he let them down by being himself? And who was David—really?

David was a skier. David lived to ski more than anything. His whole life was skiing and when he admitted that to himself, he realized he couldn't stay on the journey he was on any longer.

David is now married to a ski school instructor and they live in Incline Village, California. And what does David do now? He is on the National Ski Patrol. In the summer David and Debbie teach skiing in New Zealand and they are making ski adventure movies. They live, love and laugh together. They are happy doing what they love to do and being who they really are. (And they make a good living, too.) Their lives are full of the Riches they never could have had by staying on the journey that David's background prescribed. David would not have been true to who he really was.

WHERE WERE YOU SUPPOSED TO GO?

Is your journey where a New York Jewish boy is "supposed" to go? Is this where an Iowa farm boy is "supposed" to go? Is this where a Chicano boy from Mexico City is "supposed" to go? Is this where a young black girl from Mississippi is "supposed" to go? Is this where a Smith or a Jones or whatever your family name happens to be "supposed" to go? Is this the ticket of the child of a famous personality, or just whose ticket are you holding on your Road to Riches? We seem to feel that we must fit into certain roles that we are born into dictated by family, geography, ethnicity, economics and heritage. But is that who you really are? Maybe that's who you are only because you accepted this image as a child from the many authority figures in your life—parents, church, neighbors, teachers, grandparents, or whoever may have had an agenda concerning your life. *Well, maybe that's not who you really are at all.*

Maybe there is a "butterfly" inside you after all just waiting to grow into what it wants to become. All you have to do is to allow it to happen naturally. I recently heard a story about a caterpillar crawling along a dusty trail. He looks up to see a butterfly flying above him and he turns to his friend and says, "You'll never get me up in one of those."

Bill Cosby, one of the highest paid entertainers of all time and one who has earned a Doctorate in Psychology, believed his role was one of a shoeshine boy—and that's what he was. He used to shine shoes outside Temple University when he was a young man. Then he realized the name on his ticket to life didn't really fit him. Someone was to be a shoeshine boy at that stand, but he knew he wasn't the one.

It's vital that you allow yourself to know who you really are. You are the only one who can decide who you want to become and what you will be happy doing for the rest of your life. When you close your eyes, there is no one else in there with you. You are the master of your identity. You have been placed in charge of you. Only you can plan out the ideal itinerary for you.

YOUR DESTINATION

If you were to look back at your life from the end of the "Richest life," what would have made it so wonderfully "Rich?" What were the many facets that put the brilliance and sparkle on the "diamond " that was your life? Each of those facets was a part of the journey. Each of them was an important part of your life. If you want those wonderful results in your life, you have to make room for them. You have to allow them to happen by choosing and including them in your itinerary deliberately. That's how you live your life on purpose.

In the next chapter, *The Power of Purpose*, we will plant a seed about seeing your life from its end; your funeral. In Charles Dickens' classic story, "A Christmas Carol," Scrooge is given a look at his life from the perspective of his funeral. The ghost of Christmas Future shows him how his life will be if he continues doing what he is doing. This scares him and makes him unhappy to see what a miserable life he has led. That was his feeling of dis-satisfaction talking to him through his dream. After he listened to it, he looked at his life again from the perspective of how he wanted his life to be—how it could be if he made some changes.

RICH WITHOUT RICHES

He looked at his life from the perspective of the results he wanted in his life. Now remember, Scrooge was a wealthy man and could have all the things money could buy. So where was the source of his dissatisfaction? He had only one facet to his life—money. His life stood for nothing. He was unfulfilled, miserable, lonely, unloved, unwanted, scorned, ridiculed, mocked, hated, feared, tolerated, miserly, overbearing, unhappy, friendless and fearful. But he was rich. Yes, he was rich, but he had no Riches.

Now, look at your "perfect" life with all the facets that give it luster and brilliance. Picture your "perfect" funeral. Who is there from your family to speak for you? Who is there from your business life to speak for you, and what are they saying? Who is there speaking about your spiritual life? Who is there speaking about your contributions to society? There are many facets to a life full of Riches and someday there will be a final celebration or memorial service to sum it all up.

We are all moving toward that final destination of our lives. So why not make some course-corrections now for the journey ahead. After all, you will *spend the rest of your life on this journey.* You want to arrive at your destination feeling fulfilled, happy, proud, with no regrets, full of love and able to take a final bow to a packed house. You want a standing ovation. Anything less is just cheating yourself. Make today the first day of the rest of your "new" life. Or, as I've said before, "Make today the first day of the Best of your life."

YOUR TRAVEL AGENT

As you visualize your destination, select your itinerary, and purchase your ticket for your exciting life's journey, as with any trip, you may want to seek the assistance of a travel agent. One who knows the in's and out's, up's and down's and how to avoid the pitfalls as much as possible. There are many helpful people who might act in this capacity, as your "travel agent," such as counselors, professors and ministers. For me I have come to find that there is only one choice to make for this important role—and that is God! My life changed significantly when I discovered and accepted my creator. My purpose became clearer, I felt more fulfilled, purposeful—it just worked a whole lot better when I began using the Ten Commandments as my personal itinerary.

Through a relationship with a spiritual "travel agent," I believe you can gain great insight into what's most beneficial for you and others in the world. It's a win-win relationship for all concerned. Everyone knows the golden rule; "Do unto others as you would have them do unto you" and I believe it is true that what you give out comes back (what goes around, comes around).

What the caterpillar calls a tragedy—the master calls a butterfly

RICHARD BACH
(b. 1936)
American author

What's the use of running if you're not on the right road?

GERMAN PROVERB

Most people are about as happy as they make up their mind to be.

ABRAHAM LINCOLN
(1809–1865)
16th President of the United States

It is not the mountain we conquer, but ourselves.

SIR EDMUND HILLARY
(b. 1919)
New Zealand mountaineer

As I grow in my relationship with my God, I grow in the realization and experience of all that I want to be and to do. Many people come to this spiritual relationship as they search out their dreams, their mission, and their purpose in life. You may discover this to be true in your own experience. In a sense, you have been on a mission the minute you were launched into this world. Realizing that your mission is actually from your heart, placed there by your God, gives you an added motivation to fulfill it with class and reflect the image of God to the world through all that you are and do. It works for me!

For those who believe in God no explanation is needed; for those who do not believe in God no explanation is possible.

FATHER JOHN LAFARGE
(b. 1880)
Of the Cures at Lourdes

Now turn to Step #12 "Focus on Your Destination, Not Your Problem" in your *Roadmap to Riches* workbook.

CHAPTER 13

What Is My Purpose in Life?

It has been said that this is life's most powerful question. I am convinced that everyone has a purpose planted inside them. It's like an inner label that only you are able to determine, no one but *you*, can tell you what your purpose is. You are the only one who is able to look deeply enough inside yourself to discover that inner dream and desire of your heart. Finding out the answer to the question of what your purpose is should be easy, but it sure wasn't for me and it hasn't been easy for any one I have ever known.

Seeking your purpose is not like searching for gold. You will not "discover" it by exploration using maps, instruments or geological studies. It is also not going to be "revealed" to you by a teacher, fortuneteller, your horoscope in the paper or even by divine revelation. It is already known to you. It's deep down inside of you.

If purpose—your heart's desire—is so important, then why does it seem so difficult to discover? To many people it seems deeply *hidden*. Some people never even think that they may have a purpose, are never encouraged to think about it, or are so distracted by other life issues that they don't get around to focusing upon it.

To many other people their purpose is effectively *denied*. Have you ever had a dream pop into your mind, something you really want to do? And have you shared that dream with another person only to have them throw up all kinds of obstacles to accomplishing that dream? They say things like, "How could you do anything like that without more education, more money, a miracle, etc.? You're just dreaming. Come on back to earth, pal!" You become intimidated by the thought of having a life purpose. You begin to believe that it is presumptuous on your part to have these grandiose dreams. It doesn't take much resistance to stifle your dreams and send them scurrying back to the "wish" area of your mind. After a while, you don't need any help at all in denying your dreams—you can do it all by yourself.

WHAT KEEPS YOU STUCK?

My purpose was hidden from me for a long while until the need to answer the puzzle of what my life was all about became overwhelmingly strong. The clue to solving it came when I began to examine why my life didn't work, what were the dissatisfactions in my life. I started looking at those things that don't work for me; things that I denied existed at all. The things that I disliked and refused to deal with. You probably have your own list of these kinds of things—the things that keep you stuck. Looking at my dissatisfactions and choosing to deal with them took a great deal of courage. Once I did, I was able to open a door and walk through it into a new world

> A mans main task in life is to give birth to himself.
>
> ERIC FROMM
> (1900–1980)
> German-born American psychoanalyst and philosopher

> When we can't dream any longer, we die.
>
> EMMA GOLDMAN
> (1869–1940)
> American anarchist

> And from the discontent of man the world's best progress springs.
>
> ELLA WHEELER WILCOX
> (1850–1919)
> American poet, novelist

where I could start looking for dreams that would take their place. And take their place they did!

The "what" in the question of "What do I want?" is already known to you. It resides within you! You were uniquely created to be who you are and to do what you can do. You can access it either rationally by observation (detection or discernment) or through your intuition, by what we call "hunches."

Hunches are creative thought. In this society we were taught that logic is the better thought process, but most creative thoughts don't come from logic at all. Logic takes us from step to step, from idea to idea, from concept to concept, and from detail to detail. Hunches skip all that and just jump to a conclusion.

So what am I saying here? Simply this! In order to create the answer to the question of "What do I want?" the "what" is just something you **"make up!"** Whoa! Did you get that?

You just make it up! It's really that simple! It's the Lazy Man's Way—and it works! It works because what you think you made up, was really inside you all the time and your conscious mind finally heard it. Where does it come from? Some say it comes from your soul, other say it is your inner voice, some say it's in your DNA. What's important is how to get in touch with it so you can hear it, because once you hear it you can then act on it, and from then on your life will never be the same.

"LISTEN TO THE FORCE, LUKE"

In the *Star Wars* movie trilogy the hero, Luke Skywalker, needed to do something immediately—it was seemingly impossible to do and it was something for which he had neither adequate training nor skills to do. His mind went blank from fear and overload and then he heard a voice in his head saying, "trust the force, Luke." The voice was telling him to trust himself, to trust his instincts, to not think about it—just do it.

I believe that what you want wants you. Once you get to the point of admitting what you want, the "how" of getting it becomes almost automatic. At one time or another all of us experience momentary flashes of what we really want. But most of the time, we are too timid, unaware, not sure or embarrassed to accept those flashes so we don't share them with anyone. These "silent sentences" in your heart are valuable gold mines where you will discover the key to all the riches you are looking for! Listen for them.

One of the easiest and simplest ways to hear your inner voice is to quiet your mind and focus it through meditation. Almost all religions offer ways to quiet your mind. Christians call it going to the silence and listening to the still small voice within. If you are not religious, and if meditation doesn't appeal to you, try taking small decisions and letting go of your usual approach to handling them. Just let go of them—don't try to do anything about them. Trust that your inner voice will tell you the best course for them. As you build trust in your inner voice you will quickly learn to hand over bigger decisions to it.

THE "WHY" OF YOUR LIFE—THE PORTRAIT OF PURPOSE

Focus on your purpose—the *"why"* of your life! What does your life stand for? Develop a personal mission statement that focuses on what you want to be (your character and values) and to do (your performance and achievements). Turn to your workbook for help with your personal mission statement.

Dr. Viktor Frankl was a prominent German psychiatrist who survived the holocaust of the Second World War. While imprisoned in the Nazi death camp at Auschwitz he had to focus on something to maintain his sanity amid the horror and terror of the death camp. He wondered why some people were surviving in that hell hole and others would just give up and die, or even commit suicide. Eventually he realized that the people who survived had a sense of meaning and purpose in and for their lives—they had something to move forward to, something to live for.

He said, "Everyone has his own specific vocation or mission in life—he cannot be replaced, nor can his life be repeated. Thus everyone's task is as unique as is his specific opportunity to implement it." He goes on to say: *"Ultimately, man should not ask what the meaning of his life is, but rather must recognize that it is he who is asked. In a word, each man is questioned by life; and he can only answer to life by answering for his own life; to life he can only respond by being responsible."* In other words, your life communicates a message whether good or bad, effective or ineffective. You have a life message—a purpose for being and doing. Find out what it is!

You can look at your purpose as a personal constitution much like the Constitution of the United States. The U. S. Constitution formulated a road map for our living together. This road map has given us our primary direction for the life of this great country. It serves as a guide for knowing who we are and what we are all about, what our values are, what we stand for, what we want as a nation. Doesn't it make sense to do the same thing for you and your life?

By allowing yourself to *access* (detect and discern) your purpose, you will become involved in taking control of the direction of your life. Personal involvement is crucial in obtaining your Riches. You can't allow anyone else to suggest, define, set, or in any way become involved in your purpose. This is a job only you can do. It demands your total commitment! No involvement means no commitment, and no commitment means no results!

MY LIFE MATTERS!

Because your purpose is such a personal issue and there is no one answer as to what your purpose might be, I will talk on this subject from my personal experience of finding my purpose. I believe that my life matters and this thought lead me to strive to be useful and feel useful. My life is really empty without feeling useful and fulfilled and I feel I deny a primary purpose of my existence if I am not useful! By not being useful, I am wasting my gifts and talents. By not being useful, I allow my creative forces within to wither and even be destroyed. By not being useful, I would feel that I had sacrificed my purpose and with it my sense of fulfillment, peacefulness, contentment, happiness and joy. I would have sacrificed my Riches!

I also believe that I was born to be thoroughly used up when I die—not to go to my grave with my music still in me. Getting your music out, whatever it is, is the beginning to acquiring the great Riches you desire. It will empower you! It will inspire you! It will propel and compel you! Your "music" is your message, your meaning, your purpose in life! I like the statement, "It's not how long you live your life, but how well you spend it that counts"! A well-spent life is a life lived on purpose!

If a man does not keep pace with his companions, perhaps it is because he hears a different drummer: Let him step to the music which he hears, however measured or far away.

HENRY DAVID THOREAU
(1817–1862)
American essayist, naturalist, poet

I cannot believe that the purpose of life is to be "happy." I think the purpose of life is to be useful, to be responsible, to be honorable, to be compassionate. It is, after all, to matter: to count, to stand for something, to have made some difference that you lived at all.

LEE C. ROSTEN
Pen name of
LEONARD Q. ROSS
(b. 1908)
Polish-born American writer, political scientist

For some, purpose means achieving extraordinary things! For me the examples are everywhere. Buckminster Fuller; thinker, teacher, inventor and scientist—he was a man who could have gone in many directions and been outstanding in all of them. Frank Lloyd Wright, one of the finest architects of all time, who strove for new horizons with a burning vision. Walt Disney who dreamed of wonderful, imaginative worlds and made them come true for all of us. And so did President Abraham Lincoln who went through repeated failures but persevered to become one of the most effective and memorable men of all times. All had apparent extraordinary purpose.

Do all of us have to achieve these kinds of monuments to history with finding and fulfilling our purpose? As Robert Kennedy pointed out: "Few will have the greatness to bend history itself, but each of us can work to change a small portion of events. It is from numberless acts of courage and belief that human history is shaped." Regardless of the scope of our purpose, finding out what our purpose is and pursuing it is what is really important.

AN EMPTY LIFE IS A CLUE

When you don't have a purpose or mission (or worse yet, don't follow the one you have), you may experience an empty life without a sense of meaning and joy. This is where the daily objective is simply a struggle to solve one problem after another to survive. This lack of purpose shows up as apathy, fear, low self-esteem, and often leads to disease, alcohol and drug abuse, crime, and becoming a burden to family and society!

I believe the purpose of life is to be a growing, contributing involved human being and that life is at its best when you are willingly and happily contributing to other people and society. The idea of service and contribution is not new, but to many people the idea of serving suggests an inferior status. To the great leaders of our world the notion of service is evident in the contribution that they make to the world and to themselves. Social philosopher, Marshall McLuhan suggested that, "On Spaceship Earth there are no passengers—only crew." As a crewmember each of us is free to choose our assignment.

I feel the power of a purpose is what makes living more worthwhile, more meaningful, regardless of the challenges that come your way. It's a Richer life that will give you access to the inner confidence you need to move forward through any and all obstacles in your path. Purpose gives you the power to handle life's "piles and pits" more easily!

PURPOSE IS A CONTINUUM

A first grader told his preschool sister, "Don't ever learn to spell cat, once you do that, they keep on giving you harder words"! Good advice, but life still goes on! Life is a process that progressively builds. You are the sum total today of all of your prior experiences, whether you interpreted them to be good or bad. And no matter what your experiences have been, your purpose is best discovered through those lenses. For many, their purpose is developed out of a past trauma, an indelible mark upon them that now drives them to be more sensitive, more impassioned, more focused, more driven.

People who have had an illness as a child may develop a purpose in life to work with children suffering from disease or a physical disadvantage. A person who was embarrassed may incorporate a great sensitivity or compassion for anyone who might find themselves in the same situation. People who have experienced loss in their past have a greater sense of appreciation for those who are experiencing similar loss, therefore they have a "message" for people in the same situation. Not only does purpose build upon your past experiences, it also continues to be in process throughout your entire life. It's a continuum!

THE "WHERE" OF YOUR LIFE—YOUR SENSE OF DESTINY

In order to answer the question "What do you want?" most fully, you must walk through the process of the "Why" of your life (purpose) and the "Where" of your life (results). Your purpose will become even clearer by picturing the results you want for your life!

An ancient Chinese proverb states: "If you don't know where you are going, you won't know when you get there." Deciding what results you want—not just the *things* you want—is the vital step toward achieving the Riches you are looking for. This all helps to define your purpose or mission in life.

As the architect begins with a clean sheet of paper or the artist with an empty canvas, so I suggest you begin in the same way. Start with nothing. Start fresh with a blank sheet or an empty canvas. Fill in the blank sheet and canvas by "making up" what you want out of your life. Listen to your heart of hearts.

The best place to begin is to look at what the end might look like. The results you want! If you were an observer at your own funeral, what would you expect you would say about the results of your life? There are two possibilities to you. One is—you liked your life. It worked for you because you experienced joy, happiness, and excellent health, and felt satisfaction. Or, like Scrooge, you didn't like your life. It definitely didn't work for you. You were dissatisfied. You spent a great deal of energy and time doing those things you disliked and you missed out on a lot of joy and happiness. You missed out on experiencing loving relationships. Are you hearing the result of your life that you want to hear? Were you treating your life as if it mattered? Did you take your life into your own hands to create the life you wanted? You can. If not you, who?

The amazing thing I've discovered over the years is that virtually everyone already possesses a picture of the desired results he/she wants to achieve. Those pictures are down deep inside you.

They were placed there when you were originally created. The images of those dreams, those intended results for your life, were implanted within your very soul. They are waiting for you to develop them into pictures of reality. It's your **personal sense of destiny!**

IT'S AN APTITUDE PROBLEM

When you were in school, you probably learned how to do things. Therefore, it's natural for you to approach your life like all of the assignments you were given in school. It's what you were taught to do. You were taught how to do things: *how* to

> You can only have two things in life, reasons or results. Reasons don't count.
>
> ROBERT ANTHONY. Ph.D.
> American psychologist, writer

> Great minds have purpose, others have wishes.
>
> WASHINGTON IRVING (1783–1859)
> American essayist, biographer, historian

read, *how* to spell, *how* to solve math problems, how to play football, how to use a computer, etc. What you learned in school was *process*—the how to do things! You probably never learned about finding your dreams—the "what" you want. There were no classes in vision—creating a purpose.

Even if you think that what you want isn't possible for you or you can't possibly have what you want, that you aren't worthy, or don't have the education, or whatever limits you put on your true wants—*you still want them!* So, be honest with yourself; allow yourself to have them—at least, in your thoughts and dreams. Thoughts and dreams are seeds. At least plant them!

Even though Riches primarily come from within, other people make a major contribution to your Riches as they help you build and develop them. So if you want Riches, it's wise to fully understand that other people are going to play an important part in your getting what you want. It has been said, "You can get everything in life you want, if you will just help other people get what they want."

Before we do a simple exercise, let's sum up the basic truths about purpose:

1. Your goals are not your purpose. Your purpose drives and threads your goals together; by your purpose you know what you are to do and what you are not to do.

2. Your purpose must have a people connection. Who will you serve?

3. Your purpose may, or may not, have anything to do with your job. It enables you to abandon the job you hate and find the vocation you love. It creates the excitement that keeps you awake at night and gets you up in the morning with anticipation and eagerness.

4. Your purpose may emerge out of your life-struggles and pain.

5. You never retire from your life purpose. You may have more than one purpose throughout the course of your life.

6. Your purpose will continually be revised as you go. It is made out of patchwork experiences—the latest added on to the list.

YOUR RICHES AND YOUR SUCCESS IS TO BE AND TO DO ALL THAT YOU WERE CREATED TO BE AND TO DO.

Now let's look at a simple exercise that will show you what you are all about—your values—your purpose or mission in life! All you do is write it down. You fill in the blanks of the assignment we offer. Sounds easy doesn't it? But there is just one hitch. There is an outer you and an inner you. I don't want you to do the assignment in a surface way using the outer you. Use the inner you, your heart of hearts, your conscience—the private you. This will insure a more honest expression of your feelings. The outer you has been tinted, colored and conditioned to behave in certain ways, but these very ways are the "identities" that got you where you are today. Listen to the inner pangs of dissatisfaction down deep inside that are trying to express themselves. It needs to be heard, if you are to resolve the cause of the dissatisfaction in your life and move forward to the Riches you know you want.

No horse gets anywhere until he is harnessed. No steam or gas ever drives anything until it is confined. No Niagara is ever turned into light and power until it is tunneled. No life ever grows great until it is focused, dedicated, disciplined.

HARRY EMERSON FOSDICK
(1878–1969)
American theologian

The great and glorious masterpiece of man is to know how to live life on purpose.

MICHEL DE MONTAIGNE
(1533–1592)
French moralist, essayist

So how do you do this? Start with identifying the things in life that make you feel good, that make you come alive, and that make you say "Yes!"

They may be small things, large things, everyday things or extraordinary things. It doesn't matter as long as they "speak" to you. They are the "hunches" I spoke of at the beginning of this chapter. You continue by putting those feelings together with activities that when you think about doing them, bring about these same feelings. Once you get a sense of that, then take practice runs in filling in the blanks to this question:

FILL IN THE BLANKS

"My purpose in life is to _____ to
_____ .

As an example, an elementary school teacher might answer the question in this way:

"My purpose in life is to <u>inspire children</u> to <u>learn</u>"

Remember, anything you dream can be yours. Most often, however, we need a little help in allowing those dreams to become evident to ourselves.

A lofty vision stated clearly contains the power to move mountains! It helps you to focus on your goals and bring them into existence! The goals that make up that clear path that will take you to your purpose like a rocket to the moon! Operating from a clear sense of purpose assures that all your efforts are directed toward doing the right thing in the right way for you.

Remember, you have the right to live your life to its fullest, so be involved in your own life. If you want to live, not just exist; a vision of what you want your life to be will make it a rewarding, rich experience. Actively create that life rather than be created by the circumstances around you. Instead of being manipulated by various life-molds, manage your own life by making your life happen. It's called living your life on purpose!

The exercise in Step 13 "What is My Purpose In Life" in your workbook gives you that help. Consider both the possibilities offered on the page in the workbook as well as the possibilities that "pop" into your head for these are those messages coming from the inner you. Listen to them! After you finish reading the exercise, just sit quietly for a while and let the blanks be filled in by that inner you. You will know when the words are truly yours.

Alright, let's get on with filling in the blanks. Because this is such a critical step in moving your life forward we have provided numerous resources and aids to help you uncover or discover your propose in the workbook. Please go there now.

> When I look into the future, it's so bright, it burns my eyes.
>
> OPRAH WINFREY (b. 1954) African-American television talk show host, actress

Now turn to Step #13 "What Is My Purpose in Life?"
in your *Roadmap to Riches* workbook.

14

Setting Unbelievable (but Attainable) Goals

Setting goals is one of the most popular topics in the business world and in the psychological arena as well. And yet the selecting, setting and securing of goals is still one of the most frustrating of life's experiences. The goals path is filled with frequent disappointments and is littered with all sorts of wreckage due to misplaced, un-attained and abandoned goals.

Here are some ways you might be using to solve the problems of goal setting in the absence of tying goals to a purpose.

First Aim at nothing! The problem with this method is that when you aim at nothing you'll hit it every time and get nothing accomplished. Using this method of goal-setting is for those who have come to adopt the "couch potato" approach to life that is best lived by sitting around as a spectator—going nowhere! This approach will prevent you from making any kind of mark on your world or ever having what you want!

Second Aim at everything! This was my best method for years. I shot at everything I could. And then, when I happened to hit a somewhat significant target, I'd be quick to point out that I had been aiming at that goal all along! Using this method of goal setting is for those who have chosen to live by the roll of the dice—by accident going everywhere. This approach will enable you to make an indistinguishable mark on your world by scattering and splattering bits and pieces of you everywhere!

Third Aim at things! This is a most common target as people set goals. Accumulating things is neither right nor wrong, but if it is all you are out to do, you will eventually feel most empty. Just remember Mr. Scrooge. There is more to a quality life than just money and the things money can buy. AIM HIGH!

The most common problem with goal-setting is best stated in the following way: "The problem with most people is not that they aim too high and miss it, but that they aim too low and hit it!" Most people long for an arrival point, but when they do "finally arrive," the process of death and dying begins! So, in too many cases these people "die" at 35 or 40 and we bury them at 75 or 85! This is the world of the uninvolved—the "walking dead." It's a world of boredom and monotony, dissatisfaction and depression. But this doesn't have to be your reality. To be fully involved in life, set, select and secure your goals by aligning them to your purpose.

DR. JOHN GODDARD

"To dare is to do, to fear is to fail." This philosophy has characterized John Goddard since he was 15, when he listed 127 challenging lifetime goals, such as

> The person who makes a success of living is the one who sees his goal steadily and aims for it unswervingly That is dedication.
>
> CECIL B. DEMILLE
> (1881–1959)
> American filmmaker

> Make no little plans; they have no magic to stir men's blood . . . make big plans, aim high in hope and work.
>
> DANIEL H. BURNHAM
> (1846–1912)
> American architect

> Not failure, but low aim, is a crime.
>
> JAMES RUSSELL LOWELL
> (1819–1891)
> American poet, critic, editor, diplomat

living with pygmies and other tribal people in Africa and the headhunters in Borneo and New Guinea, driving a dog sled in the winter snows of the High Sierras, exploring the world's greatest rivers, and climbing the world's highest peaks.

He led the first expedition in history to explore the entire length of the world's longest river, the 4,200-mile Nile River, which the *Los Angeles Times* called "the most remarkable adventure of this generation," matched later by his becoming the first man to explore the entire length of the world's second largest river, Africa's 2,700-mile Congo.

John likes to lead tours to exotic places such as the remote parts of Africa, the Amazon and the Galapagos Islands. Those lucky enough to have John as a guide enjoy the fellowship and amazing personal attention provided for them on his tours. His fascinating enrichment lectures prepare the traveler for each day's activity, and he frequently leads impromptu excursions into the wilds for those willing to follow.

I took a two-week trip to Africa with John in 1995 and I had the chance to see first hand how this ordinary man has accomplished so many extra ordinary things. In the brief time I was with him we did more than I have ever done in any other two-week time period in my life. The man is a dynamo of energy and enthusiasm and he has the curiosity of several preschool children.

In recent years he has climbed lofty peaks in Africa, South America and Asia, including 22,000-foot Huascaran, the highest mountain in the Peruvian Andes, and 19,000 foot Mt. Kilimanjaro in Tanzania. Also, he has piloted a USAF B-1A bomber, as well as the Air Force F-15 "Eagle" and the F-16 "Fighting Falcon," two of the world's fastest and most sophisticated fighters.

John has been the subject of numerous articles in magazines such as *National Geographic, Life,* and *Reader's Digest,* Dr. Goddard has also been the featured guest on over 200 television shows, including "This is Your Life," has published a book recounting his first major expedition, *Kayaks Down the Nile,* and is presently completing a second book recounting 21 life-threatening adventures in his career as an explorer, pilot and undersea diver.

In 1972, *Life* magazine published a story depicting the adventures of John Goddard. His story was one of undying determination filled with personal purpose. When he was fifteen, he overheard a visiting friend of his parents lament, "If only I had done this when I was young." Determined not to spend his life playing the "if only" game, John Goddard sat down and decided what he wanted to do with his life. When he finished writing, 127 goals existed.

First say to yourself what would you be; and then do what you have to do.

EPICTETUS (c. 55–c. 135)
Greek stoic philosopher

John Goddard decided there were eight rivers he wanted to explore, along with sixteen mountains he wanted to climb. He decided to become an Eagle Scout, visit every country in the world, learn to fly an airplane, and dive in a submarine. He wanted to retrace the travels of Marco Polo and ride a horse in the Rose Bowl parade. This was just the beginning. John Goddard committed himself to reading the Bible from cover to cover, reading the entire works of Shakespeare, Plato, Dickens, Aristotle, Socrates, and several other classic authors. He planned to read the entire Encyclopedia Britannica and yet have time to learn to play the flute and violin. Marriage, children (he had five) and a stint with church missions were also in his plans, along with a desire for a career in medicine.

As of 2004, John Goddard has accomplished 109 of his original 127 goals along with more than 300 others, totaling over 400 remarkable achievements.

John Goddard exemplifies the excitement of determining a purpose in life, setting goals and pursuing them with determination. The goals that John Goddard wrote out at age fifteen were unbelievable, but he still wanted them. How do you go about attaining your goals?

Napoleon Hill in his classic work, *Think and Grow Rich*, presented a bold theme: "Whatever the mind can conceive and believe, it can achieve!" *Belief is the key!* And all truly lofty goals start out as unbelievable. It is the dynamic of "picturing" that transforms your unbelievable dreams into the realities of the Riches you will find along The Lazy Man's Way! That's the way John Goddard taught me how to set and achieve unbelievable goals.

But here is the most important lesson John Goddard taught me about setting big goals. He said "to set big and lofty goals not for what you get by reaching them, but *for what you become* as you strive to reach them." (You can see John Goddard's original goals in Step 14 of the workbook.)

PICTURING

Picturing is the first part of the process of bringing desired results into physical reality. You do it naturally, almost automatically, literally thousands of times each day. Take, for example, the turning on of a light switch. That's a very modest and simple function, but it's picturing at its most basic level.

You think, "turn on the light," and the mind commands the body to perform this act. The goal is realized. It's one thing to set a modest goal for oneself and reach it, but it's quite another to set a lofty goal to be reached. Yet by analyzing the first (the modest goal) process you can gain insight into the second (the loftier goal). The modest goal of switching on a light switch is a most certain process, because there is no credibility gap. It requires no faith—no stretch of the imagination—to believe this goal can be achieved. The possibility is unquestioned, so the results are certain. This is in agreement with Napoleon Hill's theme of *"Whatever the mind can conceive and believe, it can achieve!"* In cases where the possibility is beyond question, then to conceive is to achieve! Where your belief is not an issue, where there is no credibility gap, then to will it, is for you to own it.

When asked how he accounted for his amazing inventive genius, Thomas Alva Edison replied, "It is because I never think in words; I think in pictures." Edison was a master at *picturing* in his mind the objects he desired to invent.

Phenomenal achievements have been accomplished by people who were able to visualize what they wanted. Edison was told no light could exist in a vacuum, but he visualized it and believed it could be done. The experts scoffed at Louis Pasteur's theories of germ life. William Harvey's far-out notion that blood flowed through the body was rejected, and Samuel Langley's vision for a flying machine was ridiculed; however, each of these men were able to visualize their dream into reality. Conrad Hilton said, "Man, with God's help and personal dedication, is capable of anything he can dream." Visualize your dreams!

Remember, a goal is not the end. In the games of hockey or American football, a single goal generally won't win the game. In the game of life the more goals you

To dare is to do; to fear is to fail.

JOHN GODDARD
(b. Withheld upon request)
Anthropologist, explorer, author, adventurer, speaker

If you think you can win, you can win. Faith is necessary to victory.

WILLIAM HAZLITT
(1778–1830)
English essayist, critic

The Possible's slow fuse is lit by the Imagination.

EMILY DICKINSON
(1830–1886)
American poet

score towards your purpose, the Richer your life will be. A goal by itself is not the victory. It takes several goals to be a winner. A goal is a score, not the victory. As you attain one goal have another ready to tackle.

Too often one thinks of the goal as the finish line or the arrival point. The purpose is the entire journey, departure to arrival. This is especially true of very lofty goals. Picturing is a journey. There is normally a credibility gap, but somewhere along the line that gap is defeated and in its place come feelings of total confidence, assurance, and personal knowledge that the destination will be achieved. And by paying the price along the way you will arrive at your goal. The credibility gap is conquered in gradual increments—a process. The process goes from "if only" to "maybe" to "I think so" to "I know so." These are the natural stages of development for achieving your goals—the process of picturing.

NATURAL FACT

Emerson said, "Every natural fact is a symbol of some spiritual fact." Natural facts are representative of spiritual facts in the growth of people.

One of the earliest processes we all studied in grade school was the life cycle of the butterfly. Butterflies don't just happen out of an egg. Changes take place gradually and they are not the least bit perceptible to the casual observer—larval stage, chrysalis stage, pupa stage. Finally, after weeks of gradual growth and passing through stages of development, there emerges into the world one of nature's most marvelous creations, the mature, adult butterfly. This process is one of the miracles in our world. But this incredible transformation is nothing compared to the miracle of a human life finding his/her purpose and being fulfilled. Purpose attainment is like that. It is a process made up of many stages—your goals. (You will experience this miracle for yourself through the process you have already started in your *Roadmap to Riches* Guidebook.)

Here is how Paul Meyer of Success Motivation Institute sums up the goal process. "What you ardently desire, sincerely believe in, vividly imagine, enthusiastically act on, must inevitably come to pass."

TERRY FOX—AN UNBELIEVABLE GOAL

I'd like to introduce you to Terry Fox. Terry has been an inspiration and a "friend" for many years. I was introduced to him through a picture of him in a magazine. I never met Terry in person, because he died before I had a chance to meet him, but I felt his death as one can only feel the loss of a friend. Terry died at the age of 22. He lived only 22 short years, but he will be remembered by millions for years to come.

Terry was a great athlete (basketball, cross country and track) with enough talent to "letter" in several sports in college and the desire and drive to turn professional. A leg problem that bothered him caused him enough concern to have a doctor look at it. The doctor diagnosed it as cancer. It was ravaging his leg. The doctor told Terry, "I'm sorry, but we've got to amputate the leg. And since you are an adult you must sign for us to do the surgery." Terry signed off his own leg and with it his hopes and dreams of an athletic career.

The surgery was successful in that the leg was gone and Terry wasn't. Convalescing from a leg amputation is a long process that includes physical therapy and

It's not the attainment of the goal that matters, it is the things that are met with along the way.

HAVELOCK ELLIS
(1859–1939)
English psychologist, essayist, art critic

Only in men's imagination does every truth find an effective and undeniable existence. Imagination, not invention, is the supreme master of art as of life.

JOSEPH CONRAD
(1857–1924)
Polish-born English novelist

learning to walk again with an artificial leg. Convalescence was also a great time to rethink his purpose, since his original purpose of being a professional athlete was now a physical impossibility.

Terry's new purpose was to raise awareness and money for cancer research, so others might be spared the suffering and the torment he had experienced. Terry's new purpose was not only to raise money for others with similar conditions, but to raise people's consciousness for the need for cancer research as well. He wrote down his purpose and announced it to family and friends. Then, he planned the way to attain his purpose by writing down his goals. He organized what was called "Terry Fox's Marathon of Hope." He truly set out an unbelievable goal—to run across Canada on an artificial leg!

His parents suggested he first go to college, graduate, and then make his contribution. But that was their dream, not Terry's. He knew his purpose and would not be swayed from it. He went to the Canadian Cancer Society and proudly told them of his plan to raise awareness and money for cancer research through his "Marathon of Hope." The Cancer Society told him they were already involved in many other activities, but thanked him for thinking of it and suggested he forget the whole idea.

A MARATHON OF HOPE

Well, you don't just forget a purpose and go on doing the same old thing. Terry and his college roommate dropped out of school and flew to Canada's eastern coast of Newfoundland. Terry touched the waters of the Atlantic Ocean and turned around to start his "Marathon of Hope" journey to walk across the entire length of Canada to the Pacific!

Day after day he walked trying to generate interest and enthusiasm in his mission to raise awareness and money. It was difficult to get co-operation in French-speaking part of Canada for an "Anglo" from British Columbia. It was discouraging, but Terry was not discouraged. Terry had a purpose! He was walking over 30 miles a day and it wasn't getting any easier. The artificial leg was awkward and painful. The constant walking caused sores that brought a grimace to Terry's face. There were times the sores opened and bled. People slowly began to notice this man with a mission. Media attention began to build. Radio stations talked about Terry as he came through their towns. Local papers talked about him and ran his picture and his story. Local TV stations picked it up too.

His notoriety caught the attention of politicians including the Prime Minister of Canada, Elliott Trudeau. The Prime Minister and Terry shook hands for the press. Terry suggested that he had revised his original goal from raising $100,000 to $1 million!

The attention Terry was getting spread from Canada to other countries as the story of this young man with an *unbelievable* goal was told. The wire services carried his story to local papers all over the world and quickly Terry's story was featured in the national press and media throughout the USA.

By the time he got to Thunder Bay (about half way across Canada) he developed breathing problems which required him to see a doctor. A thorough examination showed Terry's cancer had spread to his chest. The doctor told Terry he had to stop

How far is far? How high is high? We'll never know until we try.

FROM THE CALIFORNIA SPECIAL OLYMPICS THEME SONG

He knows not his own strength that hath not met adversity.

BEN JONSON (1573–1637) English playwright, poet; "Timber"

his run. Terry told the doctor he obviously didn't know him or the purpose of this run. Both Terry and his purpose would go on.

He explained to the doctor: "My folks said I couldn't do it, but I chose to go on anyway. The Canadian Cancer Society told me no; but I chose to go on anyway. The provincial government told me to stop because I was disrupting the roadways, but I chose to go on anyway. The Prime Minister offered me no help, but I chose to go on, anyway. Well, the provincial governments are now behind me, the Prime Minister is behind me, the people are behind me and we have exceeded our goal of $1 million! So, when I leave your office today, I plan to continue and I'm going to raise a dollar for every single, living Canadian. That's $24.1 million!" The doctor protested that Terry had already accomplished his goals of raising awareness and money for his cause. Terry had already exceeded all expectations and had become a worldwide hero and an inspiration to all. He pleaded with Terry to go home and rest. The doctor's sound advice and concern along with Terry's weakened condition persuaded Terry to go home. Terry never finished his "Marathon of Hope," because he died of the cancer.

DID TERRY FAIL?

Did he meet all of his goals? No. He met the goals of raising awareness and of raising over $24 million for the cancer research fund, but he didn't reach his goal of walking across Canada. Did he fulfill his purpose? You bet he did! He raised our awareness. (Note: as of 2004, more than $340 million has been raised worldwide for cancer research in Terry's name through the annual Terry Fox Run, held across Canada and around the world.)

I "met" Terry through an article in *Time* magazine that showed a picture of him in his running shorts with his artificial leg. The story was an inspiration to me, which has marked my life. I taped that picture to my bathroom mirror where it reminds me to this day of the power of purpose. Terry achieved his purpose without being able to fulfill all of his goals. His purpose was so strong that most of his goals were "assumed" and attained almost automatically, like learning to walk on an artificial leg. But for Terry, that was an assumed goal if he were to achieve his purpose! (To see the picture of Terry, and find out more about him, just click on Step 14 in your *Roadmap to Riches Guidebook*.)

Terry never viewed his circumstances as terminal. He saw them as a new supply of raw material with which to build a new purpose. Terry looked inside himself for a new purpose for his "ruined" life and found that his "problems" were not going to keep him from accomplishing it. He chose to "accept" his purpose, which, in turn, revealed to him the goals that to us seem so extraordinary.

You don't have to lose a leg to know that you need a "purpose" in life or a new purpose. Your dissatisfaction tells you that! Some call it Divine Dissatisfaction. I've often felt that I was "on the wrong bus" in life, because it just didn't feel right, nothing was working, nothing was going my way. I couldn't get a break and my life felt out of my control. I wasn't driving my own life. I wanted off, but didn't know how. I continued on "hoping" and "wishing" that "it" would get better. If only someone or something would rescue me. Let me repeat, maturity starts when you accept that there is no one out there to rescue you, so you plan to rescue yourself.

The only measure of what you believe is what you do. If you want to know what people believe don't read what they write, don't ask them what they believe, just observe what they do.

ASHLEY MONTAGUE Ph.D.
(b. 1905)
American anthropologist, educator

The courage we desire and prize is not the courage to die decent, but to live manfully.

THOMAS CARLYLE
(1795–1881)
Scottish-born English prose writer

I was stuck. There is a profound piece of Texas wisdom that says, "When your horse is dead, get off!" I should have gotten off, but didn't know *where else to go or how to get there!* Now I know. "Purpose" is where to go and "goals" are how to get there! Don't confuse purpose and goals—a purpose is not a goal. Your purpose can never be reached and then checked off like a goal. Your purpose is fulfilled, continuously, in every moment. Goals can be defined, obtained, reached, satisfied but they are just milestones along the way to your life's purpose. But your goals must be big enough to fulfill your purpose—your mission in life. This is the answer to the questions: "Why am I here?" "What is my job as a crew member on Spaceship Earth?" "What is my contribution to humanity?"

Big enough goals will give you thrust and momentum all by themselves! Big enough goals will give you the opportunity to get your Riches! Big enough goals will motivate you to make changes. Big enough goals will be unbelievable goals!

Ask yourself four progressive questions about what you want:

WHY?!

WHY NOT?!

WHY NOT ME?!

WHY NOT NOW?

The buck stops here.

HARRY S. TRUMAN
(1884–1972)
33rd President of the
United States
(handwritten sign on his
White House desk)

The American economy
cannot be revived without
someone getting rich:
why not me?

RUSH LIMBAUGH
(b. 1951)
American radio and TV
talk-show host

Now turn to Step # 14 "Setting Unbelievable (but Attainable) Goals"
in your Roadmap to Riches workbook.

Attitudes—Your Biggest Roadblocks

Greetings. Ready for the next step on *The Lazy Man's Way to Riches?* You are if you finished up to here in your *Roadmap to Riches*—Your Personal Guidebook.

Please don't tell me you haven't got enough time to do the steps, or that it's too much trouble to log on to the Guidebook.

I can't tell you how many failures I've met who were too busy to be successful. Joe Karbo said it this way "Most people are too busy earning a living to make any real money."

Most of the steps in the *Roadmap to Riches* workbook will take you less than 15 or 20 minutes to complete. Over a month's time that's only 10 hours. Suppose that all you want to get out of this book is to discover a way to payoff all your debts and have $10,000 in the bank. Is your time worth $1,000 an hour? It can be if you'll stay with us every step on The Lazy Man's Way. Can 15 minutes per day really make that kind of difference? Suppose I said I'd let you have all the $20 bills you could scoop in the next fifteen minutes, could you find the time? You bet you would! Well, the fifteen minutes you will spend on each step will be worth much more than those $20 bills over the rest of your life. Right? Right!

So by now you have at least one thing written down that you really want out of life in each of the seven areas, and you have listed the things that are standing in your way. (If you haven't done the same for all seven areas, do so now; if you have, congratulations.)

Now we are going to discuss how you free yourself from the obstacles and limitations that are holding you back. I am going to tell you the problem that underlies every roadblock you have experienced. I'll start you on the first step toward wiping out that obstacle, and all of the roadblocks that stand between you and the Riches you want. But first I'd like to tell you a story. A true story. A story I learned about through watching a documentary of a very important experiment conducted by a research psychologist several years ago. The documentary had a tremendous impact upon me, and I'd like to share it with you.

LEARN FROM A FISH

The experimental study begins with the psychologist putting a Northern Pike in a large aquarium. A Northern Pike is a large strong fish that feeds on smaller fish and a pike's favorite dish is minnows. When the psychologist put minnows in the

> . . . Everything can be taken from a man but one thing: the last of human freedoms—to choose one's attitude in any given set of circumstances—to choose one's own way.
>
> DR. VIKTOR E. FRANKL
> (b. 1905)
> German psychiatrist, author

> Even if you're on the right track, you'll get run over if you just sit there.
>
> WILL ROGERS
> (1875–1935)
> American actor and humorist

aquarium, the pike would just snap up a minnow anytime the mood struck. It's amazing how fast a pike can move when it wants a minnow. In a split second, the minnow disappeared. After showing how the pike feeds, the psychologist then placed clear glass cylinders in the aquarium and this time puts the minnows inside the cylinders.

Now when the pike tries to feed, something very painful happens. He can't see the glass cylinders, doesn't know they are there, but every time he tries to take a minnow—Bam. He gets a very painful bump on the nose. You can see the pike shake it off—like a fighter who takes a good one on the chin. Then he tries again—Bam. He gets another bump on the nose. He tries again. Bam. Bam. Bam. Bam. You've been hit on the nose; you know how painful it can be. Well, evidently it's painful to the pike as well, because after a while he stops trying. He has learned his lesson. He can't have the minnows. No matter how tempting, no matter how hungry he gets, he just can't have them. And furthermore, not only can't he have them, it hurts to try.

STARVE AMIDST PLENTY

When the psychologist was satisfied that the pike has stopped trying, he removed the glass cylinders, thus releasing the minnows. Now minnows apparently aren't very bright because they will swim up to the pike, look him right in the eye, practically swim into his mouth, and now the pike will not make a move to take one. His favorite food easily within his reach and he won't move a muscle to get it, because he's learned it hurts to try and thinks (or whatever fish do) "What's the use I can't have it anyway." That fish will literally starve to death in the midst of an abundance of his favorite food before he will move his tail and open his mouth to eat it.

What a shame; it shouldn't happen to a poor fish. What a tragedy—it shouldn't happen to a human being either and yet it does—constantly to more than 95 percent of the people in this world. They sit and "starve" in the midst of the greatest Riches the world has ever known. They hunger for wealth, for friends, for love, for respect, and it's all within easy reach. All they have to do is move their tails and open their mouths. They are surrounded by glass walls; glass walls that exist only in their memories, in their past, in their *imaginations*, <u>but not in the here and now</u>. Everything they could ever desire could be theirs if they could simply believe in it but they have learned that it hurts to try, and— "What's the use? They can't have it anyway." Do you see how the power of belief can keep us stuck?

YOUR ATTITUDES CAN MAKE YOU—OR BREAK YOU

A positive attitude is vital to your success. Here is a definition of attitude: a manner of acting, feeling, or thinking that shows one's disposition, opinion. It is how you respond to and approach things. Of all the skills you will develop, a positive (or good) attitude will take you the furthest. We have all heard about or have seen someone with a "bad attitude" and we know how it stands out and marks them as someone we all want to stay away from.

No one wants to hire someone with a bad attitude, no one wants to partner with someone who has a bad attitude, and certainly no one wants to marry someone with a bad attitude. A bad attitude doesn't take people very far in life; in fact it is usually what stops all forward progress for the person who has a bad attitude. Most people will agree that a "positive attitude" is a good attitude. The world is a much better place when we look at things and respond to things in a positive way.

Here is an excellent example that may help you understand how your attitude can affect how well you do things: Mahatma Gandhi said *"If I believe I cannot do something, it makes me incapable of doing it. But when I believe I can, then I acquire the ability to do it, even if I did not have the ability in the beginning."* That's a powerful statement and it is one that I believe to be true from my own experience.

I think you will agree that a good attitude toward yourself is one where you believe and trust in yourself. Once you believe in yourself you will respond to things a lot differently and in a way that gets better results. Here is another example of having a good attitude, this is from Henry Ford: *"Don't find fault, find a remedy."* Again, powerful words that have the ability to change your world if you chose to adopt them into your attitudes.

Ever have a "rotten" day? One of those days where nothing goes right, and everything seems to go wrong? You oversleep, you run out of toothpaste, you burn your mouth on a cup of coffee, traffic is worse than ever, you arrive late to work, your computer crashes, and so it goes for the rest of the day.

The day I just described would qualify as a "rotten" day in most people's book. I know it would in mine. And most people would spend a good portion, if not all, of that day in a foul mood. That's only natural, right? A person couldn't help but have a bad attitude when everything is going wrong, right?

Wrong.

One of the greatest gifts you possess as a human being is Your attitude. I write it like that to emphasize that it is Your attitude. You own it. You control it. You are responsible for it. You can change it at will. Your attitude is not dependent on your surroundings, not ruled by events, not tied to the stock market, the weather, your boss, traffic, or even the government and, most importantly, not excusable when everything is lousy.

If you are not in a good mood it is only because you choose not to be. I have no quarrel with deciding to be in a bad mood and then acting on that decision. A little self-pity is probably therapeutic from time to time. Just realize that it is always **your choice**. If your attitude is poor and you find that unsatisfactory, then it is incumbent upon you to make a change to a positive attitude. Here is how to do that.

A GOOD ATTITUDE STARTS WITH A SMILE

A good attitude starts with a smile. OK, it sounds corny but you would be surprised how far a big smile will take you into the world of positive outlooks. The next time you are in a bad mood I challenge you to smile for two minutes. But you have to do it right—you have got to make it look real. Even if you are the only one around to see it—look in a mirror and give yourself a great smile.

Next, apply the principle of positive self-talk. Talking to yourself in a positive manner is a powerful tool. At first you may feel silly. That's OK. (Just think how often you say things to yourself in a negative manner and you don't feel silly then, do you?). All you need to do is change the wording a bit. I start with the time honored "Damn, I'm good!" and then back it up with other positive utterances such as; "Man, this is going to be a great day!" or "I'm going to have a great workout!" Your mind responds positively to positive input and it doesn't care where the input comes from.

Focus on the present and future, not the past. What you do, or don't do, right now determines your future. How you approach the present moment is up to you and you alone. The future you envision and dwell on for yourself is your guiding light as to how to approach the present. If you visualize great things for today, this week, this year and this lifetime you will have a hard time not being enthusiastic about the present. On the other hand dwelling on past misfortunes and allowing them to be harbingers of doom will just as certainly make your present miserable.

Promote your enthusiasm to others. Try the following—from now on when someone asks you "How're ya doing?" answer with an enthusiastic and convincing "I'm doing great!" or "fantastic!" The more believable you make this to the other person the more believable it will be to you. People who are enthusiastic about life and activities are more attractive to others.

GLASS WALLS MADE OUT OF ATTITUDES AND BELIEFS

Let's look at the obstacles in your way. I asked you to decide if they were in your attitude or your environment. What did you come up with? Look at your list of obstacles and think about that pike. Without even looking at your list, I can tell you that any obstacles which you have, that refer to your past experience, lack of experience or to your current situation, are entirely in your attitudes and belief. Are you thinking, "Now wait a minute, the fact that I'm heavily in debt is my attitude? You're crazy. My debts are real." I know your debts are real. But your debts are not the thing standing in your way; it's your attitude about your debts. Your belief is that they are holding you back. That's the imaginary glass wall that's keeping you from the Riches you need the most.

The same logic applies to every single obstacle you have written down. It's not what you have or haven't. It's not the interest rates or the economy. It's not who you know or don't know. It's what you believe about these things that are standing in your way. Change your attitude and your external circumstances change.

Now there's good news and bad news in this. The good news is that you don't have to change a whole lot of circumstances in your present, or past, in order to become successful. All you have to do is learn to change your *attitudes* about those circumstances and they will no longer block you, even though they still exist. Now here is the bad news, it seems to be pretty hard to do. As Master Motivator Zig Ziglar often says, "Hardening of the *attitudes* is more common in this country than hardening of the arteries." Have you ever said, "Sure I know I would be more effective if I would do such and such, but I'm just not good at that sort of thing." Or, "That's the way I am." Those are words of power—tremendous negative power that freezes you in a self-defeating attitude. Just eavesdrop on our friend the pike's men-

---

Men can starve from a lack of self-realization as much as they can from a lack of bread.

RICHARD WRIGHT
(1908–1960)
American novelist and short story writer;
Native Son (1940)

The meaning of things lies not in the things themselves but in our attitudes towards them.

ANTOINE DE SAINT-EXUPERY
(1900–1944)
French novelist, essayist, aviator

The greatest discovery of my generation is that a human being can alter his life by altering his attitudes of mind.

WILLIAM JAMES
(1842–1910)
American philosopher, physiologist, psychologist, teacher

tal process, "Oh boy am I hungry—I'd sure love to have a minnow, but I know I can't. I've tried and tried and all I got was a sore nose. That's the way it is with me; I just can't have any minnows."

Look at the list of the things standing in your way. You can't change the events of your past, and you can't really alter the circumstances you are in right now. You can change your attitudes about those things and when you do, you can do anything you want with your future. Unless, of course, you think that changing your attitudes is impossible, in which case, move over brother pike, you've got company.

CHANGE YOUR ATTITUDE—CHANGE YOUR FUTURE

Unless you are willing to accept the reality that everything—including you— is constantly changing, and that you can take charge of that change, and cause it to go in any direction you want, you will never be able to walk The Lazy Man's Way to your own Riches. You'll just flounder and starve like that fish—everything you want and need within easy reach, but forever kept from you, no matter how hard you work, by glass walls that exist on in your imagination. On the other hand, if you'll accept one of the fundamental principles of all existence, you can take another easy step on *The Lazy Man's Way to Riches.* You see, the major differ- ence between the struggling Joe Karbo who was deeply in debt, and with no job and no hope, and the Joe Karbo who started getting everything he wanted, cer- tainly wasn't hard work. It wasn't an invention or any idea no one else had ever had. It was a change in attitude, coupled with the simple steps I am going to teach you in the next few chapters that made the difference. Suddenly he was working less and making more progress.

Formerly impossible things became easy. The new T—Bird he wanted, but thought was impossible to obtain was his within a few days. The sailboat and the home on the water had seemed ten years away or more. Yet he had the sailboat with- in a couple of months and the home on the water within three years. How? By fol- lowing the simple steps I am going to layout for you in the Roadmap to Riches guidebook. Are you ready for the next step?

CAN YOU CHANGE YOUR MIND?

Good. Go back over the obstacles you've written down earlier in your Guidebook. Focus on the ones you thought were environmental—outside you. Try to identify the attitude that's really creating the obstacle. For example, suppose one of your obstacles is, "Not having enough money to develop my ideas." Actually the real obstacle is your belief that you don't have and can't get enough money to develop your ideas. See what I mean? Take each of your roadblocks and rephrase it. Accept the responsibility for your thoughts. This is a tremendously important step. Because if you'll accept that the roadblock is in your mind, and not in the outside world, then all you have to do is change your mind to get you on the straight track.

I don't ask you to buy all this at once. It was a struggle for me at first, but do it even if you don't believe me. Look at each of your obstacles and tell yourself—"This is holding me back only because I believe it is holding me back. If I change my atti- tude, this will no longer stand in my way."

Success or failure is caused more by mental attitude than by mental capacity.

SIR WALTER SCOTT
(1771–1832)
Scottish novelist, poet

Nurture your mind with great thoughts.

BENJAMIN DISRAELI
(1804–1881)
English statesman, novelist

In Step 15 of your Guidebook, I've written this sentence and left blanks for you to fill in your roadblocks. Write each of your own roadblocks in the blank spaces but this time after each of them; repeat the sentence at the top of the page. It might stick in your throat a couple of times. You might even feel a bit foolish doing it. It will get easier each time. Do these at least twice today, once right away and once before you go to bed tonight. Believe that it works, and it will!

Now turn to Step # 15 "Attitudes—Your Biggest Roadblocks"
in your *Roadmap to Riches* workbook.

16

Everything Changes, Why Not You?

Remember that fish I told you about—the pike who starved to death with abundant food all around him? He starved with plenty of food all around because he did not understand the most important and fundamental principle of all existence; and most people I know are struggling for the same reason. They are beating their brains out against glass walls that exist only in their imagination and in their yesterdays—not in their todays.

The most exciting step on The Lazy Man's Way is when you understand the full implications of this simple principle—EVERYTHING CHANGES. You are saying "I know that all I have to do is look at myself now and ten years ago and realize how much I've changed physically." And you have, just as everything else has changed and is changing constantly.

I'm not saying that there are no absolute, no eternal truths. There are; but in the physical world, in relationships between people and in your own mind, change is the natural order. Physical objects age. Relationships between people deepen and mature as we grow in wisdom and experience. Everything is constantly changing and yet most people refuse to accept that premise in one crucial area of their lives— their attitudes about themselves and their abilities. Have you ever said something like, "I know I could be more successful if I was just more organized but I've always been disorganized, that's the way I am." Or maybe in your case you're organized, but you are not outgoing, or you think you don't have enough drive or you have never done really well at anything in the past, so why should you expect success now? After all, if you are a failure you are a failure! Right?

TEAR DOWN THOSE WALLS!

Wrong! "That's the way I am" is one of the most negatively powerful sentences in the English language. Every time you say it or think it you are reinforcing the attitude that everything changes BUT YOU! That everything changes but those glass walls, the walls that are keeping you from the things you want and need the most, the Riches you are looking for.

You are not entirely responsible for the walls being put there in the first place any more than the fish I told you about was responsible for putting the glass wall between himself and the minnow. Your walls were erected by well meaning friends or relatives, by teachers and classmates, coaches, bosses, and by situations in your past in which you tried something new that didn't quite workout.

There are thousands of events in everyone's life that can result in a glass wall. People who laugh at you when you express your dreams; people who, out of love,

Change is the law of life. And those who look only to the past or the present are sure to miss the future.

JOHN F. KENNEDY
(1917–1963)
35th President of the
United States

We change when the pain to change is less than the pain to remain as we are.

ED FOREMAN
(b. 1933)
American entrepreneur, engineer, author, speaker, member of U.S. Congress

The absurd man is he who never changes.

AUGUSTE BARTHELEMY
(1796–1867)
French poet and satirist

warn you not to get your hopes too high so you won't be disappointed; classmates who make fun of you when you make a mistake reading aloud; or loved ones who tell you hurtful things in anger—things that are not true and are not really meant but which you take as gospel. As a result a wall is formed. It is a wall that can last forever, if you let it.

IT'S YOUR CHOICE

Now you know you have a choice. You can sit around and blame your parents and teachers and the other people who helped to build your glass walls and stay right where you are. Or, you can let the past go and get on to the more important business of tearing those walls down so that you can get at the Riches life has to offer you.

You see, while you may not be the one who put those walls there in the first place, you definitely are the only one who keeps them there, and you keep them there by denying the fundamental principle that everything changes, including you, and your attitudes. Not only is everything changing, but it's possible to take control of and guide that change in any direction you want.

You can let go of these walls and keep new ones from appearing if you'll just accept, understand, and believe The Lazy Man. There is no amount of physical work you can do to knock down those walls but with a few simple mental exercises you can make them disappear. That's the key to doing things The Lazy Man's Way. Don't work harder, work smarter!

ARE YOU A VICTIM THAT NEEDS TO BE RESCUED?

Are you still hoping and waiting for someone, somewhere to come to your rescue, wave a magic wand and instantaneously change your life for the better?

Do you pray that you will one day win the big lottery and dramatically alter the financial quality of your life?

Do you sit at your desk, daydreaming and hoping to one day rise to the next level of management without much effort and hard work?

Do you hide in the background, silently praying and hoping that you will find favor, get noticed and be thrust into the limelight of your destiny?

If you are tired of hoping and endlessly waiting for something positive to happen or someone to come to your rescue, make a deliberate decision today to take charge of your own life and begin to lead a fulfilled and productive life.

HERE ARE SOME THINGS TO HELP YOU
CHANGE YOUR LIFE FOR THE BETTER

VALUE YOURSELF HIGHLY

Value yourself, your life and your time. Value what you represent. Don't compromise what you are worth for anything. Your current position may not accurately reflect who you are, but if you place a high value on yourself, you will not only have greater expectations for yourself, but also be open to more possibilities and opportunities.

> For they can conquer who believe they can.
>
> JOHN DRYDEN
> (1631–1700)
> English poet, dramatist, critic

People who place a high value on themselves can confidently walk into any arena of success and take their place comfortably. They fit right in because this is what they have been waiting for their whole lives and they know that they deserve it! They think positively.

TAKE RESPONSIBILITY FOR YOUR OWN DESTINY

Be practical and stop expecting other people to rescue you from your current distress. People can only do so much…the rest is up to you and your God given abilities and resolve. Get rid of the dependency syndrome! It incapacitates and blinds you from doing great things with your life and getting the success you so much yearn for.

If you are not going to be the recipient of a large inheritance or if you have not yet won the lottery, begin to do the right thing by charting your own road map to success and working intelligently, meticulously and persistently to achieve your success.

STOP DOING WHAT DOES NOT WORK FOR YOU

When you desire to change your life for the better…take a minute to consider specific aspects of your life over the last five years. Have you seen any improvement in your business? Have you lost weight? Are you still working at the same place that stifles your creative abilities? Are you still in the dreaming phase of that project you wanted to accomplish? Are you still procrastinating about going back to school? Are you still doing the same things that produce unproductive and dissatisfying results?

How much longer can you keep doing the same things that don't work? You only have one life to live and if you plan to live a fulfilled life, stop doing what doesn't work, start doing the things that work and change your life for the better. A definition of insanity is doing the same thing over and over and expecting a different result.

MAKE A PRODUCTIVE ACTION STEP TODAY

Changing your life for the better means doing something today that produces results! If you can't take radical steps, take small deliberate steps towards the change you desire. One of the greatest impediments to success is procrastination. It is so often used as an excuse for inaction to the point that it has become mind-numbing!

No one wants to hear that the only reason why you have not managed to turn your idea into reality is because you have been procrastinating! People want to stand and cheer for the doer and the achiever who has taken positive steps to improve the quality of their lives. These are the inspiring stories that we read about every-day—you too can be that success story. Believe it and work toward it.

BETTER LATE…?

Let me tell you about someone who learned this concept in her late life. Dorothy was the kind of person who always got stuck with the menial jobs—you know the ones with lots of work and no glory. She was always the secretary in the clubs she joined. She always had to make the coffee and clean up the mess. In the civil service job she held, and hated for over twenty years, she frequently did work for which

A living thing is distinguished from a dead thing by the multiplicity of the changes at any moment taking place within.

HERBERT SPENCER
(1820–1903)
English philosopher and
social scientist

It is better to live rich than
to die rich.

DR. SAMUEL JOHNSON
(1709–1784)
English lexicographer,
essayist, poet

others got credit. She accepted all this because deep down inside she really didn't think too much of herself. Besides, that's the way it had always been.

When Dorothy finally retired she was worn out, depressed, bitter and physically ill. She was "dead" but just hadn't discovered it yet. Well, not totally dead because there was some spark left and there was a dream. That spark led her to The Lazy Man's Way at the age of 67. She grasped the principle that everything changes and applied it to herself. She learned to use the three simple tools that I'm going to give you, tools that will give you immediate results.

You should see Dorothy now after using these tools to achieve her dream. She went back to college when she was 69, and earned her master's degree—her life long dream—at the age of 72 with straight A's. Not only that, but this woman who had been part of the background all her life suddenly found herself center stage. She was elected president of the senior citizens student body and became a university spokes-woman for other senior citizens thinking of returning to college. She also served as a consultant to the president of the university on problems of returning students.

The Riches Dorothy went after weren't financial. They involved self-respect and self-appreciation. She achieved every one of her goals and at the age of 72 is now looking for new worlds to conquer. Dorothy's first step and yours too, if you want to attain your Riches the Lazy Man's Way, is to accept the full implications of the state-ment—EVERYTHING CHANGES. And everything is possible for you now!

When she grasped the meaning, as it applied to herself, she was able to shake off over forty years of frustration. Forty years of putting herself down in comparison with others. Forty years of wishing but not having. After forty years of bumping her nose on the glass walls, she easily began to achieve her lifelong dreams that had seemed impossible. And you can too once you've dissolved the barriers. Remove the road-blocks and you've got a clear road to your Riches. How? Very simply. So simple you may not believe it can work until you try it.

Now turn to Step #16 "Everything Changes, Why Not You"
in your *Roadmap to Riches* workbook.

17

The Turning Points

In this chapter I'm going to talk about your greatest gift and your greatest power, the power that can change your life and take you anywhere you want to go once you know how to use it. But first I'd like to ask you a question. Did you find it hard to complete the assignment Step 16 in the Roadmap workbook? Did you find you were talking to yourself—telling yourself it was silly to do all that writing, that it wouldn't work anyway? Well don't feel alone; most of us have the same response in the beginning. What's happening is that you are beginning to run up against the biggest roadblock of all . . . namely YOU!

You see, there is a constant flow of thought moving through your mind at any given time. I call it self-talk! These are the *silent sentences* within you. Some self-talk is positive; your inner dreams, your unrealized purpose, your wants, your secret desires for your life, loved ones, and your livelihood. I have been encouraging you to listen to this self-talk throughout our experience together. I warn you that some self-talk is negative; the brainwashing of the past that has gotten you nowhere.

It brings you down, limits you, discourages your dreaming process and it posts "STOP" signs in your path at most every turn. How do you tell the one from the other? It's simple! Negative, destructive self talk is just that . . . negative and self-destructive! Avoid this kind of self-talk and listen carefully for the positive dimension, where the seeds of your personal success have been planted. In a couple of chapters I'll tell you how you can take charge of your "inner voice," your self-talk, and start it working for you, instead of against you!

WE ARE ALL CREATED EQUAL!

Here is a point that many would wish to debate from a political standpoint, but politics aside let me explain what I mean here because it is an important point in achieving the success you want. When I say that we are all created equal I mean it from the bottom of my soul. My Grandma Rose taught me that lesson when I was a child and here is how she got me to understand it and apply it to my life.

I was having trouble with math and had all but given up on learning multiplication tables when Grandma Rose offered to help me. I was very relieved. She worked with me and drilled me on the multiplication tables but I still wasn't getting them. I finally declared that I was a dunce and too stupid to learn. She asked me if I thought that was really true and of course I said "yes it was true," "I was just a dope." Here is how she handled the situation.

She told me that we are all created equal. She said that if anyone of us could learn to walk, then we could all learn to walk. She asked if I believed that was true, and

Respect yourself if you would have others respect you.

BALTASAR GRACIAN
(1601–1658)
Spanish prosewriter and
Jesuit priest

People are always blaming their circumstances for what they are. I don't believe in circumstances. The people who get on in this world are the people who get up and look for the circumstances they want, and, if they can't find them, make them.

GEORGE BERNARD SHAW
(1856–1950)
Irish playwright, critic,
social reformer

because I did not know anyone who could not walk, I had to admit it was true. She said that if anyone of us could learn to talk, then we could all learn to talk. Did I believe that? Well, not knowing anyone who could not talk, I agreed that it must also be true. And on it went. If anyone of us could learn to walk, talk, whistle, read, ride a bike, sing in church, whatever—then we all could. I couldn't dispute her convincing logic. We returned to the math lesson and as I learned one set of times tables she praised me. And of course she reminded me of the greater lesson I had just learned. We all can do anything that any of us can do. **We are all created equal.**

Through the years she was to reinforce that same lesson to me, over and over again. When I later admitted that I didn't think I could learn to dance she had me repeat the lesson that "we are all created equal." If you can learn to dance then I can learn to dance. I learned to dance.

What is important about this lesson is that I have learned to apply it to all aspects of my life and it has served me well. It served me well in college, in the military, in my personal life, and in business. It has served me especially well in business. The belief that we a*re all created equal* has helped me become a pilot, get advanced degrees, become a published author, become a public speaker, start and build companies, take two companies public, and accomplish so much more than I ever thought I was capable of doing. It is not a matter of being smarter, bigger, richer, or better looking. It is simply a matter of understanding that if you can do something— I can do it too.

The examples are everywhere. On May 6th 2004 the world celebrated the 50th anniversary of a "miracle" sports event. On May 6, 1954, Roger Bannister ran the first sub-four-minute mile in recorded history. The 25-year-old native of Harrow on the Hill, England, completed the distance in 3:59.4 at Oxford. The current mile record stands at 3:43.13 to the Moroccan Hicham El Guerrouj, and today even top-level club athletes routinely break the four-minute barrier, but in 1954 it remained a magical barrier.

Now let's talk about your greatest gift and how most people throw it away without realizing what they have. I'll start with the second fundamental principle of life. Like the first fundamental principle—EVERYTHING CHANGES, the full meaning and importance of the principle is easy to overlook. Maybe you're like Joe Karbo used to be and can't even accept the truth of the statement at first. Joe really worked to understand and accept this, because all around him he saw evidence of inequality—some people were born rich, some poor, some healthy, some challenged with physical infirmities. Some who seemed to come into the world loaded with talent and some seemingly had no talent whatsoever. Some were born into freedom and some into slavery. "Where is the equality?" he kept asking. How can you possibly accept the truth of this statement when all the evidence of your experience seems to contradict it? It just seems that life isn't fair. Well, its not, so get over it and move on or chose to stay stuck—the choice is yours.

Initially Joe discarded the principle that all people are created equal and with it any chance he had at finding his Riches. Around him he saw people who were successful and happy, who had truly found the Riches that life offers to all of us, and had overcome what seemed to be enormous challenges. He also saw people who had what seemed to be every advantage and were frustrated in their efforts to be successful. And he saw others who seemingly had little natural ability and few advantages of birth or position who became enormously successful.

As time went on and the more he studied, the more convinced he became that the apparent inequalities of birth were only some of the many factors and not the most important one. Then he realized the obvious—the people who attain the Riches they desire are the ones who use their greatest gift well, even though they don't always understand the power they are using. The ones who become bogged down are the ones who throw their gift away, not realizing the power they possess.

YOU ARE FREE TO CHOOSE

What is this gift? Very simply it's FREE WILL, or if you prefer, FREEDOM OF CHOICE. The freedom to make a decision, to choose the road you wish to follow. It is the freedom to sit still and wallow in your own failure or the freedom to change and move ahead. You have freedom to accept your so-called limitations or freedom to find a way around them. You have the freedom to deny the realities of change, or freedom to accept change and make it work for you. Every day of your life you are faced with thousands of decisions, and in every case you have a choice of which way to go. Your life is the sum total of the consequences of all your decisions. When Joe accepted this principle—when he understood and began to apply the power of the gift of the freedom of choice—his whole life began to change faster than he ever could have dreamed possible!

INCH BY INCH—IT'S A CINCH

The major problem for most people in taking charge of their decision-making gift is that they fail to realize that a lot of small decisions, which are usually made without thinking, are more important than the few major ones that they really think of as life-changing decisions.

Everyday we make thousands of decisions. 95 percent, no, 99 percent of these decisions are made with little or no conscious thought. In one way that's good; it would be terrible to think about which shoe you were going to put on first or how much sugar you were going to put on your cereal or what route to take to work. We make these decisions out of habit, and rightfully so, to free our mind from the trivial details of life. It's a marvelous capacity of the human mind that we can reduce even complex procedures to habit. It is unfortunate, however, that we do this with many decisions that are not trivial in terms of their impact on our lives.

How often have you made a New Year's resolution to make a radical change in your life—perhaps to stop smoking or to lose weight or to become more organized? And how often have you failed to follow through and had to make the same resolution the next year, and the next, and so on? Your major decision did not affect your life the way you wanted it to because you didn't realize that the major life-changing decision is really the end result of a lot of little decisions, most of which you make out of habit.

> One change leaves the way open for the introduction of others.
>
> NICCOLO MACHIAVELLI (1469–1527)
> Florentine statesman and political philosopher

BURIED IN A PAPER TRAIL

For example, one of the best and fastest ways to become more organized in your business or profession is to minimize the number of times you handle any particular piece of paper and to always know where to find it. This, in turn, requires that you have a good filing system.

Suppose you decide to use these principles in your life. That's a major decision. So you buy the file cabinets and folders and spend a week setting up your system and getting it in order. But none of this does you any good if you don't make the right decision every time a piece of paper crosses your desk. If you don't develop a new set of habits for making decisions each time you handle a document, all your expense and effort will go for nothing.

The same thing is true of *The Lazy Man's Way to Riches*. You made a decision to purchase this material, and then make a much more important decision every day when you reach out and open the book. You make another important decision when you follow through by actually performing the next step in your Roadmap Guidebook. If you don't decide to reach out and open the book and don't complete the steps in your Roadmap, you cancel out all these decisions you made in starting this journey; and you have to live with the consequences of your decision. Remember, "if you just keep doing what your doing, you'll just keep getting what you're getting."

WHAT TRIGGERS THE TURNING POINTS?

One of the easiest ways to understand the importance of the little decisions is to examine the so-called turning points in your life. Were they really the result of clear-cut decisions where you knew exactly what the outcome would lead to? Or were your turning points the end result of a lot of *little* decisions that were made with hardly any or no thought of the consequences? For example, two of the most significant events in most of our lives are marriage and the choice of a career. But are these cases of major decisions made after a great deal of analysis? Usually not. Most people arrive at these turning points in their lives as a result of earlier decisions that were made without any idea of the consequences.

Joe said his decision to marry Betty, and hers to marry him came as a result of a lot of little decisions about going out together and working out the conflicts in their personalities; so by the time they decided to get married, it was the only logical thing to do. Zero in on the little decisions that affect your life.

Your next step on your road to Riches is to examine the turning points in your life. Try to exam the little decisions that added up to a major change. Pick out the major events in your life and write down all the reasons you made the choices you made. Then, look closely at your reasons and try to figure out what little decisions really created the situation that influenced your choice. In Step 17 of your Guidebook you'll find an example of a turning point and how to dig down to find the key decisions that really made the difference.

He who is outside his door already has a hard part of his journey behind him.
DUTCH PROVERB

Now turn to Step #17 "The Turning Points" in your *Roadmap to Riches* workbook.

18

Post-Hypnotic
Suggestions

(AKA Behavioral Triggers)

Congratulations! You just made a very important little decision that's going to mean a lot to you. You decided to complete the steps necessary to continue your journey on *The Lazy Man's Way to Riches*.

Was Step 17, "The Turning Points", in the Roadmap Guidebook a revelation to you? Are you getting an idea of how crucial the little decisions are in your life? It's kind of scary isn't it to think how a bunch of little decisions can really add up to a big change in your life. Scary—but also very exciting because that means you have a lot of chances every day to influence your life in a positive way.

Have you ever made a mistake, recognized it as a mistake, and turned right around and made the same mistake again? If you are human you have. We all have this experience—making the same mistakes over and over again and basically for the same reason. Habit. We get into the habit of making certain decisions without thinking. That can be great if the decisions are success decisions, but it can be disastrous if they are (and they usually are) failure—oriented decisions. Now why does this happen? Why do we make the same blunders over and over again?

God will not look you over for medals, degrees or diplomas, but for scars.

ELBERT HUBBARD
(1856–1915)
American businessman,
writer, printer

THE POWER OF SUGGESTION

Joe was convinced that we act as though we have been hypnotized. Have you ever seen a hypnotist work, especially on stage? Pat Collins was a famous hypnotist, who once owned a nightclub in Los Angeles. In her act, she asked for volunteers from the audience whom she determined were good hypnotic subjects. She hypnotized them and suggested certain situations to them. The hypnotized volunteers behaved as if her suggestions were true.

During the show Pat demonstrated a technique called "post-hypnotic suggestion." She told her volunteers that after they came out from under hypnosis, each time she mentioned the name of her club they would jump up and start shouting "The British are coming! The British are coming!" She then brought them out of their relaxed state and thanked them for helping her at the "Pat Collins Celebrity Club." Immediately they jumped up and started hollering "The British are coming! The British are coming!" Of course the audience thought it was hilarious. Each time she mentioned her club she got the same result. One of the volunteers said, "I was aware of what I was doing and each time I did it, I decided I wouldn't do it again, and yet each time Pat mentioned the name of the club, I found myself reacting the same way."

SUGGESTION GAINS IN INTENSITY!

Doesn't that sound familiar; haven't you felt that way, repeating the same mistakes over and over again? This simple nightclub gag really explains a lot of human behavior. All of you have been hypnotized at various times in your life. All that means is that you have accepted certain suggestions about yourself and your behavior as a result of your experiences. You get a certain cue or trigger and off you go shouting, "The British are coming! The British are coming." Of course, it is more subtle than that. Often the trigger is a certain kind of situation rather than a word or words.

For example, let's say you have a great idea for doing a certain part of your job more effectively. If you can sell your employer on the idea, it will probably mean a promotion and a raise; but each time you try to approach the boss with the idea you become nervous and tongue-tied. You begin to doubt the real value of your idea and as a result you really don't get it across. Your whole presentation is a shambles and you lose out. A couple weeks later, one of your co-workers gets the same idea. Worse yet, "borrows" your idea, takes it to the boss and sells it. He gets the credit and the raise and you wonder why you can't seem to communicate effectively with someone who is above you.

Well, now you know. Sometime in your past you accepted the suggestion that you don't do well talking to "The Boss" or "Authority figures." Maybe it was a bad school experience with a teacher or principal or other authority figures, or maybe it was a problem speaking to your parents. It doesn't really matter, because the damage has been done. The important thing is learning how to break the pattern. We start that process in the next chapter.

THE WINNING EDGE—PREPARE TO WIN

Why do you have these problem areas in your life, such as not winning with authority figures? According to the very successful basketball coach, Bobby Knight formerly of Indiana University, it is because you are not prepared to win. He was asked how he instilled the will to win in his players. He replied, *"Everybody has the will to win. What I work to instill in my players is the will to **prepare** to win!"* That's a key step in *The Lazy Man's Way to Riches*. If you have the will to prepare to win and engage in the right preparation, you will make the right little decisions automatically. Those little decisions really add up into a winning way of living your life.

One of the roadblocks that stop a lot of people from getting the things they want out of life is the belief that to be really successful in life you have to: work much harder, be much smarter or be luckier than the average guy. And it just isn't so! For one thing, if you had to work much harder than average, Joe would have been out of it—because he was the *original* Lazy Man.

THE WINNING EDGE—BY A NOSE!

Actually, the winning edge is much smaller than you think. Some years ago Nashua became one of the first million dollar racehorses. Now you don't have to know very much about horse racing to know that a million dollar racehorse is not a hundred times faster than a ten thousand dollar racehorse. In fact, he is not even twice as fast. If you have ever seen a horse race you know there usually isn't very much space between the winner and the rest of the pack. In Nashua's case 60 percent of the races he won were by photo finishes. In racing that means the horses were only inches apart as they crossed the finish line after more than a mile of racing. In other words, Nashua became a million dollar racehorse even though 60 percent of the time he was one or two inches ahead of his competition after over seventy thousand inches of running. That's a difference of less than 1/100 of 1 percent. It's just as true in life. The winning edge is not a matter of miles. It's often just a fraction of an inch.

THE WINNING EDGE—A FEW EXTRA HANDS!

There's not a salesperson in the world who doesn't want to make or exceed his quota. They want to win. But whether they make it or not will often depend on as small an effort as one extra call a week. Dick Johnson relates the story of his own business experience.

"In several small wholesale distribution companies this truth is clearly illustrated. The figures show that people who put at least fifteen hours per week into the development of their business succeed spectacularly. They often develop $50,000 to $100,000 incomes annually within three or four years. The figures also show that people who put less than eight hours per week into the development of their business usually struggle to make anything and often fail completely. In this case the winning edge is an extra seven hours per week—just one hour per day—and that little extra makes an enormous difference in income. How big a decision is it to make an extra call or to spend an extra hour each day developing your future? Not too big and yet it's this kind of decision that really makes the difference. There's one big problem with little decisions—they are usually made out of habit."

In the next step of your Roadmap workbook, I want you to go back over your experiences and identify the post-hypnotic patterns that are blocking your progress. In other words, where are the areas in your life where you are making the same mistakes over and over and over again. Mistakes like: "Somehow I always spend more than I make," or "I'm still in the same dead-end job that I vowed to get out of last year." In the Guidebook I've listed some more examples to get you started.

Action may not always bring happiness, but there is no happiness without action.

BENJAMIN DISRAELI
(1804–1881)
English statesman and novelist

Now turn to Step #18 "Post-Hypnotic Suggestions (AKA Behavioral Triggers)" in your *Roadmap To Riches* workbook.

Change Your Habits, Change Your Life

It really opens your eyes, doesn't it, to see how post-hypnotic suggestions or habits are dominating your life? Day after day, most of us make virtually all our decisions, important or unimportant, out of habit. If the decision is not made automatically, as some are, the thought processes that go into our decision–making are dominated by our attitudes which are just habits of thought about ourselves, our abilities and our environment.

Most, if not all of our attitudes, are not valid most of the time. I will explain that in more detail later, when I tell you about your Reality Map in your Roadmap Guidebook. You have probably already realized that you are not always 100 percent right about everything.

CHANGE YOUR HABITS AND CHANGE YOUR LIFE

Since habits dominate your life, to change your life you have to change your habits. It has been observed many times that successful people are those who make a habit out of doing the things unsuccessful people won't do. But what are those things? W. Clement Stone, who certainly has one of the twentieth century's most exciting success stories, has pretty well narrowed it down. W. Clement Stone started in the insurance business at the age of sixteen with a one hundred dollar investment. When Mr. Stone died in 2002 he had an estimated net worth of over a billion dollars. Mr. Stone is also the founder of *Success* magazine and the P.M.A. (Positive Mental Attitude) seminars and rallies.

Stone's striking appearance was something that he became noted for; his pencil-thin black mustache, vibrant suspenders, polka-dot bow ties, and spats. His charitable endeavors of over $275 million to mental health and Christian organizations are also well known. Stone was also a gifted inspirational speaker, and would shout "Bingo!" at board meetings if attention lapsed. Overall, Mr. Stone's most often used quote was "All I want to do is change the world."

Mr. Stone said that in his experience, successful people all exhibit the following characteristics.

DO IT

First, when faced with an opportunity where they have a great deal to gain if successful and little or nothing to lose if they fail, they try. How often have you seen people with a clear opportunity in front of them paralyzed by indecision and fear? And what are they afraid of? The fear of failure itself, not the consequences of it. The

It seems, in fact, as though the second half of a man's life is made up of nothing but the habits he has accumulated during the first half.

FYODOR DOSTOEVSKY
(1821–1881)
Russian novelist

We are all of us failures— at least, the best of us are.
J.M. BARRIE
(1860–1937)
British playwright

sad thing is that often there is no real risk. No risk of losing their savings, or self-respect, or good name or anything of value.

DO IT NOW!

The second of W. Clement Stone's attributes of successful people is they have a "do it now" attitude. Procrastination, putting things off—is the greatest destroyer of success that I know. And I should know, because in the past I was one of the greatest procrastinators ever known, and it has cost me dearly. Opportunity is almost always lost when people put things off and usually become much worse when they are not solved immediately. There is another negative aspect of procrastination—it saps your energy. Usually when you put something off you don't forget about it—it nags at you constantly. You run over the situation several times a day in your imagination. The amazing thing is that you burn up just as much, or more energy *thinking* about the problem as you would *solving* it. So the longer you procrastinate, the more tired and frustrated you get as you go over and over and over it in your mind. You will be astonished at how much more energy you have when you start developing a "do it now" habit!

DO IT PERSISTENTLY

W. Clement Stones' third attribute of successful people is that they have persistence. In his words, *"Success is achieved and maintained by those who try and continue to try with a positive mental attitude."*

Life has a way of testing your desires by setting some obstacle in your way. Too many people give up at the first setback. The history of failure is full of stories of people who quit just inches away from success. And the history of success is full of stories of people who failed more than once before they finally clicked.

Developing these three habits—willingness to try, do it now, and persistence with a positive mental attitude is certainly fundamental to your progress in The Lazy Man's Way. But let's be realistic. Just recognizing the desirability of a new habit is not enough. Developing habits takes attention, time and effort, especially if you are trying to replace an old habit that conflicts with a new one. Habits such as these can take a long time to establish. That is why you need some tools to help you keep on track and moving. You will have a lot of powerful tools before you are through.

DRAW UP A CONTRACT

And here is the first one. The Habit Contract. The idea of The Habit Contract is simple. We are usually motivated by rewards and our nature is such that we are usually motivated more by near-term, easily achievable, tangible rewards than by more distant, less tangible rewards. It is important, therefore, that you set up some near-term rewards, so you may become aware of the progress you are making, and to teach you to be good to yourself.

The process is simple. First, *identify* the habits you want to develop. And second (because you always develop new habits—you don't break or give up old ones) you must *develop a new response* as a substitute reaction for the old one. Changing a habit is like changing the course of a river—you must divert the flow into a new channel. The old channel is there, and in the beginning, it is fairly easy to revert to it, but as time goes on the new channel becomes deeper and deeper. The old one fills in and there is less and less likelihood of going back to it—your old ways. It would be easier to change a habit if your mind automatically made you stop and make a conscious choice about changing. You need something—a symbol- to trigger you to remember you are no longer responding in the same way to situations—to your old habits. I call this a Habit Trigger. For example when you pour yourself a cup of coffee in the morning, it could trigger you to remember the new habit you are trying to establish.

To adopt a new habit, you must first identify the long-term payoff that will result from adopting it. It may be more success, higher income, better health, more self-esteem, more freedom, peace of mind or whatever long-term benefits appeal to you. You are probably feeling it would be nice if you could have all those things but you are also not really excited about the prospects. They are too far away, not sufficiently specific to get you excited enough to generate the energy it takes to develop the new habit. That is why you need the specific award aspect of The Habit Contract to inspire you to put out the effort to change now!

REWARD YOURSELF

This is the way the Habit Contract works. You select something as a reward for yourself. Something you will give yourself as a special treat for accomplishing a milestone towards your goal of developing a new habit. To be effective, this reward must be something you really want, but would not ordinarily get for yourself. It could be something that would cost a little more than you would normally spend on yourself; perhaps a custom-made suit or dinner at a very fine restaurant. It could be something that costs very little, but seems a little selfish.

One woman's choice of the height of luxury was to have her husband and kids take off on a camping trip for three days, so she could be totally alone in her home for that time. That was a great reward for her. It was something she had always wanted but had never felt right asking for so it made a perfect reward for establishing a new habit. The habit she was working on developing was a "do it now" attitude. When she successfully performed thirty consecutive acts of completing tasks rather than putting them off, she rewarded herself with three days of peace and quiet.

So what kind of habits should you be adopting? The number one habit I want you to adopt is faithfully performing the steps in your *Roadmap to Riches—Your Personal Guidebook*, and particularly, Daily Declarations and Super Suggestions. (There is also an audio program available in cassette, CD and MP3, so you can listen to *The Lazy Man's Way to Riches* any time you want, even in your car. You can order it online at http://www.thelazymansway.com/). If you will do that, I am confident you will start developing the other habits you need.

To help you develop the habit of continuing on your *Lazy Man's Way to Riches*, I have put a Habit Contract in Step 19 of your Roadmap workbook. I have filled in a Habit Contract with reward as an example. You are then to go to the next page and fill in the Habit Contract as indicated. Keep in mind while deciding on your reward to make it something that really motivates you; and make it something you would not ordinarily do for yourself, unless you felt you had earned it.

The nature of man is always the same; it is their habits that separate them

CONFUCIUS
(551–479 BC)
Chinese Philosopher

So select your reward, and then earn it by carrying out your journey in The Lazy Man's Way. By the way, do not feel limited to just one Habit Contract. You can probably handle up to three habits simultaneously, but do not try to change everything at once. You have plenty of time; trying to do too much at once will diffuse your concentration and defeat your purpose.

How long does it take to develop a new habit pattern? Psychologists tell me that a rat can learn a new behavior in about 30 repetitions. So draw your own conclusions. To help you measure your progress, I have included the numbers one through thirty so you can check off each time you are successful in reinforcing the new habit.

Now turn to Step #19 "Change Your Habits, Change Your Life"
in your *Roadmap to Riches* workbook.

Today's Inadequate You—Tomorrow's?

A very wise man once said that there is a gift which all our true friends would love to give us, a gift which we probably need desperately, but a gift capable of utterly destroying even the deepest friendship. That gift is criticism. And, the more personal the criticism, the greater the sting it carries.

At the risk of endangering for the moment your sense of self-satisfaction, let me tell you something about your inadequacies. How do I know they are your inadequacies? Simply because you bought this book/program, the odds are overwhelming that you suffer from some feelings of inadequacy. (But if it makes you feel any better, almost everybody does.) However, you also proved that you were willing to make some important changes in your life. You've already taken the most important step!

Now when I speak of inadequacies, I am not concerned with your size, weight, physical appearance, strength, manliness or femininity. The concern here is with the most important inadequacy from which any person can suffer; an *Inadequate Self-Image*. For brevity I will refer to it as ISI.

This ISI is one of the first things formed in your life. It has an influential and lasting effect on your failure or success. It plays a more prominent role than *any other single factor*. This is true because it is the giant controller of your personal destiny. If that seems hard to believe, let me ask you this: Would you like to try to face the daily task of your present world (job, friends, love-life, etc.) knowing and believing only what you knew and believed when you were *five or six years old?*

Think of the mess you could make of even the simplest tasks assigned to you, functioning as a grown person with the knowledge and beliefs of a young child! Think of the impossibility of a mature relationship with others if your capacity to "get along" was that of a kindergartner!

Well, your ISI, in all those areas that are important to us as adults, was largely set in concrete by the time you were six years old! Challenging though that statement may seem to some, there is overwhelming scientific evidence to support it.

Once we have ascertained the point of woeful inadequacy at which ISI was established, surely you must wonder if it doesn't change as you get older. The answer (and we'll see why later) is " No, hardly ever," unless you deliberately set about to change it!

Your next question might be, what does this ISI control or affect? The answer: To a greater or lesser extent, *every single activity of the human being!* And it does this by

Wherever we go, whatever we do, self is the sole subject we study and learn.

RALPH WALDO EMERSON
(1803–1882)
American poet, essayist, philosopher

I believe that it is harder still to be just toward oneself than toward others.

ANDRE GIDE
(1869–1951)
French novelist, critic, essayist, editor, translator

placing a clamped–down, nailed–down, ceiling on success! It prevents the adult from ever reaching a potential beyond the concept of the child.

The direct result of this ISI is that the average person uses less than 10 percent of his/her potential! And it's no wonder. At the age of five or six, few of us were convinced of our own great strength, power and abilities. We didn't feel very *effective*.

HUMAN CONDITIONING

That feeling of ineffectuality was the result of the many pressures that were applied to us in those first few years. These pressures were the "do's and don'ts" of our early years as expressed in the *habits* we established. Scientifically these things are referred to as "conditioning."

Those pressures can be divided into two categories; those which *help* us in later years and those which *hinder* our progress. The *helps* of those years was the conditioning we acquired which today lets us perform many of our daily tasks almost without thinking. In this group are included such diverse things as tying our shoes; using a knife, fork and spoon; walking; talking, etc.

But what of the conditioning which hinders our effectiveness? Consider this example: As a very little boy, Johnny goes out to the garage where his father is working in his woodshop. Fascinated, he watches his father as he is "making something." Soon, watching is not enough. He wants to "help." At this point two things may occur. One will result in a conditioning, which will *help*; the other will *hinder* the self-image structure and the later—life development as well.

If his father gives him some safe but satisfying task of the utmost simplicity to perform, lets him do it, guides him to some small success, and then praises his efforts, the lad's self image has received a tremendous boost. If this pattern of events is repeated again and again, confidence is built through the *habit of success* in this area of activity. It will *help* him build a better self-image.

If, on the other hand, "Daddy's" time and/or patience is short, if the lad's interest and desire to participate result in only an irritating interference with the work at hand, no such helpful image building results. The repeated efforts to participate (for little ones are not easily discouraged) may result in a final rejection by the father as he is banished from this fascinating scene or punishment for what the father sees as deliberate disobedience.

Either way, the child has been taught a lesson. He has been "taught" or conditioned into a belief that he is "no good" at a certain kind of manly activity, or that he is "no good" merely because he has wanted to participate—"*bad*" because he was *ambitious*. His self-image has taken a blow; his fear-factor (of which we will talk later) has received a great boost.

To the same degree that this was an occurrence charged with *heavy emotionality* (loud voice, a physical punishment, lasted a long time), it will have a proportionately large and lasting effect on the self-image.

Few of us have been so fortunate as to have had only *helpful* ego forming, or self-image, experiences in our early years. That is why today it is a scientific evaluation that the average person is working at only 10% *of his/her potential!*

We are so constituted that we believe the most incredible things; and once they are engraved upon the memory, woe to him who would endeavor to erase them.

JOHANN WOLFGANG VAN GOETHE
(1749–1832)
German Poet, playwright, novelist

Creative minds have always been known to survive any kind of bad training.

ANNA FREUD
(1895–1982)
English psychoanalyst, daughter of Sigmund Freud

Where does that put you? Well, since you care enough about the future to buy a program like this, to read it, to TRY to improve your chances of success, you are already considerably *above average!* But the fact that you are not already a smashing success means you are still not functioning near the maximum of your potential power.

Now turn to Step #20 "Today's Inadequate You—Tomorrow's?"
in your *Roadmap to Riches* workbook.

21

I Can Be My Own Worst Enemy—or My Own Best Friend

Hello. I'm Richard Gilly Nixon and the reason I am introducing myself to you again is that I am not the same Richard who talked to you earlier, anymore than you are the same person you were when you started this book. You and I are constantly *changing* and can be constantly *improving*. It is usually hard to see the changes from day to day, yet just look at how you have changed since we started our page-by-page get together.

How have you changed? Well, for, one thing, you know a lot more about yourself than when we began. You know that you have all the qualities you need to be an outstanding success. You know that the roadblocks that used to block your way are really products of your attitude. And you know that you and everything else in the world around you is constantly changing, so those attitudes that block you from the Riches you want can be changed, too. You've been thinking about where you want to go in life and you have begun to identify some patterns in your life that lead you to make the same mistakes over and over again.

The knowledge you have gained in these pages makes you a new person. As you start learning to apply that knowledge, you will begin to see changes take place. And this raises a very important question. Are you willing to change? I know I asked you this question at the beginning, but I find that in the beginning, most people don't realize how significant these changes will be. Are you willing to release some old attitudes? Admit some of your most cherished beliefs aren't working for you? If you are not, it is going to be very difficult to release the barriers between you and the Riches you want.

YOU CAN PREDICT YOUR FUTURE

Look at it this way. You can absolutely predict your progress in the future by looking at the progress you have made in the past, *if you choose not to change your thinking*. But, when you change your thinking you can make your future anything you want. Resist change in your attitudes and your future will be just like your past. Post-hypnotic suggestion explains our habitual behavior.

How many mistake patterns can you find in your life? Let me check for a few you might have overlooked. How is your temper? Do you find that you often lose it when a little diplomacy would really help the situation go more smoothly? How is your procrastination level? How often do you put things off and compound a problem that could be solved by a simple action? How is your confidence? How often do you let someone else talk you out of your good ideas? How about your impatience? Do you find yourself doing things impulsively when a little patience

> Progress is impossible without change; and those who cannot change their minds cannot change anything.
>
> GEORGE BERNARD SHAW
> (1856–1950)
> Irish playwright, critic, social reformer

> Laws are never as effective as habits.
>
> ADLAI STEVENSON
> (1900–1965)
> American statesman, politician

would make things work smoother? How forgetful are you? How often do you forget an important appointment or a person's name, or a priority task that must be done? Quick temper—habit; procrastination—habit; low self-confidence—habit; impatience—habit; forgetfulness—habit. All habits, all post-hypnotic suggestions which have you behaving in ways that contradict your reason and intelligence. Fortunately, all post-hypnotic suggestions can be removed once you understand and use the process I am going to teach you.

Earlier when I was telling you about the Pat Collins Show, I left out an important part. Before Pat finished her show she was very careful to remove all post-hypnotic suggestions. After all, it could be embarrassing to suddenly jump up and shout, "The British are coming" at a dinner party just because someone happened to mention the Pat Collins Celebrity Club. Pat Collins is a conscientious professional and would never fail to remove post-hypnotic suggestions.

But suppose that one night she forgot? No need to worry. The results would not be too serious because a very important feature of hypnotic suggestions is that eventually they wear off, if they are not renewed or reinforced frequently. In other words, if you go to a hypnotist and ask him/her to help you stop smoking, the hypnotist might suggest to you that cigarettes taste terrible. They will for a while. But unless the hypnotist teaches you how to reinforce that suggestion, it will soon wear off. Because smoking is such an ingrained habit for most people, they will continue to smoke even if the taste is bad; and after a very few cigarettes their minds will begin to forget or throw off the bad-taste suggestion and soon everything will be back to normal. Just as one of Pat Collins' volunteers has been able to resist or forget that "The British are coming" within a day or so, any post-hypnotic suggestion will lose its effect within a very short time unless it is reinforced frequently.

Right about now you may be thinking, "Wait a minute, you just told me that my repetitive mistakes were examples of post-hypnotic suggestions planted in my mind years ago and now you tell me post-hypnotic suggestions wear off quickly unless they are reinforced? That's a contradiction. How come my habit patterns have not worn off?" Very simple. They have been and are continually being reinforced by you.

YOU ARE YOUR OWN HYPNOTIST

Who is the most influential person in your life? Who do you listen to more than anyone? Who do you always agree with even when they put you down? Your spouse, your parents, your kids, your boss? No. None of the above. The most influential person in your life is YOU.

When someone else is talking, you may or may not be listening. If you are listening, it is probably not to them but to your inner voice translating and restating what they are saying. And as your inner voice tells you its translated version of what it is hearing, you will attach more importance to that information than what is actually being said. You may or may not believe what others tell you, but you will always believe what your inner voice tells you, even if it puts you down—*especially* if it puts you down.

The fact of the matter is there is no such thing as being hypnotized by another person. You can only be hypnotized by yourself. All the other person does is make certain suggestions and you either accept them or reject them. For example, if the

I know you believe you understand what you think I said, but I'm not sure you realized that what you heard is not what I meant.

ANONYMOUS

hypnotist says, "Your eyelids are getting heavy," you have two choices. You can either accept the suggestion by saying, "Yes, my eyelids are getting heavy," in which case your body will respond to you and your eyelids will feel heavy, or you can say, "No, my eyelids are not getting heavy," in which case, nothing will happen. So, in fact, you hypnotize yourself. All the hypnotist does is tell you how to do it.

If that is true, then how do we develop all of our bad habits? Simple. This process is going on all the time and much of it happened when you were just a child. A lot of your limiting programming came from your lack of understanding of the world around you and the natural inclination of children to look up to and accept what bigger children and adults tell them. You accepted all kinds of suggestions about yourself and the world around you. Some were valid and helpful, many were false and worked against you and continue to work against you.

You can't really go back and change the kind of programming you received as a child. Nor is there any point in blaming your parents, teachers, brothers, sisters, other children, or anyone else. They were all going through a similar process and they did not know what was going on anymore than you did. So, if you cannot go back and change your past, does that mean you are stuck with who you are? When I was going to school, that was pretty much what psychologists believed. Supposedly our whole lives were influenced by things that happened to us when we were infants. There was not much we could do about it without a lot of very expensive psychoanalysis.

Events in our childhood do influence us later in life; but the idea that we are stuck with our behavior and attitudes just because we were not toilet trained correctly is nonsense. We can change any aspect of our personalities or behavior if we want to; but we must want to and then learn the process for doing it.

SELF TALK

There is a constant stream of chatter that goes on in our heads. It is called self-talk and all it is, is you talking to you.

I'd like to suggest you pay attention to what you say to yourself and how you say it. Do you constantly criticize yourself inside your head? Or do you constantly criticize others? Or complain about your life, your faults, or how life "treats" you? Or internally rant about the injustices of life? Do you constantly tell yourself you're fed up, you're at your wits end? Or that you can't cope with this much longer? Or that you'll fail at something? Or that you're going to have a panic attack?

Can you imagine if you had a friend that went around with you all day, every day, and was constantly whispering comments like these in your ear! How would you feel at the end of a day. How about at the end of a week? Or, after a month of such negative indoctrination? I don't know about you but I couldn't run fast enough from that type of negativy.

Well, guess what! You're already doing this to yourself—and in a far more effective manner that this so called friend would do it. After all, if a friend treated you like that you likely would tell them to stop or you'd drop them like a hot rock. But because you are doing this to yourself—and have probably been running such mental "programs" since childhood—you no longer even notice them and, as a result, they have powerful impact on your mood and on your attitude toward yourself and toward life.

Our negative self-talk is harmful, unsettling and debilitating. And because we are so used to it we don 't consciously pay attention to it and therefore do not challenge it. It goes on and on in the background and the effect is that we are giving ourselves powerful hypnotic suggestions to feel bad!

GENTLY REPLACE YOUR NEGATIVE SELF-TALK

I suggest "gently" because there's no point in adding to the inner stress and discomfort further criticising yourself "I must not say this," or "there I go again," etc.—that would be only reinforcing you negative self-talk once again.

Each time you recognize that you are doing your self-criticising or self-undermining, pause a bit, remind yourself that it's just that old habit you've gotten into, and that from now on you're changing this nonproductive habit.

Use a soft and patient tone of voice for this. Your inner voice should sound as if you are calming an upset child. Reassure yourself. Calm yourself. Remind yourself of the rationales and facts of the situation. Remind yourself of the value of handling things in a cool, calm, and confident manner. I model on someone who behaves the way I want to behave and I ask my self, "How would Ronald Reagan have gone about doing what I want to do?"

Doing this only once or twice won't make any real difference. It takes quite a while to replace the habits of a lifetime—but it's definitely worth doing. Journaling is an excellent tool for becoming aware of your self-talk and gradually reducing the intensity of negative self-talk.

You begin this process by becoming aware of how you talk to yourself. How often do you use the expression "I AM" as in statements like, "That's the way I AM" or "I AM temperamental" or "I AM lazy" or some such expression which means the same thing as, "I can't do it." To utter such statements is the same thing as saying, "I AM the kind of person who can't do it," or " I don't know," which is just another variation of the same thought. Almost anytime you use the word "I," you are making a statement about your talents and abilities—a statement that reinforces a false and limiting attitude about yourself. In Step 21 of the *Roadmap to Riches* Guidebook, you will find several examples of the kinds of statements that reinforce your attitudes and tend to lock you into being just a product of your past training—good and bad.

For the next few days, I want you to become very self-aware. Pay attention to what you say to and about yourself. Read the examples in your Roadmap Guidebook in Step 21, and check off the ones that you find you use. Add any you use that are not on the list. As you go through your day, keep track of how many times you reinforce your past training with one of these phrases or a similar statement.

What is this self inside us, this silent observer, / severe and speechless critic, who can terrorize us. / And urge us on to futile activity, / and in the end, judge us still more severely: / For the errors into which his own reproaches drove us?

T. S. ELIOT
(1888–1965)
American-born English poet, critic, editor, playwright

Now turn to Step #21 "I Can Be My Own Worst Enemy—or My Own Best Friend" in your *Roadmap to Riches* workbook.

22
Making Your Life as Good as It Can Be

Riches are yours when you really believe you are entitled to them—when you just *allow* yourself to have them and can freely *choose* to have them in your life. A true belief in your ability to attain your purpose, and the fundamental goals that support your purpose, will grow in direct proportion to your level of positive self-esteem and even to your self-images. It's been said that belief is the foundation upon which our lives are built. If that's true, then a healthy, positive self-esteem and the many self-images we have of ourselves are the bedrock upon which the foundation is built!

SELF-ESTEEM DEFINED

Self-esteem is a confidence and satisfaction in oneself. It's that deep down, inside-the-self feeling of your own worth. Our self-esteem is a total picture of how we see ourselves—a unique concept of who we are. It's the value you place on yourself—a favorable appreciation or opinion of yourself. It is the level to which you respect and value yourself as a worthwhile and important person.

- Self-dignity!
- Self-sufficiency!
- Self-assurance!
- Self-respect!
- Self-possession!
- Self-confidence!
- Self-responsibility!
- Self-pride!
- Self-reliance!

BELIEF IN ONESELF!

SELF-IMAGE DEFINED

Self-image is a conception of oneself or of one's role in a particular and singular area. It's the way you see yourself—viewing yourself as an exact likeness of another. It's a tangible or visible representation of oneself. It's a view of self *based* on an *ideal*.

We have many self-images and they are based on our beliefs or ideals of how things should be. We have an image of ourselves in every aspect of our make-up!

As a student	I'm good in math, but I'm lousy in history.
As a swimmer	I tell myself I'm a poor swimmer, so I am.
As a cook	My belief is that boys don't cook, so I don't.
As an employee	I'm a good employee.
As a spouse	I'm a so-so spouse.
As a speaker	I'm terrified as a speaker.

A man can stand a lot as long as can stand himself. He can live without hope, without friends, without books, even without music, as long as he can listen to his own thoughts.

AXEL MUNTHE
(1857–1949)
Swedish physician, author

You've got to take the initiative and play your game. In a decisive set, confidence is the difference.

CHRIS EVERT LLOYD
(CHRISTENE MARIE)
(b. 1954)
American tennis player
(#1 worldwide 1974–1978)

As a seamstress	Boy's don't sew.
As a football player	I'm a good center but a lousy tackle.
As a parent	I do my best to be a responsible parent.
As a child	I'm learning how to handle my parents.

IT'S YOUR BELIEF

We view ourselves from the perspective of the ideals or beliefs we have come to accept about each role in our lives. We tell ourselves I am a good cook, but a lousy mechanic; a good tennis player, a good golfer, but a bad swimmer. We see ourselves either competent or incompetent in every role and then we perform to the standard we set up for ourselves. We live out our self-fulfilling prophecies that are based upon the image we have of our competence in any given area. That's a wonderful concept! It's only your belief that you buy into, that affects your performance in your role as a dancer, swimmer, mechanic, etc. Therefore, you can freely, willingly, and easily **change your belief!** You can replace failure—belief (I can't dance, I can't swim, I'll never understand mechanics) with a factual—belief that you can do or have or be something that you had previously denied yourself. That's The Lazy Man's Way. Because the human experience is universal—that which any human being can do, we all can do. I call it a "factual belief."

You can't go wrong if you remember these two things. First, all of the potential of the universe is inside you. Second, it's inside every other human being, too. As Joe always said, "All men are created equal."

A word of caution here: Whenever there is a conflict between your burning desire and your self-images, self-images will win every single time. That's why it is important to look carefully at the results of your life, objectively and truthfully. Is your life as good as it could be in each of the seven goal areas you listed in Step 7 of your Roadmap workbook?

CHANGE YOUR PRESENT SELF-IMAGES!

A self-image that will work for you can easily be created in any area of your life to replace the present self-image that isn't working for you. You simply determine which areas just aren't working by simply asking yourself, "Are these the results I really want?" If they aren't, it's not the desire that's at fault or too weak; it's the idealized self-image of false belief that's getting in your way. Replace the image and the false belief it's based upon, with a new image based on the new belief that "I can dance" (or whatever). Why not? Four billion other human beings can and do dance. Why? Simply because they think they can. You can, too; and you probably did as a two year old. You then work in an easy progression toward your new image, until you are able to develop the experience and self-confidence necessary to change your new ideal image into a real self-image. You won't start out as well as Fred Astaire, Janet Jackson or Britney Spears, but neither did they! They started out just like you. You have to go out and do the things you're not very good at doing, yet!

JESSE JACKSON SAYS:

Reverend Jesse Jackson teaches people to say, "I am somebody!" That's a wonderful start! But suppose for a moment you were switched at birth with the

---

Take charge of your thoughts. You can do what you will with them.

PLATO
(428–327 BC)
Greek philosopher and prose writer

It may be all right to be content with what you have; never with what you are.

B. C. FORBES
(1880–1954)
American publisher

They can do all because they think they can.

VIRGIL (70–19 BC)
Roman Poet; *"Aenied"*

child of the rulers of your ancestral homeland. Your parents got the ruler's kid and the rulers got you. How would your life be different? You would have had the best of everything life had to offer—food, clothing, education, private tutors, arts and sports. You would have power, prestige, wealth, fame, and confidence galore! Could you dance, ride polo ponies, race cars, fly airplanes, or whatever the children of the super rich do? Of course! And so you can! You are still you regardless of how you grew up. You are somebody! **You get to create that person.**

MUHAMMED ALI SAYS:

Muhammed Ali used to proclaim "I am the greatest!" and he was. He proved it over and over. But he knew it deep in his soul even before he became the boxing champion of the world. His claim of "I am the greatest!" was not an idle boast or self-delusion. He worked for it! His claim was based upon the experience of success, after success starting out as a beginner and moving up in weight class to better opponents. You can start out doing what you want to do also (dancer, swimmer, whatever), and process!

SO WHAT'S THE DIFFERENCE?

There is a difference between "I am somebody" and "I am the greatest!" The difference is between mere existence, and existence with a purpose backed by *action* toward that purpose. *It is your performance.*

To establish real self-esteem, concentrate on your *growth* toward your idea of success. Look at the stumbles and tumbles (and sometimes even outright failures) as corrective and necessary feedback—course corrections that get you back on target again! Instead of comparing yourself with others, see yourself in terms of your abilities, your ideals, your new beliefs, your growth and your goals. You can start now by making a conscious effort to change your life, raise your sights, and become more aware of your behavior, your personal habits, your posture, and appearance—in whatever you do, try to do it just a little better each time—always try for your personal best performance. Doing your best will boost your self-esteem. Successful people believe in their own worth, even when they only have a dream to hold on to. The dream is based on a purpose and a plan! More than any other quality, a healthy, positive self-esteem is the key to your Riches!

High self-esteem must always include self-trust because when we trust ourselves we have no need to control anything or anybody. High self-esteem also includes self-respect because when we respect ourselves we find within ourselves all that we need and have no reason to fix things outside of ourselves (other people, possessions, etc.). Of course, high self-esteem can only exist in a state of genuine self-love. For in a state of genuine self-love there is no fear.

BE CAREFUL NOT TO KID YOURSELF!

What happens when you have a conflict between the ideal you hold for yourself and the opposing belief you also hold about yourself? Suppose you believe you are just a bad person. You might then try to balance out that belief with the ideal of being a "good" person in your mind. You will then attempt to fulfill the ideal image of a "good" person by doing what a "good" person does. Your behaviors and actions would thus be motivated by avoiding or moving away from the problem of being a bad person. No matter how many "good deeds" you were to do to contradict the

Many persons have a wrong idea of what constitutes true happiness. It is not attained through self-gratitude but through fidelity to a worthy purpose.

HELEN KELLER
(1880–1968)
American memoirist and essayist

Self trust is the essence of heroism.

RALPH WALDO EMERSON
(1803–1882)
American poet, essayist, philosopher; *"Heroism"*

belief of being "bad," you would only be kidding yourself! Why do that? You'll just be hurting the self-esteem you are building up.

Look at your motivation. Being good is not just the absence of bad any more than being healthy is just the absence of illness. You don't become healthy just by moving away from bad habits, although that helps. If you want to be healthy, you must believe that you are a healthy person (it's a state of mind). That motivation will cause you to then do the things that a healthy person does, moving you toward good health automatically. You will no longer have to think about not doing things that are bad, because as a healthy person you will only do those things that are good for you. Self-esteem is self-love! It is a vital step along your journey to Riches.

YOUR SELF-FULFILLING PROHECY
(The Pygmalion effect)

You are what you *think* you are.
What you think you *can* be is what you will become.

In an ancient myth as told by Ovid in the tenth book of Metamorphoses; the sculptor Pygmalion, a prince of Cyprus, sought to create an ivory statue of the perfect woman he named Galatea. She was so beautiful that Pygmalion fell desperately in love with his own creation. He prayed to the goddess Venus to bring Galatea to life. Venus granted his prayer and the couple lived happily ever after.

That's where the "Pygmalion Effect" originated, but for a better illustration of the "Pygmalion Effect" look at George Bernard Shaw's famous play *My Fair Lady* based on Pygmalion, in which Professor Henry Higgins insists that he can take an uneducated Cockney flower girl named Eliza, and with some intensive training pass her off as a Duchess. The plan works and the flower girl becomes a Duchess in the eyes of all who meet her. Her transformation from flower girl to Duchess is amazing. But her transformation is validated by the other people of royal and regal stature who then seek her out to listen to her, and to enjoy her company.

Now, listen to her commentary on the transformation. *"You see, really and truly, apart from the things anyone can pick up (how to dress, and the proper way of speaking and so on), the difference between a lady and a flower girl is not how she behaves, but how she's treated. I will always be a flower girl to Professor Higgins because he always treats me as a flower girl, and always will, but I know I can be a lady to you because you always treat me as a lady, and always will."*

That's a great insight. But there is more. I believe that we train others how we expect to be treated by them. We bow to a queen, we salute an officer, we kneel to the Pope, we hold the door for the boss, we hold out our arms for a child. Those are conscious signs of deference, respect, or love and acceptance.

A young man will get all puffed up when he sees a pretty girl. The older guy stands up straighter and holds his stomach in when he sees a pretty woman.

When we hold ourselves up to be different, or better than we are, we just *pretend* to be better than we are. And it works—because it shows. The glint in an eye, the tilting of the head, the raising of an eyebrow, the slight flaring of the nostril, the reddening of a blushing cheek. These are obvious clues and people pick up on them. We all live up to our own expectations. And we get to set those expectations.

Set them too low or keep them where they are and nothing will change for you. Set them higher and you will easily grow into them.

ACT AS IF...

Actors are taught to act as if they were the character they are playing. It helps them get into the role. It can help you to become more of anything you want to become.

One of the ways I was taught to solve tough or perplexing problems was to imagine how the person I thought *could* solve that problem *would* solve that problem. Then act as if they had to go about solving that problem. I use several people as unsuspecting role models to emulate when it comes to doing something new, different, frightening or simply something I don't know how to do. Maybe that's where the "What would Jesus do?" craze came from. He would be a great model to follow. I use Ronald Reagan, Ferris Beuller, Yoda and Billy Graham, among others.

Now turn to Step #22 "Making Your Life as Good as It Can Be"
in your *Roadmap to Riches* workbook.

Is Fear Holding You Back?

Now we are going to talk about one of the biggest roadblocks most people face on *The Lazy Man's Way to Riches*. We have already discussed the fact that all it really takes to get what we want out of life is a burning desire and the belief that we can have it. So why don't we have everything now?

It is not that we don't have motivation, and it is not that we don't have the right kind of experience. It is not that we don't have the right basic equipment with which to start. The problem is not what we don't have at all. It is something that we *do* have that gets in our way. And that something is FEAR.

Here is something that helps me get over my fears and makes it easier for me to take the positive actions that conquer my fears. This is a definition of FEAR that I like.

False

Evidence

Appearing

Real

False Evidence Appearing Real. Once I realize that my fear is just **F**alse **E**vidence **A**ppearing **R**eal I can generally move forward to conquer that particular fear.

I am not talking about the kind of fear that keeps us from placing ourselves in danger or risking our lives unnecessarily. There is nothing wrong with being afraid of stepping in front of a speeding car. There is nothing wrong with being afraid if someone is holding a gun on you and robbing you. Fear, in this case, plays a very important role—it is protective. Also it is generally short-lasting.

Once the real danger is gone, the fear usually disappears. There is another kind of fear that is not valuable to us. In fact, it is always destructive to our success and happiness. It does not involve any real danger or life threat. It usually arises in anticipation of something that almost never happens, and this kind of fear can hang around for a long time and be a continuing blight on our lives and happiness.

Suppose you have a great idea. It is an idea for making a lot of money and it has tremendous potential. Suppose that you tell me your idea and I am impressed by it. A week or so later I call you up and say, "I would like you to come over and go through your idea again in front of some friends of mine." Your feeling would probably be "Great, I would like to do that," and you would look forward to it with some anticipation.

People are afraid of the future, of the unknown. If a man faces up to it, and takes the dare of the future, he can have some control over his destiny. That's an exciting idea to me. Better than waiting with everybody else to see whats going to happen.

JOHN H. GLENN, JR.
(b. 1921)
U.S. astronaut, senator

No passion so effectively robs the mind of all its powers of acting and reasoning as fear.

EDMUND BURKE
(1729–1797)
English statesman, orator, writer

So let me assert my firm belief that the only thing we have to fear is fear itself-nameless, unreasoning, unjustified terror which paralyzes needed efforts to convert retreat into advance.

FRANKLIN D. ROOSEVELT
(1882–1945)
32nd President of the United States *First inaugural address, March 4, 1933*

It is hard to fail, but it is worse to have not tried to succeed. In this life we get nothing save by effort.

THEODORE ROOSEVELT
(1858–1919)
26th President of the United States

But suppose I go on and say, "The group of people to whom I want you to explain this is a group of the most successful people in the country. There will be about 200 of them there, and you will be on a stage in front of this group." Now what happens? How do you feel? What changes? All of a sudden it becomes something frightening. "How will I ever impress the most successful people in the country? What have I got to say that they will be interested in? Suppose I goof up?" All kinds of things go through your mind that have nothing to do with the actual situation. But they have everything to do with the kind of fear I am talking about.

WHAT DO YOU FEAR MOST?

I read a national survey some time ago in which people were asked to identify their greatest fears. Believe it or not, the number one answer was fear of speaking in public. Ahead even of the fear of death. More people were afraid of speaking in public than dying. Now I have spoken many times in public and it is neither dangerous nor life threatening so why are people afraid to do it? Why are they so much more afraid of public speaking than of real dangers? They are in the grip of non-essential fears. What are these fears? There are a lot of variations in the area of non-essential fears but there are three that seem to be the most crippling. Starting with the *Fear of Criticism*, this leads to the *Fear of Rejection*, this in turn, leads to the *Fear of Failure*. And these three—Fear of Criticism, Fear of Rejection and Fear of Failure—are the biggest roadblocks that stand in most people's way to success.

ORIGIN OF FEARS?

So where do you get these fears? And if they are so limiting and so destructive to us, why don't you just get rid of them? It all starts when you are young and defenseless. As a baby you do not want much. You are not afraid of anything when you are born, except loud noises and falling.

All you really need is to be held fairly often, to be fed and changed, and basically left on your own to sleep and just "be" the rest of the time. But as you begin to grow up, life begins to make demands on us and in the process of meeting those demands you sometimes make mistakes. You encounter the anger or disapproval of your parents, who are extremely important to us, which results in a feeling of rejection—and it hurts. You begin to experience pain. You believe that when things go wrong, it is your fault—that there is something wrong with us. Now that is a very painful feeling to a child.

Because you are criticized for making mistakes and feel the pain of rejection, you grow up with the false idea that making mistakes is failing. And because failing is the biggest mistake of all, what do you do if you feel there is any risk of failure? You don't try. And what happens when you don't try? Then you fail absolutely. That really puts us into a trap, doesn't it? You're damned if you do, and damned if you don't. To escape the criticism of others for trying and failing, you procrastinate and don't try at all which opens up to self-criticism. That is the worst kind; because there is no way you can escape that.

FEAR CONDITIONING

Although few people ever realize it, fear plays an overwhelmingly important role in the early-child conditioning. Since you have that early conditioning to thank for our later Inadequate Self-Image (ISI), it is important that you understand two unique qualities of fear as a conditioning factor:

1. Fear is always a "hindering" force.

2. Fear is generally a "buried" force.

Let me illustrate those two qualities by two specific examples of fear-conditioning.

Praise for a job well done, as in the case of the wise father with the child who wants to participate in the workshop project, is a "helping" force. It is positive in nature; it is a happily remembered experience. Praise is something to be sought after. You want to repeat the pleasure of the feeling of being praised so you try again and again to do something that earns more praise.

What of the other side of the coin—the rejection or punishment unwisely meted out? It is designed to be and operates as a "hindering force." It is negative in nature. It creates fear. It creates fear of the painful experience being repeated; and, since it is unpleasant to remember, it is shut out of the conscious mind as soon as possible. Notice I said the "conscious" mind; for with the strong impact of fear, *it is not lost entirely*. It plays its conditioning role long after the conscious remembrance is gone. It is suppressed and slips down into the subconscious mind.

So, we have fear, which hinders us in years to come, but which is *hidden* from our conscious thoughts.

To observe this in action, let us assume that some years after the child had been rewarded or reprimanded (perhaps on several occasions) in the manner outlined, a new situation arises.

The father calls his son and announces the time has come to "learn how to handle tools." Father anticipates great joy on the part of his son at this announcement. He is looking forward to the fun he and his son will have working together in the wood shop. But such will not be the case.

The son does not *remember* the things that happened so long ago when he was young, but he feels uneasy. He has been conditioned to fear the woodworking, or anything in connection with it. Is it surprising that the son probably won't be very excited about the idea, will have trouble trying to do what his father asks, will be prone to fail when he tries (thus releasing him from having to continue)?

Some prime examples of the kind of deliberate remarks that become conditioning for the very young carry in their own terms the fear-factor they will create.

> "You're stupid."

> "You never do anything right."

> "You're always so clumsy."

> "You'll never learn anything."

> "You'll never be as (smart, nice, good etc.,) as your (brother, sister)."

> "I know you're always lying, I'll never believe you."

When we add to this the number of unintentional conditionings that come about accidentally (through spilling things, breaking objects, saying the wrong thing,

Feelings of inferiority and superiority are the same. They both come from fear.

ROBERT ANTHONY, Ph.D.
American psychologist and writer

various other childhood mistakes) it is not surprising that many, many fears of failure have found a permanent home deep in our subconscious minds. All of these fears help shape our view of ourselves. And so fear is largely responsible for our ISI.

Why is the conditioning of the early years so effective in shaping today's image and even activities of an adult? Because the subconscious levels of the mind, while powerful, are non-critical. What is fed into them is all accepted as fact without any regard to logic or later learning.

NEW CONDITIONING

To alter conditioning of this sort, you must bring new conditioning to bear. It does not matter that we know *today* that a failure at the age of four does not decree similar failures as an adult. The conscious mind uses logic, the unconscious does not.

The best way to understand this is to think of dreams you have had in the past in which impossibilities seemed quite reasonable while you were asleep. "I was flying through space," "I was in this house, but it became a boat," "I fell off the cliff but I just floated to the ground."

None of these things seem unreasonable while we are sleeping, but awake we would recognize them immediately as impossibilities.

They are accepted while asleep because the lower level of consciousness has no critical judgment or logic. This means that all those fears you have suppressed to the below-consciousness level stay there unchallenged by reality as you have grown and matured in your conscious mind.

The fears and repressed impressions of your childhood years, based on the most childish lack of understanding, often rule your activities today!

You can give yourself *new conditioning* thru Dyna/Psyc to replace that faulty old conditioning that is blocking your way to success.

That conditioning permits *you* to both be a more adequate person and also to see yourself as more adequate. These two things accomplished, you are a success!

For realizing to the maximum your true potential, instead of limiting yourself to the ISI view of your potential, will make all the difference in the world.

THE CHAIN OF FEAR—A DEAD END

How do you get rid of the fears that are so destructive to your life? How do you avoid hanging on to the dead-end of the chain of fear? The answer is really quite simple: You have to take control of the chain by becoming aware of it and how it is formed. This is not to say that you can wave a magic wand and banish fear forever; but understanding where the chain starts—with criticism—and how the next links are formed, you can take steps to stop forging those links.

REDEFINE REJECTION

The first linkage in the chain of self-limiting fears you can break is the idea that criticism necessarily means rejection and there is something wrong with you. Again, nothing could be further from the truth. Most of the time criticism from others really comes from one of two things. They may be feeling self-critical and vulnerable and criticize you before you have a chance to criticize them. Or maybe they are angry about something and criticism is simply their way of venting that anger. In either case, the problem is theirs, not yours, and that is important to realize. When someone criticizes you, remember, their criticism is probably an expression of their own insecurity and doubt or of their own anger, which is not necessarily directed at you. You just happen to be there at the time, and if it weren't you it would be someone else experiencing their anger and frustration.

REDEFINE FAILURE

Second, you can break the chain by taking a good look at what it means to try and fail—to understand it intellectually. What is failure? Most of us have the idea that failure is a sin. Our schools tend to reinforce the idea. We study the final results of people's lives and don't look at their early mistakes. We look at Leonardo Da Vinci or Michelangelo's masterpieces and not at their initial attempts. We don't look at the poems that did not work for Keats and Shelley, only the masterpieces that survive. Their first efforts wound up in their wastebaskets. We get the impression that these people were somehow born with a mature talent, fully developed skills, never made mistakes, and that everything they did was perfect. Nothing could be further from the truth.

I'll bet their wastebaskets were as overflowing as yours and mine are. Every great artist, every great scientist, and every businessman made thousands of mistakes before they made the masterpieces that we study and admire.

Thomas Edison is a great example. He tried thousands of different ways to make the light bulb work. And once when an interviewer asked him how he could continue to go on after thousands of failures, Edison replied, "I haven't failed thousands of times. I succeeded in finding thousands of ways that the process won't work." That's how you have to learn to regard failure, as attempts, that just didn't work—*or as another way to define experience!*

Failure is nothing more than a successful way of finding out how a process won't work. If you try, make a mistake, and then analyze why you made the mistake, and through that analysis find out how the process really works, you will have learned a great deal! There is no shame in failing. Failing is a necessary part of growth and development. If you have never made a mistake it means you have not really tried anything new—that is the biggest failure of all. You see, the only real failure occurs when you stop trying.

BUT YET ANOTHER FEAR

Now that we have looked at the fear of failure, lets take a look at the opposite side of the coin—the fear of success. How can success be something you are afraid of? Easy, you have been programmed that way and you may be reinforcing that bad programming everyday. Most often it is the fear of success that is the cause of our failures rather than tangible reasons. You can see abundance all around you. It's there for you to enjoy. You can even understand the ideas necessary to claim your share of that abundance and still not make a move to get it, if you don't understand how to root out this fear.

One of the keys to overcoming the Fear of Success is what I call "Just Consequences." In this world there are no rewards or punishments. There are Just Consequences. And just means both only and fair. If you believe in a Creator who

Everything we say about other people is really about ourselves.

MERRITT MALLOY
American poetess

Never confuse a single defeat with a final defeat.

F. SCOTT FITZGERALD
(1896–1940)
American novelist and short-story writer

Experience is the name so many people give to their mistakes.

OSCAR WILDE
(1854–1900)
Irish-born English poet, playwright, novelist

Failure is only an event in your life—not a life.

ANONYMOUS

We fear the thing we want the most.

ROBERT ANTHONY Ph.D.
American psychologist, writer

is responsible for all life, as you believe that our Creator gave us free will, which is a fundamental belief in every major religion, if you believe that our Creator is just and fair, then it's essential to accept the principle of "Just Consequences." Does it seem reasonable that our Creator would give us free will and then slap us down if we did not make the right choices? I am not talking about the after life. I am talking about the here and now. I believe God does not reward or punish us for our choices. With God's blessing we can make any choice we want and then live with the consequences of our decisions. That is what our lives are—the total of all the consequences of all the decisions we have made.

LEARN TO ENJOY

I also believe that our Creator intended us to enjoy the fruits of his creation—not to suffer in this life in hopes of reward in heaven later on. I realize I may step on some toes with this concept, but this is important to your progress down The Lazy Man's Way. Some religions teach that the requirement for heaven is suffering and pain in this life. You may likely have picked up some of that kind of teaching at least down in your subconscious.

How many times have you heard expressions like "Poor, but happy," or "Poor little rich kid?" How many times have you seen news stories about some rich person or family that suffered some kind of loss or catastrophe and thought to yourself, "I wouldn't want to be in their shoes for any amount of money?" Sure, there are rich people who suffer, and you read about them because it makes a good story.

But there are a lot more wealthy people who are very happy. They raise families of wholesome kids, who contribute significantly to our society, and about whom you don't read because there is no news value in their lives. Every one of the tales you have heard about the sufferings of the rich or successful people is a roadblock, a speed bump, on your way to Riches.

Whatever the source of your beliefs, most of us have been taught to fear success or distrust it. Haven't you heard expressions like, "You have to pay your dues," or "Sure you can be rich if you want to do nothing but work all the time," or "I would rather have health than wealth." As if you can't have both!

These statements create an attitude of fearing success and if you have that sort of attitude, you have a mighty big roadblock to get past. It is difficult to sustain the effort required to change your course in life if you are afraid you will lose something of value along he way.

There's no doubt that you have to pay a price for your success, but the essential truth of The Lazy Man's way is that you actually learn to enjoy that price while you are paying for it. You don't make sacrifices. Besides, it is also a fact of life that you pay a price for failure as well. The difference is you never learn to enjoy the price of failure and you never stop paying for it.

THE PROCRASTINATION HABIT

We have discussed how the three big fears lead to the habit of procrastination—a big problem in anyone's life. There is no question that putting off until tomorrow things that could be done today is one of the most serious obstacles you encounter on your journey through life.

Living courageously is taking action in the presence of fear, making a conscious growth choice rather than a fear choice. Part of the fears that produce this habit lie buried in your subconscious. To get at them on that level, you will need the Power of Super Suggestion, which is available to review in Chapter 9, as well as other simple tools you can start using right now that will begin to break the procrastination habit.

As in all changes of habit, you need to be reminded that you are changing that habit. First, make a positive statement about the attitude you are trying to develop. Step 23 of your Roadmap Guidebook has a note for you to put up in a prominent place. Someplace where you will see it often during the day to remind you that you are becoming a different person, and that you are doing things differently. Each time you see this sign take the time to read it. Plant it deeply in your mind and think about what it means.

The note is very simple. It contains three words "Do It Now" and it applies to any situation or problem that you meet that needs resolution. Remember, each time you read the words "Do It Now," that good judgment is the result of experience—of learning from your mistakes. So accept mistakes as a necessary part of your development.

Men never plan to be failures; they simply fail to plan to be successful.

WILLIAM A. WARD
(1812—1882)
English theologian, writer editor

One of these days is none of these days.

ENGLISH PROVERB

Now turn to Step #23 "Is Fear Holding You Back?"
in your *Roadmap to Riches* workbook.

24

Eliminate the Negative

Y ou can use the material in this book to get everything you really want out of life. The only thing that's in your way is you: The old you; the old habits; the old attitudes.

The reason it's so hard to be free of these negative forces is that they're *comfortable*. You've had them a long time. You've grown used to them. You've accepted them.

You've brainwashed yourself, or more likely, someone—your parents, your friends, your teachers, and your boss—has done it for you. They meant well. They wanted you to be "happy," and their notion of happiness is that you should be satisfied with things as they are.

You accepted their definition of "happiness" because you wanted to please them. Well, I want you to be unhappy. Or more to the point, I want you to be *creatively unhappy*. I don't want you to accept things as they "are." I want you to make life what it can and *should* be for you.

How will you do that? By letting Dyna/Psyc take over your life! Right now. This minute. If you say you "will" do it, you've postponed making a decision until some future date. Now is the time to act, because today is the first day of the rest of your life.

Don't waste time looking back, savoring old regrets, cherishing old mistakes, crying over lost opportunities.

When Eleanor Roosevelt was asked how she had so much energy for so many different projects, she replied, "Because I never waste time looking back."

Let's say that you had your choice of two routes to take you to work. Both were the same distance and took you the same time; one route was along a tree-lined freeway with little traffic, and the other route was ugly, choked with traffic, bristling with stop signs—and ran right alongside a garbage dump. Which one would you take?

The first one, of course! Then why, as we go through life, do most of us take the second route—inhaling deeply as we pass yesterday's garbage, bringing the stink of yesterday's waste into today?

The answer? We don't know that there's another, more pleasant route to get where we're going. It doesn't take the same amount of time—it's faster! And the destination can be the one you choose—not the one you thought you had to accept.

> Knowledge of what is possible is the beginning of happiness.
>
> GEORGE SANTAYANA
> (1863–1952)
> Spanish-born American philosopher, poet, novelist, critic

Give me where to stand, and I will move the Earth.

ARCHIMEDES (287-212 BC)
Syracusan mathematician, astronomer, Inventor

Don't tell me you "can't." What you really mean is you "won't." And that's not you talking—It's that Inadequate Self-Image—your ISI.

Let me show you, once again, how ISI works:

A number of years ago I handled the advertising for a Ford agency. One day, when the manager was making out the salesmen's paychecks, he commented on something that, at first, seemed unbelievable. He noted that each and every salesman earned just about the same amount each month as he had made the month before. If there was a monthly variance, the salesman would almost always earn, within a few percentage points, during the current year what he had earned the year before.

I checked into it further and found that there was an even, stranger "coincidence." The Ford agency divided its sales-month into three 10-day periods. About 50 percent of the salesmen plugged along each day and ended up with the commission check they expected to make. Another 25 percent made enough sales during the first 10 days to provide what they anticipated as their monthly income and never made another sale.

Oh, they showed up for work all right and went through the motions; but nothing ever clicked. If you asked them what had happened, they would have told you it was "bad luck" or someone else was getting all the "buyers." The last 25 percent made little or no sales until the last 10 days of the month. Then suddenly, during those final 10 days, these salesmen got "hot."

The fact is, regardless of the pattern of sales, each salesperson made what they expected to make. Not what they wished they could make or would like to make (and really didn't think was possible)—but what they expected to make. Without exception, people got what they really wanted!

LET ME GIVE YOU ANOTHER EXAMPLE. Another advertising account of mine was a real estate firm. They were expanding and wanted to attract some new, top-flight salesmen. So they placed an ad that stated, truthfully, that people who were willing to come to work for them could earn $100,000 a year. The ad laid an egg. So they changed one word and had so many responses that they could pick the cream of the crop.

The word, or rather the figure, they changed was "$100,000." They made it "$40,000."

And now that you know a little bit about ISI, you can see why, the first ad failed and the second ad was successful. Very few people can imagine what it would be like to earn $100,000 a year, or more important, truly believe that they're worth that much, so they didn't even bother answering or investigating the "impossible" (for them) ad.

That's why the prettiest girls spend a lot of lonely nights; most of the boys think they're "unattainable."

And here's the payoff on my true story about the real estate firm. Many of the people who couldn't imagine themselves making $100,000 a year wound up making that much and more because the real estate firm had a training program to raise their ISI!

I mentioned that the real estate firm "picked the cream of the crop," They did—but the standards were not age, education, or experience. They picked those people who were willing to change, to accept the "possibility" that life could be a lot better.

Once you've picked your destination, Dyna/Psyc is the vehicle capable of taking you there swiftly and pleasurably, it requires only routine maintenance and that you do not cripple its performance with an ISI governor.

You don't have to understand the principle of internal combustion to drive a car, but you do have to turn on the key. I've given you the key, It's called Dyna/Psyc. Use it.

ACCENTUATE THE POSITIVE

I talk a lot about money. That's because it's an easy way to measure "success." As Pearl Bailey said, "I've been rich and I've been poor, but rich is better."

Not that money solves all problems. Some of the most miserable people I've known have been millionaires. They were miserable because they thought that money would make them happy. But they weren't miserable because they were rich. If they lost their money, they'd just be poor and miserable.

That's why it's important that you let Dyna/Psyc change all of your life, let it make you the kind of person you want to be and can be.

You can be a loving, forgiving, and generous person. (In fact, you can be one heck of a nice person to be around.) You can be an understanding but firm parent. You can be a true friend. You can be a trustworthy, hard-working, and loyal employee. (And if you can't, fire yourself and get another job. You'll be doing the boss and you—especially you—a big favor.) You can be a good neighbor.

You can be anything you really want to be.

And as you change, so will the people around you. Remember that if you want to teach someone to love, give them affection. If you want them to have confidence, give them encouragement. If you want them to be truthful, tell the truth. If you want them to be generous, share. If you want them to be patient, be tolerant. If you want them to be happy, give them understanding.

You can't affirm for other people. You can—and must—affirm how you respond to them. If you allow someone to "bug" you, it's your problem. You may not be able to change how they act, but you can change how you *react*.

Remember Dr. Eric Berne's *The Games People Play*? You'll be surprised at how often people stop throwing the ball to you, if you never make an effort to catch it.

Finally, accept yourself as an imperfect, fallible human being—not that you ever stop trying to improve; but you recognize that you'll probably never quite attain 100 percent in all of your zones.

When you realize—and truly accept—that you're imperfect, isn't it easier to accept and understand other people's imperfections?

To illustrate, I'd like to tell you about a friend of mine in Los Angeles.

Late one night, he received a phone call that his son was confined in a mental health clinic in San Francisco. The boy, about 19 years old, had made an unsuccessful

I don't like money actually, but it quiets my nerves!

JOE LOUIS
(1914–1981)
American boxer

Do what you can, with what you have, where you are.

THEODORE ROOSEVELT
(1858–1919)
26th President of the United States

Learn what you are and be such.

PONDAR
(522–438 BC)
Greek poet

attempt at suicide. The psychiatrist on the phone reassured the father that his son was in no physical danger but suggested that a personal interview with the father might be helpful. Could he fly to San Francisco?

When the father arrived the next day, in the late afternoon, the son was angry because the father had "taken so long." He demonstrated his anger by refusing to speak to his father.

When the psychiatrist had them both in his office, he asked the boy why he was giving his father "the silent treatment." The boy told him.

"I see," said the psychiatrist. "So you've made up your mind as to what your father should have done. And you won't settle for any less. You think that a good father—a 100 percent father—would have taken an earlier plane. So you're discounting him for every hour he was late, by your standards."

"Well, the fact is that he is here. So he must care at least a *little*. Maybe 10 percent? Are you saying that, if you can't have a 100 percent father, you won't take any less?"

My friend told me later: "I flew up to San Francisco filled with guilt and anger. 'How had I failed my son? How could he do this to me?' But the psychiatrist's question started me thinking. 'Maybe I have been a 10 percent father. And he's been a 10 percent son.' O.K. I'll try to do better. But starting right now, I'd better accept his 10 percent instead of rejecting all of him because he hasn't entirely lived up to the standards I've set for him." It was the start of an understanding between father and son.

People like people who like them. After all, anyone who has such good taste must have other redeeming qualities. And people reward the people they like with favors, love, promotions, business—everything. But they can't like you unless you like you —and them. I'm talking about your genuinely admiring that percentage of the whole person—in yourself and others—that you find likeable.

The amazing thing is that, as you reprogram your life through Dyna/Psyc, you'll find that everything else literally falls into place. One day, very soon, something you are affirming—something you thought was "impossible"—will happen. You will have made it happen.

You are indeed the cause of all your effects.

All things are possible until they are proved impossible—and even the impossible may only be so, as of now.

PEARL S. BUCK
(1892–1973)
American novelist and humanitarian

Now turn to Step #24 "Eliminate the Negative"
in your *Roadmap to Riches* workbook.

25
Balancing Your Life—What a Concept

At the beginning of our journey together I was telling you what this program was all about. I mentioned that there were three basic questions we were going to ask that are fundamental to all existence, ask yourself the following:

1. Who am I?

2. Where am I going?

3. How do I plan to get there?

Most of what you have done up to now has been working on the question "Who am I?" And you still haven't quite finished answering that question. I'll cover some important parts of the answer to that question in later chapters, but right now I want to talk about exactly where you want to go. Before you answer that question, let's examine the limits of your potential. Of what are you really capable? If you really don't see yourself as successful at this point, you may have a limited view of your capabilities. Let me tell you about some people who started out with several strikes against them and still became exceptional human beings and achieved tremendous things in life.

EINSTEIN—GREAT SCIENTIST

We have all heard of Albert Einstein, Ph.D. discoverer of the Theory of Relativity. He was awarded the Nobel prize in mathematics in 1921 and the Royal Society Copley Medal in 1925. The advances in mathematics and physics that Einstein made will affect human lives for generations to come; yet Einstein was a notoriously poor student. Teachers could not communicate with him. He had difficulty in getting his ideas across, and he nearly flunked the eighth grade.

LINCOLN—GREAT PRESIDENT

Another name you will recognize is Abraham Lincoln. Lincoln is almost universally recognized as one of the greatest American presidents. Still he lost more elections than he won and at one point in his life suffered a complete nervous breakdown. Mr. Lincoln had a notoriously bad track record in business and politics that would have stopped the average man from trying for the presidency. And we all know where he started—in a humble cabin reading by candlelight, going barefoot. If Lincoln could rise from that, to the presidency of the United States of America and become one of its greatest leaders of all time, what are you capable of accomplishing in your life? (More about Lincoln in the Guidebook)

> Never look down to test the ground before taking your next step; only he who keeps his eye fixed on the far horizon will find his right road.
>
> DAG HAMMARSKJOLD
> (1953–1961)
> Swedish statesman,
> U.N. secretary general
> (1953–1961)

> Some men succeed because they are destined to, but most men because they are determined to.
>
> ANONYMOUS

> Few great men could pass personnel.
>
> PAUL GOODMAN
> (1911–1972)
> American writer, educator, psychoanalyst

Nothing great will ever be achieved without great men, and men are great only if they are determined to be so.

CHARLES DE GAULLE
(1890–1970)
French general and statesman, president of the 5th Republic of France (1958–1969)

God gives the nuts, but he does not crack them.

GERMAN PROVERB

It is not easy to find happiness in ourselves and it is not possible to find it elsewhere.

AGNES REPPLIER
(1858–1950)
American essayist

Our duty as men is to proceed as if limits to our ability did not exist.

PIERRE TEILHARD DE CHARDIN
(1881–1955)
French Clergyman, philosopher, paleontologist

ROCKEFELLER—RESPECTED NATIONAL LEADER

Let's look at another person, one of whom you may have a more recent memory, Nelson Rockefeller. When Rockefeller was a child he was classified as "learning disabled." Now I suspect that if the Rockefeller family had less money he probably would have been called "dumb." But Nelson Rockefeller overcame that learning problem to become a respected national leader. So if you had people call you "dumb" in your life, you are in good company. Perhaps learning did not come easily to you. Your grades in school may have reflected indifference or a mental block, which kept you from being a super achiever. That does not need to hold you back now!

EMERSON—GREAT THINKER

One hundred and seventy years ago the great thinker, Ralph Waldo Emerson, wrote that there is nothing capricious in nature. Nature will not plant a burning desire in your mind if you do not have the innate capability to achieve that desire. Whatever you truly and sincerely want out of life, you can have because it is within your reach. *You do, however, have to reach out for it!*

If I asked you to name the happiest person you know, who would you name? If you did not respond with "Me"—why not? Why are you not the happiest person you know? If you are not, a lot of reasons come to mind. Stop and think for a minute. How can you measure someone else's happiness? Don't we usually measure someone's happiness relative to ours by the things they seem to have that we don't—good or bad. How can you possibly know what their life is really like? How can you appreciate someone else's problems? If you put someone else's name down, it is an indication that you think you could be happier. Even if you put your own name down as the happiest person you know, certainly you will accept the idea that life can be better for you. You wouldn't be reading this book if you didn't.

AND YOU—????

Well, how can you be happier? The key to happiness lies in understanding two concepts. One is the *need for balance in all areas of your life*. And the other is the *need for continuing expansion in those areas*. What do I mean by the areas of your life? What are they? All of us have certain basic needs in many areas. You probably responded to this book because you felt a need in the financial area of your life. But that is only one of many areas as we discovered when we did Step 6 and dealt with the seven basic areas of life: Financial, Mental, Emotional, Social, Vocational, Physical and Spiritual. Let's look at these areas more fully at this time.

The **Financial** area is obvious. We all have needs here. Strangely some people will deny those needs and live in poverty and for some this is possible. For some people it is possible to become a hermit and live away from society. But most of us have basic financial needs. We need to feed and clothe and to shelter our families and ourselves. That takes money.

What is the **Mental** area of our life? Our needs in this area are our needs for stimulation and growth, for challenge to make our mind work and keep it active. All of us benefit from the stimulation and challenge of developing our character and our skills as we continue to grow.

The **Emotional** area is of prime concern for most of us. It is the area in our life that determines how we feel inside about ourselves. And because this feeling dictates how we make most of our decisions, it is extremely important to be "whole" in this area.

The **Social** area. This is about your relationship to your fellow man, your communications with him and his communication with you, your mutual support and cooperative progress toward understanding one another and achieving harmony. Most of us feel that our family is the most important part of the social area of our lives, so growth here is paramount. Too often I've heard people say, "If only..." as regards to a departed loved one. Have the relationship you want now.

The **Vocational** area. As I said earlier, we are ultimately our own boss, so if your career isn't all you want it to be, do what any good boss would do for an employee who needs help—get it for them! Coaches, mentors, tutors, additional education, retraining—whatever it takes for your vocational growth and prosperity.

The **Physical** area of our life is obvious. It is our physical health and fitness, our bodies, our sense of well-being, our energy level, how we feel. With a healthy body everything else seems more easily obtainable.

Finally, there is the **Spiritual** area of our lives. Our need to understand our spiritual mission in life, our relationship with our God, and our place in the universe.

I feel it's vital to realize the importance of *balance* in all of these areas. It makes no more sense to deny your spiritual needs than it does to deny your financial needs. They exist. And if you do not put some effort into this area, your life will be out of balance no matter how financially successful you are and you will miss out on a lot of the Riches that life has to offer. In fact our experiences have shown, when the spiritual area of your life expands, the other areas seem to develop and balance out much more easily.

It is indeed from the experience of beauty and happiness from the occasional harmony between our nature and our environment, that we draw our conception of the divine life.

GEORGE SANTAYANA (1863–1952) Spanish born American philosopher, poet, novelist, critic

---

**Now turn to Step #25 "Balancing Your Life—What a Concept"
in your *Roadmap to Riches* workbook.**

26

Who's Drawing Your Reality Map?

L et's go on to an examination as to why fears have such a hold on us. The reason is the way you actually think and act. When we observe something, we go through a process that virtually involves our entire mind and experience, but we do it so fast that it is usually completed before we are aware of the process. It works in four steps: We see something, we compare it with all the information we have stored in our brain, we make a decision based on this stored information and then we act on that decision. SEE, COMPARE, DECIDE, ACT.

In a sense it is kind of like using a road map. Suppose you wanted to visit our office. You have a map of the area with some intersections marked and the directions you should turn. When you see an intersection coming up, you compare it with your map and decide which way to go and then act on your decision. All of our stored information is kind of like that road map. It is our whole concept of reality: The whole ball of wax; what we think of everything in the universe including ourselves. It is our map of the world, our reality map, and like any map that you have ever seen, it is inaccurate and incomplete. "What's that?" you may say. "Everything I do in life is based on this reality map that I have, and you tell me it is inaccurate and incomplete? How can I ever expect to get anywhere?" Relax. Joe Karbo's map was just as inaccurate and incomplete as yours and it didn't keep him from getting where he wanted to go.

The *key* is to know when your map is accurate and when it isn't, and how to clean it up in the critical areas. For example, when that pike I told you about bumped his nose against the glass wall enough times, his reality map contained a road block that permanently prevented him from getting to the minnows.

Now as long as those glass walls were there, the pike's reality map was accurate. He saw the minnows and he associated it with the pain of his bumped nose. He knew he could not get to them. But the instant the glass walls were removed, the pike's reality map became tragically inaccurate. Like that pike, you have locked into your reality maps certain obstacles and roadblocks—detours that are no longer there. When you think about how your reality map was drawn, it's amazing that it works at all.

As we talked about earlier, as far as we can determine, a baby comes into this world basically neutral. He or she has certain physical needs and some emotional needs, but there are no real fixed attitudes about the world that the child has entered —good or bad. If you liken the baby's mind to a balance scale, it starts off perfectly balanced. As you develop from infancy and encounter a concept or a new idea you do not know quite where to put it on the scale.

The great thing in this world is not so much where we stand, as in what direction we are moving.

OLIVER WENDELL HOLMES SR. (1809–1894) American physician, processor, man of letters

How do you form your attitudes? Well, when you first encounter a new concept or experience you tend to rely on the reactions of other people. Here's a simple example:

SPINACH—YUK! Let's go back to your childhood, say around age six or seven. Suppose you have never had spinach or have never been aware that what you were eating was spinach. You're out playing with some friends and one friend says, "Hey, wanna eat over at my house tonight?" Then the friend adds, "Uh oh, maybe you better wait until tomorrow night. Tonight we're having, yuk, spinach."

Now what has happened? Your friends have given you their value judgment with respect to spinach. You had no previous experience with this thing, so you make a decision based on your friend's judgment and your assessment of your friend's credibility as to whether spinach is a good or bad thing. You put some sort of weight on either the positive or the negative side of the balance.

Let's say your friend previously told you that ice cream was good and you tested that out and found that the friend was right—it was good. You probably respect that person's judgment in the area of food and so you slightly tip your scale in the direction of thinking the spinach is not such a hot idea.

Now let's suppose that your next experience with spinach some days later when your mother serves it. You see this green stuff on your plate and you say "What's that green stuff, mom?" And your mother says, "That's spinach." So you say, "I don't think I want it." And your father, who has had a trying day, says, "What do you mean you don't want any. You eat your spinach or I will smack you one."

Now something very important has happened. Spinach has been associated with something very negative. A heavy weight comes down on the negative side. Even though you have never tasted it, you already know it is something that has caused you stress. That is the way most of our attitudes are formed. You encounter something and make a decision as to which side of the scale the rock goes on. It's a turning point.

Once you have made a decision, positive or negative, the next piece of information relating to the same subject is going to be evaluated and influenced greatly in *respect to the first decision.* And if the experience has been a strong emotional one, it will further reinforce biases that influence the forming of this belief, as in the case of the desirability of spinach.

Your friend's assessment of spinach was probably not that important; but when your father threatened you with a spanking if you didn't eat your spinach, it had a lot of emotional impact behind it which caused the weight that you put on the negative side to be much heavier.

The impact that emotion plays on forming your reality structure is really critical. The stronger the emotion, the heavier the judgment you will develop as a result of the incidence. And the stronger the emotion, the more likely it is that it came from irrational behavior. Here is an example of how this can happen.

REMEMBER YOUR REPORT CARD?

Suppose as a child you bring home a report card and your parents are sitting there assessing it. They say, "Hmm, you got a 'B' in arithmetic, that's OK; 'A' minus

> What you think of me is none of my business.
>
> TERRY COLE-WHITTAKER
> (b. 1939)
> American evangelist, author

in English, that's fine. You got 'D' in science. What's the matter with you?" And suddenly there is big issue.

Here is an area where strong emotional impact can be made. Now whatever your reasons for getting a 'D' in science, it is probably not the result of any incompetence in that area. Perhaps you felt bad on the day of the test. Maybe you misunderstood a concept that later you would have been able to grasp.

Or perhaps you simply have difficulty with that particular teacher. But once your parent comes down on you for your inability in science, the result is a very negative feeling toward the concept of science. You may even accept the irrational conclusion that, "I'm just not good in science." And there's another turning point.

When you feel negative about something it is hard to like it and pay attention to it. So, you find it much more difficult to study which in turn makes your grade worse and so on down the line. So the initial impact of an incident augmented by emotion can add up to a very strong negative bias and a very false impression of your true capability.

The other area where you have to be careful is that part of your reality structure that is formed by things that you vividly imagine. One of the worst villains in this area is the so called comedies that we see in the movies or on television. Have you ever noticed how much comedy is derived from putting someone down or making someone look ridiculous?

Now, I'm not against humor. Laughter is one of our greatest blessings and I do not think any of us should take ourselves too seriously. You need to guard yourself against a lot of garbage that is thrown at you. That is really the role of your conscious mind, to filter out our experiences. When you relax, such as when you are watching TV or a movie or reading a book, you tend to let your guard down. Your imagination becomes involved in what you are seeing, and you start adding these impressions to your reality map without really thinking about what you are doing.

EVALUATING YOUR ROAD MAP

Evaluating the road map you have created may be one of the most challenging things to do as you walk The Lazy Man's Way. Seeing if it is as true and accurate as you think it is will take some examination. Is it a true representation of who you are and can be? Comparing one's mental roadmap, based in fact on how one imagines himself, with one's actual personality and capabilities will reveal the areas of distortion in one's reality road map.

HOW DO YOU PICTURE YOURSELF?

I call the pictures of ourselves that are stored in your reality map, your self-images. Actually your reality map has three pictures of you: You as you see yourself, you as you want other people to see you, and the real you. And the real you most likely is someone you hardly know is there.

The real you probably has capabilities far beyond even the picture of yourself you try to present to others. Unfortunately, the real you is the picture you usually believe in the least. Like everything else in your reality structure, your pictures of yourself create feelings in you. These feelings about yourself create your self-esteem.

I grew up to have my father's looks, my father's speech patterns, my father's posture, my father's walk, my father's opinions, and my mother's contempt for my father.

JULES FEIFFER (b.1929)
American cartoonist

What you think of me is none of my business.

TERRY COLE-WHITTAKER
(b. 1939)
American evangelist,
author

You've no idea what a poor opinion I have of myself—and how little I deserve it.

W. S. GILBERT
(1836–1911)
English dramatist, librettist, writer

Now you have come to a very important step in the *Roadmap to Riches*. This is where you really examine your self-esteem and self-images, and start locating some of the biggest inaccuracies in your pictures of yourself. Step 26 in your Guidebook is a questionnaire that will help you find out where you are really short-changing yourself.

Complete the questionnaire and follow the directions on the next page in your Guidebook for scoring your answers. We will then talk about your results and see what you can do about them.

Now turn to Step #26 "Who's Drawing Your Reality Map?"
in your *Roadmap to Riches* workbook.

The Cycle of Destruction

If your experience with your self-esteem questionnaire was the same as mine when I went through it, you might be feeling pretty low about yourself about now. One of the toughest things in the world is to look at yourself and see what is really there.

The questionnaire you just went through doesn't do that. What it does, is show you what you *think* is there. What you have to do is get to what is really there. If your score was low, don't let that worry you. After all, this questionnaire is only one person's idea of what high self-esteem really means. Also if your self-esteem score is low, it doesn't mean you are doomed to failure. All it really means is that you need to do some extra work. You can make best use of this questionnaire in a very important way.

As you went through the scoring you probably noticed that certain things indicated high self-esteem while others indicated low self-esteem. Go back and look at the questions in which you show low self-esteem and ask yourself why the question and your answer are important. Why does this indicate that you don't think as highly of yourself as you might? Make a decision as to whether or not you want to change yourself in that area. For example, if you put down on the questionnaire that you are constantly sensitive to other people's opinions about you, you may feel that this is a virtue. This can be a desirable characteristic but the degree to which you are sensitive to other people is also very important.

Some people are so sensitive to other people's feelings that they give no thought to their own. They worry constantly about what others will think and are never able to take care of their own needs. As a result they live inhibited and bitter lives. You have to make a decision. You can be considerate of other people's feelings, but at the same time you must recognize that you have a right to your own feelings. In Step 26, of your workbook "Who's Drawing My Reality Map," true answers to the odd-numbered statements reflect high self-esteem. True answers on the even-numbered statements show low self-esteem.

As we go on, and particularly as you begin to practice utilizing Super Suggestion, you are going to develop some specific tools that help you raise your self-esteem and self-images in a hurry. The tools that will help you release those false and limiting pictures of what you are really capable. Tools that build in your feelings of confidence and self-appreciation of what you really can do. The reason your self-images and self-esteem are so critical to your development and growth along The Lazy Man's Way is because of a basic self-defeating cycle that all of us get trapped in at one time or another.

It is easy to live for others; everybody does. I call on you to live for yourselves.

RALPH WALDO EMERSON
(1803–1882)
American poet, essayist, philosopher

In Step 27 of your Guidebook, there is a drawing that indicates a very basic human process. When you encounter a new situation, one that challenges you to take some action, to grow and develop as a human being, you create in your own mind an expectation as to how well you will handle this challenge. This is all looked upon as previous experience by your self-image and self-esteem. On a conscious level, you may anticipate success; but your self-images and self-esteem will subconsciously determine an expectation that is lower than what you state you would like to achieve.

EXPECTATIONS DETERMINE PERFORMANCE

Now the interesting thing about your expectations is they absolutely determine your performance. If you wish to accomplish something, and your expectation is below what you would like to achieve, your performance will also be below that which is necessary to achieve the results you wish. And what happens then? You evaluate your performance. You sit in judgment of yourself not based on your expectations but rather on what you wanted to achieve.

The net result is that you did not live up to what you really wanted to do, so you put yourself down. You become critical of yourself. This self-criticism lowers your self-esteem and self-images and the cycle begins again.

YOUR TOUGHEST CRITIC—YOU

How often do you praise yourself for something you have done and accomplished, as opposed to the number of times you put yourself down for not really measuring up to what you wanted to achieve? That is the real key as to how the self-defeating self-image cycle works. When you evaluate your performance you rarely praise yourself. Usually you cut yourself down and are harder on yourself than you would be on any other human being. How many times, for example, have you patted yourself on the back for sticking with *The Roadmap to Riches?*

When you pick up this book and start listening to me talking to you, do you give yourself a little congratulatory pat on the back for doing it? I hope so. When you complete each of steps in your Guidebook do you acknowledge that you have just done an important step for your own improvement? I hope you do. From this point on, I would like you to do that for yourself.

When you successfully accomplish any task, do you give yourself a congratulatory pat for doing it well? Probably not. Suppose you do *not* do something that you feel you should have done. Do you take the opportunity to jump all over yourself for it? If you are human, the answer is probably "YES." Most of us have been conditioned to put ourselves down more often than put ourselves up. You have been taught somewhere along the line that patting yourself on the back is a bad character trait. You have also been taught somewhere along the line that to be self-critical is a valuable trait. That is a bunch of nonsense!

As you can see from your understanding of the cycle I just described, it is extremely important that you put yourself up more than you put yourself down. And when you are in a situation where you are evaluating performance that does not measure up to what you felt you wanted to accomplish, don't be too hard on yourself. I am not saying that you shouldn't evaluate yourself at all. It is essential that you evaluate yourself and learn from your mistakes so that you can grow. But it is not essential that you put yourself down in the process.

If you think you're a second-class citizen, you are.

TED (ROBERT EDWARD) TURNER III (b. 1938) American sportsman, businessman

After all, when you try something new, the chances that you are going to make a mistake are much greater than the chances that you are going to do things perfectly. This is especially true if what you are trying is really new to you.

If you are reaching out and trying to change your life, you are going to make mistakes. You have two choices. When you make a mistake or fall short of what you are trying to achieve, you can stamp all over yourself with hobnail boots and use words like "You dummy, you always make mistakes." Or you can say, "I made a mistake. I was trying something new, I can learn something from that mistake and next time I will do a better job." Which do you think will have a more positive effect on your self-image and self-esteem?

If you jump all over yourself, it is not going to help because you believe the things you say to yourself. That's true even when you say such things in fun. Your subconscious has no sense of humor and it accepts them as deadly serious.

But if when you make a mistake, look at it, evaluate it, figure out why you made the mistake and then tell yourself: "OK, I made a mistake. But I was trying something new. It was a stretch for me and I have learned something from it, so next time I will do a better job;" then what happens to your self-esteem?

You have grown. You have learned. You have improved yourself. That improves your self-image and self-esteem. You know a little more than you used to and this in turn will increase your expectations and pulls you in a positive direction toward better performance the next time. ***Put yourself down, you diminish your performance. Put yourself up, you increase your performance. It is that simple.***

CHILL OUT! EASE UP!

What is not so simple is to break the habits of a lifetime. Especially if you have the habit of jumping all over yourself when you make a mistake. Learn to look at what you have done wrong, recognize the mistake, and approve of yourself for learning from that mistake. Learn that when you do something right, even if it is an everyday sort of thing, to give yourself a pat on the back; and never, never, never, under any circumstances, miss an opportunity to praise yourself for doing something significant and new correctly.

Too often when we do something right we think, "Oh anybody can do that." But you *actually did it!* You have to pay conscious attention to the process of building your self-images and self-esteem so that you can raise your expectations and improve your performance. And if you keep making the same mistake over and over again, remember, you have just been at the effect of a habit trigger; and if you jump on yourself for making that mistake, you are just aggravating the problem.

BE CAREFUL WHERE YOU SET YOUR THERMOSTAT

The reason our reality map is so important, especially our self-images and self-esteem, is that our reality map works like a thermostat. If you want to raise the temperature in a room, you turn up the thermostat. You don't build a fire in the middle of the floor. Trying to improve your performance without raising your thermostat is like building a fire. It may work for a while, but it sure isn't the easiest way to do it.

> Do not find fault; find a remedy.
>
> HENRY FORD
> (1863–1947)
> American Industrialist

> What it lies in our power to do, it lies in our power not to do.
>
> ARISTOTLE
> (384–322 BC)
> Greek philosopher

You see this often with people in the area of making money and you see it again with another common American problem, losing weight. You have an image of yourself and you consistently do things to live up or down to that image.

People have a picture of themselves. Let's say they weigh 180 pounds and they would like to weigh 160, but the mental picture they have of themselves is at the heavier weight. So they diet and diet and try to lose the twenty pounds. Maybe they even succeed or at least get most of it off. But since they haven't changed their mental thermostat, they still see themselves at that heavier weight.

So within a short time, they pop right back up. How do you change your weight? How do you change your income? You do it by changing your thermostat. How do you change your thermostat? You do it by becoming conscious of the way you talk to yourself about yourself.

Your exercise in this step in your Roadmap Guidebook is really very simple. It amounts to six words—PUT YOURSELF UP OR SHUT UP. This means that when you are talking to yourself or to anyone else, find a way to put yourself up, put them up, or don't talk at all. My mom used to say, "If you can't say something good about someone, don't say anything at all!"

> He who undervalues himself is justly undervalued by others.
>
> WILLIAM HAZLITT
> (1788–1830)
> English essayist, critic

Now turn to Step #27 "The Cycle of Destruction"
in your *Roadmap to Riches* workbook.

Accepting "Response-Ability"

D o you find it easy to put yourself up? Or do you find that all those years of conditioning make you feel a little self-conscious and a little silly every time you gave yourself a thumbs up or a pat on the back? Don't let those years of negative conditioning get in the way of doing something positive about your future.

Don't be a pike surrounded by glass walls. One of those walls is that you are not worthy of praise, and you shouldn't praise yourself. Don't let that glass wall stop you. It does not exist. It is just the echo of past training.

Nobody likes a braggart, it's true, but we are not asking you to brag about yourself to yourself or to other people. We are simply asking you to recognize the true value of your own accomplishments; a very important step if you are going to walk *The Lazy Man's Way to Riches* and success.

Isn't today a wonderful day? Don't you feel full of energy and enthusiasm on a day like today? What's that? You don't think it is such a hot day? And you're not full of energy and enthusiasm? Why not? So the weather outside isn't the greatest, what difference does it make? And why should the weather determine your attitude? And if you're not exactly bubbling over with energy and enthusiasm today, why not?

Who determines what kind of a day it is for you? Who is responsible for how you feel? The weatherman? The alarm clock? Your spouse, or any other family member who happened to get up on the wrong side of the bed? Or maybe it is the morning news broadcast with its unbroken chain of disasters.

Just who is the most influential person in your life? Here's a flash for you—YOU ARE. And you are the one who determines what kind of day today is going to be for you. What if you are one of those people whose bones ache in a certain kind of weather. Well, then they will ache. But you still have the choice between focusing on your aches and pains and letting that destroy your day or focusing on living today to the fullest extent, accomplishing and advancing toward your goals.

Our minds are amazing. When you concentrate in one area, you tend to block out other things. Focus on your aches and pains and they will get worse. Focus on the woes of the world and you can easily get depressed and tired. Focus on your purpose and where you are going in life, reinforce your plans with some activity, and the aches and bad news will fade into the background.

Your moods and feelings are the direct result of the thoughts on which you choose to dwell. You have the choice, so you are responsible for the way you feel and what kind of a day today turns out to be for you. You cannot control your

> One of man's greatest failings is that he looks almost always for an excuse, in the misfortune that befalls him through his own fault, before looking for a remedy— which means he often finds the remedy too late.
>
> CARDINAL DE RETZ
> (1614–1679)
> French prelate and writer

> With most men, unbelief in one thing springs from blind belief in another.
>
> G. C. LICHTENBERG
> (1742–1799)
> German
> physicist, writer

The highest possible stage in moral culture is when we recognize that we ought to control our thoughts.

CHARLES DARWIN
(1809–1882)
English naturalist

environment, but you are absolutely the only one who controls how you react to your environment. There are several things you can do to make it easier for you to focus on the excitement of the day, instead of the negative aspects.

START YOUR DAY EARLY

Actually, your attitude toward today started yesterday with the instructions you gave yourself about today. You probably were not aware of them. If you worked long hours yesterday or stayed up too late you may have told yourself, "I'm going to be exhausted tomorrow," and sure enough you were. Or maybe on last night's weather report you heard that today was going to be cold and damp and you told yourself, "That kind of weather always makes my joints ache."

And sure enough, it does—and they do.

It is a fact of life and an essential part of The Lazy Man's Way to realize that you control the power of your mind. What you plant in your mind about yourself, you will experience; whether it be physical, "I always catch a cold about this time every year," or emotional, "Rainy days get me down," or mental, "I know I can't figure this problem out." Your mind will respond. Joe used to say that more people catch colds as a result of the five o'clock news and TV commercials shouting that this is the flu season, than for any other reason. He knew that what you plant in your mind about your emotions is the most important factor in determining how you feel. Your mind, particularly the part of the mind we refer to as the subconscious mind, has tremendous power over you. It can make you wealthy or keep you in poverty.

Rich people live on what they earn and save a little regularly, poor people spend everything they earn, bankrupt people spend everything they earn and borrow to live.

ED FOREMAN
(b. 1933)
American entrepreneur, engineer, author, speaker, seminar leader, U. S. congressman

RESPONSIBILITY—YOU ARE IN CONTROL

To sum it all up, you are responsible. I see the word as response-able, because you are able to be responsible. You have the ability to control your responses to any situation. Fortunately, the subconscious does only what it is told.

Fortunately, you are in control of this mighty power because you, the conscious you, can totally control the instructions the subconscious receives. That's the good news. The bad news is that you do not always pay attention to the kinds of instructions your subconscious receives either from you or from others, without your consent and that results in actions of habit we talked of earlier.

For example, have you ever found yourself getting angry with someone over something that wasn't all that important and then wondering afterwards why you made such a fuss? Have you ever found yourself in a situation where you knew exactly what should be done and yet couldn't make yourself do it? And afterwards you wondered, "Why couldn't I have just done it? It would have been so easy."

God helps those who help themselves.

ALGERNON SIDNEY
(1622–1683)
English politician, author

It is extremely important for you to take control of the way you program your subconscious. In fact, it is the single most important secret of *The Lazy Man's Way to Riches* and you can do it with Daily Declarations, Awareness and Super Suggestion. You have already begun part of this. Every one of the steps in your *Roadmap to Riches* workbook is designed to help you take over the programming of your subconscious, using the Daily Declaration and Awareness steps.

PLANT THE SEEDS OF SUCCESS

Remember in Step 16 of the Roadmap workbook, "Everything Changes—Why Not You," we asked you to write the following declaration.

"I, (Space for your name) accept that everything changes including me. I am free of all past limiting attitudes."

That statement is what we call a Daily Declaration. Suppose I am trying to plant in my mind the firm belief that I use my time efficiently. And let's suppose that at the present I do not use my time as efficiently as I would like. I might design an affirmation like this:

"I, _____ (always use your own name in your affirmation. It gets your attention) use my time efficiently. I plan and perform my activities so that, whether at work or at play, I always make the best use of my time."

PLANT POSITIVELY

Notice a couple of things; I state things as positives. I didn't say I am not disorganized. I talked only in terms of the result I plan to achieve. And I talked as though the result is already true. After all, I am not trying to build the attitude that I will become efficient. I am trying to reinforce the attitude that I am efficient.

When I've planted this affirmation enough times, cultivated it with the Awareness principle that I will talk about shortly, and nurtured it with the Super Suggestion process, I will soon become exactly the kind of person that I have described. This is because that is what I believe about myself and I always behave consistently with my beliefs.

Furthermore, I won't have to think about it—it is automatic and therefore easy. Notice I did not have to spell out all the little things that go into being efficient. I simply have to develop the attitude that I am efficient and my subconscious takes care of the rest.

Your next step in your Roadmap Guidebook is to apply the Daily Declaration process to an important concept, the concept of—"Response-ability." This is the ability to control your responses.

The mind is like a clock that is constantly running down and must be wound up daily with good thoughts.

FULTON JOHN SHEEN, BISHOP (1895–1979) American religious leader, author

Freedom is the will to be responsible to ourselves.

FRIEDRICH NIETZSCHE (1844–1900) German philosopher

Man is not a being who stands still; he is a being in the process of becoming. The more he enables himself to become, the more he fulfills his true mission.

RUDOPLH STEINER (1861–1925) Austrian philosopher

Now turn to Step #28 "Accepting 'Response-Ability'" in your *Roadmap to Riches* workbook.

29
Turn Your "Have-To's" into "Choose-To's"

Today is another beautiful day, isn't it? A day in which the whole world can change for the better—especially for you. Today is a day you can look forward to with energy and anticipation. Of course, as the day progresses and challenges arise, as they usually do, it gets a little tougher to believe. I can just hear you say, "I knew he wasn't telling the truth. He said I could make some Daily Declarations and my whole day would be better. Now look at this mess. Maybe it works for him, but I bet he doesn't have the problems I have," and so on. *No*, I don't have your problems.

I *do* have my own and Joe had his, but he taught me that problems are not necessarily something to be avoided. You see, our problems are teachers, when we learn to look at them correctly. And our problems are also the source of opportunity.

That is because problems generate needs; and anywhere there is a need, there is an opportunity to provide a product or service to fill that need—that means opportunities to make money. Besides, the challenge of new problems everyday keeps us alive, keeps us developing our minds, our talents and our skills, keeps us stimulated. There is nothing quite like the feelings of accomplishment you get when you take on a challenge and successfully handle it. So, when you encounter a new problem, welcome it. It is an opportunity.

While you need new challenges to help you develop and to provide you with opportunity, what you don't need are the same old problems coming back day after day after day. Life is constantly handing you new ones and if you can't dispose of the old ones, the burden begins to overwhelm you, and then you really have a problem.

So what do you do when you run into an old problem today? Welcome it; treat it as a new opportunity, one you have never seen before. At least, the you of today has never seen it before, because you are changing. You are not the same person who battled this problem day after day without success.

You are someone who can take a fresh look at it. You can work through the problem/opportunity because you now know who is responsible for the recurring problem—namely you. And you are someone who already knows the solution to any problem—it is locked inside you. Locked for the moment behind your own glass walls. But you know the solution is there; and like our friend the pike, you are probably overlooking it because it seems to be out of reach. You are going to find out how to remove some of those glass walls and get at the answers you need.

Let's talk some more about responsibility. Who is responsible for your problems? Especially the ones that keep recurring in your life. Your parents? Your spouse?

From error to error one discovers the entire truth.

SIGMUND FREUD
(1856–1939)
Austrian psychoanalyst

A wise man will make you more opportunities than he finds.

SIR FRANCIS BACON
(1561–1626)
English philosopher, statesman, essayist

A thought is often original, though you have uttered it a hundred times. It has come to you over a new route, by a new and express train of associations.

OLIVER WENDALL HOLMES SR.
(1809–1894)
American physician, professor, man of letters

Your kids? Your boss? Your creditors? The economy? Some oil company? The government? God?

If that is the case you are in real trouble because you have little or no control over any of those entities. The only person over whom you really have any consistent and total control is *you*. So if you are going to work through your recurrent problems, you are the only tool with which you can really work.

BEWARE OF FROZEN ATTITUDES

It has been my experience, in my own life and in the lives of all the people I have worked with, that at the core of every recurring problem there is a frozen attitude. It is locked in a position that guarantees the problem will occur again and again and again. Invariably, in my own life, I found that the old problems I consistently faced were the result of mental blocks. Blocks that kept me from even seeing, let alone doing the obvious things that would solve my problem.

One such frozen attitude you are already working on. That's the attitude that tomorrow will be no different than today. You are addressing that attitude with the knowledge that everything changes and that you can take control of that change.

Another source of recurring problems is buried in what you call the Fear of the Unknown. Many people would rather keep a problem around that has been there for a while, than solve it and have to face some new problem that might be worse.

"HAVE-TO'S" ARE "HATE-TO'S"

And finally, many recurring problems are the result of what you call the "have-to." Time after time in advising someone with a recurring problem, Joe heard the words, "I can see that Action 'A' is the way to solve my problem but I HAVE TO DO 'B' instead."

Let me give you an example. A long-time friend went to Joe for advice about his continuing problems on his job. It was quickly obvious to Joe that he hated the work he was doing. When Joe suggested this, his friend agreed that a career change was the solution to his dissatisfaction.

But then he said, he "had to" stay in his current job because he had invested so much time in getting to his current level. He couldn't start over. "Besides," he said, "I have a family to support. If I went into something else, they would have to give up too much. I cannot do that to them."

What a string of "have-to's" and what a ducking of responsibility. The solution to his problem was obvious, but it was behind a whole lot of glass walls. You might say, "Now wait a minute. Are you saying this guy did not have an obligation to his family? He has to support them." Sure he has obligations to his family—to love and to cherish and to support them—Yes. But to maintain some arbitrary standard of living for them if it means sacrificing his health and happiness? . . . NO.

Besides, he never asked them what they wanted. He just *assumed* their lifestyle was more important to them than he was. He had put himself in a box because he really didn't understand the difference between "have-to's" and "want-to's." When it comes right down to it, there are very few "have-to's" in life. In fact there is only one. We have to die eventually, and except for that, there are no others.

"WANT-TO'S ARE "CHOOSE-TO'S"

What our lives are really full of are not "have-to's" but "want- to's." You might want to call them "choose-to's." We choose to do certain things in order to produce certain results or to avoid certain kinds of consequences, but it is still a choice.

Are you thinking "Aw, come on, you're making a mountain out of a mole hill." What is the difference if I think I "have to" do something instead of thinking I "choose to?"

There is plenty of difference. When you think you have to do something, you have no motivation to look for an alternative or even to investigate why you have to do this thing. You put a very high glass wall between you and some of the things you desire.

When you realize that you always have a choice, you are mentally open to other alternatives and you will be astonished at the difference that makes. Saying you "have to" do something is a way of ducking responsibility, that someone or something is making you do it. Realizing you are choosing to do it makes it a voluntary act and places the responsibility squarely on you, which is where it belongs and where you want it.

When you choose to be responsible you can do something about it. But when you transfer that responsibility onto someone else, not only are you powerless, but eventually you will come to resent the person to whom you have given the power. In every recurring problem the major obstacle to the solution of that problem is generally one or more "have-to's."

Pick a problem in your life that is forever popping up to bother you. Write down the nature of that problem. This is extremely important. Often just writing down the problem will put it in a different perspective. Then try to identify the "have-to's." Force yourself to consider the "have-to's" as "choose-to's."

Accept the truth that your problem does have a solution and that the solution will come to you once you have eliminated the "have-to's." In Step 29 of your Roadmap workbook you will find the guide to help you locate the "have-to's" in your life and to help you change them into "choose-to's."

> If you look at life one way, there is always cause for alarm.
>
> ELIZABETH BOWEN
> (1899-1973)
> Anglo-Irish novelist

Now turn to Step #29 "Turn Your "Have-To's" into "Choose-To's"
in your *Roadmap to Riches* workbook.

30

Self-Talk, a Rut or a Rocket

Has it occurred to you as you have gone through the steps in the Roadmap Guidebook, that *The Lazy Man's Way to Riches* is a lot of work, and that some of the steps are not all that easy? You're right. It is a lot of work in the beginning, because you have a lot of changes to go through and that does take some effort. You will be glad to know that it gets a whole lot easier from here on out.

CHANGE YOUR ATTITUDES

We are going to talk about the second of the three tools that are necessary to permanently change your attitudes. The first is Daily Declarations, which involves your conscious mind and the decision to change.

The second is called Creative Self-Awareness or simply Awareness. It involves becoming so aware about what you say to and about yourself, that you are constantly building yourself up, instead of tearing yourself down. Remember the story about Pat Collins and post-hypnotic suggestions and how they need to be reinforced frequently in order to have any lasting effect? In your Roadmap Guidebook in Step 18, you started looking for examples of self-limiting post-hypnotic suggestions in your life and for statements you make that reinforced these mental blocks and barriers.

Well, that was your first step toward becoming aware, of really focusing on you and the power you have to affect your behavior either positively or negatively. You probably made some interesting discoveries. Did you find that a lot of your statements were self-limiting? That they reinforced your mental blocks?

When I first started utilizing these concepts I was amazed at how much I put myself down in my own speech and in my own thoughts. In looking for reinforcement of self-limiting ideas be careful of the hidden and implied reinforcements. Things like, "There I go again," when you have made a mistake or "I always do that."

Questions are important too. "Why can't I do that?" or "Why am I so clumsy?" "Why can't I learn?" Statements that imply a feeling of envy or jealousy are also self-limiting. "I wish I could do that" or "What does he have that I don't?" It really takes a determined individual to dissolve all the self-limiting statements that he or she makes.

For a long time, one goal Joe had trouble achieving concerned his weight. One of his goals was to get his weight down to 170 pounds and keep it there. For the longest time he didn't realize what was holding him back. Finally he became aware that he was actually programming himself to be overweight.

Self-love, my liege, is not so vile a sin as self-neglecting.

WILLIAM SHAKESPEARE
(1564–1616)
English playwright, poet;
Henry V

It is doubtless a vice to turn ones eyes inward too much, but I am my own comedy and tragedy.

RALPH WALDO EMERSON
(1803–1882)
American poet, essayist, philosopher

Take charge of your thoughts. You can do what you will with them.

PLATO (428-347 BC)
Greek philosopher,
prose writer

To enter one's own self, it is necessary to go armed to the teeth.

PAUL VALERY (1871–1945)
French poet, critic

Time and again he would use statements like "It is really hard for me to lose weight. I just can't do it" or "Every time I eat something sweet it sets me off on a craving." You really have to be careful with the things you say to and about yourself. Actually Step 18 in your Roadmap Guidebook was only the beginning. From now on you will have a continuing assignment to recognize and eliminate self-limiting statements from your speech and thoughts.

FILL THE EMPTY SPACES IN YOUR MIND

Because it's important to continue your effort to become conscious of how you talk about yourself and it's hard to develop a new habit, we are going to reinforce the importance of this tool.

I want you to become extremely self-conscious. That may surprise you. I don't mean to say that self-conscious is being worried about how you look and act but rather to be self-aware. Aware of your power statements, the; "I am's," the "I can't's," the "I haven't's," and so on. These are the statements that reinforce your limiting attitudes. Unfortunately, you can't just eliminate a whole bunch of sentences like this from your daily routine. It leaves a lot of empty space.

Learn to fill that empty space with positive self-supporting statements. Instead of saying "I can't do that" or "I am not good at that," say "I have never done that, but I am sure I could learn to if I want to." Instead of saying, "I have a poor memory" say, "My memory is constantly improving." Instead of saying, "I can't afford it" say, "I am accumulating all the money I need for this or anything else that I want."

STOP LAUGHING AT YOURSELF

Another area of real importance that many people overlook is what I call the "Ha-Ha Put-Downs." Many people have developed a defense mechanism against the fear of criticism and rejection. This defense is to make fun of themselves before anyone else can.

These people will pick on areas where they feel insecure about themselves such as their looks, their weight, and their intelligence (or what they think is their lack of it), they think that if they laugh about these things first, then others will laugh with them and not at them. The only problem with this is that our subconscious mind has no sense of humor. It treats those disparaging things we laughingly say about ourself as deadly serious and reinforces the very insecurities we are trying to hide.

If you have fallen into this trap of laughing at yourself, you are probably going to experience considerable conflict at the idea of trying to change what you are doing. Most people who do this have come to rely on this part of their personality as a way of being accepted by others and it is scary to think of giving that up. Maybe you choose not to give it all up at once, but if there is an area of your life that is distressing to you and you find yourself making jokes about it, realize that the condition will never change—as long as you keep reinforcing it.

PROGRAMMED BY SELF-TALK

Just like everything else in life, you have a choice and you have to live with the consequences. In making your choice about changing your self-talk there is a very important fact of life I would like you to understand. Other people will react to you the way you tell them to.

If you really do put a small value upon yourself, rest assured that the world will not raise your price.

ANONYMOUS

What you do, how you act, the way you dress, or the way you introduce yourself, tells other people how to treat you. They will, in almost every case, go along with you. If you expect respect and consideration, you will get it. If you expect condescension and laughter, you will get that. If you expect to be ignored, you will get that too.

The important thing to realize is that you are in control. You determine how other people respond and you determine how you respond. The voice in your head may be telling you right about now that this is a lot of nonsense. How could harmless jokes and statements about you be so important? Let me tell you a story that illustrates how powerful the mind can be when it accepts a suggestion.

PARALYZED BY SELF-TALK

I was told by my mother that none of the men in my family ever lived past the age of 40. Although it wasn't a conscious thought, I truly believed I would only live to age 40. So, I retired at 40, not knowing why; I just had to. My belief acted like an instinct.

It drove me, but I didn't understand why. It's as if I had been programmed. My retirement was the beginning of the end for me—or maybe I should say the beginning of the end of the role I was playing that was getting me nowhere fast. I was just drifting on the currents of life without any purpose or direction. And as the old saying goes, "Idle hands are the Devil's workshop." I became self-destructive.

Then a very significant encounter happened to me while I was vacationing on my boat. I was on a subconscious self-destruction plan and that plan was headed for success. I had no life plan whatsoever. After all, when you only expect to live to 40 and you are now past 40, there isn't any reason to set any future goals or make plans. There's just no future. (See your Guidebook for more about a life plan.)

During one of my perpetual parties on the boat, a couple of new-found acquaintances (psychotherapists from New York) gently, but bluntly, pointed out that I seemed to have no purpose or life plan, no goals for my life at all. And they also made the comment that I could live another 50 years or more. "What are you going to do with the rest of your life?"

"The rest of my life?!!!" You mean there is more?????

It was a question I had not asked myself. It wasn't even something I had considered. Wow!

A MAJOR WAKE UP CALL

This was a major wake-up call. I consulted a doctor for a thorough physical exam. He pronounced me as healthy as I could be. It was at this point that I was confused and a bit terrified. I never realized the incredible power of the belief that I would only live until I was 40.

That "belief" had been a map I had followed subconsciously. Amazingly enough, I later found out the true nature of this belief that had charted the course of my life for 40 years. It was absolutely false. Many of my male ancestors lived well into their 90s. I essentially allowed the power of that negative, false belief to nearly destroy my life. I had accepted false programming and virtually believed it.

Our life is what our thoughts make it.

MARCUS AURELIUS ANTONINUS (121–180) Roman emperor, Stoic philosopher

Experience is not what happens to a man. It's what a man does with what happens to him.

ALDOUS HUXLEY (1894–1963) English novelist, essayist, satirist

You are today where your thoughts have brought you; you will be tomorrow where your thoughts take you.

JAMES ALLEN (1849–1925) American author

As a man thinks in his heart, so is he.

SOLOMON
(10TH CENTURY BC)
King of Israel, reputed author
of biblical books

Dr. Barbara Brown, a leading researcher in the area of bio-feedback, is convinced that we have the ability to control the activity of our system right down to the cellular level. The only thing that stops us from learning how is that we cannot measure the effects of our thoughts accurately enough.

How do you form your reality map? How much of your concept of reality is not really true? How accurate are you in evaluating your limitations and insecurities. I was way off in mine. If you want to change your mind, you have to change what you tell yourself is true.

You've seen how Super Suggestion speeds up the process tremendously. But, Super Suggestion is just part of the process. You need to involve your conscious mind through the use of the daily declarations and through constant attention to your self-talk. Step 30 in your Roadmap workbook is designed to make you aware of how you talk to and about yourself. Back in Step 21, "I Can Be My Own Worst Enemy or My Own Best Friend," there were examples of limiting self-talk. You may want to re-read those examples and look for these kinds of statements you make about yourself in other instances in your life. Try to turn each example into a self-expanding statement.

Now turn to Step #30 "Self-Talk, a Rut or a Rocket"
in your *Roadmap to Riches* workbook.

31

Taking Charge of Your Mind

Now you are going to explore how to use the tools you have been learning about to start *eliminating* some of the really tough roadblocks on your way to Riches. There is no question that the conflicts caused by the unnecessary fears we talked about stop more people than anything else.

Fear of criticism, rejection, failure, and success lock us in a vise preventing us from following through promptly and thoroughly on the good ideas we have. They make every bit of progress a real struggle. A struggle with ourselves. I call this struggle "The 2000 Pound Telephone;" because when you have this problem, the telephone seems to weigh 2000 pounds when you have to make a call that you keep putting off. Sales people suffering from call reluctance call it the "red hot door-knob."

Earlier we talked about the unnecessary fears and how they grow. You saw how fears can become conditioned reflexes causing emotional distress, even physical distress and upset. Now you have the tools to attack these fears, both in your conscious and your subconscious minds.

WHAT'S BUGGING YOU?

Back in Step 6, we asked you to write down your burning desires. And I have also asked you to examine your fears of success. By now your exercises have started developing your awareness of your feelings, so the process you are going to go through now will be fairly easy for you. The first thing to do in releasing yourself of any conflict is to get in touch with your conflict by bringing it out into the open. You did some of that when you wrote down the pros and cons of achieving your desires. You did it again when you evaluated your attitudes toward success.

Now that you understand more about these fears, go back into the pro and con process and see if you can come up with any additions to your list. Search yourself and be brutally honest. Don't try to edit anything. Just get it all on paper. A good technique is to keep asking yourself "What else bothers me?" until you have run out of things.

Once you have all your obstacles and doubts down on paper, an interesting thing may happen. Some of your obstacles won't look as bad written down as they do when they are floating around in your head. We all tend to enlarge our problems with our imaginations. Writing them out helps to *see them clearly and reduce them to their proper perspective*. Some of your obstacles will not just melt away. These take more effort; both consciously and through the power of Super Suggestion.

There is no terror in a bang, only in the anticipation of it.

SIR ALFRED JOSEPH HITCHCOCK
(1899–1980)
English-born American film director

Life hardly ever lives up to our anxieties.

PAUL MONASH
American television producer, writer

Hope is brightest when it dawns from fear.

SIR WALTER SCOTT
(1771–1832)
Scottish novelist and poet;
"The Lady of the Lake"
(1810)

We have more ability than will power and it is often an excuse to ourselves that we imagine that things are impossible.

LA ROCHEFOUCAULD
(1613–1680)
French writer

Change is not made without inconvenience; even from worse to better.

ROBERT BROWNING
(1812–1889)
English poet

If one advances confidently in the direction of his dreams, and endeavors to live the life which he has imagined, he will meet with a success unexpected in common hours.

HENRY DAVID THOREAU
(1817–1862)
American essayist, naturalist, poet

Your next step is to exercise your greatest gift. Look at what you have written and decide whether you're giving up your freedom of choice by treating some things in your life as "have-to's" rather than "choose-to's." If you need to, go back and review Step 29 for a refresher on this process.

The next key step is to remove the obstacles that are rooted in fear of criticism and failure. Often these are stated in terms of what will happen if you try and fail. In other words, your expectation is not success but failure.

LOOKING AT HIDDEN CONFLICTS

Joe's friend, Dick Johnson tells how Joe helped him see the kinds of conflicts generated by his unnecessary fears:

"I had an excellent job in the Aerospace industry. Good prospects for advancement. The only problem was my heart wasn't in it, even though I had a Masters degree in Mathematics and had worked for almost 15 years to attain my position. I really liked working with people better than figures. I am a hard worker, but I hated a regimented schedule. The idea of turning 40 years of life over to a boss really distressed me. I wanted the freedom of being my own boss.

Joe suggested that I write out the pros and cons of changing careers. So I did. I wrote out both sides of my dilemma—my feelings about my job and current career and my feelings about the alternate option I was considering. After I had written out my feelings, I told Joe it hadn't helped me out a bit. I was still unable to make a decision.

When Joe looked at what I had written he wasn't surprised. Everything I had written about both options was negative. About my current career, I had expressed all my frustration and boredom. About my alternative choice I wrote of the uncertainty and the lack of security, of starting at the bottom and giving up all the training and experience I had worked so hard to attain. Of course, I was paralyzed. In my own mind both choices were totally unattractive.

I had actually managed to turn the positives such as freedom and working with people that supposedly were attracting me to the new career into negatives—insecurity and giving up my training in the area I didn't like. When Joe pointed this out to me I began to re-orient my thinking.

With the aid of Super Suggestion I started working on my fears and my goals. Within a short time I made my career change and I did struggle at first, but I knew where I was going. Soon I was earning twice the income of the job I had left, and within three years we were able to buy a beautiful home in the Colorado Rockies.

Within five years I had increased my net worth more than twenty times over what I had accomplished in the previous fifteen years. Even more important, my life improved in every department. Free from the career I hated, my emotional outlook, my energy, and my health all improved. I feel like I am hardly working because I enjoy myself so much. I feel ten years younger and every day of my life is an exciting adventure for me."

So one important key to resolving your conflicts in this area, is building your expectations of success while at the same time understanding about hidden fears of what success can mean. Now let's concentrate on dealing with your fears.

On the conscious level you can help this process by reading biographies of successful, happy people. (See the suggested reading section of the Guidebook.) You will experience their feelings of success and will realize that even the most successful people have human failings and make lots of mistakes. In this way you can begin to build the feeling that if they can do it, so can you. You will realize, at least on the conscious level, that success in itself is not something to fear, and that successful people have had to overcome the same fears and challenges that you face.

Finally, to deal with the useless fears, you have to get on the level where they do the most harm—the subconscious mind. And we do that through Super Suggestion. Remember back in Step 26, we talked about how your reality map was formed. Some of your map is a result of conscious choices you have made, but there is another way information gets in.

Vividly imagined events can also become part of your map, bypassing the conscious mind completely. With this book you are learning how to use your *imagination* to change your reality map in four important ways: by reducing the strengths of the useless fear, by increasing the belief in the attainment of your goals, by improving your self-images and by building your self-esteem.

> The only reason they come to see me is that I know life is great—and they know I know it.
>
> CLARK GABLE
> (1901–1960)
> American Actor

Now turn to Step #31 "Taking Charge of Your Mind" in your *Roadmap to Riches* workbook.

32

Rehearsing Success

C an you imagine a football coach spending several hours a day having his players practice fumbling? Can you image a baseball player practicing striking out? Do you see any sense at all in a person spending hours each day practicing failure?

And yet that is exactly what most of us do. We spend a substantial part of every day rehearsing failure. Take the salesman who mentally visualizes rejection before he picks up the phone. Or the person who has a speech to make who constantly worries about forgetting his talk. Or the businessman who, under the impression he's being conservative, constantly worries about every conceivable disaster that could occur.

All of them are practicing in their imaginations. Practicing failing before they have ever given themselves a chance for success. Therefore, they are guaranteeing that the thing they are most afraid of will happen to them because *what you practice and think about mentally, you will do.*

YOUR SUCCESS MACHINE

Your mind is an incredible success machine. Whatever you program it to do, it will accomplish. Mentally rehearse and practice success and your mind will figure out a way to do it. Mentally practice failure and your mind will figure out a way for you to fail. It is very accommodating. What you tell it you want is what you get.

The power of mental rehearsal has been known for some time. Championship athletes have used this technique to improve their performance and some, not understanding what they are doing, have used it to degrade their performance. Recently an article in the *Los Angeles Times* described the astonishing experience of an American psychologist who also happened to be a weight lifter. He was intrigued by the tremendous progress of the Eastern European countries in sports in general and at an international conference he had an opportunity to talk to some leading German scientists about how this was being achieved.

They performed a demonstration for him. His personal best in the bench press was 300 pounds. They asked him what he would consider to be a significant improvement and he said even ten pounds more would be an outstanding improvement. Using a technique **virtually identical to Super Suggestion** they taught him how to use his imagination to experience lifting a much heavier weight. Within an hour he bench-pressed 365 pounds, a 20 percent increase in just one hour. That is phenomenal.

When the mind is thinking, it is talking to itself.

PLATO (428-347 BC)
Greek philosopher, prose writer

We become what we habitually contemplate.

GEORGE WILLIAM RUSSELL (1867–1935)
Irish poet, dramatist, editor

You say you don't want to be a weight lifter or football star. "What does this have to do with achieving your goals?" Just this. The same techniques will work in every aspect of your life. As part of the same demonstration, the American psychologist also worked on imagining himself to be an excellent writer, an area in which he was not particularly good. The results astonished him. People who had no idea of what he was doing began complimenting him on his writing skills and how they had improved.

MENTAL REHEARSALS

I am frequently called upon to make speeches, give talks and give radio and TV interviews. As a business and personal development expert, I have spoken to YPO (Young Presidents Organization) groups, TEC (The Executive Committee) groups, trade association groups, seminars, and conventions. I have also been a keynote speaker for sales organizations, non-profit organizations, government agencies, and major corporations throughout the world. As much as I have done it, I am still always nervous before any talk or interview.

The audiences vary in size from small groups to several thousands in our seminars and for major corporations. Of course, I want to be at my best during these talks, so I rehearse. Not by writing out my speech and practicing it. In fact, I don't write out my speech at all. I make a few notes about the ideas I want to get across and then program my subconscious to do the rest.

I mentally rehearse the feeling of giving a good talk, of being articulate, and having a constant flow of ideas. I visualize the happy response of the audience, their enjoyment and enthusiasm so that I approach the date of the talk with anticipation of success and my subconscious knows that it must produce the desired results. So when I am actually in front of the audience, I get the results I rehearsed. I am usually surprised at some of the things I say. Some of my best ideas have come out during a speech—ideas that my conscious mind had not fully formed.

You can use your subconscious minds in the discovery and development of business ideas. It is extremely important to grasp the idea of mentally rehearsing success as well, when you begin to develop your ideas. One of the tragedies of the way you were raised is that most of you are conditioned to expect disappointment and failure. "Don't count your chickens before they are hatched" is a perfect example of negative programming.

As a result you learn to dread the future rather than look forward to it. And you find it too easy to rehearse failure and extremely difficult to rehearse success. Remember the self-defeating self-image cycle in Step 27? The only way to increase your performance is to raise your expectations—in other words, to rehearse success. Are you thinking "But I can't rehearse being successful when I'm not successful. How do I pretend to be successful, when the reality is I have nothing going? And, besides, if I get my hopes up and it doesn't work then I will really be disappointed."

So what! Disappointment is hardly ever *fatal*. In fact, it is rarely even dangerous. Yet, we let the fear of disappointment rob us of one of the greatest sources of energy we have—anticipation. Have you ever watched a child as Christmas gets closer and closer? When does Christmas really start for a child? Sometime between late October and early November they usually start getting excited.

They begin looking forward to that exciting time. They begin dreaming. Their behavior starts to improve. They may start doing a lot of chores around the house because they want extra money for Christmas presents. They have more energy than usual because they are excited. Then Christmas Day arrives. The gifts are opened and in just minutes it is all over. But was Christmas just those few minutes on Christmas morning or was it those weeks of excitement and anticipation leading up to it?

If you don't learn to anticipate and rehearse Success, you rob yourself of the energy and determination that you need to be successful. After all, how much effort will you put into a project if your mind is telling you that you are going to fail?

How heavy will the telephone be, if in your mind you are already rehearsing a "NO" on the other end? Rehearsing failure puts tremendous roadblocks in your road to Riches. You can remove those roadblocks using the three basic tools I have discussed: **Daily Declaration, Creative Self-Awareness, and Super Suggestion.**

What you are going to do in this next step closely resembles the rehearsal period an actor goes through in preparation for a play. Have you ever wondered how an actor can laugh or cry on cue? Do they actually think what they are doing on stage is real?

Hardly. But through hours and hours of rehearsal the actor behaves as though the play were reality. He uses his imagination to explore how the character he is portraying would respond if the situation were real and most importantly, he builds a conditioned reflex or rather a whole set of conditioned reflexes that take over when he is on stage. The situation in the play triggers feelings—anger, tears, joy—and the actor experiences and projects these feelings automatically without having to think about them, whenever the proper cue occurs.

You see, the actor is doing his own version of Dr. Pavlov's conditioning by practicing cue response over and over again. That is just what you are going to do. Only, instead of rehearsal, you will be using the three powerful tools—Daily Declaration, Creative Self-Awareness, and Super Suggestion.

> The future belongs to those who believe in the beauty of their dreams.
>
> ELEANOR ROOSEVELT
> (1884–1962)
> American humanitarian, columnist, lecturer, wife of President Franklin D. Roosevelt

Now turn to Step #32 "Rehearsing Success" in your *Roadmap to Riches* workbook.

33

Dumping Your Excess Baggage

I f you were starting out on a long hike and you personally had to carry every bit of your baggage, how much time would you spend making sure you got rid of all excess baggage before you started? Wouldn't it be worth the time in the beginning to pack carefully, so you wouldn't be burdened every step of the way? *The Lazy Man's Way to Riches* is a journey; a journey that will last you the rest of your life.

Doesn't it make sense to dump your excess baggage now? Because, believe me, if you don't, it will drag you down every step of the way and wear you out before you achieve everything you want. Oh, you will make progress, but it will be a lot easier if you learn to lighten your load.

What kind of excess baggage am I talking about? The kind we all carry into every new venture—the negative emotions and fears that act like a brake on our tremendous potential, making every step forward a tremendous effort. I have already discussed the fears for criticism, rejection, failure, and success and how to get rid of them.

Now I want to talk about some emotions that are *not* such *obvious* obstacles but can be even bigger roadblocks than these fears, especially since you probably will want to hold onto them with a vengeance and deny that they are holding you back. Believe me, they are among your worst enemies. What are these emotional roadblocks? Envy, jealousy, greed, revenge, bitterness, resentment, hatred, prejudice, guilt. Get the picture? You may say, "Now wait a minute, what do these emotions have to do with success? I am not bitter about much, but believe me I have the right to be."

Do you have any of those thoughts? Are you cherishing thoughts of *revenge* for some wrong that has been done you? Are you a little *bitter* at the hand life has dealt you? Are you a little *envious* of the person who inherited a fortune? Do you feel like you have a right to those feelings?

Well, you are welcome to hang on to them, but I can tell you right now, they are excess baggage and eventually will wear you right into the ground. You may go and achieve some of the good things of life, but you pay a much higher price than the person who is willing to spend a little time to drop some of the excess baggage of the negative emotions.

You will draw to yourself that which you most persistently think about.
ROBERT A. ANTHONY, Ph.D.
American psychologist, writer

Nothing vivifies, and nothing kills like the emotions.
JOSEPH ROUX
(1834–1905)
French priest, writer

A brave man thinks no one is his superior who does him an injury; for he has it then in his power to make himself superior to the other by forgiving it.

ALEXANDER POPE
(1688–1744)
English poet, satirist

How unhappy is he who cannot forgive himself.

PUBLILIUS SYRUS
(1st century BC)
Latin writer of mimes

Begin somewhere: you cannot build a reputation on what you intend to do.

LIZ SMITH
(MARY ELIZABETH)
(b. 1923)
American journalist
(gossip columnist)

LET GO OF THE ESSENTIAL DEAD WEIGHT

I can just hear some of you saying, "Now, are you telling me I have to be a saint to walk The Lazy Man's Way?" No, or none of us would ever make it.

I am suggesting that you can make your progress a whole lot easier by letting go of some emotional dead weight. Let's take a look at these negative emotions; The first set, bitterness, revenge, resentment, hatred, and guilt is leftover from the dead past. And there is one absolute fact about the past. *It can't be changed* and these feelings ruin your precious "now" time—the only time you really have to work with. Every minute spent wallowing over a past wrong or beating yourself for a past mistake is wasted time and wasted energy. Thoughts of revenge do nothing to the person or persons you think wronged you. They only harm you, by distorting your view of life in the present and preventing you from focusing on where your life goes by keeping you looking over your shoulder all the time.

And what good does it do to continue feeling guilty about a serious mistake you may have made that hurt you or someone else? Ask for forgiveness. Do what you can to repair the damage, learn the lesson of your mistake, and then *forgive yourself* and go on. Remember, unlike the past, you can change the future. You are not the same person who made that mistake.

Chances are the mistake was made because you didn't or couldn't possibly predict the consequences of your actions. Or maybe you were simply acting out some post-hypnotic suggestion. But you are treating yourself as though you deliberately set out to cause harm. I am not saying you are not responsible for your actions. You are. Everything I have told you in these chapters should make it clear that I do believe in personal responsibility. So accept your personal responsibility. Do what you can to correct the problem. Ask for forgiveness. Forgive yourself and go on. Wallowing in guilt is not accepting responsibility. It is usually a way to avoid living in the here and now.

But what about envy, jealousy and greed? These are rooted in insecurity and low self-esteem. Why envy someone else's possessions? You can easily get your own The Lazy Man's Way. Jealousy? It is probably the most destructive of emotions. Certainly it destroys the love that it is supposedly trying to protect. And once again, it is a symptom of insecurity and low self-esteem.

The solution is not in restricting someone else's behavior; it is raising your own concept of yourself. And how about greed? The person who is truly greedy, who can never get enough money or power or whatever, really has a problem. His life is out of balance and he is attempting to make up in one department for what he is lacking and really needs in another department.

If you feel that you can never get enough money to satisfy you, you are right. Because you can never get enough of what you don't really need. It is not the money you want and need. Money has simply become a symbol for love or respect or acceptance. Stop wasting your energy, sit down and look at yourself and go after what you really want.

HOW YOU CAN LET GO

Now, how do you get rid of all this excess baggage? Don't worry, you don't need seven years of psychoanalysis, you simply have to work on removing these emotional dregs every single day. How? By using the tools you have been learning in these chapters.

Your emotional reactions are simply a product of your attitudes and your attitudes can be changed, *if you really want to change them*. After all they are just your attitudes, they are not carved in stone, so just change those that don't work for you.

That may be the hard part where these emotions are concerned. (Giving them up, releasing those feelings of revenge, that bitterness.) "You mean I have to let that so-and-so get away with what he did to me?" No, you don't have to, but everything will be a lot easier for you if you do. And not only let that so-and-so get away with whatever it was, but forgive that so-and-so as well.

Simply release all feelings of anger, bitterness, and revenge no matter how justified you think they are. And while you are at it, forgive yourself as well for all your past mistakes. Let go of your past and go on with your life; it's a choice you make. It's a conscious choice.

TAKING YOUR EMOTIONAL INVENTORY

You're already working on any feeling of jealousy, envy or prejudice that you may have, because you are building your self-images through Super Suggestion. The better you feel about yourself the less you will need these drags on your energies. In the next step of your Roadmap Guidebook there are steps to do that help you free yourself from these downers.

Begin by taking an inventory of all your negative feelings. Write down all the people at whom you are angry, the ones whom you feel have wronged you, the ones you feel you hate and why you feel that way. Write down the names of people of whom you are envious and why. Add any jealousy you are feeling and all the people, races, or organizations you have prejudice against. And finally, write down any reasons you feel guilty. Get it all out . . . all of the garbage. Be totally honest.

No one will ever see this list but you. When you are sure this list is complete, very carefully burn your list and, as you burn it, realize that all the feelings that you put down on your list as you were writing it are burning up, too. Release them and let them go up in smoke.

This is more than just a symbolic act. In writing your feelings down you release some of the pent up energy behind your emotions. You may also realize how silly some of them are. At least, that has been the experience of hundreds of thousands who wrote down all their grievances. If you do this exactly, you will be amazed at how good you feel.

You may find that some of your suppressed grievances still hang around. After all, these emotions can be deeply buried in your subconscious. That is why I have given you a Super Suggestion exercise in Step 33 of your Roadmap to help you in this area.

Forgiving is the answer to the child's dream of a miracle by which what is broken is made whole again, what is soiled is again made clean.

DAG HAMMARSKJOLD
(1905–1961)
Swedish statesman,
U.N. secretary general
(1955–1961)

The ineffable joy of forgiving and being forgiven forms an ecstasy that might well arouse the envy of the gods.

ELBERT HUBBARD
(1856–1915)
American businessman,
writer, printer

It is no exaggeration to say that using this exercise regularly can be one of the most important steps you will ever take along the way to Riches in every aspect of your life. Remember the good feelings that come from letting go of these emotions and use them to beat back any of those downer emotions that try to come back. And work with the Super Suggestion exercise frequently.

The next step is to look at what you may want to start dumping and how to dump it all.

Now turn to Step #33 "Dumping Your Excess Baggage" in your *Roadmap to Riches* workbook.

34
Man Does Not Work for Bread Alone

Y ou have just talked about getting rid of the excess baggage; habits, downers and emotions that zap your energy and divert your attention from your *chosen direction*. Now I want to give you some ideas on how to avoid taking on new downers by making the best out of all your relationships with others.

SUCCESS DOESN'T HAPPEN IN A VACUUM—
SUCCESS IS NOT FOR LONERS

When you study the lives of successful people, you rarely find a loner—someone who did it all on his or her own. In fact, it's hard to think of a single one. Success is a cooperative effort, especially when you do it The Lazy Man's Way.

Moneymaking ideas nearly always need the financial and emotional support, the advice, the talent and the skills and labor of others to blossom and grow. To turn your ideas into reality, will greatly facilitate gaining the enthusiastic cooperation of others. Some people think you can get others to cooperate through manipulation and a lot of people try this. To me the major problems with trying to manipulate people are: first, you can't feel good about yourself if you are not completely honest with people, and second, as Mr. Lincoln said, "You can't fool all of the people all of the time."

Eventually your manipulation is discovered and the people you have used tend to get downright hostile. With all the internal challenges and fears you have to overcome, the last thing you need to do is to make enemies. Perhaps you are thinking, "Wait a minute, you just got through saying that I need people to make my projects go, and now you say I can't use people."

You can use people, *but only with their knowledge and consent and in a "win/win" setting.* You can gain the enthusiastic cooperation and support of everyone you need to make your ideas productive. It is very simple. Help people get what *they* want and they will help you get what *you* want. Help enough other people to get what they want out of life and your success is assured.

GIVE PEOPLE WHAT THEY WANT

So, what do people want? Of course, it varies. For some it might be a job with a decent wage. If development of your idea requires that you have employees, remember, you get what you pay for. Always pay a fair price for the job you want done and hire someone whose skills, abilities, and interests match the job. It's better to have someone in every position that has to stretch a little to accomplish the job than have someone whose abilities are not fully used.

> When you make a world tolerable for yourself you make a world tolerable for others.
>
> ANAIS NIN
> (1914–1977)
> French-born American novelist, dancer

> Long-range studies imply that doing something with other people, especially something for them is the most powerful of all stimuli to longevity and health.
>
> JON POPPY
> (b. 1942)
> American health columnist

If you are short on cash, you could offer equity or profit sharing and performance bonuses as incentives. Don't fall into the trap of believing that money is the only thing your employees require or even the most important thing. Sure, money is a necessary part of our lives, but haven't you heard about the thousands of people who leave excellent paying jobs each year to work for less because they are looking for something else.

That something is called *satisfaction*. Satisfaction is a basic human need, which has nothing to do with money. When you ask these people why they changed careers they often mention their desire to make a contribution or to do something meaningful.

Many said they felt like they were just lost in a big crowd—that nobody knew or cared what they were doing. Others talk of a desire for more freedom or more independence. What these people are expressing are fundamental human needs for appreciation, recognition, and opportunity for personal development. How many times have you seen people work at low-paying jobs because they knew their efforts were valuable and necessary? (We all know people like that; nurses, teachers, devoted secretaries, and the key man in a company who gives 40 years of loyal service.) These people are working for something other than financial gain and they accept less in the financial department, because they feel needed or important or valued.

Don't ever make the mistake that people can just be bought. Give value for value, but go an extra mile and give appreciation and recognition as well. You get a lot more than just an employee in return.

GIVE AWAY MORE THAN MATERIAL THINGS

The importance of intangibles such as appreciation and recognition and respect go far beyond the employer/employee relationship. It extends to your family, your day-to-day associates and all your business dealings. People want to be around you and support you in your efforts in *direct proportion* to how good you make them feel about themselves.

This doesn't mean you should falsely flatter people or be insincere; that is manipulation and it always rings false. Find some quality that you admire in each person you meet and especially each member of your family. Do the same with all your close associates and praise them for their good qualities. Look for ways to show your appreciation, not for what they do for you, but for what they are, and offer your appreciation freely without expecting anything in return.

Don't worry, you will get results. Remember, its best not to tie your appreciation to any specific favor or other return. If not given freely, it is meaningless. A short note expressing your feelings is usually much more meaningful to the person than a 15 minute eulogy. Suppose you receive the following letter from a friend or a member of your family:

> *Dear Hal,*
>
> *Just a quick note to tell you how much I enjoy your friendship. You are the kind of person that is a pleasure to be around. Let's get together soon for some good conversation.*
>
> *Regards, Richard*

Happiness is mostly a by-product of doing what makes us feel fulfilled.

DR. BENJAMIN SPOCK
(1903–1998)
Physician, writer

Everybody forgets the basic thing; people are not going to love you unless you love them.

PAT CARROLL
(b. 1927)
American actress, comedienne, Emmy and Tony award winner

What is your first thought? As a human being with negative training, your first reaction might be, "Hey, what does he want?" If you realized that the note is simply what it appeared to be, a sincere expression of appreciation for you as a person, then what would your first thought be? "Wow! What a terrific person this is to write me such a nice note."

Wouldn't you like people to feel that way about you? Just show them a little appreciation and you will be pleasantly surprised with the results. In business, and also in your personal life, try catching people doing something *right* and complimenting them on it. It works for me.

APPRECIATION—IT'S AN ART

A woman friend of mine tried this approach with her mother whom she had resented for years—she actually found it difficult to be around her mother. Most of this tension was a result of misunderstandings during her childhood. But the resentment carried on into adulthood and, as a result, their contact as adults continually aggravated the problem. One day, having learned the principles we have been talking about, she had a floral arrangement sent to her mother with the message "You are loved." Her mother was deeply moved and when she called to say "thank you," the years of friction started to turn into a warm relationship that "enriched" both of their lives.

Make a list of the people who are important in your life—your spouse, your children, your family, friends, and business associates. For each one, make a list of all the qualities you appreciate about that person and then write a short note expressing that appreciation. Not for the things they have done, but for what they are. Don't flatter them; be honest and objective.

Now, this may take a little more time than most of your Roadmap steps, but it will be worth it. And you probably won't have time to do it all in a day. Make a habit out of it. Start with those closest to you. It will be easier and you will feel less embarrassment. Don't cop out with, "I don't have to tell my family how I feel. They already know." If that is the way you think, they probably don't know, because it is probably difficult for you to show your feelings.

We are all a little insecure and we all need reassurance from time to time, so even if you think they know, tell them anyway. If you are afraid they will think you have gone crazy, I have given you a little paragraph to insert in your note, so they will understand what you are doing. You don't have to use it, but if it helps, go ahead and do it. Here it is:

> *Dear Donna,*
>
> *I am in the process of going through a course in self-development and improvement. Each day I have an exercise to complete. Today I'm to write a note of appreciation to someone I care for. I chose to write to you because of all the things I appreciate about you. This isn't a thank you for past favors; it's a thank you for all the things our friendship has meant to me.*
>
> *Richard*

For some of you, this may be the hardest step on The Lazy Man's Way, but don't skip it no matter how hard. Remember, what you freely give in this world always comes back multiplied many times over.

Never lose sight of the fact that the most important yardstick of your success will be how you treat other people—your family, friends, and co-workers, and even strangers you meet along the way.

BARBARA BUSH
(b. 1925)
Wife of President
George Bush Sr., mother of
President George W. Bush

By now, if you have faithfully followed the steps in your *Roadmap to Riches* Guidebook, you have papered the surfaces around you with lots of messages and reminders; and it must be getting pretty cluttered by this time. So to make things a little easier and neater, you are going to introduce a concept that will take care of this clutter and at the same time helps you get the necessary reinforcement that you need every single day to remind you of the habits you are changing.

After you have been looking at the messages for two or three days put them on little file cards, 3 × 5 inches is a convenient size. They fit into most pockets and handbags. Three times a day make a practice of reading through these file cards one at a time, taking a moment to think about the meaning of each message.

This way you continue to get the reinforcement. From now on when we ask you to put up something on the bathroom mirror or on the dashboard of your car, go ahead and do that for several days and then transfer it to a file card. Once again, what I am trying to do is get maximum saturation of all of your senses in this process of changing.

Now turn to Step #34 "Man Does Not Work for Bread Alone"
in your *Roadmap to Riches* workbook.

35
The World's Most Exciting Business!

You've come a long way on your journey to Riches and have been exposed to all kinds of wonderful principles, ideas and suggestions. They were designed to open you up to new ideas, new ways of growing and thinking. They were designed to help you grow beyond your old limitations and to help you grow beyond where you are now, and to help you keep growing for the rest of your life. My Grandma Rose put it this way. *"To have more, to achieve more—one must first become more."* Now that you are becoming more than you were, and you know how to become even more than you are, what can you do in a practical sense with all of this information?

No matter what your gender, age, interest, talents, and needs, what you're about to learn can make all your financial dreams come true.

MAKE YOUR FORTUNE—THE LAZY MAN'S WAY!

Turn it into dollars, lots of dollars—just like Joe Karbo and I did. We are now going to show you **exactly** how we made our money so that you can easily replicate our successes—The Lazy Man's Way. We made our fortunes in the direct response business.

Some say there is no such thing as the direct response business and they are technically correct. Direct response is a merely a way of doing business that can be used in *any* business. And you can use it with any product or service. It simply means dealing direct with your customer without: salesmen, clerks, retailers, wholesalers, or anyone else between you and your customer.

You make an offer to the customer and they respond directly to you to purchase your products or services. You control the entire transaction from start to finish so you can satisfy your customers/clients every need in an ethical, top quality environment, and build a lasting relationship with your customer that would not be possible with traditional business methods.

It's one of the last frontiers where, starting with very little capital, you can build a worldwide business almost overnight.

DIRECT RESPONSE WORKS

Direct response can be done by; mail, flyers, newspapers, telephone, magazines, coupon packs, radio, television, cable, or on the Internet by E-mail, E-zines, or on your own website. I don't know of a single product or service that hasn't been sold this way. There are people sitting at home right now making money selling hand made quilts, wine, shoes, computers, computer repair, automobiles, pens and pencils, comic books, jewelry, clothing, electronics,—you name it and it is being sold right now by direct response. Skeptical? Just log on to E-Bay and see for yourself that practically everything is being sold on E-Bay. Everything that you can buy on E-Bay you can also find in every other direct response medium.

WHY SHOULD YOU LISTEN TO THESE GUYS?

What you may not know is that Joe Karbo was one of the largest and most knowledgeable advertisers in the world specializing in print media. His specialty was newspapers and magazines with direct mail not far behind. My specialty was electronic media – television and radio, and now the Internet with direct E-mail, E-zines (newsletters) and websites. Joe was the most successful direct response practitioner of his time and perfected many of the techniques we all now use.

I have been called the father of the infomercial and have done more TV & radio spots than anyone else I know of. Between the two of us, we have more direct response experience than virtually anyone on the planet. The chapters that follow can help make you a few extra dollars or—set you on the road to vast wealth accumulation for the rest of your life.

No matter what your gender, age, interest, talents, and needs; there are all kinds of ways to make it happen for you. In the following chapters, Joe and I will share with you all kinds of wonderful information to make your dreams come true. Joe felt passionately about the subject and shares that with you next; particularly his specific passion, what he called **The World's Most Exciting Business.**

I'm going to tell you about the most exciting business in the world. It's just about the last frontier for the "little guy." It's a business you can start in your garage or bedroom, right in your hometown. And, if things go right, you can build a national—even a worldwide—business almost overnight. Yes you can! We'll show you how to start where you are, with what you've got.

It takes very little capital to get started; and if you play your cards right, it's self-financing. You can have thousands of salespeople working for you—some on a straight commission basis. In other words, you pay them only for what they sell, so your profit is assured.

GET INTO A GROWING BUSINESS

It's called Direct Response. Virtually no other business has so many people who started from scratch and became millionaires. You know some of the giants: Sears, LL Bean, Dell Computer, Spiegel's, Fingerhut, Sharper Image, Neiman Marcus, Victoria's Secret; and I'm sure you could list a dozen more household names. And there are thousands of less familiar names who are raking in the profits from direct response business, what *Barron's*, the financial journal, described the as—"the fastest growing business in America." Now almost a **trillion** dollar a year industry in the United States and perhaps three times that globally. And you can compete in it because we will show you how.

The greatest thing is that you can be, if you pick your spots, on an equal footing with the giants. The discounts they get, through buying power, can be relatively insignificant, and you can more than offset their advantages by "cutting corners." What's more, because you don't have to filter your profits through layers of people and acres of overhead, you can act more quickly and efficiently.

A BUSINESS WHERE CUSTOMERS ALWAYS WIN

Here's why the Direct Response is growing—and will continue to grow. It offers your customers convenience. It's a lot easier to cut out a newspaper or

It is probable that in no other business have so many people who've started from scratch become millionaires.

magazine coupon, write a check and stick it in the mail box, or simply make a phone call (have your credit card ready), or fax your order, or get on-line and pay by credit card, than it is to drive to a store, find a parking place and try to get a clerk's attention.

It's efficient. Most stores have to pay clerks to stand around during the slack hours, just so there'll be enough—or almost enough—to handle the peak periods. In the Direct Response Business, you can spread your workload throughout the day, getting maximum production from every employee.

Customers save by reduced handling costs. The average product has to go through the hands of wholesalers, distributors, and jobbers before it even reaches the retailer. Each one takes his cut—and adds to the cost. And the retailer has to take a good chunk just to cover the cost of prime real estate, to say nothing of a whopping investment in fixtures; and there's the cost of merchandise that's damaged as it's shipped, reshipped, and shipped again. Those are just a few of the costs that are eliminated or reduced in the Direct Response Business.

That's why almost anything you can name is sold, using Direct Response methods, and more items are being added every day. Here are some estimates on sales volume—the number of units sold—in various categories. The figures came from the trade magazine *Ad Age*: Kitchen appliances—6,100,000; Tools, under $30—5,200,000; Tools, over $30—1,600,000; Watches under $40—2,500,000; Watches, over $40? 1,000,000; Luggage sets, under $30—2,200,000; Tableware sets, under $30—1,600,000; Vacuum cleaners—1,200,000; Radios, under $80—1,200,000; Cookware sets, under $40—950,000. And those figures do not include sales from catalogs.

Here's more proof that Direct Response is a growing, multi-billion dollar business: Ninety-five percent of the major corporations listed on the New York Stock Exchange chalk up an important part of their sales, using direct response techniques. And the biggies—American Express, IBM, Ford, General Foods, General Mills, ITT, and Avon—are all now into it.

THE BEST BUSINESS FOR THE LITTLE GUY

But don't let the size of the competition scare you off, because, unlike any other kind of business I can think of, in the case of the Direct Response Business, your smallness is an advantage. Your direct, personal control and your low overhead work for you.

The president of some corporate octopus is not going to go into the business. He's going to have to hire and pay experts, who are going to hire other experts—all in the hope that they'll know what they are doing. And they'll make mistakes because they're not spending their own money—and never have. They'll have monstrous expenses I'll show you how to avoid.

Not the least of which are advertising agencies that take 15 percent off the top. The discounts that are available in the two most important areas—advertising and shipping and mailing costs—are available to anyone. In fact, I'll show you how you can pay far less for your advertising than the big boys pay using identical media (including radio, TV, and newspapers) simply because they are big.

> It's convenient, it's efficient, it's very competitive, and almost anything can be sold using these methods.

> Though it's a growing multi-billion dollar industry, your smallness is an advantage.

> I'll show you how to slash your ad costs and in fact, how to pay far less than what the Big Boys have to pay simply because they're big.

Furthermore, in the pages that follow, we're going to share "trade secrets" that cost us, literally, hundreds of thousands of dollars to discover—information that has never been published before.

WE PROMISE TO HOLD NOTHING BACK!

As for us, we're not going to hold anything back. If you follow the procedures we outline, step by step, you can have any degree of success you really want; anything from a comfortable "second income" to more money than you ever dreamt was possible.

I'll hold nothing back. Follow my advice, step-by-step and you may end up with more money than you ever dreamt was possible.

Why are we willing to do this? Well, because you paid us for it. The amount of money you spent might be a ridiculously low figure for the value of what you're about to receive, but I think that there are a hundred thousand like you. And twenty dollars times a hundred thousand people is two million dollars. So we'll make a lot of money doing what we like best. As for you, you've already had your first—and most important—lesson in the Direct Response Business.

**YOU CAN HAVE A LOT OF FUN
AND MAKE A LOT OF MONEY
GIVING PEOPLE WHAT THEY WANT
AT A REASONABLE PRICE.**

Now turn to Step #35 "The World's Most Exciting Business!"
in your *Roadmap to Riches* workbook.

CHAPTER

36
Techniques for Getting Unusual Ideas

The Direct Response Business can be divided into these six major categories: Radio, TV, Newspapers, Magazines, Direct Mail, and the Internet. But these are really only the means you use to tell people about what you have for sale.

We've used them all successfully. I'll show you how you can, too.

There are other methods of communicating—and making sales—that require little or no investment, and I'll tell you about those, too. And what may be the greatest method of making sales is just aborning. It's the Internet and it is the best way to make money I have ever seen in my entire life. Let's start with the other five and work our way to the Internet because all the lessons and skills needed for the other five work on the Internet.

WHAT ARE YOU GOING TO SELL?

The first thing you're going to have to consider—and it's really the hardest part of the problem—is what you're going to sell.

The best thing to sell is something unique: a better product, a greater service, at a lower price. What you're looking for could be anyone of these or could include all three. The crucial element is that people should have to come to you when they want it.

WHAT DO YOU DO WELL?

Make a list of what you enjoy doing and do better than most people. Are you a great cook? Are you a genius at fixing things around the house? Are you a sharp poker player? Does everyone admire the way you refinish furniture? Is there something special you know about attracting people of the opposite sex? When you're on a fishing trip, are you the one who usually ends up with the biggest catch? Are the parties you give the ones that people talk about? Do you get a kick out of meeting new people? Are you the one person in the neighborhood everyone tells his troubles to? Are you the guy people call for advice when they're having trouble with their cars? Are you a whiz at math? Can you make people laugh? Do you know how to butcher a cow? Do people admire your garden? Do you have a good memory?

A million dollar Direct Response Business has been built on every one of these, and there's a lot of room for competition.

Start your own list. Use those that are applicable from the examples I've given and add your own—things you do better than most people. Notice I didn't say "better than anyone." You just have to be better than average.

Radio, TV, newspapers, magazines, direct mail and the Internet—I've used them all successfully. I'll show you how you can too.

The best thing to sell is a better product, with greater service at a lower price.
JOE KARBO
(1925–1980)

We all do something better than most, and a million dollar direct response business has probably already been built on it—but there's plenty of room for competition.

Even if you're just a little bit better than average— that still leaves you with a potential market of over one hundred million people in the U.S. alone.

YOUR MARKET IS HUGE

Because if you're just a little better than only half the people in this great country and they want some skill, product or service that you can do better or more easily than they can, that's a market of more than one hundred forty five million people. Surely those are enough prospects to start with here at home.

But let's not forget the people in Canada, The European Common Market, Asia, South and Central America, Oceania, (Australia, New Zealand, etc,) and the Peoples Republic of China, and the new consumers in The Commonwealth of Independent States in Eastern Europe. (The former Soviet Union). It is now a global village and we can reach it all . . . especially with the Internet.

When you've completed your list (and if it's not a long one, work harder on your ISI), try mixing it up to produce an unusual combination. For example, if you can make people laugh and you're a great fisherman, you could make a good living as a guest speaker at service club meetings—or writing for *Field and Stream*—or printing signs and cards for the tourist trade of fishing resorts—or . . . .

Or if butchering a cow and throwing great parties are the two things that really turn you on, maybe you could go into the business of catering barbecues for organizations—or you could set up a "party plan" for selling meat wholesale—or . . . .

SELL AN IDEA OR A PLAN

Keep in mind, you don't have to sell a product. You can sell an idea, a plan or a better, faster, cheaper way of doing something.

* On Jan 1, 1992 Mikel Pippi of I.C.E./ Videospec and Richard Gilly Nixon broadcast the Tournament Of Roses Parade live to an estimated audience of 100 million in Poland and the former Soviet Union.

Richard has also helped bring Peter Kimball's Emmy Award winning T.V. Show " The Nashville Skyline" to television viewers in the former Soviet Union. It is now a global village, and we can reach it all.

Anyway, you get the point. Fool around with it. Have fun. And keep in mind that you don't have to sell a *product*. You can sell an *idea* or a plan; a way to do something better, or faster or cheaper. There are a lot more people who got rich selling cookbooks than running restaurants.

Paper is cheaper than plastic. And people will pay you well for a good idea—any idea that will make them healthier or happier, or stronger, sexier or richer. Certainly as you've gone through life, you've learned something that people would like to know—and will pay you to find out.

Another way to get ideas is to use Creative Unhappiness or your dissatisfactions. Make notes of the things that bug you: long lines in the supermarket, a gadget that won't work, surly waiters, paperback books that are printed too close to the margin, cluttered TV commercials, the kids leaving the lights on in every room of the house, your spouse snoring, cleaning up after the dog, dripping faucets.

Remember that the things that annoy you, bother other's too. And, if you can find a way to get rid of some petty annoyance, people will be glad to pay you for your solution.

TURN WORRY INTO WAMPUM

If you have a serious problem, attack it. Don't just let it whirl round and round in your head, making you miserable and robbing you of sleep. Look at it as a challenge—an opportunity—because it is. When you figure out the answer, you could have a profitable business on your hands.

Let me give you an example:

When I was head-over heels in debt, I knew that there were two things I could do: (1) Declare bankruptcy or (2) Work my way out. The first alternative would be a "legal" solution to my problem, but, in my eyes, it would not be an honorable one. My creditors had "loaned" me money in good faith. If I didn't pay them back, I would be betraying that faith. I'd given my word and I wouldn't break it. It was as simple as that.

TAKE A PERSONAL AND FAMILY INVENTORY

But I also had an obligation to my family—to house, clothe, and feed them decently. Not luxuriously—just decently. So, obviously, any repayment program would have to take that primary obligation into account. It had to be something we could live with—and for a long time—because a $50,000 debt wouldn't be repaid overnight. (It took us eight years.)

So I started to find out everything I could about getting out of debt. I interviewed four lawyers and a judge to find out what my legal rights were—what my creditors could and couldn't do.

My wife and I inventoried the material things we had and the qualities of our life that were essential to us as individuals and a family. We decided which were important to us and which we could do without. We discovered, of course, that the things that were truly meaningful to us; the beach, the parks, the forests, the museums, reading, the picnics, and good conversation, were all free.

LOOK FOR BARGAINS

The other things we enjoyed—an occasional evening at the theatre or a dinner out could be budgeted and the pleasure actually enhanced. It was more fun to find "bargains" in these areas: The movie houses where you could see a good feature for a few dollars at off times such as twilight or after midnight or the first movie of the day. The offbeat storefront restaurants where you could get an excellent meal for less than ten dollars. (Someday I'm going to write a book, The Gourmet's Guide to Budget Restaurants. There are hundreds of them in every large city. Why don't you write one for your town?)

As we compiled our list of all the things we had to have; including shelter, utilities, furniture, food, transportation, clothing, medical and dental care, etc. . . . we researched how to get the most for our money. Incidentally, Christmas is not an "Emergency." It happens every year and has to be saved for in advance.

SET UP A BUDGET

When we finished our list of essentials, we made up a budget, allotting the necessary Emergency Fund, a Savings Fund, and one called "We're Just Human Beings." The last was a small amount set aside so we could buy or do something "foolish" (and human) once in while.

USE THE ENVELOPE METHOD OF ACCOUTING

Then we made up envelopes for each category and put the necessary cash in an envelope every week. There are two important elements in that preceding sentence: "cash" and "every week." "Cash" because you can see it and touch it. It's real— and much easier to keep track of than a bank balance. "Every week" because when you provide for your monthly payments on this basis, it's a lot easier than having to come up with a lump—and 4⅓ times larger—sum at the end of the month.

The rules we set up were; (1) You couldn't borrow from one envelope if you developed a shortage in another. (2) If you had an overage, it had to go into the

I had a problem. I was head over heels in debt, yet I couldn't declare bankruptcy. So I found out everything I could about getting out of debt. I even interviewed four lawyers and a judge.

I set up a budget I could live with. One that would allow me to take care of all the family bills, as well as a small amount set aside so I could even do something "foolish" once in a while.

Emergency Fund or the savings fund. (3) We bought nothing on credit cards. Because when you buy on credit you usually can't always make as good a "buy" and you have to pay interest on the money you're borrowing. That meant we had to anticipate our needs for major purchases and/or repairs, furniture, appliances, a car, whatever—and budget for them in advance so we'd have the money when we needed it—by setting it aside every week.

INVOLVE THE ENTIRE FAMILY

Each of the kids has his/her own envelopes: for "School Expenses," for example, for "Snacks" (this kept us from being "nickeled and dimed" to death), for "Clothing" (this kept us from being nagged for the faddish clothes that "all the other kids" had. If they really wanted it, they could buy it, and figure out what they were going to do without).

The most pleasant by-product of all this planning was that it brought us closer together as a family. The kids actually felt more secure, more a part of the action. And we think they learned valuable lessons about money—where it comes from and where it goes. All of us derived more pleasure from the things our money bought because we were in control. We didn't have to make dozens of little decisions every day.

Could we—or couldn't we—afford this or that? We could afford anything we really wanted as long as there was enough money in the envelope—and we had decided what we could do without. In simple terms, we could have steak for dinner any day of the week, but it could mean some corner cutting on the other six days and occasionally, it was worth it.

The Budget Plan eliminated most of our careless "impulse buying." In other words, it stopped us from buying a lot of things we didn't really want or need. We didn't just "buy" things; we shopped for them. And it was fun—pitting our skills against a whole world of businessmen who were bombarding us with advertising, sometimes trying to mislead or cheat us, always anxious to separate us from our money.

KEEP GOOD RECORDS

I found out that setting up a Budget Plan and making it work is crucial. Dun and Bradstreet, the credit-reporting firm, says that over 90 percent of all businesses fail within five years after they've opened their doors. Most of these failures have one thing in common—*they don't keep good records!* And, without records, they don't know what they're doing, where they've been, where they are, or where they're going. I think that most family finances fail or stay in hot water for the same reason.

These are some of the other things about getting out of debt, staying out of debt, and having more money to spend that my research uncovered:

- How you can make yourself judgment and attachment proof.
- How you can have thousands of dollars in assets that creditors can't touch.
- How to use the little-known Law of Debt Relief to protect what you have (your home, car, salary, possession) from grasping creditors.
- How to payoff debts—on your terms.
- How to avoid bankruptcy—by preparing for it.
- Why there are certain old bills you'd better not pay—or even acknowledge.

- Why not owing enough money can be worse than owing too much.
- How to beat a greedy merchant out of excessive interest charges and even collect damages.
- Where to get free legal advice.
- How to win a lawsuit.
- Which creditors to pay first. (The ones who are bullying you probably have the least chance of collecting.)
- How "going bankrupt" may actually improve your credit rating!
- Where you can legally deposit your savings so they're probably safe, even if you do go bankrupt.
- How and where to borrow at "wholesale" rates.
- How to get your hands on money you may not know you have.

All of these things and a lot more, are perfectly legal—and honorable. They are based on laws and facts that the Easy Credit Merchants, Finance Companies, the credit card companies and the Collection Agencies hope you won't find out about. But an honest man can use this information to payoff his bills in an orderly fashion without living in fear or being sick with worry.

I LEARNED ENOUGH TO WRITE A BOOK

Which brings us back to the original point: How to turn Worry into Wampum. When I'd worked out a plan for getting us out of debt, I realized that there had to be a lot of people in the same boat. So I wrote a book entitled *The Power of Money Management*. (© 1967, © 1993 LazyMan Publishing Co. . . . available for purchase on our website http://www.thelazymansway.com/) I then wrote an ad, headlined "Get out of debt in 90 minutes—without borrowing." (The 90 minutes referred to the legal steps you can take, with or without a lawyer that stops creditors from badgering you.)

Some newspapers and magazines refused to publish the ad. (The Easy Credit Merchants and Finance Companies are big advertisers.) The Bar Association investigated the ad and the book, and cleared both . . . somewhat reluctantly. (After all, lawyers have to make a living too.)

The net result was that I sold over 100,000 copies.

In solving my own problems, and sharing the solution, I made a lot of money and, not so incidentally, helped a lot of other people with debt problems.

So I'm going to hand you a great opportunity. Make a list of your worries. Pick your biggest, meanest Worry. Then make a list of alternatives—the ways the problem might be solved. Next, gather all the information you can about the possible solutions. Usually, at this point, the answer will be obvious. If it's not, or even if you don't like the answer, simply turn the problem over to your Subconscious Computer.

When you get your solution . . . and you will, you could be on your way to getting rich. First, because you have proven to yourself how easily you can rid yourself of your own worries. Second, if it was a really Big Worry, one that a lot of other people share, they'll be glad to pay you for telling them how to solve it.

TURN WORRY INTO WAMPUM—Part 2

If you don't have any worries of your own, here's a list of subjects that other people are concerned about. They represent a compilation of the questions (almost

---

I found out some very interesting things in this process, such as: how to make myself judgement proof; how to pay off my debts—on my terms; where I could go for free legal advice; and how going bankrupt could have actually improved my credit rating.

I then realized that there were probably a lot of other people in the same boat I was in. So I wrote a book, "The Power of Money Management" and the net result was that I sold over 100,000 copies.

Solving a problem, and sharing your solution with others, not only helps them, but can make you a lot of money in the process.

There are plenty of problems that still need solving. Just because someone else may be making millions from their solution, there's still plenty of room for yours.

300,000) sent into the research division of the Encyclopedia Brittanica. The list is in order of most popular reports requested through December 2004 and the greatest number of questions. They are:

Establishing a Small Business, How to Prepare a Business Plan, Terrorism, Recycling Trends and Potentials, Debate Over Capital Punishment, Acid Rain, Euthanasia, Abortion Issue, The Right to Die, Ocean Dumping, Water Pollution, Animal Experimentation, Garbage Crisis, Child Abuse, Adolescent Suicide, Effects of Marijuana, Ozone Depletion, Air Pollution, AIDS as a Public Health Problem, Tobacco Smoke, the Effects of Crack Cocaine.

That's what other people are worrying about. I think it's obvious that millions of dollars are already being made, providing some of the answers. But I assure you that they haven't scratched the surface. So go to it . . . pick a worry you really like, and get rich!

When you're problem solving, don't overlook the obvious. The best answers are usually brilliantly simple. Don't fret that "It's so obvious that someone else must have thought of it," with the inference that "It's so easy; something must be wrong with it." Chances are that someone else *did* think of it . . . and abandoned the idea for that very reason. Don't make the same mistake.

UNGRATEFUL—BROKE AND MAD

Let me tell you about a modest, personal experience with the danger of overlooking the obvious.

When I got out of the service, I was 20 years old, married, and had one child. I went over to UCLA to enroll and saw the long lines of students queuing up in front of the Registrar's window. I decided that 2 years, 9 months and 13 days of waiting in line for food, crew-haircuts, supplies, and the latrine had been enough. I wasn't going to wait in line for an education. I was going to get a job.

But I found out there wasn't really a big demand for ex-Third Class Pharmacist's Mates with a high school diploma. The only job I was offered at what we called 52 weeks Club (because for 52 weeks an unemployed veteran could draw minimum wage) was as a Toy Assembler. It paid minimum wage for a 48-hour week. When I turned it down, the 52 week man told me that I was ungrateful and cut off the minimum wage.

SURPLUS/RECYCLING = BUSINESS OPPORTUNITY

Now I was not only ungrateful, I was broke. And I was mad. For years, an older friend of mine had been telling me about all the money that could be made in the surplus business. Not War Surplus, but the surplus goods acquired by manufacturers and businesses. Things they'd sell cheap because they couldn't dispose of them through their normal channels. You didn't buy anything until you had a customer.

Well, I was scared—but desperate. So I took a bus into downtown Los Angeles. The first big building I saw was the May Company Department Store. I went up to their purchasing office. I told the lady that I was in the Surplus Business—did they have anything they wanted to sell? She thought for a moment, and then said there was one thing. The May Company had about 20,000 small cardboard shipping cartons. It seemed that all packages sent overseas to servicemen had to be shipped in this kind of carton. Now, with the war over, nobody was buying them. Would I like to make her an offer?

I swallowed hard and told her I would have to call my "associate," who was our company expert on shipping cartons. In a daze, I wandered out of her office and into a phone booth. I held the phone book dumbly in my hands. Who would want to buy 20,000 shipping cartons that weren't being used to mail packages overseas anymore? The one obvious answer was a "paper jobber," who would sell them to small manufacturing companies for their shipping needs. But surely the Purchasing Office lady would have thought of this outlet. It was too simple. There must be some reason the paper jobbers didn't want them.

But, out of sheer desperation, I looked in the Yellow Pages and found the largest ad. (It turned out later to be a very small company.) Sure enough, a line in the ad assured me that they bought and sold cardboard cartons. I called them, described the carton as best I could, and asked what they'd pay me for 20,000. The man told me one and one-half cents a piece—$300 for the lot. I thanked him and told him I'd let him know.

I went back to the Purchasing Office and told the lady I'd pay her $250. She accepted the offer. I was in the surplus business and I had made $50 the very first day—the equivalent of a week and a half's pay as a Toy Assembler in those days.

NEVER OVERLOOK THE OBVIOUS

Most important, I'd learned my lesson: never overlook the obvious. Sure, the Purchasing Office lady could have made the same phone call. However, she had a lot of other things on her mind—and it wasn't her money. But, I was concentrating on that one little problem—and it was easy money if I could solve it. I did find out later what the boxes were really worth at "wholesale" about a nickel apiece or $1000 for the lot, and about $2,000 at "retail," and that they were easily saleable because there was a paper shortage. No matter, my business career was launched—and I'd learned a lesson that would profit me a thousand fold.

The windup on this story is that in less than six months we moved out of my in-laws' house into a handsome apartment, paid cash for a brand new car, and had four years income in the bank. All because it occurred to me that if the May company had a large inventory of these "obsolete" boxes; the same must be true of every major department store and dime store in the country. I didn't have the capital, so I had to buy one batch, sell it, and then parlay the profits to buy a bigger batch. Storage space was scarce and expensive so I rented private garages in my neighborhood for next to nothing. It was slow and a lot of hard work, but it sure beat assembling toys.

Incidentally, there's still a lot of money to be made in the Surplus Business (only now it's called recycling.) Is it something you'd enjoy doing? The only basic it requires is imagination.

Imagination is the key to all success. Which brings us to the next point. It's the counterpoint to "Don't overlook the obvious." This lesson is entitled "Don't accept the obvious." To illustrate, I'm going to ask you to change the following figure into a "6" using only a single line:

IX

Work on it before you go to the next page for the answer.

Don't overlook the obvious. Just because your solution may seem so easy—so obvious—it still doesn't mean that anything has been done on it.

Though ungrateful, broke and mad, I had an idea for making money in the surplus business. It suited me well; I didn't need to buy anything until I had a customer.

By using the obvious—most simple—solution, I was able to earn in one day what would take a week and a half at a normal job.

The bottom line? By applying the obvious solution, in less than six months I was able to get a new apartment, buy a brand new car, and had the equivalent of four years of income in the bank.

Here's the answer:

SIX

Simple wasn't it? But only one out of 500 will get it right. The trick is that most people immediately see the "IX" as a Roman numeral, and they're trapped. Or they think only in terms of a straight line, not a curved one. They accept what is "obvious."

In trying to find an imaginative solution to a problem, examine what "everybody else" is doing. Don't assume that, with their wider experience, "they" must be right. They may just be playing "follow the leader." Instead, apply what I call "Operation Zig Zag." Determine what everyone else is doing—and then ask yourself what would happen if you did just the opposite—when "they" zig, you zag.

COME ON DOWN—LOUSY FOOD—BAD SERVICE

Successful restaurant businesses have been built by advertising "lousy food, bad service" or something to that effect. True, nobody believed the sign or they just had to find out for themselves. But it worked. It got people to try the food and service—at least once.

When I started doing advertising for the Ford Agency I mentioned earlier, we looked at what our competitors were doing. You can tell me what it was, because they're still doing it. Everyone was the largest, offered the best trade-ins, practically gave cars away; and if you didn't have enough money to buy a car, they'd lend it to you. On TV, they always sponsored old movies so they could have frequent, long commercials and show lots of their used car "bargains."

They did all this because that was the way it had "always been done" and the techniques had apparently worked very well for some of the car dealers. (Happily, most of the competitors we surveyed at that time have since gone broke. In fact, all except one—which only proves that you can't lose 'em all.)

So, how do you go about advertising for a small car dealer, in an inconvenient location, who has a few green salesmen?

TRUTH WORKS WONDERS

Well, when all else fails, tell the truth (it works wonders in advertising). In our advertising, we told people that we were a small car dealer in an inconvenient location, with a few green salesmen. Then we also admitted that we were in business to make a profit-at least enough so that we could be around long enough to give them the service they had coming.

We didn't show any used cars or quote any "bargain" prices. We shared our feeling that if a car was priced way below the marked price, it must be because that was all the car was really worth or the dealer was losing money—and why would a dealer add the cost of advertising to the loss he was already taking on a sale—unless he really didn't intend to sell it?

We interviewed numerous customers ("live" so we couldn't be accused of editing) who told how they'd saved money or had a financing problem solved. We guaranteed that we'd do anything within reason and a few things that were unreasonable—to keep a customer happy.

When searching for an imaginative solution, sometimes by doing the opposite of what everyone else is doing, you can come out a winner.

DARE TO BE DIFFERENT

Instead of having many long commercials in one movie, we bought a number of comparatively short commercials in many different kinds of programs.

In other words, where our competitors zigged, we zagged. The whole campaign was directed towards building confidence and believability because we thought that people distrusted car dealers in general. And you have to be trusted if you are going to sell something to anyone. And you have to live up to that trust if you're going top sell them again.

The result: The Ford agency netted over a million dollars in the first three years.

Moral: Don't accept the obvious.

There are two reasons why you should welcome problems:

1. As you solve them, you rebuild your self-esteem. It's powerful help in correcting your ISI. And the knowledge, the skill, and the practice in problem solving you gain as you solve each problem make it easier to solve the next one.

2. When you solve a really big problem, in an imaginative way, you could be laying the foundation for an exciting, enriching business.

Problem solving is an adventure. It'll take you places you've never been before. It'll make you see things you've only looked at before. One of the curious things that happen when you start researching your answers is what I call "Tuning In."

"Tuning In" works like this: When you get interested in a subject, you "tune in" to sources of information you would have otherwise missed. Articles in newspapers and magazines, TV and radio programs, the conversations of friends, the sermon at church—all of these things and more—suddenly start coming into your awareness. You get vital input you would not have seen or heard if you hadn't been "tuned in." In my own case, I'm not sure whether the information was there all along and I had missed it, or whether some kind of magnetism I've unleashed is drawing the new material and attracting people who can be of help to me. It doesn't matter. It works.

The correct definition of this phenomenon is *Selective Perception.* You selectively perceive what your subconscious is searching for. A common experience in "tuning in" or in Selective Perception is when you buy a new car . . . all of a sudden you notice lots of the same make you never noticed before. Or when you find out you are about to become a parent . . . all of a sudden you notice babies and pregnant women.

When you're tracking down answers, do it with energy and enthusiasm. Don't be afraid to ask questions. No one will think you're stupid. Remember what Will Rogers, the cowboy philosopher, said: "We're all ignorant . . . only on different subjects." Experts are flattered by your interest in "their" subject.

MAKE YOUR MISTAKES WHOPPERS

When you make a mistake, make it a WHOPPER. Anyone can make a careless or thoughtless mistake. All that shows is that you weren't paying attention or weren't interested.

"Lousy food, bad service," the motto for a successful restaurant?

If all else fails, tell the truth in advertising. It works wonders.

By doing the opposite of what everyone else was doing, I helped build a local Ford Agency into one of the most profitable in the nation.

Welcome problems, because when you solve them: 1) you rebuild your-self-esteem and 2) your solution can become the foundation for an exciting business.

Selective perception: you buy a new car. Suddenly you notice how many others are driving the very same make.

If you make a mistake, make it a BIG mistake. Babe Ruth held records for both home runs AND strike outs!

But a BIG mistake—one that you've put a lot of thought, heart and sweat into—a mistake that you made after carefully weighing the alternatives and energetically implementing the conclusions. Now, that's a mistake to be proud of.

Babe Ruth held two records: one for home runs and the other for strikeouts. But he isn't remembered for his strikeouts.

I don't know of any advance in Science that was made without a whole series of mistakes being made. What's "science" but a systemized approach to solving problems? Each "failure" brings you one step closer to the right answer.

I know one insurance salesman who used the phone to "prospect." He figured out that for every ten "cold calls" he made, he got nine "No's" and one "Yes." So each "No" was not a rebuff. It was just a step up the ladder. He could hardly wait to go up the nine steps so he could get what he was after—the "Yes" at the top.

My only question is: Could he, with Dyna/Psyc, have raised his expectation say, one "Yes" for every five "No's"? My experience says yes!

Now turn to Step #36 "Techniques for Getting Unusual Ideas" in your *Roadmap to Riches* workbook.

37

Formula for Sales Success

A few years ago I helped set up a sales training program for real estate salesmen. Through interviews with the most successful salesmen, we had been able to determine what they did to find prospects, make presentations, and close sales.

We distilled the best techniques and taught them to the new salesmen. This was a Formula for Success. Because we were able to prove to them that, if they followed our program, step by step, they would get the following results: For every five phone calls they, made, they would make one appointment.

> One out of three people would keep the appointment and two would cancel.

> One out of three of the people who kept the appointment would visit the property being sold, and . . .

> One out of three who visited the property would buy.

So all the new salesmen had to do is make 135 phone calls to wind up with one sale. And if the average commission was $1700, that made each phone call—whether the particular answer was "Yes" or "No"—worth $12.60. If they made 30 phone calls a day, worked five days a week, took a two-week vacation, their income for the year would be $94,500!

Success is a matter of viewpoint. The pessimist sees the bottle as half empty. The optimist sees it as half full.

My wife is the most optimistic person I know, I tease her that if she found a pile of manure in the middle of the living room, she'd clap: her hands and say, "Oh boy. Somebody gave me a pony."

She bounces out of bed each morning, eager to discover the delightful surprises she knows the day holds.

She knows that everyone loves her and that they delight in her enthusiasm and curiosity. If, infrequently, she meets someone who isn't taken with her charm, she's disturbed at most, only momentarily. She wonders (if she reacts to it at all) what's wrong with *them*.

NOTHING HAPPENS UNTIL SOMEBODY SELLS SOMETHING

You may wonder why I dwell so much on salesmen.

Because we're all salesmen. It has been said that nothing happens until somebody sells something.

> Success is a matter of viewpoint. The pessimist sees the bottle as half empty. The optimist see it as half full.

We are all in sales. The infant wanting to be fed. The child wanting a toy. The housewife wanting respect. The employee, a raise. The business owner, more customers. And the good salesmen get more because they expect more.

When you were a "helpless" infant, you had to occasionally convince your mother that you needed to be fed. When you were a child and growing up you had to use sales techniques on your parents to get what you wanted. You had to "sell" yourself to your lover, your boss, your customers, and your friends. The technique was always the same. All you had to show them was that you had something they wanted—even if it was "only" your respect or admiration—even if it was only the self-respect they achieved by doing their duty.

So we're all salesmen—good, bad and indifferent. And the good salesmen get more because they expect more.

DON'T JUST GET ALONG—GET AHEAD

Don't be afraid to ask "Why?"

It's no accident that children learn most during their first six years—before we start "educating" them and getting them to memorize "facts" instead of youthfully pursuing their interests and satisfying their curiosity.

The persons who ask "Why?" show that they're not just "doing"—they're thinking.

The two subjects our schools teach best are "Sitting Still" and "Being Quiet." A child can "pass" if he does very little else. Then we wonder why adults are so passive. Why they have so little energy (call it ambition or "get up and go"). Why they accept the "rules" without question.

That's because they've learned their lesson—"That's how you get along—and they've learned it well."

Well, don't just "get along"—Get Ahead.

The persons who ask "Why?" show that they're not just "doing"—they're thinking, and they'll probably find a better way to do it. Business is hungry for Thinkers. They'll shower them with rewards because there are so few Thinkers...Many "Doers" but very few Thinkers. And all you have to do to be a Thinker is use the magic word..."Why?"

Don't be afraid to take chances.

The only things I regret... are the things I didn't do.

How many people do you know who have starved to death? You won't starve either.

When you've figured out where you want to go—jump. If there's a two-foot chasm between where you are and the next peak, the only way you'll fall in is by taking a timid step.

My father-in-law, in his late seventies, told me something I never forgot; I was a little nervous about having bought our new home. I thought I could swing the payments, but what if...

He said, "What's the worst that could happen? You might live in your beautiful new house for a couple of years and then lose it. But you'll have had it for a couple of years, and you can never lose that memory. Isn't that better than never having had it at all?" He paused for a moment, and I could sense that he was looking back on his own life. "You know," he said quietly, "the only things I regret are the things I didn't do."

DAILY BUILD UP

Set aside a definite, prescribed time each day to build your new life. Include your Daily Declarations in the morning when you get up and just before you go to sleep. Time: 20 minutes. Super-Suggestion once each day. Time: 10 minutes. Then take a half-hour, an hour—whatever you can spare—to make your purpose and supporting goals a reality. **R.S.V.P.**—**R**ead. **S**tudy. **V**isualize. **P**erform.

That's an average of an hour and a half out of your 16 waking hours, 9 percent to discover what you have that other people want. And that 9 percent of your time is probably time that you're frittering away worrying or watching TV or something else that's meaningless. But 9 percent of your life is seven years. And even if you've lived more than half of it, that's three years. Can you think of many problems that couldn't be solved in three years of concentrated effort?

So don't tell me you "haven't got the time." The wisest man I ever knew told me "Most people are too busy earning a living to make any money." Don't take as long as I did to find out he was right.

Every newspaper and magazine is crammed with Business Opportunities—and I don't mean the ads or the ones that appear in the Classified Section. Newspapers and magazines report the things that people are interested in and concerned about. Today. Right now.

SCAN THE NEWSPAPER FOR IDEAS

Here are one day's headlines and some rather obvious products they suggest—most of which could be or are being sold by Direct Response methods.

"Free Rides for Elderly"

The Senior Citizens have millions of dollars to spend for leisure, gifts for their grandchildren. They're concerned about property taxes, hospitalization costs. How can you help them?

"Sued Firm Agrees to Cancel Subscriptions"

How about a consumer newsletter warning people in your town about rackets.

"8 Day Gospel Convention to Be Held Here."

Conventioneers need places to stay and places to go, souvenirs.

"Family of Gang-War Victim Makes Appeal."

So much violence. What about a personal alarm that people can carry.

"Credit Card Fees Deductible"

How about a pamphlet listing overlooked deductions.

"Panel Says Autos Can Meet Smog Goal"

How about lightweight gas masks that people can wear. More serious answer. Natural gas is a practically smogless fuel. It triples engine life and the life of your oil and lube jobs. Its only drawbacks are that a car loses about 10% in speed and acceleration and you can only go about

---

Don't be "too busy" earning a living to make any money.

The ideas are there for the picking. All you have to do is take the time to look for them.

Every newspaper and magazine is crammed with business opportunities.

Here is something for you to think about. I believe it was Emerson who said it: "The creation of a thousand forests is in one action."

120 miles on a tankful. So who needs to go from 0 to 60 in 90 seconds? Ten seconds is fast enough for me. And there are dual fuel systems available for about $1500 installed. So you could still go on long trips, using the natural gas for the trips around town that rack up 90% of your mileage. Mileage figures are about the same, and natural gas costs fewer cents a gallon. (It's apparent that I've done some research on this. But I'm not greedy. C'mon in; the money's fine.)

"Traffic Snarled as Drifting Snow Covers Midwest"

Could roads be heated like an electric blanket by "planting" wires when they're paved—and melt the snow?

"48 Meat Plants Called Unclean"

Could you start a maintenance service to take care of this problem for them?

SELL IT BETTER BY DIRECT RESPONSE

So much for the news. When I look over the ads, I really can't see a thing that couldn't be sold better and cheaper by Direct Response. Even cars are being sold that way, and I'm told that a buyer can save several hundred dollars.

I've told you a few of the ways that you can develop a unique product or service. Probably the best ones will crop up when you open up your mind to the possibilities.

For example:

1. We were testing some "invisible" powders that would help trap thieves. That didn't work out the way we hoped. But we suddenly realized that a process we'd developed would make it possible to produce Christmas ornaments that would be shatterproof, glow in the dark, and sell for less than a buck. Through the years we've sold millions of them.

2. I was talking to my best friend. I found out that he had a manuscript telling all about "How to Build Your Own Swimming Pool for Less than $500." I arranged to have it published. The booklet cost us about 50 cents and we sold them for $10. The people who bought them got more than their money's worth and we made out all right.

3. One of the newspaper sales representatives who called on me, kidded me about what an easy way I had of making a living. He said that he'd like to find something to sell—and get away from punching a clock. I asked him what he liked to do best. He grinned and told me, "Play the horses." So I asked him if he was any good at it; he told me "Yes." So, I suggested that he write a book. I needled him for about two years, but he never did write the book. But he did run into a guy named Larry Voegele, who had a fantastic record of success at picking the winners— and had written a book, *Professional Method of Winner Selection*. I bought the rights, and in our best year we sold 130,000 copies at $10 a piece. (It's available on our Web site; www.thelazymansway.com)

The former newspaper sales representative, quit his job and became my associate in a Handicapping School. At the Handicapping School

There's hardly a thing that couldn't be sold better or cheaper than by Direct Response—even cars.

The importance of this process of opening up your mind to new possibilities was best put by Oliver Wendell Holmes when he said, "Man's mind stretched to a new idea, never goes back to it's original dimensions."

(which later became a home study course), Larry Voegele (The Master) taught what he knows in a three-night course that cost $200. The fellow who introduced us was the Administrator and probably made more money working from 9 to noon than he did peddling space full time—and still had plenty of time to go to the track.

4. My wife read a newspaper article about a new kind of diet plan developed by a doctor. We investigated and saw the possibilities of marketing it. The circulation of that newspaper is over a million.

But one person who read the article did something about it. The result: The Northwestern Weight-Loss Plan was the largest selling product in its field, and sold for almost 20 years.

5. A client of mine gave me about 200 door-viewers. (You know the things they put in doors so the person inside can see who's outside without being seen.) He'd imported about 500 from Germany; these were the remains and he couldn't seem to sell them. He thought maybe I could figure out what to do with them. At any rate, we moved them out of his warehouse into mine. There they gathered dust for two years.

One day, the shipping clerk told me they were in the way and asked if he should throw them out. Well, I was too cheap to do that, so I called a wholesale hardware company and a couple of retail hardware stores. They all gave me the same story. They weren't interested in an odd lot of what was, at best, a slow moving item. They already had regular suppliers of "name brand" merchandise. The challenge nagged me, and I finally assigned the problem to my subconscious computer. A few days later, driving home, I got the answer.

Why should a door-viewer be installed in just a front door? Why not any door? Or in a fence? Or even a wall?

So, I pulled off the freeway, into a gas station. I scribbled out an ad. I can't say I "wrote" it. It just came to me. (That's one of the creepy things that happens when you use your subconscious computer)

The headline was "Super-Spy Lets You See Through Walls, Fences, and Locked Doors." The ad resulted in interviews on national radio and TV; was reprinted by a Los Angeles Times columnist (who hated it) and by New Yorker Magazine (who thought it was funny). Most important, it sold over 140,000 door-viewers.

Don't get me wrong. I've had my share of flops. Can you figure out what to do with a game that tests your ESP quotient? Or some beautiful Christmas Cards with a sculpted medallion that glows in the dark? We sold some of these items, but not enough to make it interesting. But someday. . . .

The secret of success in this business (or maybe any business) is to milk your winners—and when you lay an egg, cut your losses. If you've taken your best shot, and it hasn't worked, forget it and go on to the next project.

Since you can test your potential so inexpensively (and I'll show you how) you can have an awful lot of losers before you can have one winner. And the winner will make up your losses—and then some.

> A man, to carry on a successful business, must have imagination. He must see things as in a vision, a dream of the whole thing.
>
> CHARLES M. SCHWAB
> (1862–1939)
> American industrialist

> The secret of this business is to milk your winner—and when you lay an egg, cut your losses.

Here are some more ways to develop a product or service: when looking at something, play "What Would Happen If."

What Would Happen If...

It was larger?

It was smaller?

It was upside down?

It was inside out?

You charged more?

You charged less?

You used it in a different way?

It was made out of a better kind of material?

It was made out of a cheaper kind of material?

S-T-R-E-T-C-H your imagination. It's a muscle and develops with use.

I've told you a lot of different ways you can find a product or service to sell. Now I'm going to warn you about a couple of things I do not recommend.

1. Don't become a "distributor" for some gadget unless you get an exclusive from the manufacturer. Even if you do, be careful. Just the other night, a magazine sales representative told me this true story:

A small businessman had a modest success selling a wooden chest for coasters for $7.95. A larger firm noticed that the ads were repeated and deduced that it was a success. So he played "What Would Happen If" it was made of a simulated wood and offered for $ 4.95. Then a larger firm played the same game, produced it out of plastic and sold it for $ 2.95. Recently a very large firm produced the same item in a very cheap Styrofoam and is selling it for $1.49.

Don't be too reassured if the gadget is patented. There are plenty of unscrupulous people who know that patents don't hold up or can be changed slightly. In any event, patent litigation is very costly and it takes a long, long time to get to court.

2. Don't fall for "Mail Order Course" or "Get into the Import Business; Buy at Wholesale" approach. Mostly for the reasons I have already enumerated (lack of exclusivity, etc.). But even more important, because you'll be paying too much for the merchandise. (I'll go into that at greater length later.) Most of these outfits are primarily interested in charging you for having your name printed on a catalog. Then you have to dig up the mailing list (more about that later too) and pay the postage costs.

Any orders that do straggle in result in a sure profit for them...and a doubtful one for you.

Besides, if you use the techniques I've described, you can come up with enough products of your own. And they're the best—and most profitable—kind.

Stretch your imagination. It's a muscle and it develops with use.

Don't become a "distributor" or fall for those "get into the import business;" or "buy at wholesale" approach.

There are opportunities all around—and within—you.

FIRST, MAKE UP YOUR MIND TO MAKE MONEY.

SECOND, CHANGE YOUR MIND WITH DYNA/PSYC.

THIRD, OPEN YOUR MIND SO YOU CAN TRULY SEE WHAT YOU'VE ONLY "LOOKED AT" BEFORE.

Don't forget: "All things come to him who goes after them."

Now turn to Step #37 "Formula for Sales Success"
in your *Roadmap to Riches* workbook.

38

Evaluating Your Ideas

If you are faithful in using the principles of Dyna/Psyc for creating ideas, you are soon going to find out that the problem is not getting the idea. It's evaluating the idea and carrying it through to completion. Now, how do you determine whether the idea you have come up with is the right one for you to pursue and how do you launch it successfully?

You'll soon find the problem isn't coming up with ideas, it's evaluating and following through with them.

SHARE YOUR IDEAS CAREFULLY

One of the first things Joe became aware of, when he consulted with people who had read his book, is that most people haven't the slightest idea where to go and who to ask for help in evaluating and developing their ideas. Many times Joe heard people tell about good ideas they had, but which were not pursued, because someone gave them bad advice.

When a new business idea is born in your subconscious computer, like any new-born baby, it tends to be a little delicate and fragile. The wrong treatment in its infancy can destroy what can become a really tremendous idea. The worst thing that you can do with an idea in its formative stages is to expose it to too many people, especially the wrong kind of people.

It never ceases to amaze me how many people will expose their ideas for evaluation to people who are negative and uninformed. The first rule for nourishing and developing your ideas is: *Don't talk about them to your friends, spouse, brother-in-law or next-door neighbor unless they have extensive special experience that can be helpful to you. Or they have already shown that they are successful entrepreneurs and you know from past experience that they are supportive of your ideas.*

IDEA KILLER

You have two problems when you expose your ideas and plans to someone else. The first is, unless you choose very carefully, your "expert" may have absolutely nothing from which to base his opinion about your idea, even if he is successful in his own profession.

Your second problem is what I call the "Second Crab in the Bucket Syndrome." When you go crabbing, you don't have to put a lid on your bucket once you have at least two crabs in it, because as soon as one tries to climb out the other will pull him back. Some of your friends are professional second crabs and they will put down your idea or plans, no matter how good they are. Does that mean you

There never was an idea started that woke up men out of their stupid indifference but its originator was spoken as a crank.

OLIVER WENDELL HOLMES SR
(1809–1894)
American physician, professor, man of letters

Should you never seek advice? No. Expert advice can be extremely helpful after your idea has had a chance to develop.

The beautiful part of a good idea is that it's self-financing.

The ideas I've conceived in a white heat and pursued with enthusiasm succeeded 50% of the time. Its been enough to make me rich.

should never seek advice? No. Expert advice can be extremely helpful after your idea has had a chance to develop some substance and you have had a chance to build some confidence in it.

Also, when you consult an expert you have to know the right questions to ask. Otherwise, you will not get the answers you need. And in getting expert advice, remember, free advice is usually worth exactly what you paid for it.

BACK TO JOE RE: CREATING IDEAS

The same gentleman who told me "Most people are too busy trying to earn a living to make any money," gave me a business maxim I never forgot:

A GOOD IDEA DOESN'T TAKE MUCH MONEY.

It's proved to be true for me and I'll prove it can be true for you too.

You can spend a lot of money on a good idea, but that doesn't make it any better. And all the money in the world won't salvage a bad idea.

The beautiful part of a good idea is that it's self-financing. You can, and should, expand by plowing part of the profits back in. "Seed" or "venture" capital should be small, something you can afford to lose. Not because, as every gambler says, "Desperate money doesn't win." Because desperate money does win... *sometimes.* But you've reduced your odds for success.

I can think of a number of deals that I literally worried to death. Instead of going with my original concept, I kept changing it around, hoping to hedge my bet. I was playing a destructive game of "What would happen if...?" The ideas that I worked and reworked failed. No exceptions.

The ones I conceived in a white heat and pursued with enthusiasm succeeded about 50 percent of the time. That's a .500 batting average, and it's been enough to make me Rich. Rich enough that when a friend I told you about (the one who made 11 million dollars in this business in eight years) jokingly asked me if I wanted a partner, I could honestly tell him, "No. I don't have any problems that money can solve." And you shouldn't want a partner either. Because you don't need one.

I told you before and I'll tell you again, "You can have everything in the world you really want."

Nothing would give me more pleasure than to see you succeed.

And you will, if you do nothing more than apply what you're learning in these pages.

And, since you're still with me, maybe you will at least try it. I know it sounds "too easy" but it works! Every successful person uses some of these methods. The most successful use more of them. These successful people may not follow the form, but they surely follow the substance because they couldn't succeed without it.

Dyna/Psyc is a systemized method for releasing creativity. All you have to do is follow the system. That's all you have to do. What have you got to lose?

I guess that two kinds of people will respond to that challenge. The first will be the person who's open-minded enough to admit that he's seen some evidence that the principle works, even in his own life, and the refinements we've offered might make it work better.

The other kind of person is desperate, but not without hope. As one man wrote to me, "I'm a truck driver. I realize that the best I can get out of life right now is some overtime. There has to be something better than this." There is. I promise.

But I'm worried about all those people in between. The ones who are saying, "Oh yeah, all that Positive Thinking stuff. I know all about that." Oh no they don't! If they really knew—and put it into action—they wouldn't be in humdrum jobs, or making "some" money, but not enough.

And what you have in your hands is not "just" Positive Thinking. I know. I took the Dale Carnegie course. I read Norman Vincent Peale and Napoleon Hill. And I got a lot out of them.

But Dyna/Psyc takes over where Positive Thinking leaves off. Dyna/Psyc gives you everything that Science and Psychology have discovered about the System for Success. **Work the System—and the System will work for you**.

Maybe you're not interested in the Direct Response Business. I love it, because I think it's one of the last areas where a little guy can get a start, live where he pleases, work when he wants, and have virtually unlimited income.

But, regardless of whether the Direct Response Business or any other idea appeals to you, I assure you that, using Dyna/Psyc and getting the kind of help you need, the freedom and pleasure of a business on your own can be yours. And you can't say that you "don't know how to go about it" because you know a lot more than I did when I got started.

EVALUATING YOUR IDEAS

Joe was right on. Using the principles of Dyna/Psyc does work! Let's expand on this process in regard to the next step in creating and developing ideas—evaluating that idea. How do you determine whether the idea you have come up with is the right one for you to pursue?

DEVELOP CONFIDENCE IN YOUR IDEA

Develop confidence in your own judgment and the power of your subconscious mind to come up with the details necessary to fill out your idea. That means you must continue to ask your subconscious computer to expand and develop the idea just as Joe did. It also means that you use your conscious mind to collect as much information as possible to feed your computer. This information should be factual, not feelings of doubt.

FINANCIAL CONSIDERATIONS

Let's look further at the financial aspects of your idea as we continue our evaluation process. As Joe said, "It doesn't take much money to create an idea." But it is crucial to manage and budget what money you have wisely.

Every successful person uses some of these methods. The most successful use more of them.

Dyna/Psyc takes over where Positive Thinking leaves off. You do what you can, Dyna/Psyc will do what you can't.

Believe in your idea. Ask your subconscious computer to help you expand it.

More enterprises fail because of cash flow problems than for any other reason. Don't commit yourself to large expenditures.

Cash flow is the first thing to consider. Good cash flow means that you always have enough in the till to meet current expenses. More enterprises fail because of cash flow problems than because of any other reason. And usually it could have been avoided with a little planning.

Don't commit yourself to large expenditures, until you know the idea will work. Don't buy the product, until you know you can move it. If you need to secure your position, take a short-term option for as little money as possible. Better still; try to work out an agreement that doesn't cost you anything, until you actually need the project.

IDEAS THAT ARE SIMPLE

The best ideas are the simple ones.

There are three other general principles to keep in mind in evaluating your ideas. The **first** is: the best ideas are the simple ones. The cleverness comes in thinking of them. If you find your ideas really complicated and they become even more complex as you try to solve the problems that arise, then they are probably not the best idea for you to go with—especially your first time out. It was Joe's experience that the really good, highly profitable, low risk ideas are always based on a simple concept with only minor variations.

IDEAS THAT MULTIPLY

A good idea must give you leverage on your time, your efforts, or your money.

The **second** principle in evaluating your idea is: How much leverage will it provide? Leverage means the ability to multiply your efforts or your money, or the value of your time. A good example of leverage on your money is buying your own home instead of renting. Suppose you buy a piece of property for 10 percent down. If the total value of the property appreciates at least 15 percent per year, which it has in many areas of the country, you will earn three or four times that much on your investment even after your interests costs. This is because the appreciation is on the total value of the property, not just on your 10 percent down payment.

Multi-level direct sales plans such as Amway and Shaklee Corporation are examples of programs that allow you to multiply your efforts by building a sales organization. The multiple listing approach to real estate sales is another example. You can have hundreds of agents trying to sell your listing.

Of course, Joe's baby was direct response marketing: direct mail, magazines, television, radio, newspapers. A good ad in the right place turned Joe into thousands of salesmen making calls. Your idea should provide you some leverage. A good idea must give you leverage on your time, your efforts, or your money. If you can get sufficient leverage on your money and you have some capital to play with, you can live without leverage on your efforts.

Don't fall into the trap of building your idea around yourself as the indispensable person unless there is an opportunity for tremendous leverage on the value of your time. Otherwise, you will find yourself worked to death to keep the thing going.

IDEAS HAVE OBSTACLES

Your **third** principle to remember in evaluating your ideas is to be aware of a potential obstacle to avoid, and that is: *too* much planning. I call this the "Green

Light Syndrome." If you are in a hurry to get across town, you don't sit in your car, in your driveway waiting for all the traffic lights on your route to turn green. There will be times when you should go ahead with an idea, even though there is a potential problem down the road that you haven't completely solved. Remember, you have a powerful tool working for you. Your subconscious computer is a tremendous success mechanism. If you program it properly, by the time you reach that problem, it will come up with the answers you need.

FILL IN THE DETAILS OF YOUR IDEA

Now, let's examine how you use your subconscious computer to fill in the details of your idea, and to solve the problems associated with the development of your idea. The key here is to assume that the solutions and answers you need actually exist and are available to you.

Your subconscious takes its instructions literally. If you say "I can't figure this out" or "this is impossible," your subconscious will take your word for it and not even try to find the solution. So, as usual, you have to be careful of the way you talk to yourself and put your negative input into the proper perspective. I found that I had to tell my subconscious to search for the answers I need. I told you how Joe programmed his subconscious to provide him with the advertising approach that made his first million dollars.

There is one final thought. If the idea you are evaluating came as a result of the proper programming of your subconscious, then you can be sure that the additional help you need will be available to you, too. And it is a pretty good indication that the idea has a strong possibility for taking you to your goal. Otherwise your subconscious computer would not have come up with it in the first place.

BRING YOUR IDEAS TO COMPLETION

The care and development of a new moneymaking idea is extremely important. Like a newborn child, your idea is fragile at first. Treat it gently and don't expose it to harsh treatment—such as the criticism of others—until you have had a chance to strengthen the ideas and develop some confidence in it.

1. Start by writing out your idea in as much detail as you can. You won't know all the details at first, but get everything you know down on paper. Break the project down into its major parts—the product itself, whether you are going to buy it or make it, what it will cost you. Your marketing strategies: What market you are going to reach? How you are going to reach that market? What type of approach you are going to make? How you are going to handle the distribution? And so on.

2. Make a list of the questions you need answers to. Identify an area in which you feel you need more information. Try to figure out where you need to go for the information. By the way, the public library is often an excellent place to start, because they have reference and research materials available online for free, that you can't get access to at home without spending a fortune.

3. Figure out how many and what kinds of people you'll need to get your idea going. Try to identify the people you need and work out the kind

> Assume that the solutions and answers you need actually exist and are available to you.

> Like a newborn child, your new idea is fragile at first. Treat it gently until you've had a chance to strengthen it.

of participation that is best for each, such as investors, partners, consultants and employees.

Above all else, remember these two things: 1) Ideas are the root of creation; and 2) no army can withstand the strength of an idea whose time has come.

4. Estimate the amount of money required to get your project successfully launched. Work out a strategy that will generate the maximum amount of progress for the least amount of money. Test your project, marketing approach, and market demand before you make large commitments.

5. While you are doing the above steps, keep asking your Subconscious Computer for the answers you need. Outlining your project, asking questions, studying available information will help to load your Subconscious computer with all the information it needs. Be sure to tell your subconscious computer exactly what you want. For example, suppose you can't quite figure out how to finance your project. Each day before your Super Suggestion period, give the following instructions to your Subconscious Computer:

"There is an ideal way to finance this project that I am becoming aware of. This financing approach is simple and within my ability to work out. The details of this plan are becoming clear in my mind."

6. Remember, to be really productive, an idea must provide you with some leverage; that is, a way of multiplying either your money or your efforts, or the value of your time. If the idea of leverage is not clear to you, reread the last chapter again.

7. When your plan has taken shape and your Subconscious Computer has given you what you need to get started, then start. Don't let your idea die—as many die—because you can't get started. Even if you haven't solved all the problems you can foresee, get your program moving.

8. Remember that all the best ideas are usually the simple ones. Avoid the "band-aid approach." When you are always running into a problem, take the necessary time to gather the information you need and then ask your Subconscious Computer for the best solution. Then act on your solution promptly and effectively.

9. Avoid distractions. Focus on your goal.

Now turn to Step #38 "Evaluating Your Ideas"
in your *Roadmap to Riches* workbook.

Setting the Best Price

The most common (and usually fatal) mistake that the amateur in the Direct Response Business makes is in the area of pricing. He simply doesn't realize how much he has to charge in order to make a profit. **The inflexible rule is this: Your selling price must be at least three times your actual cost.**

"Actual cost" is defined as:

1. The cost of the product

2. The cost of packaging (materials and labor)

3. The cost of postage

4. The cost of refunds/bad checks/credit card processing

Not to mention the cost of doing actually business, rent, utilities, business license fees, taxes, insurance, computers, phones, credit card processing, internet fees, pay-per-click and search engine optimization, etc.

For example, if you're going to sell a Widget and the actual total cost is ten dollars, your sales price must be a minimum of thirty dollars.

Now using that minimum as a base, how much can you charge for it without running into buyer resistance? That depends, of course, on the item. What do similar or competitive products cost? What's it readily worth to a buyer in terms of what it'll do for them or save them? How important is the problem that your Widget solves?

The price you want to charge is the one that gives you the best return on your investment. And the best way to determine that optimum price is by testing.

ALWAYS TEST THE PRICING

Let's say that you're undecided whether to charge thirty, forty, or fifty dollars. To test, you prepare ads that are identical in every detail, except one—the price.

Then, for this purpose, you divide your prospects into three parts. Let's say that you are going to mail 3,000 letters to people who should be interested in what you're selling. (I say 3,000 because the larger the "sample," the more you can rely on the results.) What you do is mail a thousand letters offering the $30 price; a thousand letters quoting the $40 price; and another thousand giving the $50 price. (This is much easier on the Internet but we'll get to that in later chapters.)

Be sure that the only difference between the letters is the price and that they're all mailed at the same time. That's because when a person receives a letter this can have a strong influence on whether they respond to it or not. Furthermore, when

> As a minimum, your selling price must be at least three times your actual cost.

> To determine the best selling price you must test.

The selling price that generates the greatest number of dollars is the one you will most likely use.

you're testing, be sure that the different offers are equally distributed if there's an economic differential within the areas you're mailing to.

When you get the orders, tabulate the results. The price offer that produced the greatest number of dollars is the one you'll probably want to use from then on. (There's another factor to weigh, which I'll go into at the end of this chapter.) However, if the difference in response is less than five percent, you usually go with the lower price. For example, let's suppose you get 100 orders at $30 ($3000); 90 orders at $40 ($3600); and 74 orders at $50 ($3700). The price you'd set would be $40. First, because the difference between dollar returns on the $40 offer and $50 offer is statistically insignificant. (Statisticians tell us that you have to allow for a 5 percent "error.")

Second, your $40 offer produced almost 22 percent more customers. And those names are valuable for your own use in mailing similar or related offers in the future and renting to other people in Direct Response Business. In fact, there are many firms in this business who get the major portion of their income from renting their customer lists to firms with noncompetitive offers.

I said the names were valuable, and I'll prove it. We have one highly specialized list of about 330,000. I wouldn't take an offer of $2.50 per name on an outright sale! Why? Because I expect to make more than that this year alone, just "renting" the names—and I'll still own them.

3-TO-1 MARKUP

Back to Pricing. What do you do if you can't get a minimum of three times your actual cost? I can tell you the answer in two words: Forget it. And go on to something else.

A 3-to-1 markup doesn't assure you of success, it just gives you a fighting chance.

Now the 3-to-1 markup doesn't assure you of success. It just gives you a fighting chance. I'm simply stating, flatly, that you have little, if any, possibility of succeeding without it.

Are there any exceptions? Yes, one: When you're handling a high priced item and the number of dollars of profit generated by each sale is sufficient. What do I mean by "sufficient?" Let's say that you're selling a computer by mail for $1000 (assuming that that's a bargain price). Furthermore, let's assume that the manufacturers will absorb all of the delivery, installation, service and warranty costs. In that case, your only "product" costs are your overhead (including rent, phone, utilities, insurance, etc.) and salaries for people to write up and process the orders. And let's say that all that comes to $2500 a month.

If the manufacturer is paying you $100 for each sale, you'd have to sell at least 75 computers a month for a gross profit of $7500 before you could hope to make a decent profit.

So the exception isn't really an exception at all. You still have to have at least that bare-bones minimum markup of 3-to-1 ($7500 income for $2500 of overhead cost). And if you have to stock any of the computers or perform any of the services that the Theoretical Manufacturing Company was absorbing in our example, those added costs have become part of your "product" cost—and you have to get that same 3-to-1 markup on those added costs as well.

Incidentally, if you thought that the idea of selling computers by mail was outlandish, keep in mind that thousands of Dell Computers have been sold by Direct Response. And Sears, Best Buy, Staples, Office Depot, Office Max, and the hundreds of discount catalog operations sold quite a few more.

If you think that a 3-to-1 markup is exorbitant, let me point out a few facts:

The average manufacturer figures the retail price will have to be at least five times his manufacturing cost. If he doesn't, he'll go bankrupt just as sure as accountants use red ink.

The Brand Name vitamins that the manufacturer recommends you take once a day sell for about $3.95 for a bottle of 100. I can buy the identical product (in large quantities of course) for about 39 cents a hundred—and the man I buy them from makes a profit.

The finest lipstick that money can buy costs the manufacturer just pennies. The case costs anywhere from a few cents to over a dime, if it's really fancy. Check the retail prices of lipstick at the discount stores and the hoity-toity department stores.

In fact, almost every pharmaceutical or cosmetic manufacturer knows his product has to sell for 10 times—or as much as 20 times—his cost. Does that mean that all the pharmaceutical and cosmetic manufacturers who do provide for the price structure get rich? No, just a few of them. The others quit or go broke because they fail to take into account the enormous cost of doing business in America today.

If you have a Widget that retails for ten dollars and you want to sell it to a chain of Auto Supply Stores or Discount Drug Stores, here's what you'll have to face (if they agree to buy your Widget at all): They'll pay you three dollars if you agree to pay the shipping costs, pay for the advertising, agree to take back any Widgets that the customers return, and sell your Widgets on what they call "On Consignment" or "Pay on Reorder." That means that they'll pay you when and if they sell the Widgets and will return the ones that are unsold.

Some time ago I read that Kodak gets a 6-to-1 markup on its film. And do you have any idea of the actual product cost of toothpaste, mouthwash, cigarettes, cereal, or laundry products? It's pennies.

The only time that a major store will operate on less than a 3-to-1 markup is when the merchandise is so highly advertised that they feel they have to stock it. Or it's a high-priced or "Big Ticket" item with enough profit dollars to make it worthwhile. Or they want to use it for a "loss leader." And with all this apparent profit gouging, most of the successful businessmen in this country end up with a net profit of a little more than five percent!

Now do you feel better? Do you see why that minimum 3-to-1 markup is not only "in line," but necessary.

Unfortunately, it's not really enough. It's only a minimum, only the rock-bottom kind of markup you have to have before you decide to try selling something.

PUSH IT TO 5-TO-1 IF YOU CAN

Personally, I feel much more comfortable with 5-to-1. And with 10-to-1, I haven't got a sure thing, but the odds are sure on my side!

If you think that a 3-to-1 markup is exorbitant, consider this: There's a brand name vitamin that you take once a day that sells for about $3.95 per 100. I can buy (in large quantities) the very same product for about $.39 per hundred.

Did you realize that the actual product cost of many of the popular toothpaste, mouthwash, cigarettes, cereal, and laundry products you buy is just pennies on the dollar?

A minimum 3-to-1 markup is not only "in line," it's necessary.

Personally, I prefer a 5-to-1 to 10-to-1 markup on most of the items that I sell.

Why do you and I need as much markup as we can reasonably get?

First, so we can afford to make mistakes. Show me a man that doesn't make a mistake, and I'll show you a man who isn't doing anything. In this business, as in any business, you have to keep trying: new products, new approaches, and new media. And you can't do that unless you can afford to be wrong. The richest rewards go to the people who aren't afraid to take a chance. Even the turtle knows that he can't get ahead unless he sticks his neck out.

The second reason that we need the 10-to-1 markup, if the product merits it, is so that we can afford to spend a lot of money on advertising. So we can sell more product. So we can make more money. But if you lowered the price, wouldn't you sell more? Not necessarily.

Sometimes the public equates quality with price. They feel that if it's too cheap it can't be any good. Want to find out? Test your prices in the way I outlined at the beginning of the chapter. The public will tell you how much, or how little, they're willing to pay. All you have to do is ask them. And when they tell you what your product's worth, you'd better pay attention.

How much do I budget for advertising? I go into a deal prepared to spend 50 percent on advertising—50 cents out of every dollar that comes in. Now my actual advertising may cost me a lot less.

Right off the top, you've got to be prepared to allocate 50%—50 cents out of each dollar that comes in—to advertising.

I've spent as little as 3 percent—and as much as 300 percent. In other words, I've had some cases where a $30 order cost me 90 cents in advertising cost, and I've had other cases where every $30 order cost me $90. One offsets the other (hopefully), and the average is about 50 percent. The advertising cost to get a $30 order is $15.

That's not just my advertising cost. Give or take a few percentage points, that's the advertising cost paid by every successful company I know in this business. You'd better count on it and plan on it. If you can advertise for less, good! You can put the profits aside and use them the next time you try something and it bombs. But be prepared to spend 50 percent.

Now turn to Step #39 "Setting the Best Price"
in your *Roadmap to Riches* workbook.

Running a Smart Business

A lawyer friend of mine told me why he thinks that the big companies survive and the little companies go under. It's not because the presidents of the big corporations are so smart. (I worked for a big corporation for nine months once. I couldn't believe that that many scared, stupid people could be gathered under one roof.) The secret of success for large companies my friend said, was that they could afford to do inefficient, dumb things. They're rich enough to survive their mistakes.

I might add that that's not how they got big. It's just how they stay alive. Herman Wouk, who wrote *The Caine Mutiny*, described the operation of the Navy to this effect: "A master plan conceived by geniuses and executed by idiots." The Navy doesn't want their plans executed by idiots. But they have to allow for the possibility.

50 PERCENT ADVERTISING COSTS

And you have to be financially prepared for the fact that you or someone who works for you will, from time to time, do something idiotic. Realistic planning helps—and 50 percent for advertising is realistic. Just how realistic it is can be emphasized by this bit of information: There are many, very successful advertisers in the Direct Response Business who are willing, even eager, to pay advertising costs of 100 percent—or more—for an order!

Why? Because they know that the customer—and what he'll buy in the future—is worth a lot of money! Video Clubs, Tape/CD Clubs, and Book Clubs (and similar promotions) are just three examples of Direct Response advertisers who lose a lot of money on the initial sale—but profit very handsomely in the long run.

The better example of this however is the TV infomercial that offers a product with such a high perceived value to price, that you just can't believe they can make a profit at such a low price. Items generally sold at $19.95, such as soldering gun kits, sewing machines, steamers, spaghetti strainer pots, and microwave cooking sets where they also include additional great bonuses. "How can they do that?" you wonder. The secret is they can't. Not without the long-term sales potential or selling your name. And not unless they sell you something else when you call in . . . such as an immediate up-sell or add-on sale when you place your order.

But I'm not suggesting, at this point, that you go in the hole on your initial sale. I don't think you should because it requires tremendous capital.

Now, let me tell you a couple of other things that should put your mind at ease about that 50 percent advertising cost.

The secret of success for many large companies is they're rich enough to survive their mistakes.

Fifty percent for advertising may seem like a lot, but there are many very successful direct response businesses who are more than willing to pay advertising costs of 100% or more for an order. (But only the first order.)

Even with 50% for advertising, direct response merchandising is still one of the most efficient methods of distribution.

First, it's just about your total "distribution" cost. It's the force that moves a product from you to the customer and there's no middleman in between taking his cut. You can allocate that 50 percent, and the product can still cost the consumer less than he would have to pay for something comparable in a retail store.

That's because the retail item has to go through so many hands (and each hand has to reach into the customer's pocket and extract both costs and profits). In retail sales there are most or all of these middlemen taking their pound of flesh between the manufacturer and the eventual buyer: Wholesalers, Distributors, Brokers, Jobbers, and finally, the Retail Outlet.

The retail product is sold again and again and again in ever-decreasing quantities until the customer finally completes the chain—and pays all of the expenses and the profits of the purchasers who preceded him. The retailer takes the biggest chunk. He has to, to recover his costs: advertising, display in an expensive location, "free" parking, breakage, shoplifting, clerks and what have you.

That's why Direct Response merchandising is the most efficient, most direct method of distribution. It gets the greatest number of products to the most people at the lowest possible cost.

So let's take a final look at markup. If the actual cost of a product is ten dollars, here's how the various prices you might charge break down:

Sale Price	Product Cost	Advertising Cost	Gross Profit
$30.00	$10.00	$15.00	$ 5.00
$40.00	$10.00	$20.00	$10.00
$50.00	$10.00	$25.00	$15.00

The profit margin on a 3-to-1 markup is actually quite slim.

You can see that the profit margin on a 3-to-1 markup is painfully slim; because, out of that $5.00, you're going to have to pay your own overhead costs and have something left over for yourself. If you're selling Widgets, you'd better sell them by the carload.

But, as soon as you raise the price to $40, your advertising cost goes up only by one-third, but your profit margin doubles. Ahhh, that's better.

And if you can get $50 for your product, your advertising cost goes up by two-thirds—and your profit triples! The net effect is that you'll make more money selling half as many Widgets at $50 as you would if you sold them at $30! Let's see how that works out:

1,000	Widgets at $30 each	Gross profit: $5000
500	Widgets at $50 each	Gross profit: $7500

So you can do half the work and have half the trouble, and make 50 percent more profit! Now the only thing that could offset your apparent windfall of profit is this consideration: Your prospect for "add-on" or "bounce-back" sales—additional sales to the same customer.

Will people be so pleased with your Widget that they'll want to order more for themselves and their friends? Did they buy an "Economy" Widget and do you have a "Super-Duper" Widget that they'll find irresistible when you describe it in the brochure you include in their package?

Is your Widget something they'll use up and buy again next month—and every month? Will they buy lots of attachments for your Widget to increase its usefulness? Will other Direct Response Businessmen want to rent your list of Widget buyers?

If any or a number of these things are true, and the quantity of "add-on" or "bounce-back" orders is sufficient, then 1,000 customers at a smaller profit could be more profitable in the long run than 500 customers at a higher profit.

BUYER RESISTANCE

Here's why: Because you have little or no advertising cost for a reorder; you're making a $20 profit on each $30 sale and a $40 profit on each $50 sale.

Now, let's assume that 50 percent of your $30 customers reorder. That's 500 reorders and you make $20 apiece. That's a total of $10,000.

Now if 50 percent of your $50 buyers' reorder, that's 250 sales, times your $40 profit—or the same $10,000. But the fact is that if 50 percent of your $30 buyers reorder, it's likely that a smaller percentage of your $50 purchasers will! If your $50 reorders drop to only 30 percent, the profit picture changes drastically. Now your profit on your $50 reorder drops to 150 sales times $40 for a total of $6000.

That means that your total profit from your $30 customer (the original order plus the reorder) is $15,000. Your total profit from your $50 customer is only $13,500.

Why is it likely that you'll get a lower percentage of reorders on your $50 sale? Because, usually, the greater the amount of money involved, the harder it is to get the customer to part with it.

That's why you have to figure that it'll only cost you $15.00 to talk your prospect out of that first $30, but you'll need $25.00 in advertising cost to get him to part with a $50 bill.

The same kind of buyer resistance comes into play when it comes to reordering. After all, your customer has only a limited amount of money, and he has to decide who's going to get how much of it. And now that he's gotten the original order, the honeymoon is over. All the promises, all the mystery, all the anticipation have been replaced by reality. He has the product. Whether he reorders or not depends on two things.

The **first** is how well your product kept your promises and fulfilled his expectations. He'll probably forgive your having been a little over-enthusiastic. (He probably discounted some of your superlatives beforehand.) But he won't forgive you—and he shouldn't—if you're a liar and a cheat.

Supposedly, a few shysters have gotten away with advertising a "Sure-fire Roach Killer" and sending two blocks of wood, with instructions to place the roach on one block and crush it with the other. Or advertising a "Breast Developer" and sending a picture of a man's hand. And the story keeps cropping up about the man who got

If the quantity of "bounce-back" sales is sufficient, then 1000 customers at a small profit can be more profitable, in the long run, than 500 customers at a higher profit.

Once the customer receives your product, the honeymoon is over: He may forgive you if you were a little over-enthusiastic. But he won't forgive you if you're a liar and a cheat.

rich by placing an ad that said "Last chance to send in your dollar!" But I don't believe it.

I did talk to one man who said he made a lot of money selling weeds that were supposed to produce a miraculous blossom on a "money-back guarantee." He operated on the theory that many of the purchasers wouldn't get around to planting the seeds. Of those who actually went to the trouble of planting the seeds—and were rewarded for their labor with nothing at all or a few scraggly plants—most would figure that the fault was theirs or the result of bad weather.

As to the rest, by the time the plant had matured, many months after they had sent for it and planted it, they would have misplaced his address. Which was just as well because he'd moved anyway. . . and, needless to say, without leaving a forwarding address.

To me, the interesting thing is that the "entrepreneur" who was telling of his petty triumph was obviously down-at-the-heels. If he had indeed made a lot of money at his sorry little con game, he'd obviously blown it. As I listened to him, I couldn't help think of an old world curse: "May you make a lot of money and spend it ALL on doctor bills."

There was a time when the Sears catalog could unblushingly promise elixirs guaranteed to cure cancer, tuberculosis and rheumatism. But today's consumer is pretty smart. And why not? Advertisers have spent billions educating him.

He's learned at a very tender age that most of the toys that seemed so miraculous on TV are pretty shoddy in real life (and that he'll have to wait till the day after Christmas to play with them, because Mother forgot that the "batteries are not included"). He's found that he can eat a whole loaf of Wonder Bread, and he still won't be tall enough and strong enough to lick the big brother or sister who's been tormenting him. He's learned that he can brush his teeth after every meal with Ultra-Brite and still not be irresistible to members of the opposite sex.

All in all, with the help of consumer advocates like David Horowitz and Ralph Nader, he's become a little skeptical. And it's a good thing. It doesn't mean, as they say in the childhood chant "Cheaters never prosper." It does mean that the Cheater finds it very hard to prosper and, I hope, spends it all on doctor bills.

The consumer today is more skeptical than ever. And is it any wonder?

It means that you'd better have a unique product that provides a real benefit. That doesn't mean that you shouldn't make a handsome profit. In fact, you should be rewarded. But remember that no man can get rich unless he enriches others. And that enrichment can and does consist of making another's life easier, or simpler, or more fulfilling.

No man can get rich unless he enriches others.

The **second** reason that getting that reorder is a challenge is this: There are only four basic Human Motivations—what I call the 4 R's. They are: **Reincarnation, Recognition, Romance and Reward.**

REINCARNATION: All of us hope for Immortality or Life after Death . . . and a few of us really believe in it. Most of us hedge our bets by creating works, or children, or monuments that will survive our physical being, so that at least some part of us will live "forever."

RECOGNITION: We want the respect and admiration of others; even if we have to inspire these reactions through fear.

ROMANCE: Sex is the driving force, but even after the fires have been banked, most human beings have a continuing need for comfort, companionship, and tenderness.

REWARD: This can take many forms: a nameplate on the door of an office; an office with a view instead of four blank walls; the services of a private secretary. But the most common, and most eagerly sought after, reward is Money. In this country at least, it's the coat of arms of the Aristocracy—the irrefutable answer to the question, "If you're so smart, why aren't you rich?"

PROMOTIONAL BOMBARDMENT

There are only these 4R's—and they are being assaulted by 4500 advertising impressions each day! There are magazines, billboards, newspapers, circulars, letters, radio, television, E-mails, Pop-ups, and they're all appealing to any or all of these motivations, vying for the same spendable dollar.

And the more they ask for—the bigger the size of the purchase—the harder it is to get. The ease of making a sale is in inverse proportion to the money it takes to complete it. Putting it another way, the farther it gets away from what the prospect will spend "on impulse" without carefully considering the amount of money involved—the more difficult it becomes to convince a buyer to opt for your solution to his problem, or the easing of his pain, instead of your competitor's. Or to decide to attempt the solution of some other, apparently more urgent problem.

That is why it's harder to get someone to spend $50 instead of $30 for his original order. And that's the obstacle you have to overcome when you determine your sales price and go after that profitable reorder.

How do you set this optimum price?

You don't. You let the public decide. You test in the way I've already outlined. You keep records and you take the course they dictate.

Incidentally, there are other methods to test components in your advertising. Many newspapers have what they call "split runs." Because they're mechanically set up to print two identical pages at the same time, you can make what is called a "True A/B Split." Half of the subscribers will get the "A" copy and half will get the "B" Copy. In theory, if there are two subscribers in the same block, one will get a publication with your "A" advertising copy, and the other subscriber will have a chance to react to the "B" copy. By keeping track of your results, you can decide which is the most effective.

"Regional" or "Zone" editions of magazines or newspapers are not meaningful in copy testing. Even if you adjusted mathematically for the difference in the number of copies of the publication sold in each area, there may be geographical, ethnic, educational, or economic differences that could affect results.

In this discussion of pricing, here are some experiences I've had that might be helpful:

There are only four basic human motivations: Reincarnation, Recognition, Romance and Reward.

The ease of making a sale is in inverse proportion to the money it takes to complete it.

So, how do you set the optimum selling price? You don't! You let the public decide.

The 3.5.7 strategy: If the basic sale is for $30, for $50 you can get a double order and for $70 you can get a triple order.

THE 3-5-7 STRATEGY

In two of my businesses, I've used what I call the "3-5-7 Strategy." This is a strategy we have used for almost thirty years and is as valid in the 2010's as it was in the 1960's. Let's say my basic sale is $30. But I offer the prospect a substantial saving if they order double the quantity for $50 or triple the quantity for $70. I can do this because the clerical cost is the same for all three orders (it takes the same time to process the order, do the shipping, and keep the accounting records, no matter what the size of the order).

The difference in packaging (materials and labor) is increased very little for a large order. In one business, we use the same size "jiffy bag"—a mailing package—for all three sizes of orders. In the other business, we designed a package that will accommodate a single or double order. When we get a triple order, we send one double and one single. (In both businesses, our "standardized" packaging means that we can order in larger quantities and save money.)

The differential in postage does not increase proportionately.

Only the weight of the product has gone up. The packaging is the same, and one set of instructions and literature to resell the value is all you need. (Reselling is important. They might have forgotten why they ordered and what your product will do for them.)

The net result is that I'm working on a somewhat slimmer profit, but I've increased the size of my average order—generally, to about $48.40. I've also gotten the people who might not have ordered at $50 but would spend $30 to place an order, and I've picked up some who were willing to invest $70.

With the 3.5.7 strategy I'm working on a somewhat slimmer profit, but my "average" order size has gone from $30 to about $48.40.

The approximate percentages break down this way: 45 percent order the $30 package; 38 percent order the $50 package; and 17 percent order the $70 package. A thousand orders typically produce an income of $44,000 or $44.40 per order. But that's only $44.40, and I said earlier that my average order was $48.40. Where does the other $4.00 come from? I ask the buyer to "Please enclose an extra $5.00 for postage and handling." About 80 percent of them do. Even if they don't, we send the package anyway.

Why don't we return the order and ask for the amount due? Or at least enclose a bill? Because, in the first case, I believe that the extra handling would cost as much or more than it would produce in collections. Besides, the delay in shipping might antagonize the customer and cause him to say "Forget the whole thing." In trying to collect $5.00, I would risk losing the $44.40.

In the second case (enclosing a bill), I've told the customer that I've caught him trying to cheat me. Or, at the very least, I've proven that he's careless or semi-illiterate since he obviously didn't follow the instructions in the coupon. Either way, I've embarrassed him or made him angry. If that's true, he might decide to "get even" by returning the package—and I've lost a customer.

The "3-5-7 Strategy," where it's applicable, does more than allow you to offer the price that meets the lowest point of "buyer resistance" (in this instance, those who are willing to spend $30). It also enables you to capitalize on those who are willing

Chapter 40—Running a Smart Business

to spend more. Furthermore, and perhaps more important, it gives people a chance to "sample" your product. If they like it, they'll buy more. In our case, our average reorder was getting closer to $66.00.

The only time you can use the "3-5-7 Strategy" is when the choice lies between quantities or sizes. Not when the customer has to choose between products. Supposedly, you've offered the best solution to his problem. His only decision should be "how much" he wants to buy, not "which." If you're selling luggage, it's O.K. to offer small, medium or large. You can also offer "regular" or "deluxe." But don't offer a choice between a briefcase and a two-suiter or a cardboard box. It confuses the customer. And if he can't make up his mind, he will make up his mind to buy nothing. Get that—*confusion equals no order.*

The "Strategy" allows you to both offer your product at a price that meets the lowest point of buyer resistance as well as capitalize on those who are willing to spend more.

Be careful about the choices you offer the customer. If you confuse him and he can't make up his mind, he will, and buy nothing.

HOW TO SHIP

Outsourcing has become a political dirty word, but in the direct response business it makes a great deal of sense. Especially when it comes to shipping product. I suggest you use a fulfillment house to fill your orders. They are set up to do what you don't know how to do—and don't really want to do anyway. Fulfillment is so critically important that I recommend you leave it to the experts who can ship using UPS, DHL, FedEx, and all the many ways of the US Postal Service. They have the ability to scale up or down depending on order volume and the entire process can be handled via the Internet and E-mail.

There may come a time when your volume warrants bringing fulfillment in-house but there is plenty of time for that. For the time being, concentrate on building your business.

Should you ship C.O.D.? No. For the beginner, I recommend a line in the ad that says "Sorry—no C.O.D.'s." Nowadays no one really expects C.O.D. shipping and the paperwork is too time consuming.

Because of the extra costs and paperwork they involve, I don't recommend shipping COD or insuring your packages.

Should you insure packages? I don't recommend it. The costs of paper work and the insurance itself would be horrendous. If one of my customers says he never got his order (and a reasonable time has elapsed), I take his word for it and send him a replacement immediately. My records might show that we sent it, but that doesn't prove he received it.

Some time ago a Post Office official publicly admitted that nine billion pieces of mail are delayed, lost, or stolen each year—that's about 10 percent of the total! The figure doesn't surprise me. Not when I see how many little pieces of paper can get lost or misplaced in an area no larger than the top of my desk. And when I think of how many hands it has to go through and the distances traveled, I'm amazed that any mail gets delivered at all. An exception to the rule might be if you were selling a high priced item such as a computer. In this case the extra cost of the paper work and insurance might be warranted.

ACCOUNTABILITY

To establish, some control of those thousands of itty-bitty coupons we get every day, we've set up the following procedures. They serve three purposes: 1. Show us which ads are producing what income. 2. Provide an accounting method so we can

Without some sort of accountability I'd be operating blindly.

By setting up specific step-by-step procedures, you'll have control over your cash, and have immediate access to important media information.

reasonably expect to catch anyone who might be tempted to steal a cash payment included with an order. (Yes, some people still send cash through the mail.) 3. Make sure that an order is processed and shipped.

Here's what we do: When the mail is picked up or delivered, it's sorted by "department number." That number, which appears in the coupon as part of the address, tells us which ad the customer is responding to.

Any mail that doesn't bear a department number is opened. If the "code" does appear on the coupon, (but the customer forgot to put it on the envelope) or it can otherwise be identified (say, for example, that the coupon is on newsprint and the envelope or coupon bears a St. Louis address, you know that you ran an ad in the St. Louis Globe so you can reasonably assume that this order is a result of that ad) and if the payment is enclosed you put the now-identified letter in the appropriate stack. If no money is enclosed, or if it's a request for information, or a complaint, it goes in a "No Money" stack.

When the sorting has been completed, a report of mail received for that day is made up. It lists the department numbers in numerical order, followed by the number of pieces of mail received for each department, as well as the total of the number of pieces received by all "departments." Remember that, at this point, none of the mail with the "department" number on the envelope has been opened.

HOW TO "KEY" YOUR RESPONSE

We assign numbers to every publication we use. The first ad we place gives that number as the "Department," followed by the letter "A." The next one is "B" and so on. We skip sequential letters that look too much alike and will slowdown the sorting.

To illustrate, *our* alphabet is A B C D F G H J K L M O P Q R S T V X Y Z. For radio or TV, we use a Department number, or if we're using a Post Office Box address, we add a letter. For example, "Box 345-A."

For a direct mailing, I have found that using a three letter key (the first two letters for the mailing list used, the third for the product—offer—being mailed), followed by a number. For example, if I were to mail an offer for my book by Larry Voegele *(Professional Method of Winner Selection)* to my *The Lazy Man's Way to Riches* list, and it was my first ever mailing; I might "key" the mailing "LMV-1."

"LM" for "Lazy Man's" list, "V" for "Voegele" offer, "1" because it was my first mailing. My next mailing would then be keyed "LMV-2," the third "LMV-3," and so on. (By the way, this key code is usually placed on the mailing label. The mailing label is then attached to the back of the reply envelope or the coupon the customer would be using for his/her reply.)

ACCOUNTING FORM

Then, an Accounting Form is made up for each "department." It includes the department number, the total quantity of orders included as well as a space For each of the orders expected. (For example, if you're using the "3-5-7 Strategy," you'd have 7 spaces; one for $30, another for $33.50 and so on. The last space would be for an occasional "Other"—or people who order combinations or multiples of the prices offered.) There's also a space for "extending" or totaling the amount of money that a particular order represents. (For example, in the space that says $30, there's room to write the number 40 if that's what the mail produced, and another space to show that this comes to $1200. Now there's another space to show the total number of orders accounted for, and still another to show the total number of dollars those orders should produce.) Finally, there's a space for reporting the number of pieces of "No Money" mail and still another for "Not Enough Money."

The Accounting Form, together with the appropriate mail, is given to one of the people who open the mail. This person re-counts the pieces. If it's correct, he puts his initials on the Form to indicate that he's received it and accepts responsibility for it.

If there's a difference in the count, he adjusts it (with the approval of the supervisor who made the original count) before initialing the Form. (If the response to a particular ad is very heavy, the "department" is divided into bundles of 100 or fewer letters to reduce the possibility of error and make rechecking easier.) Then the person opens the mail and they first verify that the name and address on the coupon are legible. If not, he checks the address on the envelope or the check or money order, with the hope that one of them can be translated. (I'd like to have a nickel for every order we haven't been able to process because we couldn't read the name and address. And then we get a nasty letter, threatening to report us to the Post Office, the District Attorney, and the Better Business Bureau if we don't ship the order immediately—and we can't read the name or address on that letter either.)

> By following these triple check procedures you'll keep the post office, district attorney, and the Better Business Bureau off your back.

Assuming that he does solve the puzzle when necessary, he prints the corrected address on the coupon. If the payment is by check (and the address is imprinted), and it differs from the address on the coupon, he prints the coupon address on the check (so that if the check bounces, or the account is closed, we have some idea of where to look for our delinquent purchaser.)

Another technique we use when we can't decipher a name and address is this: If the payment was by an unprinted check (such as a new account, counter check or temporary check), we write to the bank giving the account number and explaining our problem.

If the customer is paying by credit card, we fill out a credit card slip. (These slips are available from your bank if you are fortunate enough to get a credit card merchant account. I say this because it has become increasingly difficult for "mail order" companies to obtain a merchant account. If you are able to get one, often times the bank will require that you have a large amount of money on deposit to offset any potential charge backs—where a customer rejects or disputes the charge. Banks are often wary of "mail order" companies as they tend to have a higher percentage of returns than "normal" businesses because of their customer friendly return policies.) All I can say is, this is something you will have to take up with your banker.

> Credit card merchant accounts—if you're lucky enough to get one—and you want to keep it—are especially accommodating to your credit card customers.

Next, the opener verifies that the merchandise ordered coincides with the payment enclosed. If it's too much, even by a penny or two, he notes the overpayment on his Accounting Form. Later a Credit Memo or refund check or credit card credit will be issued. If it's too little, but the unpaid amount is less than 10 percent of the purchase price, he notes the underpayment on his Accounting Form. (The order will still be shipped for the reasons I outlined before.)

However, if the underpayment exceeds 10 percent, he notes that fact on his Accounting Form in the "Not Enough Money" space. (The order will not be shipped, and the matter will be handled as I'll tell you in a few moments.) If there's no money enclosed, or if it's a request for C.O.D. without an appropriate deposit, or a request for information, or a complaint, he leaves the contents intact and stamps the envelope with an appropriate rubber stamp.

And all the while that he's been performing these tasks, he's been separating the orders into the necessary stacks—one for each category. When he's finished, he uses a numbering machine (they range in cost from $30 to $60) to imprint the identical number on the coupon, check, money order or credit card slip that accompanies it. If an order is paid for with cash, the name and address and the amount are written on a piece of paper and numbered in the same way as the checks, money orders or credit card slips. (You can buy numbering machines that repeat the same number in a series of three. In other words, it'll print the number "1" three times before it goes on to "2," etc.)

So now he's separated his orders by amount and numbered them in sequence. Then he puts a rubber band around each stack—one around the coupons; another around the checks, money orders, credit card slips, or cash; and yet another around the "No Money" or "Not Enough Money" mail. (Which we'll now call "Miscellaneous Mail.") The coupons, the payments, and the Miscellaneous Mail all are wrapped in the Accounting Form and given to the Accounting Department.

The Accounting Department checks to see if the actual amount of money turned in "balances" with the orders reported. They do all of the "extensions" or final totals. The Opener does none of these figures, so he has no idea of how much money should be there.

If there's a shortage or overage, the coupons are rechecked to see if one or more was placed in the wrong stack. (This is usually the case when there's a discrepancy, and the error is corrected.)

If everything is O.K., the coupons are given to the Data Entry Clerk. Since the data entry demands painstaking accuracy and is deadly dull, the sequential numbering system gives the Data Entry Clerk a safeguard against skipping a coupon or having one blown off their desk by a puff of wind.

If, as the Clerk types the number in each record, he/she finds one missing, he/she is immediately alerted. They know that two coupons have stuck together, or one has fallen to the floor, or they've been daydreaming. In any case, they can start their search for the cause. If they can't find the coupon, they can look up the corresponding missing number on the check, money order, or credit card slip. The amount of the payment should provide the information they need to replace the coupon.

If payment was in cash, hopefully they can match the missing number with the piece of paper included with the checks, money orders, or credit card slips, and the size of the order can be deduced.

It has been said that 90% of all businesses fail within the first 5 years because they don't keep good records. Follow these procedures and you'll have good records.

Let's say that the clerk didn't notice that a number was missing. For that possibility, they check the number of records they've entered and see if it balances with the number of coupons they received. If they have fewer records than the numbering system indicates, they can start a search.

ACCOUNTING FOR YOUR PEOPLE

Now let's retrace our steps for a moment. What if an Opener's Accounting Form is frequently "out of balance." Then we have to conclude that they are either unsuited to this kind of work or may be stealing. Either way, we can't afford to have that person around.

How would we know if someone took cash out of an envelope and then put it in the "No Money" stack? When we send out a form letter requesting payment, we enclose a return envelope that's coded with the "number" of the Opener. If we get back a few indignant letters protesting that the sender had enclosed cash—and we trace them to the same Opener—we advise him that his services are no longer required. He may be innocent, but we can't afford to take chances.

We take one additional step to save employees from temptation. No one opens mail or handles money in the Accounting Department when he's alone. At least two people must be present, and their desks must be facing each other. When they go to the restroom, or on a coffee break, or out to lunch, they leave at the same time. They do not leave the room until the Accounting Form they're working with has been completed and locked up for safekeeping.

Do I think that these procedures make it impossible to steal? No. A dedicated thief can always find a way to beat the system. But it does discourage amateurs. And I think that a more complex system for security would probably cost more than it would save.

> Do these procedures make it impossible to steal? No. But they will discourage amateurs.

TIME FOR SHIPPING

Now, on with our story. . . after the orders have been entered, the labels are run off and given to the Shipping Department. In the Shipping Department, there's one final check to make sure that no order has been missed. The labels are counted, and the total compared with the number that the sequential numbering system indicates there should be. If there's a shortage, back to the Data Entry Room they go. If the numbers are O.K., the labels are put on the packages. Now that our data entry and shipping is computerized that is seldom a problem anymore.

Assuming that the errors or omissions have all been corrected, and the package has been consigned to the tender mercies of the Post Office, or other shipper, back to the Accounting Department. The total amount of payment received on each Accounting Form is added up. That's how much the deposit prepared for the bank should be. If the totals, taken from the Accounting Forms, and the actual deposit are "in balance," that winds up the day.

If not, it's back to the calculator and re-counting the checks, money orders, credit card slips and cash until the error is discovered.

At this stage, if you are using a "hold the check for 30 days" guarantee, the checks are placed in the safe, in numerical order, (that's the reason for the

> The faster you ship, the sooner they'll receive, the happier your customer will be. And a happy customer will order again and again and again.

numbering machine), where they are held for a full 30 days. At the end of 30 days they are deposited in the bank. By the way, the hold the check guarantee still works, as do variations on that theme such as "we won't charge your credit card for 30 days."

POST THE RESULTS

The final activity of the Accounting Department is posting the results. What they now produce is your most important record. For this purpose you make up a sheet of paper that can go into a binder, with these headings listed at the top:

Source of Order: The name of the publication, call letters of the radio or TV station, mailing list used, etc.

Unit: The size of the ad or the length of commercial, number of pieces mailed, etc.

Key: The identifying code you used.

Day/Date Ran: For obvious reasons.

Cost: The total cost of the advertising medium, including "production" charges (to have an ad set by printer, artwork, a film or tape made, etc.—this is not applicable for direct mailing).

Product: Useful if you own a company selling more than one.

Comments: Here you write anything that could have influenced results: weather, a strike, a holiday, good or bad positioning of an ad, bad reproduction, etc.

Under the above information set up columns using these sub-headings, so the pertinent information can be entered:

Date   Day's Orders   Cumulative Orders   Day's Receipts   Cumulative Receipts

This gives you a day-by-day picture of how your advertising is doing. It shows you what your average order is (divide the Cumulative Receipts by the Cumulative Orders). It gives you the pattern of results.

For example, most morning newspapers will produce double the first three days' orders; most magazines will end up pulling twice as many orders as you get in the first 25 days; most first class mailings will reach their "halfway" point in 10 to 11 days, and most third class bulk rate mailings will reach their halfway point in about 25 days. (Note—forget anything but first class mailings in the U. S. anymore as the post office now throws away a large percentage of anything bulk mailed. They deny it but it has cost us a fortune to verify they do just exactly that.) But they differ, and you have to know what each particular medium will generate in orders.

The only way to find out is to keep meticulous records. And as you accumulate these records, you'll be able to look at what you've done in the past and be able to forecast the success or failure of a new ad in that medium. The speed of your re-

The single most important record in the direct response business is the daily posting sheet. It should give you a breakdown of the exact number of orders received from each and every ad, commercial, or direct mailer used.

action to that forecast—whether it's to expand your advertising, repeat the ad, or even cancel advertising you've already placed when that's possible—can be the difference between making or losing a lot of money.

These "Posting Sheets" can tell you "how you're doing" at a glance when you're getting started. Later, they'll tell you what you should do. I can't overemphasize the importance of keeping and using them.

For practical purposes, I keep Posting Sheets "active" for 30 days after a newspaper ad has run, for 6 months after running a magazine ad, for 45 days after a first class mailing has gone out and for two to three months after a bulk rate mailing has been mailed. Results will still trickle in after that time. (I'm still getting about $100 worth of orders every week for ads that I stopped running many years ago!) Its delicious revenue since there's no advertising cost; but statistically, it's insignificant. For Internet programs the exact same principle applies but there is now sophisticated software to do all this for you.

THE DRAG FACTOR

Incidentally, I heard about one large Direct Response firm which sold out to a large corporation for several million dollars. The large corporation acquired the business because it showed such fantastic profits, particularly in the year or so preceding the acquisition. What they didn't discover until later was the reason for the sudden jump in profits. The Direct Response firm had simply stopped advertising. So they had a large income and very little outgo!

In this business, these extra orders are called "drag." And when and if I ever retire, I expect the drag to provide my wife and myself with a very fat pension! Meanwhile, back at the Accounting Department.

What happens to requests for information and complaints? Answer them—preferably on the day they're received, but certainly as quickly as possible. Even if a complaint's unreasonable, even if the merchandise couldn't possibly have been delivered in the time that's passed since you received the order, even if you're "sure" that the customer probably received his order a day or two after he wrote, ANSWER HIM.

Let him know, in writing and immediately, that his order and his money haven't disappeared. That all those terrible things he's heard about Direct Response companies aren't true in your case. It'll pay off and, someday, make you rich.

Don't do what I saw one man do, with my own eyes. I visited this character who was running a one-man business, and watched him opening envelopes. As he slit them, he peeked inside. Some, he stacked on his desk; others he threw into the wastebasket. I asked him what he was doing. He said that he was throwing away the envelopes that didn't contain any money. He explained that the envelopes without money either wanted more information or were complaints. His experience, he went on to say, was that he couldn't sell the former and couldn't satisfy the latter. So he just threw them away.

Well, I'll tell you something. I could have made money out of his trash basket! Because people asking for information are begging to be sold. And if you take care of a complaint, you make a friend...a friend who buys. The great thing about this

---

These daily posting sheets tell you instantly and daily at a glance exactly how your business is doing.

I am still getting a $100 worth of orders ever week for ads I stopped running years ago.

Request for additional information—answer them, they are potential costumers just begging to be sold.

If you get a complaint, even if the complaint is unreasonable, answer it.

business is that you get to build a relationship with your customer so that he is yours for years and years to come.

I know another man, who's probably the best salesman I ever met. When he worked for a Real Estate firm, he asked to be put in charge of the "Complaint Desk." His philosophy was that once he'd solved the customer's problem—and most problems can be solved—the customer was pleased and grateful—and ready to buy again from someone he trusted. It worked. He sold more property than anyone else in the firm.

A long time ago, when I was in the wholesale paper business (remember, it all started with those surplus cartons), I learned a valuable lesson. At first, if an order had been goofed up, I'd tell my secretary to say I was out if the customer phoned. When I finally had to face up to him, he was mad. Frequently, the outcome would cost me money and the customer.

Your big profit comes from re-orders. Only satisfied customers reorder.

Then I decided to try another approach. If anything had gone wrong, I'd call or E-mail him. Preferably before he even knew about the mistake. I'd explain, apologize, and ask him what I could do to make it right. Nine times out of ten, he was so pleased at my interest that he'd tell me to forget it, or offer a settlement that was a lot less than I was prepared to give. As for the tenth man, I simply tried to settle as gracefully as possible and keep his business.

Now turn to Step #40 "Running a Smart Business"
in your *Roadmap to Riches* workbook.

41

Eight Tips to Save You Money

Here are some tips to keep your costs down and improve your results. These are facts that I found out the hard way—after wasting enough money to put each of my kids through college. And I have a lot of kids. (These tips apply to all methods of direct response except the Internet, which I'll cover in later chapters)

TIP #1

Watch the weight of your package very closely.

Any advertising that you insert has to pay its own way. First, from the standpoint of what it costs to produce (including printing, amortized art and all production costs). Second, what does it add to your postage costs? Sometimes, you can use a lighter weight paper stock and keep the postage scale from moving up an extra notch. Then you can mail it free!

If it's at all possible, keep the total weight under a pound. Even if you have to, ship the order in two or more packages (assuming that's feasible). Because, unless you do, you can't get the savings made possible by shipping "Bulk rate" (more about that later). By the way, shipping bulk rate is fine—sending out ads bulk rate is not fine—don't do it.

And as soon as you go over a pound, even if you're using ordinary Parcel Post rather than "Bulk rate," the postage costs skyrocket. For example, if the package weighs less than a pound, you pay so much per ounce, no matter where you ship it in the United States. But as soon as you go over a pound, the postage is based on the "zone" it's going to. To illustrate (at the rates in effect as this is written): you can mail a package anywhere in the United States for $1.79 or less if it weighs under 16 ounces. But if it weighs more than one pound, and less than two, it'll cost you $2.12 for local delivery and $2.85 for shipment to the furthest zone. All you can do is figure out what's best in your case—but don't forget the clerical and handling costs involved in computing the varying postage.

Avoid any product that's packed in glass. The increased costs in protective packaging, to say nothing of the weight of the glass, make it tough to market. Attractive plastic containers are cheap, lightweight, and virtually unbreakable. In my vitamin business, we use what's called "strip" packaging. Each pill is encased in an individual cellophane cell, and there are 30 cells in a "strip." This protects freshness; makes it easy to carry a day's supply in your pocket or purse. From our viewpoint, the feather-light flat strips can be slipped into a "Jiffy Utility Bag" (one without padding) and cushioned against breakage by putting our literature on each side.

Watch the weight of your package very closely. The difference of just one ounce can end up saving—or costing—you thousands in the long run.

Economies like this have made it possible for us to hold our prices in this business at the same level for as long as 15 years before we have had to revise them—in spite of advertising costs that have tripled and postage costs that have soared and are continuing to rise. (Remember the penny postcard and the four-cent first-class stamp?) We do it by constantly playing the game of "What Would Happen If..." And, of course, buying pills by the millions helps.

TIP #2

Use the lowest possible postage rate or shipping weight!

By using the lowest possible postage rate, you can save as much as 65% in postage costs.

If you don't have enough volume (200 or more identical packages or the number of identical packages it takes to make up 50 pounds) to ship "Bulk rate," use "Third Class." Shipping a product by "Bulk rate" as opposed to "Third Class" has saved us as much as 65 percent in postage costs.

You've heard some horror stories about the slowness of Third Class mailing, and some of them are true. But First Class mail can get snarled up too—and First Class rates will kill you.

We've done test-mailings around the country, mailing three identical packages, on the same day, to the same destination. We sent one First Class, another Third Class, and the last as part of a Bulk rate shipment. In almost every case, they all either arrived at the same time or, at most, delivery was delayed by a couple of days! Although "Bulk rate" enjoys the lowest cost, delivery is usually satisfactory because you're doing most of the Post Office's work for them in terms of sorting and bundling.

Sure, you'll have an occasional Third Class or Bulk rate package go astray. When you do, replace it promptly. It's still a lot cheaper than sending everything first class. The only exceptions I make are these: (1) Merchandise replacements are sent First Class. If I can believe my tests, they won't arrive much sooner, but I think the psychological impact on the customer is worth the added expense. That extra postage is meant to say "I'm sorry—and I value your business." (2) Sometimes, customers are in a dreadful hurry to get the product (for example, with Larry Voegele's book, *Professional Method of Winners Selection*, on how to beat the horses). So I've offered, in the coupon, to send the book by first class if they'll pay the extra cost; and if they do, I do.

The Post Office has some bargain rates for certain kinds of merchandise; books, educational material, and tapes/CDs (both audio and video) for example. Books can be sent out at a special rate. It's a bit higher in cost than "Bulk rate"—but you don't have the added expense of sorting and bundling or the necessity of identical packages and minimum shipments. All you have to do is write or rubber-stamp the words, "Special Fourth Class Book Rate," on the package. One Caution: You can't enclose any advertising literature.

Other materials such as certain films, test materials, sound recordings and the like also enjoy the "Special Fourth Class Rate." All you must do to take advantage of it is to write or stamp the magic words, "Special Fourth Class Rate."

I think it's accurate to state that no one in the Post Office will volunteer information on how you can save money on postage rates—or tell you that you're paying more than is necessary. But with these guidelines, persistence, and a thick skin, you can wheedle out the information you need. Always go to the Head Man; he's most likely to be well informed or know whom to ask.

We increasingly use other methods of shipping such as; UPS, DHL, FedEx, and even USPS Global Priority on our websites. The customer can predetermine the costs of shipping via every known method of shipping, and the computer program calculates the shipping costs and the delivery times instantly no matter where the customer lives on the planet. The customer gets to choose when he gets the product and how much it will cost him. We have the computer programmed to include our packaging materials and labor costs also. We still recommend you use a fulfillment house.

SAME DAY FULFILLMENT The one factor that's indispensable in making lowest-cost postage work is this: Fill your orders the same day they arrive...Or, at the very latest, the next day. If you're out of stock, or there's some other problem, send an E-mail, explanatory card or a letter to the customer immediately. Don't forget: he's "sent" money to someone he doesn't know for something he hasn't seen—and he's nervous. He's eager to get the merchandise, or he wouldn't have ordered it in the first place. Reassure him, before he complains.

TIP #3

Keep on top of your state's Sales Tax!

I don't know about the laws in other states, but I can tell what I think I know about California. (We've been audited three times in the past 16 years and have gotten clobbered each time. I have the uneasy feeling that every time the Governor needs money for a new State project he sends a guy around from the State Board of Equalization to pick up the down payment from me.)

The only hopeful note is that the "assessment" has been for a lesser amount each time. What's discouraging is that each new auditor tells us that the instructions given by his predecessor are wrong—and this is the way we should keep our records. I can hardly wait 'til the next time. Maybe they'll discover we've overpaid. And maybe the moon really is made out of cheese.

And don't think that Internet orders are tax-free—they aren't. Any orders from your own state are a taxable transaction and you better keep records for the taxman. As your state, county, and local politicians are increasingly spending more than they take in, this will continue to be an ever increasing problem for those of us in business. There are moves afoot to tax Internet sales in every political body and even though they haven't been successful yet—they will be, so be prepared and protect your business and yourself by automating your sales processes. See our web site for recommendations.

O.K. back to business. You'll need a resale permit number. There'll be a fee, and you may have to post a cash deposit (or a bond), consistent with the tax you'll owe, based on the volume of business you expect to do. There's even some way that you can put the money in a bank and earn interest, even though the principal is pledged to the State Board (ask your accountant—rules vary widely).

The resale permit number allows you to buy all the supplies that you resell, without paying tax. For example, you don't have to pay sales tax on your Widgets or the instruction booklet that goes with them. You do have to pay tax on the advertising literature you put in the package. There are all sorts of fascinating, trifling differentials like that, and your accountant is, again, your best source of advice.

Watch—stay on top of—your state sales tax. Here in California with the rates going up and down (mostly up), and the tax laws keep coming and going (mostly coming), I find it difficult to keep on top of it all. Three times I've been audited and three times I've been clobbered.

There is one positive side of the sales tax picture for mail order businesses. At least it's true for now. It's this: you are not required to collect—or pay—a sales tax on any sales that are in a state which you have no physical presence.

One sidelight: My wife uses our resale permit number to get into wholesale showrooms, which do business only with "dealers." She has to pay the tax, but she saves a lot of money. Or so she tells me.

How much tax do you have to collect and remit? Well, on all sales made to customers living in the city (if there's a city sales tax) or the state where you do business, you have to pay the tax. On out-of-state sales, at present you do not have to either collect or pay. (This is a fact that was reaffirmed by a Supreme Court ruling on May 26, 1992. Basically, they upheld part of the "Bella Hess" decision which stated that, "a business is not liable for sales or use tax in a state in which it has no physical presence.")

Now, if you're doing a big volume and a substantial number of your sales are out-of-state, how do you know how much is taxable—without getting buried under piles of records that you're required to keep for three years? One answer, of course, is to go on computer.

Incidentally, if you are assessed, you don't have to accept their figure. You can arbitrate or appeal; and if you're in the right, I recommend that you do. We've had assessments reduced by two-thirds.

TIP #4

Don't hold orders, waiting for checks to clear!

In the first place, it can take days or weeks—and how will you know which checks have cleared and which have not? Even more important, why should you punish all of your customers for transgressions of a few? Trust them. Most of them will justify that trust. After all, they trusted you.

Our bank has instructions to put any check that bounces through a second time before returning it to us. When a check is returned, we write to the customer, asking him to make good and reimburse us for the fee the bank charged. Most do. From time to time, we gather up a batch of checks we have not been able to collect on, and turn them over to a collection agency or our attorney. For a percentage, they try again, and we get some more of our money in. If your experience is like mine, the remaining uncollectables are a stiff figure at the end of the year, but only a tiny fraction of your sales volume.

TIP #5

Shop around for a bank!

Banks differ widely in their policies and those differences can add up to a lot of money for you. I've found that an independent bank, or one that's part of a small chain, usually offers the most advantages.

Here's what you want to compare: (1) Will there be a service charge if you maintain a minimum balance, if so…what's the minimum? (2) Will they charge you for each check you deposit? (Most large banks will make a charge for each check you deposit, if you deposit a large volume of checks of small denominations. Depending on the volume, this can be anywhere from three to five

---

Note: This can change at any time. Be sure to check with your accountant and stay on top of it.

Ship orders promptly—don't wait for the customers check to clear. The sooner the customer gets his product, the happier he'll be. And a happy customer is the kind that will order again and again and again.

cents—or even more—per check.) This seemingly insignificant amount can run into BIG money.

Before I switched banks, I was being charged about $14,000 a year for this activity—and this was the net figure, after I'd been given credit for the average balance in the account! Based on my present volume, that figure would have been multiplied again and again. (3) Will they allow you to deposit checks and money orders without listing the bank numbers and itemizing the checks? (There's a procedure for doing this, attaching only an adding machine tape after the checks have been separated. A cooperative bank will show you how.) Eliminating the bank number listings and listing each check will save you hundreds of man-hours. (4) Can you bank by mail, and will the bank pay the postage? If you have a wad of checks, the postage can be two or three dollars a day. That's over $1,000 a year—and they can afford it better than you can. Actually, I don't recommend this today. In the first place you'll lose two to three days float and besides, when your deposits are sufficient enough, your bank will pick them up on a regular basis. (5) Once you're able to get a credit card merchant account, what is the service fee that a bank will charge you? The range of fees is from 1.75 percent to as high as 9 percent with an average more in the range of 3 percent to 5 percent. The rate is negotiable so it pays to shop around. (See the guidebook for the best online merchant accounts)

After you've shopped for your best deal and weighed the other obvious considerations—like convenience of location and availability of credit for your operation—pick the one that has the most to offer. But think in terms of your future, as well as your present needs. Incidentally, your bank can also help you file a "Certificate of Fictitious Firm Name" if one is necessary.

TIP #6

Make refunds promptly.

The only thing that I can add to that is "cheerfully." We've made some so fast that we discovered that the customer's check had bounced after we'd already sent him a refund. But that's more than offset by the people who are so pleased at the speed of the refund that they ordered again. (And we got our money back in most of the other cases.) One other thing while I'm at it, even if you never received the returned product back, yet the customer claims to have returned it, take their word for it and issue a refund, Don't ever, and I mean ever, argue with a customer over this point.

I know of one competitor of mine who once told me with great pride how he would never allow any of his customers to take advantage of him. No way. In fact, there was even the time when he boasted that he'd responded to the same customer on ten separate occasions, refusing to issue the customer a refund because no product had ever been returned.

What a waste. My competitor probably spent two hundred dollars in time, energy and effort, yet saved himself from having to issue a $30 refund. How stupid! (By the way, this competitor of mine is no longer in business. I wonder why?)

Next to shipping orders on a timely basis, the single area that will get you in hot water quicker than anything else, is failing to issue a prompt—if not cheerful—refund.

Your customers are your best friends and should be treated as such. I can't tell you how many customers have continued to do business with us after we cheerfully issued them a refund. At our seminars, these people come up to us and thank us for the way we handled their problem. I love that! Now I have a satisfied customer and a friend. It's the old "Golden Rule" and you can't run your life or your business without it.

TIP# 7

Read *Direct Marketing Magazine* and *Direct Marketing News!*

I recommend looking over as many back issues as they have. You can probably pick them up at your local library, or you can subscribe. If you want a subscription you can reach them at: *Direct Marketing Magazine* www.directmsag.com *Direct Marketing News* www.dmn.com. I also recommend you join the Direct Marketing Association www.dma.org

No, I don't make a commission (although I have to admit that the thought crossed my mind).

But I want you to read them because I think you'll find them full of information you'll want and need. Each month, they describe dozens of brand-new products you might want to take on—or that trigger ideas of your own.

There are great articles by some of the best pros in the business, examining every phase in great detail. There are directories, itemizing the names and addresses of the people who provide the services and the products you'll need. And Ideas, Ideas, and more Ideas! They're invaluable—and if you're serious about taking a crack at the Direct Response Business, you can deduct your subscriptions as a business expense.

TIP# 8

Read these books.

They are all very informative and will give you many additional and valuable pointers on starting and operating a successful direct response mail order business. They are:

How I Made $1,000,000 in Mail Order—And You Can Too

By E. Joseph Cossman

Dollars in Your Mailbox (The Beginner's Guide to Selling Information by Mail)

By Ernest P. Weckesser, Ph.D.

Successful Direct Marketing Methods

By Bob Stone

Profitable Direct Marketing

By Jim Kobs

Building a Mail Order Business

By Dr. William A. Cohen

Sidebar notes (left margin):

Ideas, they are the lifeblood of this business. They are, as Frank Lloyd Wright best put it, "...salvation by Imagination."

Ralph Waldo Emerson says "Books are for nothing but to inspire."

None of this will guarantee your success. But it will (hopefully) keep you from making some of the dumb mistakes I made when I was starting out.

Some of these books should be available at your local library or, if you wish to buy them, check with your neighborhood bookstore. You can also order them from our website's Success Library.

Well, I've covered almost everything you need to know about Pricing and Business Practices. Plenty to get you started—keep you going and help you get big and stay big.

None of it will guarantee success. That depends on you and what you do about your ISI! But it'll sure keep you from making some of the dumb mistakes I made when I was starting out.

Now turn to Step # 41 "Eight Tips to Save You Money"
in your *Roadmap To Riches* workbook.

How to Write Successful Ads

I can tell you how to write an ad in one word:

Don't.

Most people who try to write ads immediately adopt a stilted style, or try to be terribly clever, or use words that they—and the rest of us—have to look up in the dictionary. The result is a special language and form that I call "Advertise-ese"— there's only one problem with it: It doesn't communicate. It's not personal. It's all skin and no flesh—and certainly no guts.

When you've found something you want to sell, here's all you have to do to create a successful ad. And I promise you that it'll work.

WHAT WILL YOUR PRODUCT DO FOR PEOPLE

First, think of all the things your product will do for people. Then pick out the one, most important, specific thing it will do. Not just "Makes Long Life a Reality"...but "Guaranteed to Make You Live to 100!" Not just "You Can Be Important"...but "How to Get a Promotion and a Raise in 5 Minutes!" Not just "You Can Be Beautiful"...but "7 Ways You Can Make Him Ask for a Date!" Not just "It's Easy to Make Money"...but (will you forgive me?) "The Lazy Man's Way to Riches!"

Every one of those "headlines" appealed to one or more of the 4R's. (Remember?...Reincarnation [immortality], Recognition, Romance, Reward.) And the strength—the drama—of your appeal to these four Basic Human Motivations will determine how successful you will be in getting the attention of your reader, listener, or viewer.

There's no mystery to it. (Although a lot of ad agency copy chiefs who are pulling down $400,000 a year would like you to think so.) I'm showing how they do it, step by step, and you can do it, too! So let's continue.

Think about what you'd like the product to offer you. What problem you'd like it to solve or pain you want to eliminate. (You're really not that much different from anyone else.)

Write down all the ideas that come to you; even if they seem silly or wild. Don't try to judge them—not yet, just write them down. Keep a pad and pencil within reach, or better yet...use the memo section of your PDA (my Palm Pilot is filled with notes and ideas). If you don't capture your inspiration and make it a prisoner, it'll escape and be lost forever.

> Successful ads communicate on a personal level.

> It has been said that an advertising agency is 85% confusion and 15% commission.

Keep a pad and pencil within easy reach. If you don't capture your inspiration and make it a prisoner—it'll escape and be lost forever.

All of my best ideas were generated when I was driving my car, reading a book, just falling asleep, just waking up, or it seems most often in restaurants. Many a business has been started with an idea jotted down on a restaurant napkin.

Do you notice what each of these activities had in common? Nothing. That's right, I was doing absolutely nothing about solving my problem—how to sell a particular product—and then the right idea suddenly popped up...not out of nowhere—out of my Subconscious Mind.

What had I done to feed the subconscious mind the information it needed, so it could spit out the answer? I'd simply thought about the product. Not so much what it is, but what it does. My wife bought a vacuum cleaner and hired a housekeeper. But what she really wanted was an easy way to clean the house. Do you see the difference?

People buy things or hire people, but what they are after is results.

People buy things or hire people, but what they're after is the result. If she could press a button and, through some miracle of electronics or ultrasonic sound waves, the house would be cleaned spotlessly—and the cost was within reason, she'd junk the vacuum cleaner and fire the housekeeper. (At least when I asked her she said she would.)

So think about what the product will do. Better, or cheaper, or faster than anything else you know about.

REASONS FOR BUYING

Think about all the reasons you *would* buy it. Think about all the reasons you *wouldn't* buy it. (How many of those objections can you overcome?) Write it all down. Read magazines and newspapers. Notice how articles about the problem leap right off the page and hit you in the eye (remember, Selective Perception). If you must, talk about the product with people who are as enthusiastic as you are. But even if you try to avoid the Wet Blankets, there's a danger. You might, literally, talk it out and release the energy you've been building up.

Because that's exactly what you've been doing; fueling the subconscious. Warming it up. So it can produce that spark you're looking for.

Fill your head with as many facts and insights as you think you can handle then let your subconscious go to work!

When you feel you're saturated with facts and insight—when you've racked your brain, simply forget about the problem. The next step is to do nothing. Go on with the other things that make up your life. What could be easier? But, at that point, the problem is as good as solved. In an hour, or a day, or a week, you'll get the idea. The one, perfect way to express exactly what your product will do.

It'll come when you're not thinking about it at all. Write it down! And keep writing. Because the "headline" or the attention-getting idea is just the valve—and it's been blown off by the pressure of the whole idea that's boiling underneath. It'll all come out now. Just keep writing. Keep writing 'til you run out of steam. Chances are that you won't until you're finished. But if you do, don't worry about it. Forget it again. When it's ready, the subconscious will let you know that it's raring to go back to work.

What about all those notes you made? Don't look at them or think about them until you're finished. That's because you want to give your Subconscious Mind a chance to "edit" them—to polish up the good ones, combine some to produce a new idea, discard the ones that are unworkable or simply don't fit into your new concept.

After you're all through writing, look at your notes. There might be a phrase or two that you'll want to include. But it's not likely. You'll be amazed at how your subconscious has sorted out your input—keeping the good stuff and rejecting the junk.

At this point, put what you've written away for a couple of days before you look at it again. Make minor corrections. Read it aloud and listen to whether it sounds like you talking. That's important. It should use the same words you'd ordinarily use in talking to another human being. If you've included something terribly clever or coined a great little slogan—kill it. Or it'll kill you. As soon as people become aware of your "style," you've lost them. They may be entertained, they may be amused, but they won't buy.

GO FOR FEEDBACK FROM PEOPLE

The next step is the hardest. Have other people read what you've written. But you're not to listen to their opinion. Not until you've had a lot more experience and know which opinions to accept and which to reject. And that takes years. At this point, the only thing you want to know is whether your ad is clear. Not whether they like it or dislike it—only whether they understand it.

If you find yourself explaining or, worse yet, defending the ad, then you know it isn't clear. If they don't know what you mean, clarify it. If they have to reread a phrase before they understand it (watch their eye movements!), change it. But don't change your approach or change a single word because they suggest one that's "more refined" or "sounds better."

After reading your ad, if they know what your product will do for them, what it's advantages and disadvantages are, if they know how much it costs and where to buy it—that's all that's necessary. Why do you tell them about the disadvantages, the small weak points? So they'll believe you. And if you've been completely honest, they'll have to believe you. Because it's the truth. The truth, told as attractively as possible, perhaps, but still the truth.

Do you still think it's hard to write a good ad? Let me show you how easy it is.

Dear Betty,

I love you very much.

I want to take care of you and our kids for the rest of your lives. There'll be good times and bad. But I'll try to do my best with what I've got.

From time to time, I'll probably exasperate or annoy you, but I promise that you'll never be bored.

I read somewhere that the contract for marriage is the only one that doesn't have a definite term—a point at which it ends or can be renewed. It just says...'Till Death do us part.' Well, I want you to know that, in our case, I'm satisfied with that arrangement. but, to be perfectly honest, I sometimes wish that we weren't married—so we'd both know, every day, that we were sharing our lives because we wanted to—not because we had to.

All my love,

Joe

Once the idea "hits" you, start writing. And don't stop writing till you've run out of steam.

If after reading your ad, they know what your product will do for them, they know it's advantages and disadvantages, they know how much it costs and where to buy it—that's all that is necessary.

Every ad should be a love letter, a personal communication.

You're saying, "That's no ad, that's a love letter!" Well, every ad should be a love letter, a personal communication. And let see if this one contains the basic elements.

You may not like the headline "Dear Betty"—but my wife will be crazy about it. It has her name in it, it's directed to her. And that's the secret of a good headline. The person reading it, the one you're trying to reach, should say, "Hey—he's talking to me."

The subhead, "I love you very much," isn't bad either. I've told her that she's a very important person, a great human being, and that I care about her.

Next, at the start of the body copy, I've made my promise—to take care of her and our kids for an unlimited time. Then I've gone on to enumerate the advantages and disadvantages of such an arrangement. (If she wasn't already so familiar with them, I'd probably have gone into greater detail and been more exact. But, after all, I made my sale some years back and am now looking for a reorder.

The rest of the copy is simply reassuring; it repeats the promise, and identifies the seller. Although there hasn't been a specific call for action, it's certainly implied. She knows what I want, which is why I married her in the first place. As you can see, you don't have to be a literary genius to write a good ad, not a great ad perhaps, but enough to get the job done.

Let me give you another example; let's say that you found the following note from a friend in your mailbox:

> *I have a new Caddilac that I got to sell because I'm leaving for the Service next week, It cost me $34,000 and only has 732 miles on it, Rather than sell it to some thief of a car dealer or going to the trouble of advertising, I'll let you have it for $24,000.*
>
> *If you don't have the cash, don't worry about it because I only owe the $24,000 and you can take over my payments which are about $397 a month.*
>
> *You know I drive careful, but I'd feel better if you'd have your mechanic check it out before you buy. In fact, if you'd like to drive it for a couple of days, I'll be glad to deliver it to you with a full tank of gas. And if you don't like the car, I'll take it back and you've had a free ride. No obligation.*
>
> *One thing—it's an awful green color (but you could have it painted).*
>
> *If you're interested, call me at (714) 555-1212 between 7 and 9 tonight*
>
> *Your friend,*
>
> *Roger Atbury*

Now, that's a good ad! It doesn't matter that your friend doesn't know how to spell "Cadillac" or that his grammar is atrocious. He's told you what he's selling, why it's cheap, how you can easily afford it, revealed its one shortcoming (correctable), offered a free trial, and told you just what to do if you want to buy.

There are still a number of reasons that you might not want to buy it—you might hate Cadillac's, or not be able to afford $397 a month—but you'll have to admit that it's an almost irresistible offer, even if you only bought it for resale.

The whole point is that a good product will almost sell itself—if you don't garbage it up with a lot of things that people think are "advertising."

I once read somewhere that advertising is simple salesmanship in print.

The best ad is a good product—as long as you don't garbage it up.

WHAT'S THE RIGHT SIZE OF AD?

Maybe you've noticed that I haven't said anything about how big or how long your ad should be. The answer to that is: as big or as long as it needs to be. It takes less space or time to sell a Cadillac at half-price than it does to sell a Widget. That's because the Cadillac has been pre-sold by General Motors, and all you have to sell is the bargain price and the terms—and make it believable. With your Widget, you're starting from scratch. I never start out to write a certain size of ad. I simply write the best, most simple ad I can. I try to describe every sales feature, anticipate and over-come every objection.

Not 'til I'm finished and am satisfied that I've done a good selling job do I decide what media I'm going to use. A very long ad can go into a letter—or be used in newspapers or magazines if you can afford the greater risk. A short one can be used in all of those and might work even better on radio, TV or the Internet.

A small ad might be "lost" in a magazine or newspaper, but every radio or TV commercial is the equivalent of a full page. Your radio or TV commercial is just as important and can be just as effective as the one produced by the biggest, richest advertisers in the country.

But I won't cut my copy down to "size"—not yet. (After all, what's the point of knocking on the door if the salesman disappears when it's opened?) So, first, I'll test the ad just as I've written it. If it works, then I'll cut it—and test it again. If the second ad is more profitable than the first, I'll cut it again and test again and make my next decision, based on results. Writing advertising copy is part art, but mostly science. You can measure the effect of what you do.

What do I cut? What seem to be the lesser points, the apparent repetitions. I'll see if something can be said more economically—but without lousing up the ad's "conversational" quality or flow. In cutting, I use what I call the "RCA principle." First, I build the best product I know how. Then I see how many parts I can remove before it stops working.

If I cut too much, the ad won't pull as well and I'll go back to the original.

But, you say, no one will read long copy. And you're right, no one will unless he's interested—unless it has his name on it. Then he'll read every word. And that's the only guy you want to read your copy.

DON'T LET YOUR AD LOOK LIKE AN AD

Do I turn my copy over to an artist so that I can get a "professional" layout? No. The last thing I want is for my copy to look like an ad. People buy newspapers or magazines to read the news. Ads are a necessary but unwelcome intrusion, and the reader's experience is that many of them are overblown or untrue. So I want my copy to look like a news story (which is what it should be), matching their editorial lay-out and typestyle as closely as the publication will let me.

So, if I want to save money, I send my copy to the newspaper or magazine, with those instructions. They'll "pub-set" it—do the job free. Or, if I'm flush, I'll take my copy to a printer or typographer and ask him to make it look like an article, not an ad. And now, with the sophistication of Desktop Publishing, you can stylize your ad to each specific publication. Ideally, the only way that the casual reader will be able to distinguish the difference between my "ad" and the editorial content will be the

Be careful about cutting down the size of your ad, simply for the sake of size. After all, what's the point of knocking on the door if the salesman disappears when its opened?

You say, "No one will read long copy." And they won't. Not unless they're interested—unless it's got their name on it.

The best layout for an ad is one that matches, as closely as possible, the editorial layout and typestyle of the medium being used.

small "Advertisement" line the publication may put at the top. I want the printer to do everything he can to achieve that effect.

Don't use small type or a typeface that's difficult to read (again, "imitating" the editorial content is your best guide). Anything that's worth saying is worth saying aloud, and small type is associated with something you're trying to hide.

For newspapers, I like to stick with a "news" format. It's cheaper and more effective.

For newspapers, assuming you can't afford the expense of a full-page ad, the "ideal layout" is usually three columns (about 5½ inches) wide and about eight or more inches deep. This size is harder for the make-up man to bury. It's likely to go on top of a larger ad. Or, if it does wind up at the bottom of the page, generally only one or two much smaller ads will be stacked on top of it. (Later, we'll go into what your position request should be.) A bottle of booze and some conversation with the make-up man are a good investment. He can tell you if there's some "shape" that's easier for him to work with, to give you the "position" you need.

I've already told you to stick with a news format. It's cheaper to produce and, most important, more effective. You won't win any art awards or get the admiring comments of your friends. But, with the money you'll make, you'll be able to buy your own trophies and be able to afford to move into a better neighborhood.

To emphasize my point about ads that look like ads—and are therefore suspect—here are some DONT'S:

The most effective ads are those that don't look like ads.

1. Don't use "reverse" printing (white type on a black background). It may stand out, but you've pleaded guilty to running an ad and it's also hard to read.

2. Don't use "Ben Day" backgrounds (a gray "screen" that artists seem to love). For the same reasons you shouldn't use reverse printing.

3. Don't use illustrations, unless they show the product in dramatic use— what it does, and words can't paint the picture. You're usually better off letting the prospect's imagination take over. (If I say the word "house" to you, what do you see? But if I show you a picture of a house, you may not like it—and I've stopped you cold.) What's more, the prospect may not be able to "identify" with the illustration—and you've lost him.

4. Don't get talked into a need for "white space" for aesthetic effect. The publication is charging you for both paper and ink. Make them use the ink. It'll imprint words that'll sell for you.

Here are some other points to remember:

RESTATE YOUR OFFER IN THE ORDER FORM The customer is signing a contract—and he knows it. And you can use the space (I summarize the deal) and "sell" him again. Incidentally, don't make it sound like a contract. In conversational language—what Rudy Flesch used to call "shirt sleeve" English—tell the prospect what he's getting, what it'll do for him, and what your guarantee is. Be sure it's clear, easy to complete, and there's enough room to write the mailing information you need.

DON'T USE A POST OFFICE BOX AS YOUR ADDRESS   It looks like you're trying to hide. Besides, giving your street address can produce an impressive number of walk-in sales. We do more than enough each year to pay the rent.

READ THE LARGE-SPACE MAIL ORDER ADVERTISING YOU SEE REPEATED TIME AFTER TIME IN MAGAZINES AND NEWSPAPER (That would indicate that the ads are successful.) See how well they've followed the "rules." If they've "broken" one, it may be an act of daring innovation that they've found improves results. Or the ad may be working in spite of the "mistake"—and the results would be improved if it were corrected. Direct Response ads have to work for a living. Every ad has to stand on its own two feet. Learn what you can from them, every chance you get.

> Look for and study ads that you see repeated time after time and in several different publications. It's an indication that they are successful. Learn what you can from them.

MUCH "NATIONAL" AND A LOT OF "RETAIL" ADVERTISING IS WASTEFUL It publicizes the "name" and does very little else. It doesn't motivate people to buy; instead, it relies on the hope that when, and if, they buy a product in that particular category, they'll remember a certain brand.

Most advertising agencies would be terrified at the thought of putting a coupon in the ad of a major advertiser; not because, as they'd like you to believe, it would "cheapen" the product, but because it would accurately measure results—and that's the last thing they want.

In some ways, it's not the agencies' fault. They have to sell every ad twice. Once to the company that's paying the bill; and after it's been watered down, prettied up and approved by the client's wife and 13 year-old son, they have to sell what's left to the public.

A case in point is the cigarette companies. After they were forced off radio and TV and saved millions and millions of dollars in advertising costs, their sales went up, which only goes to prove that if people really want to get cancer badly enough they'll find a way. Or perhaps what the cigarette companies' thought was "soft-sell" was really "no sell."

We've gone quite thoroughly into the physical production of newspaper ads. (You'll see why when you read the next chapter.)

Now, here are some tips for preparing your copy for other media.

LETTERS

> Make your letters friendly and personal. People like to get letters; they hate to get ads.

TIP #1   Send a friendly, personal letter—not advertising circular. People like to get letters; they hate to get advertising.

TIP #2   Avoid salutations like "Dear Sir," "Gentlemen," "Fellow Fisherman," or "Dear Friend." It's a "form" letter, sure, but why rub the customer's nose in it? Don't type in his name (and/or address) either. In the first place, it's expensive; in the second place, the type probably won't match the rest of the letter and he'll feel that you're trying to put something over on him (except for E-mail letters, of course). So, unless you can afford to go to the expense of a "computer" letter, what kind of salutation do you use? None. Just start right out with a headline—in this case, your first sentence—telling him, specifically, what problem your product will solve. If it's his problem, and your solution sounds good, he'll know that—the letter is addressed to him.

Keep your sentences and paragraphs short, simple and easy to read.

TIP #3 Keep your sentences short and simple. Probably no more than 10 to 12 words, with paragraphs short, and no more than five sentences. You can send a four, six, or even an eight-page letter—and you should—if the selling job requires it, but it'll look easy to read if you follow Tips #2 and #3.

Stand back and just look at your letter: It should look inviting—easy to read.

TIP #4 It'll also make the letter look easy to read—and add visual interest—if you do these things: (a) Indent some of your key paragraphs. (b) Add what appear to be hand written notations. (c) Underline some of the important words, capitalize others...but don't overdo it. Don't, for example, put a whole sentence in capital letters. They're harder to read and seem a little pushy or immature. (Overselling is just as bad as underselling. A guy has to wonder, "If this deal is so good, why is he trying so hard.") (d) If the letter is a two or more pages long, never have a sentence end on the bottom of a page. "Carry" the reader to the next page. If possible make that last sentence a cliffhanger. For example, the last partial sentence at the bottom of page one might say "Forty thousand people have found that their sex" with the balance of the sentence on the next page.

TIP #5 Use a word processor or computer with a laser or good ink jet printer, or reproduce a typewritten letter. Do NOT have it typeset. Do NOT have it mimeographed or photocopied. The first looks like an ad. The second and third unless it's expertly done, looks shoddy.

Signatures in your letters should always be signed in blue.

TIP #6 Use two colors. For the beginner, the reproduction of the typewritten material should always be in black. But the letterhead should be in a contrasting color. You can either furnish your printer with stationery if you have it, or he can give you a two-color print job. The extra expense is worth it.

TIP #7 If possible, hand-sign the letters (if the quantity is small) or have the "signature" imprinted in blue ink. (Signing with a felt-tip pen gives an impression of strength.) You can take care of Tips #6 and #7 by having the letter done in black; the letter-head and signature in blue. You can also use the blue to simulate the "handwritten" notations, but don't go wild with it.

TIP #8 Use color for added attention and a "second chance." Your letter should always be printed on white paper. But if you're enclosing a brochure or some other supporting material, use colored paper stock; a different color for each piece. Chances are your prospect will look at each enclosure before he decides to throw it away. Make each enclosure a "selling" piece. If your letter didn't "grab" him, maybe something else will.

TIP #9 Include an order form and a return envelope. (These will be at least two opportunities to add colored paper stock.) You do not have to use a postage-paid envelope. It might improve results, but that wasn't the experience of one large mailer who recently ran some tests. He reported that he got more orders when people had to buy their own stamps than when he enclosed a postage-paid envelope. He was surprised—and so am I. Including two return envelopes improves response but I don't know why—it just works.

TIP #10 Fold your letter so the printed side is out.

TIP #11 Time your mailings so they don't arrive on Monday or the day after a holiday. The mail piles up and you have too much competition.

TIP #12 Avoid mailing during the summer months. Families go on vacation and really tear through the mail when they return.

TIP #13 Use a First Class postage stamp, if you can. And if you do, rubber-stamp a big "FIRST CLASS MAIL" on the envelope. The onlytime I can't use First Class postage is when the contents are so bulkythat my cost would be doubled.

TIP #14 Test your mailings! I've known advertisers to put together a mailing they liked and mail out 100,000—only to have it flop. They could have found out it was a dud with a 2,000 mailing test—for two percent of the cost.

> Time your mailings so they arrive during the middle of the week (Tuesday, Wednesday, Thursday). There's less competition.

Does Direct Mail payoff? You bet it does!

Let me give two examples from my personal experience. On one item, after testing, we mailed 25,000 letters. Our cost was $9800. The mailing produced over $40,000 worth of orders! In another instance every batch of 1,000 letters we mailed (at a cost of $500) brought in $9000 worth of business! Now, these are unusually good results from a specialized mailing list. But, as of now, you know everything it took me years to find out about making Direct Mail work.

It's interesting that the newspapers grumble about "Junk Mail." But they use it themselves to sell subscriptions.

> Just how profitable can Direct Mail advertising be? Well, how does a 1,800% return on your investment sound to you?

RADIO

Radio commercials can be produced in anyone of three ways: (1) Live, (2) E.T.'s (electrical transcriptions or recordings), (3) CDs or MP3s.

If the announcer understands some of the rudiments of selling—and realizes, as few do, that his job depends on the sponsor's success—live presentation is best. Some of those who ad-lib, amplify, and personalize the copy can do an exceptional job. But most announcers think of themselves as entertainers and only tolerate commercials as a necessary evil. Many announcers like to demonstrate their prowess at "sight reading"... their skill in being able to go on the air with a piece of copy they've never seen before. The result of these attitudes is a singsong style of delivery, where the announcer's tongue is in gear, but his mind is in neutral. This is known as "throwing the commercial away"—along with the money that was paid for its delivery.

In the Los Angeles market, with its dozens of radio stations and hundreds of announcers, I can think readily of only two announcers whom I consider "star sales-men." The rest range from indifferent to just plain bad.

As of late 2004, there are no local announcers in Los Angeles who can deliver a commercial for a direct response product the way a national talk show host of the stature and effectiveness of Paul Harvey, Rush Limbaugh, or Glenn Beck can.

When Paul Harvey delivers a commercial message, he sells it. You believe him, and that is that.

For the ultimate in "selling" on the radio today there is no one better than Rush Limbaugh. When he breaks into his own commercial with, "Stop the tape, stop the tape!" your attention is riveted to one of the finest examples of a radio commercial you will ever hear. You just know if Rush says it, he believes it, and so do you.

You want your radio commercial to be delivered with conviction, passion and enthusiasm. And if you can't afford to hire Rush Limbaugh, Paul Harvey, or Glenn Beck, I suggest you do them yourself. That's the only way you'll get the same kind of enthusiasm and believability.

If you don't think you can do a radio or television commercial, think again. Lee Iacocca did it for Chrysler, Al Eisner for his blue toilet cleaner 2000 Flushes Blue, Orville Redenbacher and his grandson pitching their popcorn or, Sam Winston for his Winston Tires, and James Dyson does it for his line of Dyson Vacuum cleaners.

Each of these people has the special quality of believability in the product they are selling.

The difficulty with radio as a medium for Direct Response advertising is the limited length of commercial time. It's difficult, and often impossible, to create desire and tell people how to order in 60 seconds. (And I wouldn't even attempt anything less.) Einstein's Theory of Relativity comes into play here—60 seconds is a long time if you're listening and a short time if you're paying for it.

Here are some tips if you're preparing radio commercials:

TIP #1   Direct it to one person. Don't think of yourself as being in the Coli-seum, addressing 100,000 people. Think of yourself as talking to a friend and saying, "Hey! I've got something I want to tell you"...and then telling him, simply and directly.

TIP #2   Don't use music to introduce your commercial or, as a background. Not unless you're selling records, tapes and CD's. (And more tapes and CD's are sold by mail than in any other way!) But, ordinarily, music as an introduction wastes precious seconds. As background, it's distracting.

TIP #3   Allow at least 20 seconds for ordering information—the amount and where to send it. Repeat the information at least twice. If possible, three times. This repetition is annoying to the person who's not inter-ested and *vital* to the person who is.

TIP #4   Don't try to use your "3-5-7 Strategy" on radio spots. Too many num-bers confuse the listener.

When it comes to the ordering information you need to repeat the infor-mation at least twice. Though this may be annoying to the person who's not interested, it's vital to the person who is.

TIP #5 Use a very simple address. If possible, it's best that the mail be directed to the station. They announce their call letters frequently, and if the listener missed it the first time, he has another chance to pick it up. Ask the listener to "Send $30 to Widgets in care of KABC Los Angeles 4"; not "Widget Company International in care of KABC, 17242 West Hyacinth Avenue, Los Angeles 90004." Sending the mail to the station is also reassuring to the customer. He probably trusts them. He's not too sure about you.

Best of all is to use your web site address. It is no longer necessary to say the http://www portion of the address (<u>Ex: thelazymansway.com</u>)

If the radio station won't accept and forward the mail (and a few won't), it's better to use a post office box number than a complicated street address. Try to get a box with no more than three digits and, if possible, in sequence (like 3-4-5). If the post office can't give you a decent box number, try one of the private mail services (like Mail Boxes Etc./UPS Stores USA). They should be able to give you the kind of number you'll need.

TIP #6 Keep your price in even dollars. "Thirty dollars" is less confusing, and takes less time to say, than "twenty-nine dollars and seventy-nine cents."

TIP #7 Do the commercials yourself. If you don't sound like an announcer, so much the better. The only caution is this: Don't try to sound like an announcer. If you stumble and stammer a bit, that's great. (Unless you're selling a course in diction.) It only adds to your believability. And people buy things from people they trust. It'll take a little practice, but you're better off ad libbing from a "fact sheet" instead of a script. That's because you're not accustomed to reading material and making it sound as though it's coming off the top of your head. A "spontaneous" presentation is the best kind.

TELEVISION

It's too bad, but there are very few stations that will allow you to do "live" commercials any more. Live commercials are more effective because they have a greater sense of immediacy and can be varied from one commercial to the next. They're especially good if a product is being demonstrated, because the customer can see whether it really works or not. They're hoping it won't but they're impressed when it does.

However, most commercials are on tape, and a few are on film. Here are some tips:

TIP #1 Reread all the tips on producing radio commercials. Almost all of them apply to TV.

TIP #2 Don't clutter your commercial with special effects. The technicians love to show off their electronic wizardry, but it just reminds the audience that what they're watching is staged. The impression you want to give is that you're in the viewer's living room and talking only to them.

> When advertising, the three most important rules are, keep it simple; keep it simple; keep it simple.

TIP #3   Don't read your commercial. If you must, memorize it. If you can, ad-lib it. But don't ever read it from cue cards and try not to use a teleprompter either; in the first place, you'll sound like you're reading, in the second place, you'll lose direct eye contact with the viewer. And who'll buy from someone who won't look a person in the eye?

TIP #4   Don't use a "super" (printing that's imposed on a picture) unless it's absolutely necessary. It divides the prospect's attention. If you do use them, be sure that the talk matches the sign word for word. Otherwise, the prospect gets confused or suspicious because he's hearing one thing and seeing something else. What you're buying, the impact of sight and sound, is lost.

TIP #5   Ask the cameraman or director for a "medium" shot. The picture of you (if you're doing the selling) should be from slightly above the waist. That matches the way people would see you if you were visiting them in their homes, and that's exactly what you're doing. A "close-up" makes you look pushy. A "long shot" gives the impression you're afraid to come close. You may be talking in a conversational tone (and you should) but his eyes will tell him that you've raised your voice in order to be heard. It's just plain not intimate, and TV is an intimate medium.

TIP #6   Keep it simple. Keep it simple; ten thousand times repeat, keep it simple.

MAGAZINES

Almost all magazines are produced on computers for letterpress or offset printing. In either case, your preparation is exactly the same. Most magazines will pub-set your ad (Remember?—do the typography free), but I prefer to send them a finished ad for reproduction. It saves time and the chance of error. If it's "offset" (a photographic process) that's all they need. If it's letterpress (which means that a "plate" must be made), I ask them to make the plate and charge me for it. It'll probably cost me less and will certainly save me the trouble and expense of carefully packaging a plate.

Don't ever send the magazine your "original" layout. The printer can "pull reproduction glossies" or use a photographic process to make as many "velox prints" as you'll need. In the latter case, save the negative so you can order more.

All magazine (and most newspaper) space is sold by the "line." There are 14 lines to the inch—and one inch is usually the minimum.

How big should your magazine ad be? As big as it needs to be. You can use a slightly smaller type-size in magazines because the paper stock they generally use reproduces more sharply than newsprint does. But don't use type so small that it discourages the reader. I've seen ads with type so small that it looked like the typographer's hobby was inscribing Bible verses on the head of a pin. I've "seen" them— but I haven't read them.

I usually run fairly large space in magazines; two-thirds of a page or full pages. First, because I have a lot to say. Second, I think that, psychologically, it makes the

TV is an intimate medium. Have the cameraman shoot you from slightly above the waist. This matches the way people would see you if you were to visit them in their homes—which is exactly what you are doing.

More advertisers go broke by not spending enough to do the job than as a result of spending too much. Personally, I'd rather be chewed up by lions than tickled to death by ants.

offer look important and the company solvent (at least we had enough money to pay for a big ad).

I suggest that, when you're ready to try magazine advertising, you wait until you can afford to buy big space. More advertisers go broke by not spending enough to do the job than as a result of spending too much. Personally, I'd rather be chewed up by lions than tickled to death by ants.

In addition, big space gives you the muscle you need to get the positioning that can make the difference between failure and success. (More about that in the next chapter.)

WHEN TO GO FOR IT

Here's one tip that can save you a lot of money:

The best months for Direct Response results are generally January, February, March, April and May. June is shaky, and July and August can be disastrous. In September, October and November, business bounces back; and December is iffy.

> The three best months for Direct Response advertising are January, February and March.

So time your ads for those prime months, unless you have a seasonal product. For Christmas items, October is the month to advertise in magazines. And November issues are good if they're "on sale" before the 15th of the month.

Speaking of Christmas items, my experience in newspapers is to advertise after Halloween and before November 15. Period.

The thing to be careful of is, that the months you're buying in are those that the magazine goes on sale. The "issue" on the cover of the magazine may be an entirely different matter.

It may be the "January issue," but if it goes on sale (copies are mailed or put on newsstands) about December 15, you could be in a lot of trouble.

So I buy the February issues that are on sale after January 1. Some small magazines postdate their issues by several months. For example, the "July issue" hits the newsstands in April. I presume that this is to give their product a longer life before it's outdated.

So now you know how to write an ad and the basics of preparing it for newspapers, direct mail, radio, TV, and magazines.

ADVERTISING BOOKS WE RECOMMEND

At a minimum, your library should consist of the following. (I want you to read, re-read and read again each of them. Do this and you will have as much expertise and probably more—than 99.9 percent of the people working in most ad agencies. There are very few "professionals" who really know how to write good copy.) At any rate, I want you to start with these:

> Read these books! Do this and you will have just as much expertise as most so-called ad agency people.

Tested Advertising Methods

   By John Caples

Confessions of an Advertising Man

   By David Ogilvy

I simply can't overemphasize the importance of these books. Get them. Read them. Study them. Use them.

The Robert Collier Letter Book

    By Robert Collier

How to Write, Speak and Think More Effectively

    By Rudolf Flesch

My Life in Advertising / Scientific Advertising

    By Claude Hopkins

Some of these books are no longer being published, so you won't be able to pick them up in your local bookstore. However, we have found all of them and while supplies last, you can find links to them in Step 42 of your workbook.

Now turn to Step #42 "How to Write Successful Ads" in your *Roadmap to Riches* workbook.

43
How to Get the Best Buys in Time and Space

Some time back, I said that I would tell you everything I know about the Direct Response Business. And I've tried to keep my promise. But now I'm getting into an area where I can't tell you "everything." Not because telling the truth would hurt me, but because it might embarrass and harm people I do business with and who have relied upon my discretion.

The "secret" I can't reveal is the names of the newspapers, magazines, radio, and television stations that will sell your product for you on a "commission" basis—the people you pay only for the orders they deliver. With this kind of arrangement, of course, you can't lose. Every order represents a small but sure profit.

TRY A PARTNERSHIP

You'd be surprised at same of the Big Name Media who are willing to be a partner in your business, provided (and this is important) they are convinced that you are reliable and honest.

This kind of a deal is called a "P.I." The letters stand for "Per Inquiry," because you pay the media a percentage of the sale price for each "inquiry" or order they generate.

Although many of them might go along with a lesser percentage, I pay them 50 percent. In the first place, I've budgeted for this expenditure. In the second place, I want them to make money. Because, if it's profitable to them, they'll give my advertising the greatest possible exposure and increase my volume of sales without increasing my overhead. And don't forget that, although my profit on the original order is limited, the profit margin skyrockets on the reorders I'll get—because I have virtually no advertising expense!

In "P.I." deals, the mail is generally directed to the media. After they've verified the number of orders, they forward it to you.

In addition to the "P.I." deals that can be negotiated, there are two other ways to buy space or time that have almost the same effect. The first relates to magazines and is called "H.I.N." or "Help If Necessary." This means that you agree to pay for the ad, but if the results aren't profitable, the publication will run the ad again without charge. And will run it as many times, as they have to, in order for you to at least break even.

Since the orders are being directed to you, how do they know how many orders you received—and whether you need "help?" They don't. They have to trust you.

I know I promised to tell you "everything," but I'm afraid this is one area where I can't.

It would probably surprise you at some of the Big Name Media who are willing to be your "partner."

If you are a straight shooter and you've got a really "hot" offer, you may be able to let the media be your "partner" and pick up your ad costs.

And, of course, they make this deal only with people they trust. In a sense, it's self-policing. Obviously, you will want to continue buying space in a magazine that produces profitable results. And it might be a little awkward if you asked for "help"—and then came back in a few months and said that you'd like to run in the same magazine again. Why would you want to do that if the first time was unprofitable? Naturally, the best reason for playing it straight is that that's the most rewarding business practice in the long run.

The second way to reduce your risk, and this applies to radio and TV stations, is the "Guaranteed" deal. Some of the stations that won't "P.I." will go along with this one. You buy the time, and they run your "spots" (that's what broadcast commercials are called). However, if you don't get a prearranged number of orders, they'll keep running your commercials until that number is reached; again, it doesn't pay for you to be greedy or they won't make the same arrangement a second time.

Why are some of the media willing to be "commission salesmen?" Because they've made a commitment and are working against a deadline.

A publisher, for example has to decide long in advance how many pages he's going to print. He allocates a certain amount of space to editorial, and the balance to the advertising he hopes he can sell. If, as the deadline approaches, he has unsold space, he can do, one of three things: (1) Fill the unsold advertising space with editorial - which means he has not only lost the revenue he hoped for, but he'll have to pay someone to write it. (2) He can run "Public Service" ads free. "Smokey the Bear" is nice, but what's really going up in smoke is advertising revenue. (3) He can make a "P.I." or "H.I.N." deal with some Direct Response advertiser.

Why a Direct Response advertiser? Because: (1) He's the only kind of advertiser who can make an immediate decision without checking his "budget" or submitting the proposal to a committee (and don't forget, time is running out). (2) He's the only kind of advertiser who keeps exact records of his results and is willing to pay accordingly.

So the publisher gambles. He knows that he'll at least get some income—and if a deal is "hot" he may wind up making more money than if he had sold the space outright!

Radio and TV stations are really under pressure— minute by minute. The 60 seconds that just passed is gone forever.

Radio and TV stations are under pressure, not day by day like a newspaper, and not weekly or monthly like a magazine—but minute by minute. The 60 seconds that just passed is gone forever. Unlike the publisher, who can cut his product cost by reducing the number of pages he prints, the broadcaster has a fixed commitment to stay on the air so many hours a day—and his overhead grinds on.

That's why the majority of broadcasters will take on at least a few "P.I." or "Guaranteed" accounts—and why some subsist on very little else. In fact, at one time there was a big station in Texas that wouldn't take anything except "P.I.'s." They found that if they picked the cream of the crop of Direct Response offers, they could sometimes get more income from each "spot" than if they sold it to a "national" account or a retailer! And they eliminated the need for (and expense of) salesmen and were always "sold out." Not a commercial minute was wasted!

This "commission" arrangement is a great way to go if you have little or no capital.

You can use the "commission" arrangements to get started if you have little or even no capital. However, I have to be honest and say that I don't use these methods to "test" a new product or a new ad for an established product. Instead, I test in media that I've used for a long time and have extensive records on, so that I can judge the results objectively. "P.I.," "H.I.N.," and "Guaranteed" deals are in a sense artificial and don't allow me to make direct comparisons.

After I've tested, and I know that a product is "hot," I'll make a publisher or broadcaster my partner but not until then. Because, if it's a "proven" product, and the results are poor, my "partner" knows that it's the weakness of his medium and won't find the fulfillment of his obligations as painful. If it's a run-away success, we're both happy. In either case, he'll call me again when he's in trouble.

There's one other circumstance in which I use these no-risk techniques. That's when someone is trying to sell me on advertising in his medium—and I have serious reservations. Perhaps I feel that the cost is too high for the number of readers, listeners, or viewers. Or I doubt that the audience composition (by sex, age, or interest) is suitable. If he thinks it is, I ask him to prove it by taking a share of the profits: I know my offer works. The only thing that's in question is whether his medium will or won't. If he's willing to gamble, fine; if not, I probably haven't missed much. You can dribble away a lot of money, a few dollars at a time. No medium is "cheap" if it doesn't produce results, and no medium is "expensive" if you have a profit after paying the bill.

> No medium is "cheap" if it doesn't produce results. And no medium is "expensive" if you show a profit after using it.

HOW TO PURCHASE MEDIA

Now, how do you go about buying media when you're prepared to risk cold cash?

First, you take advantage of all the "discounts" that exist.

Here are some tips:

TIP #1 You buy at "wholesale." That means that you pay a rate that is far lower than the one that's printed on the rate card—the price that the medium quotes (and is being paid by the majority of "uneducated" advertisers).

Rate cards, particularly in the case of low circulation magazines, quote the "asking" price. If you know what you're doing, you can pay a lot less. I'd say that in many cases I pay 20 to 50 percent less than the "list price." In a few instances, my under-the-table discount is even more.

I'm not trying to imply that I'm getting any bargain. The price I'm paying is what the medium is really worth. At the price I'm paying, my ads will payoff. If I had to pay any more—anywhere near the "asking price"—the result would be marginal and I could lose my shirt.

> Never ever pay "rate card" rates for any advertising. I rarely consider any medium unless I'm getting a 20 to 50% discount.

I recently asked one of the magazine sales representatives who, among his clients, paid the rate-card prices. He replied, "Almost everybody does. All of the 'national' advertisers and all of the 'one-shot' mail order advertisers do."

"But," I said, "You know that a mail order advertiser can't pay those prices and make a profit."

"I know," he said, "but, if a man doesn't ask me for a lower price, am I going to volunteer it? Besides, most of the little guys don't know what they're doing anyway and wouldn't make out if they paid half of what you're paying. I'm doing them a favor, showing them that they ought to get out of the business."

"Once in awhile," he went on, "some little guy pays me top dollar and almost breaks even or maybe makes a little. Him, I'll help. I won't cut the price, because I'd be admitting I got to him the first time. But since I know that he's got the makings of a steady advertiser, I'll give him some 'free' space every so often. That way he thinks I'm a hero, and he ends up paying what he should have been paying right along."

Incidentally, this sales representative is a very nice guy, and I've never caught him in a direct lie. Some omissions perhaps, but never a direct lie. Which is more than I can say for a few of the "reps."

Now, the key words in that whole speech are "steady advertiser." And you can add to that the advertisers who buy big units of space—full pages—and lots of them. Because those are the guys, naturally, who get the deals.

"Remnants" and "bulk buyers," two other ways to get substantial discounts (up to 50 percent and more) on your media purchases.

TIP #2 If there's no discount off the rate card, here's what to ask about: "remnants." So many large magazines and newspaper supplements are putting out "regional" editions these days that there's an advantageous situation for the Direct Response advertiser. A large "national" advertiser buys one or more of these "regions" because he only has distribution in those areas. He pays a premiumbecause he's only buying a selected part of the circulation.

But you can pick up the unsold balance of the circulation at a substantial savings. However, these "remnants" are usually available only in space units of one-half page, three-fifths of a page, or full pages in the case of newspaper supplements like Parade and USA Today or two-thirds of a page or full pages in the slick, big circulation magazines. And even with the "remnant" discount, the amount you have to shell out can make you pucker a bit.

TIP #3 Buy through a bulk buyer. There are a handful of people in this business who contract with magazines to buy a large number of pages throughout the year. There are others who trade something the magazine wants in the way of goods or services for their value in advertising pages. Their gimmick, of course, is that they acquired what they traded or bartered for a lot less. In effect, these Bulk Buyers guarantee that the magazine will have a certain number of ad pages inevery issue. In return, the magazine gives them a very attractive price per page.

The Bulk Buyer fulfills his contract by running advertising for those products he owns or has a proprietary interest in and sells off the rest for what he can get. What he can get may vary from a 10 percent discount to a 40 percent discount. Or whatever. The only rule is that he can't sell to advertisers who are already using the magazine.

TIP #4 If you handle your own advertising, form an advertising agency. This is really a very complicated procedure. You will need a business license and some stationery. On second thought, you might not need the business license. As a result of this tremendous investment, you might get a 15 percent discount on any advertising you buy! (The only exception is your local newspaper. They will probably give you a much greater discount, but it will be in the form of the "retail rate" as opposed to the "national" or "general" rate they charge the out-of-town advertisers.) Your local radio station will give you a "retail" rate plus the advertising agency discount. True, some of the stuffier, old-line media may not "recognize" you as a bonafide advertising agency (there are certain criteria for financial stability and the number of accounts you service), but most of the smaller ones and many of the medium-sized ones will. Particularly if it's clear that that's the only way they're going to get your business.

TIP #5   There are still other ways to save money buying advertising. That's to make a deal with someone who's contracted to buy, say, 12 pages at a 20 percent discount (right off the rate card). But they've bitten off more than they can chew. So they'll sell you some of that space for less than you'd have to pay otherwise.

Instead of making a "P.I." deal with a broadcaster or publication directly, you can work through a broker. If you have a good product, with a proven track record, there are two or three people (generally, Bulk Buyers) who will act as a middleman.

However, they will want the mail directed to them, will open the orders, and keep all of the money till they've covered their costs. Which means that until income reaches that point (and it may never come) you don't get a dime. From that time forward, you only get a pre-arranged part of the income.

Even if you could live with the financial aspect of the deal, there's another (and in my mind, more serious) drawback. There's an unavoidable slowdown in the time it takes for the mail to go to them and then be forwarded to you. This is aggravated by the fact that they'll take anywhere from a week to a month to get around to processing it. So the longer the deal runs, the greater the percentage of complaint letters. The brokers couldn't care less. But you should.

If you've gotten the impression that buying advertising is, for the novice, like walking through Central Park at midnight without a gun, you're right. But at least I've given you a water pistol! Which is more than I had when I started. And believe me, I got mugged more than once.

But, really, I've told you more than you need to know at this stage of your career. Because you should start modestly, by testing your ads right in your own hometown before you try to slug it out in the Big Leagues. (I still do, on every project.) Here are some things you should know about it.

NEWSPAPERS

I prefer testing in newspapers. Production's easy and cheap (I've already gone into that). You can generally assess your results in two or three days (I covered that, too). And here are some tips:

Form your own ad agency and take 15% off the top of virtually all your advertising.

I said it before, and I'll say it again, never ever pay the published rate for any advertising you buy.

Start out small—test your ads in your own home town—before attempting to slug it out in the "big leagues."

TIP #1 Don't run your ad in the Mail Order Section if the paper has one. Readership is poor and, generally, your ad has to conform to a restricted size and layout. The only person I can imagine poring over the Mail Order Section is someone hoping to find something—anything—to buy. Or maybe someone who's in the business and is curious about what competitors are doing.

If you think those ads "must work" because there are so many of them, save a few issues, you'll see how few are repeated. The only ones I see, week in and week out, are the guys who invite you to "write for free information" and then try to sell you a correspondence course for several hundred dollars. And I'll bet that even this handful of successful advertisers would do better if they took this next tip.

TIP #2 Put your ad in the Main News Section. I should note that recently I've found that the absolute best position, when you can afford it, is a full page, front (outside page) of a section. The further forward the section, the better. If you can't get a front outside page, try a back outside page of a section. You'll find that some back pages work and some don't.

When buying ad space in newspapers, your best position is in the main news section, far forward, right hand page, above the fold.

For practical purposes, and in as much as a full page can be a very expensive way to go, I suggest you start out with something smaller and apply the following: If there are two or more sections of Main News, try to get it in the first section. You might think that an ad directed primarily to women should be in the Women's Section or Society Section, or if you're looking for male customers that you'll find them in the Sports or Financial Section. You're wrong. Placement in the Main News Section gives you your best exposure to either or both sexes. The only exception to this rule that I've found in 16 years is Larry Voegele's book on Professional Handicapping. These ads do best on the "Race Entries" page. Presumably, the racing fan doesn't read anything else.

Most newspapers won't give you any static about getting into a particular section. Here's where you start running into trouble, because here's the rest of what you should have, in terms of "position," for your ad to succeed. It should be on the right-hand page. It should be "above the fold" (the "fold" is the horizontal middle of the paper if it's a standard-sized newspaper). And, if possible, it should be on the "outside edge" or, as it's sometimes called, the "thumbnail position." You can see how it got its name if you'll notice where your hands are when you hold a newspaper.

Now, to the degree that the position of your ad follows this formula, it will increase your chance of success. To the degree it varies from this position, your likelihood of failure is multiplied.

Newspaper salesmen can show you all kinds of surveys to "prove" that it doesn't make any difference where your ad appears. I can only say that I've spent millions of dollars of my own money, making my own survey and my records show it makes a lot of difference!

If it doesn't make any difference, why don't they put their front-page news in the middle of the paper and the Classified Section on the front page? Believe me—the closer you get to the front page, the more likely it is that people will read the "news" of your product.

Now, how do you try to insure that your ad will appear where you know it'll do the most good? Well, you could weigh the newspaper and whichever day of the week the newspaper is consistently the lightest (has the least number of pages), that's the day you want to schedule your ad. Because that's the day that the newspaper will doubly welcome your business. The paper's lighter because it has fewer ads. Therefore, it'll be easier for the makeup man to give you the position you request and you will have less competition for the customer's dollar.

I avoid the hernia-inducing Sunday papers unless I put my ad in the Comics—yes, the Comics, or in the TV Magazine. (When I buy the TV Magazine, I request a right-hand page towards the back. That way, my ad hasn't been "lost" after the reader looked at the Sunday or Monday program listings—and I'll pick up some people who'll thumb through to see what's coming up.) And I've had some success with very large ads in the front page of the Classified Section.

TIP #3 Sign a contract—the smallest (the one that involves the least obligation) that's available. That's because newspapers have an "open rate"—which is their highest rate—and a series of "contract rates" which mean that the more advertising you run, the less it costs you per "line" or inch.

If you buy at the "open rate," you'll pay the same high price every time you run. (Although some newspapers will permit you to try one ad at the "open rate" and then backdate a contract when you run a second.) The reason you want the, smallest contract is that if you exceed it, you'll get a rebate at the end of the year on all the advertising you've bought—based on the contract level you reach.

On the other hand, if you shot too high, you'll be "short-rated." If you are "short-rated," you'll be billed for the difference per line for the contract you signed and the rate you actually earned. This can be a tidy sum. For your second year, you'll have a better idea of how much space you expect to use and can sign a contract for that amount.

Don't sign a contract that guarantees you'll run every week. Instead, sign an annual "bulk space" contract (usually 500 to 1,000 "lines" or 36 to 72 inches).

TIP #4 Don't run an ad just before or during holiday weekends or on any holiday that falls in the middle of the week, or just before Thanksgiving or Christmas.

TIP #5 Don't buy "throw-aways" or "free circulation" newspapers. They don't work.

TIP #6 Be wary of newspapers with less than 100,000 circulations. Their "C.P.M." (cost per thousand) subscribers is ordinarily too high. But I know a few that payouts handsomely.

I've spent millions and my records show that it makes a whole world of difference where your ad appears.

Avoid "thick" paper days—there's a lot more competition for the reader to see your ad.

Avoid running an ad just before or on a holiday weekend. The customers mind is probably somewhere else.

I have never found that repetition improves newspaper's results. If an ad falls flat the first time, it'll do worse the next.

TIP # 7 Don't let anyone kid you that repetition improves results. In the Direct Response Business each ad has to stand on its own two feet. If your first ad lies down and dies, a second ad will only do worse. In fact, if your first ad's results are excellent, expect the returns to decline from then on. When you run an unprofitable ad or two after a series of winners, get out of the newspaper for a while. Let the deal rest for at least a month or two—and then try it again. Sometimes a change of headline will perk it up.

The greatest thing about using newspapers—and radio and TV—in your town is that you can buy them for far less than I or any other out-of-town advertiser can. No matter how much money we spend, you have the advantage of a much lower cost. That's because these media, as I told you before, have a "national" or "general" rate for me, and a "local" or "retail" rate for you.

Despite all the money I spend, and the advertising agency discount I'm allowed to take, you still have me beat. An ad that might be barely profitable for me could be a bonanza for you—due to your lower advertising cost. Do you remember my telling you that this is where being "small" is actually an advantage?

So, if you're ready, contact the newspaper's Retail Sales Department and talk to the salesman. And when you're ready to buy advertising in other towns' newspapers, your salesman can tell you how to go about that.

RADIO

When buying time on radio, start with "talk show" or "all news" formats. People "listen" to these stations when tuned in.

TIP #1 Stations that feature Talk Shows, All-News formats, and Country and Western music are usually effective, and in about that order. Stations that program Contemporary music, Middle-of-the-Road music, and Classical music usually won't work unless your product is targeted towards that special audience, and even then they're doubtful.

The reason is that people listen to Talk Shows and News—that's why they tuned in, and they hang on to every word—even your commercial. They have what's called a "foreground" sound. I'm not sure why Country and Western formats are productive, but they sometimes are. Maybe because the fans have a loyalty to the announcers—have more confidence in them than those "fancy-talking dudes."

Unlike newspapers and magazines, repetition helps (builds) radio response.

Contemporary, Middle-of-the-Road (those "good old songs"), and Classical music stations usually aren't productive because they provide a "background" sound. There are some exceptions, but you can blow a lot of money finding out which ones they are unless you can get a "P.I." or buy on a "Guaranteed" basis.

If you're thinking about buying radio time, listen to the station. If you hear a lot of spots in which the "tag" of the commercial suggests calling a phone number, or there are some Direct Response advertisers, it might be worth a try. If these advertisers continue week after week, they know something. Because the phone calls must produce "leads" for salesmen, and the orders must be coming in to the Direct Response companies— or they wouldn't continue to advertise.

It doesn't matter whether you like the station or not. The only thing that counts is how productive it is.

If you do decide to buy some time, place your schedule where other advertisers who measure response are.

TIP #2   Run enough spots.

Unlike newspapers or magazines (where repetition often depreciates results), broadcast response builds. Maybe they tuned in on the middle of your commercial, or maybe they missed the address. They need another chance to get it all. Or maybe they just need convincing. Reading is active—they have to decide to do it. Listening is passive—they can just sit and let it happen.

But a one-week test is all you need to decide whether to continue or not. If I have enough orders at the end of the first week, so that the total gross income is at least enough to pay for the advertising, I'll renew my contract. If it's a little less, I'll either gamble and renew or take a week's hiatus to check it more carefully.

If it's a lot less, I'll cancel for good. If I do continue, I'll do so for one week at a time—and stay on top of the results. But don't forget, as you go ahead, that the weekly results have to increase sharply (because most of the mail is coming from the previous week or weeks). If they level off, cancel.

TIP #3   If the station puts more than one commercial in a "break," make sure that yours is the first. That'll give, your customer a chance to write down the address while the next commercial is on and before the program resumes.

TIP #4   Just because you go to bed early, don't forget that a lot of people don't. If you live in a metropolitan community, there's a whole army of people who don't get off work till midnight—and there are a lot of insomniacs too. Some of your most effective commercial time is after midnight, and your costs are rock-bottom. You'll be surprised at the results if there's a personable, low-key host on the show. "Night people" are lonely and they show their loyalty to the friendly host by buying what he sells.

TIP #5   If the station has some good "salesmen announcers," you'd be wise to submit a "fact sheet" instead of a cut-and-dried commercial. They'll ad-lib, covering your main sales points, and you'll probably end up with a "pitch" that's considerably longer than the 60 seconds you paid for. And the longer they talk, the more they sell. If there are several "personalities" on the station, it doesn't hurt to set up a little competition. Make your mailing address "Send $3 to Widgets, care of Michael Silvertongue, KABC, Los Angeles 90004." I've never seen an announcer yet who didn't think he was the best of the lot and was insecure enough to have to prove it.

In a big city, some of the most effective commercial time is after midnight.

Your 15% ad agency discount applies to radio advertising, too.

You'll notice that there are a lot of similarities between radio and TV advertising. Not the least of which is that TV commercials will benefit from repetition.

TIP #6   Don't run a commercial directed at men during what the stations call the "traffic hours." True, there are a lot of them listening, but it's hard to write down an address when you have at least one hand on the steering wheel.

TIP #7   You, too, can be an advertising agency and save 15 percent!

To get started, just call the radio station and ask for the Local Sales Department, and talk to the salesperson.

TELEVISION

I spent 12 years in TV running an advertising agency and working as one of those salesmen-announcers (do I hear someone saying "pitchmen?"). I made a lot of money—and blew it all, plus another $50,000, trying to produce my own TV show.

That debt was the best thing that ever happened to me. It made me desperate enough to try anything—and I found Dyna/Psyc.

I stopped working the 18-hour days, 7 days a week—a schedule that had literally paralyzed me three times. (The diagnosis was "exhaustion and nervous tension." The last time I was in the hospital, the doctor conducted a bunch of tests, including the one where they stick a tube in your scrotum and thread it through the arteries leading to your heart. After 10 days of delightful experiences like that, the doctor came to my bedside, "Well," he smiled, "I can tell you a lot of things that aren't wrong with you," When I got the bill for $2,000, I knew why he was smiling.)

With Dyna/Psyc, I did a lot less work—and made a lot more money. (The other day a friend of mine said, "You're the only guy I know who retired first and then got Rich!") The only reason I've told you all this is partly self-indulgence, but mostly to establish my credentials as knowing something about TV.

Here are some of the things I know about buying TV time:

TIP #1   Buy "fringe" time, daytime until about 6 o'clock at night; or after 11 P.M. You're right—you don't get the big audiences that the prime-time shows deliver. But you don't pay nearly as much per person for the ones you do reach. And many stations will permit 90-second or even 2-minute spots in these fringe periods. And you need all the time you can get. You have to tell before you can sell.

TIP #2   Get your commercial within the program. Not at a "station break." Not just after opening credits (the name of the show). Not just before closing credits (the names of the technicians).

TIP #3   If there are two or more commercials in a break, fight to be first.

TIP #4   Before you buy time on a station, watch the programs. Buy time in those where you see other "lead" deals and Direct Response advertisers. There may be a waiting list. Good, wait.

TIP #5   Don't buy spots in half-hour programs unless you can nail down Tips #2 and #3. Old movies are your best bet. I love them myself, but the people who watch films from England or dubbed foreign films either don't buy enough or there aren't enough of them. Adventure, cowboy, and tearjerker films work best. Comedies are so-so. Action programs, like Monster Trucks, or the WWF wrestling can be a gold mine. Talk Shows, particularly if they involve controversy, can be very productive.

TIP #6   Remember I said that, on radio, the All-News format can work. But don't buy News programs on TV. In the first place, they're terribly expensive—and that's all the places you need.

TIP #7   Like radio, and in contrast to publications, your commercial will benefit from repetition. But, for the purposes of testing, you don't need as many spots because you have both the customer's eyes and ears to absorb the ordering information. If there's a late movie five nights a week, you might try one spot in each of three nights. Since they know what movies they're going to show, pick the ones that fit the criteria I gave you in Tip #5. And if they're having a Foreign Film Festival, watch and enjoy it—but don't buy any commercials in it. And don't sign a 4-week or a 13-week contract until you've completed your test.

TIP #8   One kind of Late Night program to avoid is the one where all of the advertisers are local merchants. These are usually the result of the station selling a block of time to a promoter. He, in turn, high pressures and sweet-talks the barber, the pool hall, and the pizza parlor into advertising on TV. The price is ridiculously low—but not worth it.

TIP #9   Remember that advertising agencies get a 15 percent discount and a few of them will earn you more than they cost. Darned few.

When you're ready to try TV, call the station and ask for the Local Sales representative.

MAGAZINES

I've already alerted you to the fact there are lots of "inside deals" in this area. A few magazines stick by the rate card, but you could put them all in one stack and get over them without jumping. To clarify, I don't mean that they play footsie with the "national" advertisers (although more and more of them are buying "bartered" space) but magazines normally give a discount to mail order advertisers. And some, as I've indicated, go a lot further.

Here's a rule of thumb: if, based on the rate for a full page, the cost is about $8 per thousand of circulation, you're on pretty safe ground. I've paid a little more for a highly specialized audience I wanted to reach and I frequently pay half that much—or less. To put that $8 figure in mathematical terms: a magazine with a paid, audited circulation of 1,000,000 should have a page rate of less than $8,000 . . . less 15 percent for the advertising agency. If you're, in fact, the advertising agency, your net cost should be $6,800. To the degree that you pay more than that $8-per-thousand figure, you're increasing your risk. To the degree that you pay less, you increase your chance to make a profit. And profit is the name of the game.

> The most important factors you need to be concerned with when analyzing magazine response are: 1) Cost of the ad; and 2) gross dollars brought in. That's it.

> One of the main benefits of magazine advertising is that you can pinpoint your market.

"Edits" can be a great way to get started in business, even if you have no money for advertising.

What percentage of the readers will respond to an offer? I don't know—and I don't care. All I watch is expense (what the advertising costs) and income (how many dollars it produced). For example, if an ad cost me $8,000 (the fictional rate for a magazine with a circulation of 1,000,000), I'd want to get at least $16,000 worth of orders. Or, to put it another way, my income should be double my cost. And if you're going to grade results, that would be somewhere between "good" and "excellent." If I've budgeted correctly, that dollar income should give me a fair profit. And I can drop down some, without losing any money. But every dollar that comes in over the $16,000 figure is half profit! Because, in a sense, I've already paid for the advertising—and the rest is free!

However, if you insist on reducing this to percentages, it might be instructive. You'll see how few people you can reasonably expect to respond. (And maybe I'll never have to listen again to the starry-eyed people who say, "The circulation of the Times is over a million—and if only two or three percent send in orders...!")

So let's proceed with our conversion to percentages. Let's say that you have a $10 offer. You need 1600 orders to produce that $16,000 income. And 1600 is sixteen hundredths of one percent! If it were a $20 offer, you'd need 800 orders, or eight-hundredths of one per cent.

Now, these percentage figures are not what you can "expect" to get—they're what you can hope to get—IF the ad is successful.

Why is it so low if you're selling something that "everyone" should want? Because: (1) Some of the people who get the magazine won't read it. (2) Some of them will read only part of it—and your ad may not be in that section. (3) If they do read that section, some will not "see" your ad. (4) Out of those who see it, many will not read it. (5) Out of those who read it, some will not believe it. (6) Of those who do believe it—and mean to act on it—some will forget or never follow through.

Pretty discouraging, isn't it? Not at all, if you're prepared for it and set your sights accordingly. In other words, if you're not like those people who say, "The circulation of the Times is over a million—and if only...."

So what percentage of people will respond? Enough—if you're lucky.

Buying magazine advertising requires a lot bigger nest egg than any other media. Because, if you haven't established a credit rating with them (and they're tough), you have to pay in advance. That means 60 to 90 days before your ad appears, if it's a monthly publication. If they have extended you credit, you have to pay within 10 days after the magazine comes out to get a "cash discount" of 2 percent—and no later than 30 days if they're ever going to extend credit again.

Remember that I told you the "average" monthly magazine will, in 6 months, double the number of orders it pulls in the first 30 days? Well, that's O.K. for projecting income and making a decision as to whether to buy the magazine again. But it also means that you're going to wait quite awhile to get your advertising money back—and pay for the product, packaging, postage, and overhead—before you get into the black.

What's good about magazines is that you can pinpoint your market. Men, boys, women, girls, psychology freaks, sexual deviates, motorcycle fanatics—they all have their own little magazines, and some of the magazines can deliver combinations of these groups.

So when you've tested your ad in the newspapers (which is what I recommend) and you're ready to take a whack at the magazines, here are some tips:

TIP #1   Try to get a right-hand page. If your ad appears on a left hand page, results will be drastically diminished.

TIP #2   Try to buy enough space so you can be the only ad on the page. A full page insures it (in which case you want to request "editorialn only" on the left-hand page). A two-thirds page in a "standard size" magazine, if the other column is editorial, is a good buy. A vertical half page in a "big size" magazine (like the Ladies Home Journal) will do the same job. I've bought a couple of horizontal half-pages—to my regret. People we conditioned to look first (and sometimes only) at the top of the page.

TIP #3   If you buy enough space, ask that there be "no backing coupon." Because if there's a competitive coupon on the "back" of yours—and it's cut out—you've lost a possible sale.

TIP #4   Ask if you can get a "free edit." Many magazines will give you one or more "edits" (small "articles" in their "Shoppers Guide Section") when you buy an ad. They won't produce a whole lot of orders (about the best I've done is $800), but every little bit helps. Other magazines, particularly the magazines directed at "Salesmen," may give you a good-sized article.

Incidentally, these "edits" can help you get started in business even if you have no money for advertising. Get a good 8 × 10 photo of your product at work, write a short, punchy ad—and send both out to all the magazines that have "Shoppers Guide Sections." If your product's new and exciting, quite a few may print it—and you'll be on your way! Dozens of magazines have these "Sections."

If you want to know which they are, visit a news stand, pick out the magazines that would appeal to your prospects and look for it in the "Mail Order Section." The magazine's address will be there or, if not, somewhere in the first few pages of the magazine.

TIP #5   Base your advertising buying on circulation, not "readership." The "readership" will be three to four times as high as the circulation, and small circulation magazines often quote that figure because it's so much more impressive. But your $8-per-thousand "rule of thumb" is based on circulation.

TIP #6   Another thing to check is "newsstand sales" as opposed to "subscriptions." (That information should be given to you along with a rate card.) For the Direct Response Business, a high percentage of news-

---

The percentage of readers who respond to your offer is not what's important. Profit is important.

Get your hands on a copy of the standard rates and data service publication titled "Consumer Magazine Advertising Source." In it you will find a listing of virtually every magazine you've every heard about.

stand sales is desirable. It means the purchaser of the magazine went to a little trouble to get it—and may read it more thoroughly.

TIP #7   Have you formed your own advertising agency yet?

When you're ready to get started on your magazine advertising, go to your local library and pick up a copy of the most current SRDS (Standard Rates and Data Service, http://www.srds.com/) publication entitled, *Consumer Magazine Advertising Source*. In it you'll find a listing of every magazine you've ever heard of—and then some.

The listings include such information as the publisher's editorial profile, ad rates, circulation, discounts available, and addresses of reps and/or branch offices... virtually everything you'll need to know about a specific publication.

DIRECT MAIL

There's very little I can add here, because in terms of "how to buy it," it's a fairly simple medium. The only caution is to "shop" for printing prices because they can vary widely, and, of course, you can affect great savings by ordering large quantities. But don't step up your order until you've had a chance to test the "pull" of your letter.

To whom do you mail your letters? Well, what's the "profile" of your prospect? Man? Woman? Skiing enthusiast? Overweight? Earns $60,000 a year?

Mailing List Brokers have hundreds of lists, millions of names and a lot of information about the people on those lists. You'll certainly want to contact them when you want to "rent" out the names of the customers you've acquired; and if you want to do a mailing of your own, a conscientious Mailing List Broker can be a lot of help in "zeroing in" on your target.

Do a search on the Internet through any good search engine for mailing list brokers and you'll find more than you need. You might check the Yellow Pages for someone nearby. You'll also find "Direct Marketing" for "Co-op Mailings." These are mailings made to specific groups (such as expectant mothers). You can participate with your particular offer—if it's pertinent—for a fraction of what it would cost you to make a mailing on your own.

Also, the broker you select will be able to put you in touch with people in this business that, for about three to five cents per piece, will include your advertising in their package or follow-up mailing. (These are called Co-Op Mailings and Package Insert Programs.) I heard about one large Direct-Selling luggage company who saved its business from bankruptcy using this advertising technique.

If the company you're "piggy-backing" with has customers who should be interested in your product, you'll probably do all right.

If you're curious about the various mailing lists and Package Insert Programs that are available to you, just as with magazine advertising, you'll want to take a trip to your Public Library and pick up a copy of the most Current Standard Rates and Data Services title, *"Direct Marketing List Source"* (or get it online www.srds.com). In it you

---

Direct Mail, the favorite of many a novice in this business, allows you to focus your advertising efforts on only those prospects who are most likely to be interested in your offer.

It's now up to you. Just don't be too busy earning a living to make any money.

will find that there is a mailing list (and Package Insert Program) for just about every group imaginable. From Aircraft Owners to Zenith Book Buyers—quite literally "A to Z!"

So now you know how to "think up" a product (and a product can be a thing or a service)—how to set your selling price and control your costs—you know the business procedures—how to write and produce your ad—and how much media to buy.

**Are you still too busy working for a living
to make any money?**

Now turn to Step #43 "How to Get the Best Buys in Time and Space"
in your *Roadmap to Riches* workbook.

44

The Internet—
an Overview

AN EXCITING NEW WORLD OF DIRECT RESPONSE POSSIBILITIES

I've saved the best for last. These last few chapters of *The Lazy Man's Way to Riches* are about the Internet and they are as new and as up-to-date as it gets. They are designed to get you up and running on the Internet quickly, inexpensively, and effectively.

Why do I say the Internet is the best? Because for making money the "Lazy Man's Way" there is nothing better than the Internet, because it's all about working smarter, not harder.

The Worldwide Web didn't exist until 1993. Within 5 years it had more than a hundred million users worldwide. 2004's projected Internet sales are *2.7 trillion dollars.*

Here's why I say the Internet is the best opportunity you have to get Rich! The following facts speak for themselves:

- The number of Internet users has grown by a steady 22.3 percent every year for the past four years! No other business medium has ever come close to that.

- Almost 1.23 **Billion** people **worldwide** have Internet access as of July of 2004. That means one out of every six human beings on this planet is wired to the Internet and can access your website. It's a market 4 times the size of the United States and they are hungry for information and products not available to them where they live.

- 86 percent of users surveyed said sending and receiving E-mail was what they did most often making E-mail the Web's "Killer Application."

- Between 1999 and 2004, on-line shopping grew by a **staggering 740 percent**. And it is still growing as consumers become more trusting and computer savvy!

- More than 300 million people now buy and sell on the Internet. What other sales medium can compete with that?

- The Internet is **always open**; meaning your business on the Internet is always open. Customers come to your website from home, work, Starbucks, or any place they can make an Internet connection—any time of day or night. You are literally making money in your sleep!

These numbers are facts, and they convey a truthful message that things have never been better. E-commerce is booming in both Business to Business (B2B)

During my service in the United States Congress, I took the initiative in creating the Internet.

ALBERT GORE, JR.
(b.1948)
former Vice-President of the United States

The world is poised on the cusp of an economic and cultural shift as dramatic as that of the Industrial Revolution.

STEPHEN LEVY
Author, Newsweek journalist

You can literally make money while you sl

and Business to Consumers (B2C), and is picking up both speed and momentum as it grows.

WHAT'S DRIVING THE INTERNETS EXPLOSIVE GROWTH?

It's the Internet's remarkable ability to increase sales and reduce costs while simultaneously enabling business to deliver their products and services, with 24 hour customer support, in ever-expanding ways to a now "Global Village."

> The Internet is a telephone system that's gone uppity.
>
> CLIFFORD STOLL

Although the Internet is still in its infancy, it has the power to reshape people's lives as well as entire industries. The Internet has already changed the way people work, get news, research, do banking and pay bills, communicate with each other, buy books and music, buy cars, shop for housing and mortgages, order groceries, book travel, and attend meetings or seminars, and so much more. If you can pick up the phone to do it, you can do it quicker and cheaper on the Internet.

That's why I say the Internet is the best opportunity to achieve the Riches you desire. There has never been anything like the Internet in all of recorded human history that has the potential for making money like the opportunity the Internet presents right now and in the near future. How exciting is that?

Now, riding this economic wave requires more than simply throwing a site on the Web and hoping the world beats a path to your virtual door. It takes a keen understanding of how the web changes the nature of customer relationships and how it's reshaping the way we do business.

I assure you, if you follow the advice I'm going to give you and use the resources that I will make available to you in your *Roadmap to Riches* workbook, that you too, will become a success on the Internet.

And like any other business, it is dependent upon how much planning, thought, skill, and resources you are willing to invest. The amount of time and effort that you will spend on your current Internet project will decrease once you have built your Internet business, but you will need to stay on top of new developments in technology and new techniques in direct response marketing . . . which you will be able to do with our *The Game Plan for Success* newsletter . . . to assure your continued success.

BEFORE WE START—SOME ASSUMPTIONS

Before we get started on the details of making the Internet work for you, there are a few assumptions that I've made about you.

You have a product or service that you are eager and anxious to sell and are looking at the Internet as one of (if not the main) sales channels. (If you don't yet have a product or service, then revisit Chapter 36.)

You have a burning desire to make your online business a success— you just need a coach or a mentor to show you how. Well, what I will show you, teach you, and push you to do is not complicated, but it will take some consistent effort on your part.

You did not invest your last dime to buy this program. You will need some money, although it will be a lot less than building a traditional bricks and mortar business would require.

You have basic computer skills. You know how to e-mail, surf the Web, use a word processor, and hopefully more. If you don't, then you will have to hire someone to do those things for you. No matter how much you learn, I feel it's invaluable to have experts you can count on. (We list several sources in the *Roadmap to Riches* workbook.)

But, I hope you are an Electronically Literate Person (ELP). Beyond the basic computer skills listed previously, you should be able to operate digital scanners, digital cameras, make CDs, burn DVDs, install and upgrade software, create documents on a word processor and html editor, use search engines with the proper techniques (do you speak boolean?), upload files, set up and maintain an e-mail program, and understand bandwidth.

The first step to mastering the Internet is to become totally familiar with the basic tools and information equipment of the times.

The next step is become an advanced ELP by accepting that the electronic world of the Internet will continue to change at a rapid pace and to get ahead of the curve by doing, making mistakes, and learning from experience. I'll give you all the tools you need—but you have to use them.

Don't panic—it's all explained here and in the guidebook. You can learn anything you don't yet know. I promise you it's not rocket science. If I can learn it so can you.

I'VE BEEN THERE

I feel I know where you are right now because I've been there too. I started as a novice doing Internet marketing less than two years after the Internet became "The Internet." I wanted to learn enough about it to be able to competently tell my employees what needed to be done.

When I started on the Internet in 1995 there were precious few resources to help me learn how to effectively market on the Internet. My education has cost me time—year after year of time—and money, lots of it—hundreds of thousands of dollars to learn how to make money consistently on the Internet.

Mine was a journey of trial and error, but your journey doesn't have to be that way because I'll lay it all out for you in the pages that follow, and in the *Roadmap to Riches*.

The *Roadmap to Riches* contains everything you need to be successful on the Internet. In it:

- You get tools and resources that will enable you to do everything you need to do.

- You get in-depth articles and explanations of things I'll only touch on in this book.

- You get live hyperlinks to websites where you can get additional information and help.

- You get my personal recommendations for things that I have found to be of top value—the very things I use in my Internet business.

Correct me if I'm wrong, the gizmo is connected to the flingflang connected to the watzis, the watzis connected to the doodad connected to the ding-dong.

PATRICK B. OLIPHANT
Cartoon caption in *Time* magazine

I am always doing that which I cannot do, in order that I may learn how to do it.

PABLO PICASSO
(1881–1973)
Spanish artist

When you sell a man a book, you don't sell him just twelve ounces of paper and ink and glue—you sell him a whole new life.

ROGER MIFFLIN
Protaganist of Christopher Morley's classic haunted *Bookshop* novels.

I not only use all the brains that I have, but all that I can borrow.

WOODROW WILSON
(1856–1924)
28th President of
the United States

- You get lists of products, software, systems, suppliers, trainers, providers, articles, sources that have taken me years to assemble.

- You get the forms and checklists I use.

- You get access to the forum where you can ask me, and other experts, questions about anything in this book.

- And you get lots more. You get it all!

The *Roadmap to Riches* workbook is quite simply the most complete tool on the market today to assure that you get real success on the Internet.

Now turn to Step #44 "The Internet—an Overview"
in your *Roadmap to Riches* workbook.

45
Why Should You Do Business On-Line?

REASONS TO CONSIDER

Did you ever ask yourself, "Why am I going on-line to do business?" Of course everybody will do business on-line eventually but it's still a good question to ask yourself. Your reason is important because your reasons for doing something are stronger than the methods you use to get the job done. If you have a strong enough reason—a strong enough "Why" to create a successful on-line business, then you will persevere. You will find a way to get the job done to be as successful as you want to be.

Here are some reasons to consider doing business on-line:

- Age is of no concern—it works regardless if you are too young, or too old, for any other business.
- There is no discrimination of any kind on the Internet because no one knows who you are—and no one cares.
- Your educational level is also a non-factor as long as your website looks and functions properly.
- Doing business on the Internet gives you a "passive" income stream that works for you no matter where you go or what you do.
- You are truly your own boss—for better or worse.
- If you have the drive and determination but lack the skills and knowledge you can start slow and learn as you go.
- You can earn far more than any employer will ever pay you.
- It gives you the ability to have security regarding your financial future.
- You can operate from virtually anywhere, anytime day or night, as long as you have a computer and Internet access. You could be on a constant "vacation" working from wherever you happen to be that day!
- You enjoy the lowest start up and operating costs of any good business.

So, ask yourself again—"Why do I want to do business on-line?"

Most people answer something like, "Everybody is doing it." Or "I want to make money."

My next question to you would be, "How do you plan to make your money on the Internet?"

> Almost overnight the Internet's gone from a technical wonder to a business must.
>
> BILL SCHRADER
> CEO of PSINet.

> He who jumps into the void owes no explanation to those who stand and watch.
>
> JEAN LUC GODARD
> French film maker

That's where most people get stuck and why they never go beyond the dream of having an online business. You'd be amazed at the number of people who answer that with, "I'm not sure." I will help you answer that question and help you on the way to living your dream.

You need to be clear about developing a lean, clean Internet business that will accomplish your personal and business goals and satisfy your earthly purpose.

Before I go on, a warning...

BEWARE THE ONLINE BUSINESS OPPORTUNITY

For those who can't think of their own product or service to sell online, thousands of business opportunities tout themselves as the path to online riches. You've seen them in "opportunity" magazines for years and now they flood your E-mail inbox with enchanting tales of easy Internet money.

To cash in and get your piece of the pie, they explain that all any self-motivated self-starter like you needs to do is hand over a couple hundred dollars, and you will instantly find yourself in a proven turnkey business on the World Wide Web.

What many online business opportunity sellers fail to mention is that the real money is only for *them*, by getting people to sign up and pay *them* for the opportunity itself.

Those "biz-oppers" have multiplied like flies, and they can open and close shop on-line faster than a con man with a card table at a swap meet.

But if you have to pay hundreds of dollars to sign up for an opportunity, and the company still owns the customers, (who you found), and will make thousands of dollars from them on the backend, while leaving you out in the cold—I suggest you find another opportunity quick.

Use common sense when investing in an online business opportunity. If it looks too good to be true...it is.

Don't come across with any money until you get a chance to talk with at least 10 people who have bought into the opportunity, as well as 10 people who are unhappy with it and have quit.

If the opportunity promoters won't give you the names of both happy and unhappy clients, you need to keep looking. Or better yet, just do it yourself.

The problem with most of these "opportunities" is;

1. They don't work at all, and they have no chance of working

2. They are outdated, or

3. They are so complicated that the average person doesn't have a clue how to accomplish the first step.

Now that that is out of the way...

THE BIG FOUR

There are four major missions that individuals and companies seek to accomplish by doing business on the Internet:

> Everybody gets so much information all day long that they lose their common sense.
>
> GERTRUDE STEIN
> American writer, poet, feminist, playwright

- Revenue generation...making money!
- Cost savings
- Enhanced customer support
- Brand development

Revenue Generation. First and foremost you must generate revenue to produce the profits necessary to meet your plans and objectives—not just revenues, but profits. That's where direct response marketing comes in. You can also generate revenue from advertising and renting your opt-in list, and there are many other ways we will show you.

If you sell products and/or services on the Internet that can be delivered outside your geographical area then the world opens up to you a little wider.

But, if you can deliver your product or service on-line, then the entire globe becomes your marketplace. That's why I sell information products (e-books, special reports, etc.) on the Internet. Instant customer satisfaction—they get the product *immediately* with no postage and handling charge, and...instant reward for me—the payment is deposited into my bank account almost instantly.

Cost Savings. If you like, you might consider the purpose of cost savings as a revenue generation model. Ben Franklin recognized this revenue source when he told us, "A penny saved is a penny earned."

New Internet-only companies may not appreciate the cost-savings possible on the Web, but many traditional businesses are able to lower costs significantly by moving essential business processes to the Internet. My Internet company is virtually a "poster child" model of automation. It works for me.

It may not be politically correct, but it makes great business sense to outsource those things you can obtain cheaper and at a higher quality level by outsourcing. I have seen TEC member companies save huge amounts of money and get better results from outsourcing using the Internet.

One company got rid of its entire Human Resources department and replaced it with an H. R. Compliance Company and several top notch recruiters who are independent contractors. The former head of that H. R. department is now an independent contractor doing her H. R. business on the Internet and making more than she ever did before.

Save on distribution of sales materials. If you've ever run a catalog business, or sent sales materials to your far-flung offices, you know how much money and energy is invested in printing and postage.

The Web shines as a way to distribute great amounts of information inexpensively. Many companies put their entire catalog on the Web and then keep it up-to-date as needed, they long for the time when they won't have to print a catalog at all. Others put their sales materials on the Internet (or on a company Intranet for employees).

While there is some expense in converting text and graphics to the Web, once the material is there, it costs next to nothing to keep it there. Updating of data is simpler, too, especially on database-driven sites.

Beware of the little expenses. A small leak will sink a great ship.

BENJAMIN FRANKLIN
(1706–1790)
American scientist, publisher, statesman

Great Customer Support. Successful businesses have this in common: They focus on the customer's needs. This ought to be an important purpose for most business websites.

Pre-sales support can be listed under revenue generation, but post sales support to your customers is a category all of its own. Fortunately, the Web can provide the very best in customer support.

Your system may be as simple as an FAQ page or troubleshooting decision tree. What a great way to help your customers. The more material you have, the more valuable your searchable database becomes. Microsoft's site, for example, provides a huge amount of product support information. Epson's site links you to any driver software you may need.

Providing customer support on the Web is not only efficient for the customer, it is also a boon to company customer support departments, who can refer callers to their website for detailed and complete information, substantially shortening phone calls.

Brand Development. You may have never thought about your company as a brand, so this may be new to you, but follow me here. One of the chief reasons your company has a website is to demonstrate that you're staying up with the times, that you're on the cutting edge. You're seeking to communicate an image about your company that will register in the minds of your potential customers. Professional marketers refer to this as brand development.

Your brand is the image of your business in the minds of customers and prospects. Everything about your site—the ease of navigation, the quality of the design, the clarity of your wording, the sense of interest and excitement, the color scheme, the download time, and much more—all contribute to your image, and your image is your brand identity.

YOU WANT THEM TO HAVE A GREAT EXPERIENCE ON YOUR WEBSITE

Your primary goal is to sell them something on the first visit—and next, to have them give you their contact information voluntarily so you can start building the trust necessary to build a relationship with them over a period of time. You want them to have a great experience on your website so when they leave your site they'll remember you positively. And that the next time they come, they'll make another purchase, or pick up the phone to call in an order. Your brand image is also the trust the customer has in you.

There are no real shortcuts here. The major corporations spends millions of dollars to develop their brand image and keep it fresh in the minds of consumers. Is there any way a small business can compete?

Yes, your site can look every bit as good on the Web as a major corporation's, and without spending the big bucks they do. Even though the Web is no longer a level playing field, small businesses can still compete for a great first impression.

You need *professional* help.

Now, how can I say this without offending you? You need professional help.

> If you do it right, a website can enhance your company's image, build customer loyalty, and get information to customers and potential customers quickly and cheaply.
>
> NATALIE SEQUERIA
> Claris Corp. Spokeswoman

Relax, it's not a shrink I'm talking about, but an experienced website designer. To compete today you either need to either have graphics training and a design sense yourself, or you need to hire it. Do-it-yourself will undercut the strong brand identity you are trying to build. Sure, it's cheaper to do it yourself or to have your nephew do it with that spiffy new software he's dying to use on you, but not if it means your business won't get off the ground.

Design includes the color scheme and graphics, but also structure of the site, the all-important navigation system, the size and quality of the photos or illustrations. All these affect your brand image. Your nephew doesn't understand brand image yet.

Be very clear about this, whether you are General Motors or a one-person small business, brand development; "image," is on your list of purposes for being on the Internet. It is a precondition for sales since it relates directly to customer trust. Fail at this and you will fail at the core purposes of your site.

So, there's no need to be fuzzy about your website's purposes. Ask yourself these questions:

What source(s) of revenue can you realistically expect from your online business?

How can you achieve maximal cost savings on the Internet?

How can you provide excellent online customer support?

How can you present your company in the best possible light? (Brand development)

Answer these questions well, and you are on your way to on-line success and Riches.

> The most damaging phrase in the language is, "It's always been done that way."
> ADMIRAL GRACE HOPPER (1906–1992)

Now turn to Step #45 "Why Should You Do Business On-Line?" in your *Roadmap to Riches* workbook.

46

Riches in Cyberspace

T he lure of low startup costs (compared to brick and mortar stores) and the possibility of working from home, along with the promise of high rewards draws an ever growing crowd of entrepreneurs and established business people to the on-line marketplace.

Everyone wants to know—"What does it take to succeed in the e-commerce world once you've completed the basic steps for getting on-line?"

Now, I don't mean to oversimplify things, but I'll just tell you like it is. There are only 3 things that you need to earn a full-time living on-line.

The three vital steps in successfully earning a full-time living online are to acquire your own product or service, develop a direct response Web site, and launch a targeted marketing campaign. It's that simple. None of which are very difficult to do. In fact, they are fairly simple, as you will soon discover.

STEP 1. ACQUIRE A HIGH-DEMAND PROFIT—GENERATING PRODUCT OR SERVICE

Step one of the simple three-step system for earning a guaranteed full-time living on line is to develop your very own product that you can sell and keep 100% of the profits from. Got that?

There are lots of on-line marketers who would try to sell you on just being their affiliates and selling their products and they will send you big referral fees—sure. But, there is one glaring problem with affiliate programs—the owner of the affiliate program is generally the only one making the big bucks!

Learn this unchanging, universal fact: The person who <u>owns</u> the product is the one who makes the big bucks. Behind 99 percent of internet success stories (there are a few exceptions) there is a product that is entirely theirs. And, more than likely, there's an entire arsenal of products.

Face it; if you don't own your own product or service, your chances of earning a full-time living online are diminished greatly.

You need a quality product or service with highly evident and easily understood benefits for the consumer. In other words you need a Profit Generating Product or Service.

In our world of products/services—it's *benefits*, not the features that are the emotional spark that ignites the consumer to make a positive buying decision. The Internet magnifies the "What's In It For Me" benefits driven emotional evaluation by consumers. Products/services presented with readily understood, self-serving benefits for consumers sell best.

Savvy businesses are racing to stake a claim in cyberspace.

Inc. magazine

Most people do not believe that wealth is a lifestyle choice within their control. Indeed, many believe the only way they'll get rich is by winning the lottery or robbing a bank...ignore these pessimists!

COREY RUDL
Internet marketer

Most Internet marketing experts (those of us actually making money on the Internet) feel that selling *information* is the ultimate business to be in. In fact, with the exception of sex sites, information is the number 1 seller online today. Electronic information products (delivered digitally) are among the most sought after on-line.

Once you create your information product (more on this in just a minute) the business can easily be completely automated and requires very little monthly overhead. (I spend less than $400. a month) Since the products are electronic, there are zero reproduction costs. The products can easily be downloaded from your Web site thousands of times without spending another dime.

And the profit is incredible. If the product sells for $19.95, then you keep $19.95. I'm no math expert, but that seems like 100% of the sale goes to you, not your affiliate sponsor!

Necessity is the mother of invention.

PROVERB

And, there is no need to maintain inventory. Everything is hosted on your Web site, with instant and constant (24/7/365) access for your customers.

You can do this in a couple of ways:

Develop your own product from scratch. Most people immediately want to call it quits right there. For some reason, people think you must have been born with writers genes in order to be a successful writer. If your genes don't have the Great American Novel stored within them, then you can't write.

Wrong!

Despite what you may be thinking, you don't have to be blessed with special skills and abilities in order to create your own information product to sell online. In fact, if you can write a shopping list, you can create your own infoproduct! Don't sell yourself short here, you can do it.

It doesn't have to be 300 pages. I have written 15–20 page reports that I have sold for thousands of dollars in profits. The key is having good content.

And good content is easy to find if you know where to look.

There are many excellent resources available online to show you exactly how to get it done. I'll show you how to find them in the *Roadmap to Riches* workbook.

Purchase reprint rights to an existing product. Of course, you can also do something even easier, if you choose! Despite how easy it is to create your own product, maybe you don't have the time or would rather add more products to your arsenal.

You can purchase reprint rights to products that are ready to sell. Good products can be purchased for as little as $25.00 and as much as $25,000. For less than twenty five bucks you can own your very own product to start selling on the internet to learn how it's done. You'll make some money and have fun while you learn.

The key here is to find high-quality products to sell that are still timely.

What you want are products that...

Are high-demand. They focus on topics that are hot. Not outdated, but fresh and wanted.

Are ready-to-launch. They must have an order-producing sales letter and web-page ready for you to plug in your information and begin selling immediately.

Are written by an authority. Again, the key is content. You want material that is authored by someone who knows what they are talking about and is well respected in the industry they represent.

You can find offers all over the web, but beware of bad quality products. Focus on the above mentioned criteria and you'll find a winner.

And, to save you a bit of work, let me point you in the right direction. Just look in the *Roadmap to Riches* where you'll find some products that I personally recommend.

That brings us to step 2...

STEP 2. DEVELOP A DIRECT RESPONSE WEB SITE

Your Web site will need to load immediately, provide pertinent information to targeted customers, provide compelling sales copy, and allow them to make their purchase, pay for the purchase, and download their purchase instantly and securely.

When you visit the Web sites of the Internet "gurus" as you first begin your own adventure online, you'll found a wide variety of layouts and designs. Graphically, they are quite different in appearance. Their choice of writing style is varied, as are their offers.

Web Site Sales Letters

One thing they have in common, however, are the **sales letters** that convince people to "click here" to buy. That purpose is to...

Compel visitors to "Click" on the order button and make an immediate purchase, or...

Compel visitors to "Click" on the submit button to join an E-Zine mailing list or receive a free report or E-book, so they can follow-up and make the sale in the future.

Something conspicuously absent from these Web sites is *anything* that would distract the reader away from the selling purpose. You don't find links that lead the reader off of their sites. In fact, you don't find a lot of links period. No slow-loading graphics that force us impatient folks to leave prematurely. There is nothing that would distract the reader. Just a great sales letter that persuasively and consistently convinces the visitor to "click here." And as you can imagine, there is a whole lot of clicking going on at these sites.

SOME QUICK TIPS

Here are some **quick tips** that you can begin using immediately to improve your webpage sales letter...

A. Write your sales letter with one particular person in mind. Go ahead and pick out someone, a real person to write your sales letter to. It doesn't matter if it is your next door neighbor, a co-worker or your last prospect.

...in the end the communicator will be confronted with the old problem of what to say and how to say it.

EDWARD R. MORROW
Journalist

Write your sales letter just like you are writing it to them personally. Why? Because when your potential customer reads it, it will seem personal, almost like you wrote it with them in mind.

Most sales letters are written as if they were going to be read to a radio audience, rather than one person. Keep your sales letters personal, because one person at a time is going to read them.

B. Grab the reader from the very first line. Your first line of the sales letter should immediately create a desire in the reader to want to know more. Carefully craft your first line. If you can immediately get them wanting to know more, you've got a winner.

C. Make your sales letter personal. Make sure that the words "you" and "your" are at least 4:1 over "I" and "my." Your ad copy must be written to and about your customer. I'm not sure how the old advertising adage goes, but it's something like this, "I don't care a thing about *your* lawn mower, I just care about *my* lawn." Prospects aren't interested in you or your products; they are interested in themselves and their wants and needs. Remember, WIIFM? (What's In It For Me)

D. Use short paragraphs consisting of 2–4 sentences each. Long copy works... but long paragraphs don't. Everyone seems to have shorter attention spans in today's world. Use short paragraphs that lead into the next paragraph. Don't be afraid to use short sentences. Like this one. Or this. See what I mean?

Shorter paragraphs keep the interest of the reader. Longer paragraphs cause eye strain and often force the reader to get distracted.

E. Use similes and metaphors for effect. When the customer purchases your product, they will generate "a flood of traffic that would make Noah start building another ark." If they don't order today, they will "feel like a cat that let the mouse get away."

Use words to create a picture in the readers' mind. When you think of Superman, what comes to mind? Immediately, we remember that he is "faster than a speeding bullet, more powerful than a locomotive. Able to leap tall buildings in a single bound." See how word pictures stick in our minds?

F. Focus on one product or service. Don't try to sell your customer multiple products at the same time. It only confuses the reader—and when they're confused by choices they don't buy.

A direct response Web site always works best. Keep your ad copy directed at one specific product or service. Then, you can use other products and services as back-end products.

G. Be believable. "Earn $54,000 in the next 24 hours!!!!!" Delete. I mean really... do they think I am an idiot or something? Get real. Don't make outrageous claims that are obviously not the truth. You'll ruin your reputation. Let me tell you a simple universal fact that cannot be reversed. Once you have been branded a liar, you will never be anything but a liar.

It doesn't matter if you launch the most respectable, honest business available anywhere, people will always have doubt because they remember the crazy

> Do not let what you cannot do interfere with what you can do.
>
> JOHN WOODEN
> UCLA basketball coach

stuff you've said before. Be believable. Don't exaggerate, mislead, stretch or distort the truth.

H. Be specific. Don't generalize your information, but rather be exact. Instead of "over 100 tips for losing weight" use "124 tips for losing weight." By generalizing information, it creates doubt and questions in the reader's mind. When you use specific information, the reader begins to think, "This person must have counted. I know exactly what I can expect."

I. Use headlines over and over throughout the sales letter. A headline isn't just relegated to the beginning of your ad copy. Use them frequently—but don't overuse in the body. (They are really sub-heads.) A well-placed headline re-grabs the reader's attention, brings them deeper into the letter, and readies them for the next paragraph. You will want to spend as much time working on your headlines as you do the entire sales letter. They are that important.

J. Use bonuses to overwhelm the reader. Make them an offer they can't refuse. One of the things that I have found very effective in writing sales letters is to include bonus items that out-value the main product I am offering. This worked at K-Tel in the 60s and 70s—"But wait, there's more…" Before the commercial was finished, there were so many bonus items on the table it was hard to refuse the offer. Make sure you provide quality bonuses and not something perceived worthless, that just damages the credibility of your main offer.

There is more information on building your own direct response Web site in the *Roadmap to Riches* workbook.

And step three…

STEP THREE. LAUNCH A TARGETED MARKETING CAMPAIGN

Once you have built your Web site… where is it? It might as well be on a distant planet if no one knows where it is and exactly how to get there, but even more importantly—why should they seek it out?

What can you do to get people interested enough in your product to want to seek it out? Promote… promote… promote. You need to arouse their curiosity to the point where they are compelled to find out more. It must be intuitively simple for them to get to your Web site with one click at the point where they are ready to make a buying decision.

It doesn't matter what you want to sell, whether it's a product or service, whether high-ticket item or low-priced goods. It doesn't matter where you live or what you look like. You've simply got to market in order to produce orders. Creating a great product is the beginning. Building a Web site is the natural follow-up to that.

But, if you stop there, you're no better off than you were when you began. You've got to attract targeted prospects to your Web site in order to create paying customers. I'll teach you about that in one of the following chapter's and I'll show you how to put it all together to earn guaranteed monthly income.

Like I said, I don't mean to oversimplify things. The "Lazy Man's" formula for success on the Internet is complete and includes the entire arsenal of tools and

> If you refuse to accept anything but the best, you very often get it.
>
> SOMERSET MAUGHAN (1874–1965)
> Novelist, playwright, and short-story writer

> The best way to predict the future is to create it.
>
> PETER DRUCKER, Ph.D. (b.1909)
> Professor, author

Some people drink from the fountain of knowledge, others just gargle.

ROBERT ANTHONY, PH.D.
American psychologist and writer

resources like E-zines, joint ventures, affiliates, branding, viral marketing and so forth. And I'll teach you about all of them in the following chapters, and more completely in the *Roadmap To Riches* workbook.

But to tell you the truth, if you do the above mentioned three things, everything else will fall into place. I guarantee it.

Now turn to Step #46 "Riches in Cyberspace" in your *Roadmap to Riches* workbook.

47

Creating a Successful On-Line Presence

Establishing a successful online presence involves much more than going at it blindly, or simply asking your Internet technical (IT) person to build a Web site. A clear sense of direction and a good understanding of fundamental e-commerce principles is needed.

> Action to be effective must be directed to clearly conceived ends.
>
> JAWAHARLAL NEHRU
> (1889–1964)
> Indian Statesman

BUSINESS FIRST, TECHNOLOGY SECOND

Individuals and companies that succeed on the Web understand perhaps the most important e-commerce principle of all...although the Internet involves technology and computers, it is *not* about technology. It's about delivering value, getting paid and making a return on your investment. In short, it's all about doing business. If you lose sight of this fact at any point in the development of your Web site, you dramatically reduce your chances for success.

A WEB SITE MUST SOLVE A PROBLEM OR EASE A PAIN

A Web site must solve a problem or ease a pain that the market cares about. You also have to understand that the Web represents a very different medium. On the Internet, you **only have a few seconds to get people's attention** and convince them to spend time and money on your site. The best way to do that is to let them know right away that you intend to solve a problem or ease a pain for them immediately.

> Life isn't about finding yourself. Life is about creating yourself.
>
> GEORGE BERNARD SHAW
> (1856–1950)
> Irish playwright, critic, social reformer

What kind of pain can you ease or problems can you solve online?

- Help new and existing customers identify your products and services as solutions they need.
- Simplify the buying process by providing information and product demonstrations.
- Provide a 24-hour help desk to answer frequently asked questions (FAQs).
- Allow customers to track inventory levels and product delivery.
- Even help job seekers learn about the positions available in your company and why they should work for you.

These represent but a fraction of the potential business problems you could solve using the Internet. You must first identify the problem(s) you want to solve, and then determine how the technology can help you do that. The business plan always suggests the technologies, not the other way around.

BENEFITS—BENEFITS

Without exception, the most important component of doing business online is having a crystal-clear picture of the benefit you want to provide visitors. If you can't give people a compelling reason, laced with some sort of benefit to them on why they should come to your Web site, your Internet concept will quickly collapse.

A benefit can be anything from providing ordinary price information to leading customers through a complex transaction. The *key* is to *identify* the benefits to your target market that your online presence will provide, and then *build* everything around those benefits. Without this bedrock foundation, your Web site will rest on very shaky ground.

"BEST PRACTICE" OF GREAT WEBSITES

Good Web sites have a lot in common with custom homes. Each one has its own design and features that create a unique look and feel, but the builders use the same engineering principles and the underlying foundations are essentially the same. In a similar manner, companies that establish and maintain a dominant Internet presence all adhere to several important principles. Here's what the online winners do:

They have a highly focused Internet plan

Web sites often fail due to lack of leadership. In small business, the owner just starts building a website with no vision. He is just "winging it" so to speak. In big business, all too often, the owner says, "Build me a Web site!" and then provides little or no direction. The IT person (or whoever is unlucky enough to be on the receiving end of that command) comes back later with a technologically nifty site, full of "cool" long loading graphics, that doesn't do anything the owner expected it to do. And may even be counter productive to the online selling process.

Whether you are a one person business or a major company, to have successful Web sites, the owner first has to set the strategy, goals and objectives of the site, then secondly delegate implementation to a capable manager or start work on it yourself with a clear vision....and then hold that person or yourself accountable. This requires a focused Internet plan with timetables, roles and responsibilities, and expected corporate and marketing outcomes.

They clearly define their expectations for the site

Never build a Web site just because everyone else is doing it. Without clearly defined goals and objectives, your site will never get off the ground. Plus, unless you have a specific outcome in mind, you can't measure your success or failure. Examples of possible outcomes include:

- Increasing sales or sales leads
- Educating customers and prospects
- Driving customers to your retail outlets
- Improving customer service
- Supporting your offline marketing efforts
- Attracting qualified job applicants

How you design your site determines how well it accomplishes your objec-

---

A goal is created three times. First as a mental picture. Second, when written down to add clarity and dimension. And Third, when you take action towards it's achievement.

GARY RYAN BLAIR
Author, speaker, coach

tives. But it also impacts the *offline* parts of your business as well. For example, if you decide to conduct retail sales on your site, you have to decide how to the customer will pay for the purchases, how you will deliver the product. Plus, you had better be prepared to handle a flood of orders. We recently put up a Web site for a product that got so many online orders that we couldn't hire enough people to keep up. That may sound like a good problem to have, but it can destroy you on the Internet. People may come to your site once, but if you don't meet their expectations, they will never come back.

They define their target market

Unless you're an Amazon.com or eBay, you may not want the whole world coming to your site. But be prepared for foreign business and make sure you can fulfill and ship their orders. I suggest you use a good fulfillment house, as order filling in volume is better outsourced.

Like an author writing a book or a public speaker giving a speech, knowing your audience pays big dividends. To build the most effective Web site, clearly identify:

- Who you want to come to the site
- What you want them to do once they get there
- What benefit your visitors will gain from taking that action
- How that will allow you to profitably increase revenues or cut costs

After defining your target audience, it helps to create a customer profile. Ask questions like,

- Who is your target audience?
- How old is your target audience?
- How technologically savvy are they?
- What do they expect when they come to your site?'

Create an accurate profile and build your marketing plan and your site accordingly. If your target market involves seniors, for example, make your site simple and very easy to navigate and use larger fonts.

If you're pursuing the under-25 market, you can get away with wild graphics, state-of-the-art technology, and streaming audio. Just be aware that those fun things might also cost you sales.

They identify their "pull component"

Offline marketing is quite intrusive. It imposes itself on prospects and customers whether they want it or not; like junk mail or the obnoxious television commercial, or billboards in your face on the highway.

In contrast, Web marketing involves a deliberate, *conscious* choice to find your site. If you want people to come to your site, you must give them a compelling reason to visit and a way to get there. That compelling reason represents your "pull component."

I feel that three of the best websites at demonstrating the power of the "pull component" are; Hotmail.com, Google.com and Mapquest.com. Hotmail.com with

> You are not your target market.
>
> JOE KARBO

> You can tell whether a man is clever by his answers. You can tell whether a man is wise by his questions.
>
> NAGUIB MAHFOUZ
> (b. 1911)
> Egyptian writer, Nobel Peace prize winner

it's free email, has brought them millions of customers because of their viral like word of mouth. The word on free email spread to every corner of the globe in a remarkably short period of time, making Hotmail a powerhouse. Another great example is Google.com whose effective search engine brought millions of customers to Google, and is making the two young founders billionaires. Mapquest.com is another. Who doesn't use Mapquest.com?

You may not have the ability to have a search engine or mapping capabilities, but you can certainly have features on your website that have a "pull component" to them. Having a quote of the day, joke of the day or business tip of the day are all excellent ways of pulling people to your site. You can even have free email like Hotmail.com. Come up with a good "pull component" and the world will beat a path to your door and fill your pockets with riches.

They understand the medium

Unlike any other communication medium, the Internet has its own culture. It creates a whole new way for customers to interact with you and vice versa. So don't go into a Web site thinking you can conduct business as usual. To establish an effective online presence, pay close attention to how the Internet alters relationships and expectations. People change when they go online. Within a very short time, their expectations for free information and speed of response dramatically increase, and their trust quotient declines. They have learned to reject anything that smells like hype. They will simply go to another site where someone will deal with them honestly and intelligently.

They outsource as much as possible

Unless you're a large company with a huge Internet budget and plenty of in-house expertise, I recommend outsourcing everything except the strategy. Why? Because outsourcing:

- Can get the site up and running more quickly and effectively
- Offers significant cost savings with fixed price bids.
- Provides specialized experts who know how to avoid costly mistakes
- Allows your key players to stay focused on their primary responsibilities
- Makes it easier to keep up with the constantly changing Web environment and technology.
- Avoids the costly and time-consuming process of recruiting and hiring Internet specialists

It definitely pays to outsource the technology, but never delegate your Internet strategy to someone who doesn't understand your company's mission and objectives. Otherwise you will likely end up with a state-of-the-art site that doesn't accomplish any of your business objectives, and won't produce a profit, and you will spend a lot of money doing it . . . and then even more money un-doing it. Better to take the time to find the right person, to do it right the first time.

They measure results

Individuals and companies that succeed on the Internet pay close attention to the specific results they want to achieve with their Web site (i.e., increased sales, reduced customer service costs) and their overall Internet Return on Investment (ROI). Companies that flounder usually neglect these two critical areas.

Many experienced businesspeople forget about the basics when conducting e-commerce. They invest a great deal of time and money in building their Web sites and then don't bother to measure their ROI. They have a vague sense that they're not getting what they paid for, but they don't know for sure because they don't measure results. Every Web site should generate profitable revenue, reduce expenses or both. If not, there's no point in having the site. But you can't know one way or the other unless you measure what matters.

Success is more a function of consistent common sense than it is of genius.

AN WANG
(1920–1990)
Founder of Wang Labaratories

Now turn to Step #47 "Creating A Successful On-Line Presence"
in your *Roadmap To Riches* workbook.

48
Planning for On-Line Success

I recommend three types of plans to accomplish your Internet goals:

A Marketing Plan for the website itself.

A Business Plan for the online business.

An Implementation Plan.

THE WEBSITE MARKETING PLAN

As the owner of your web business, your job is to create and manage both the marketing and the Internet strategy, and let the technical people handle the operational details. Therefore, your Internet marketing and business plans should focus on the strategy, not the technology. I believe that the starting point for any Internet business plan begins with four critical questions:

- What problem(s) or pain(s) do we want to solve?
- Who do we want to solve them for?
- What is the value of solving these problems?
- What are we willing to invest to solve them?

If your answers to these questions make sense from a business standpoint, then proceed with the planning process. If not, you may want to reconsider your decision to go online, or find a new problem to solve.

Too many company owners put the technology ahead of the strategy because they get dazzled by the "Wow" factor of technology. But doing business on the Internet is not about technology. It's about delivering value over the Internet and getting a return on your investment. As I mentioned before, it's the strategy that always drives the technology and not the other way around, and that requires starting with a *business* plan, not a technology plan.

THE ONE PAGE BUSINESS PLAN

To outline your Internet strategy, I recommend a one-page, bullet-point business plan that covers five key areas:

- The problem(s) or pain(s) you intend to solve for your target market
- Specific goals and objectives for the Web site
- Time frames
- Budget
- Measurement criteria

Lack of planning on your part—does not constitute a crisis on my part.

PETER UEBERROTH
(b. 1937)
Entrepreneur, Former NFL commissioner, President of L.A.Olympics

The will to succeed is important, but what's more important is the will to prepare to succeed.

BOBBY KNIGHT
(b. 1940)
Passionate basketball coach

I recently worked with a company that designed its Web site to increase sales and generate leads. Its *online* business leads began placing first orders *three times faster* than leads that came through trade shows, advertising and other traditional methods. Plus, the initial order from the online leads averaged five times the size of initial orders from offline sources. Is it any wonder I love the Internet?

Those are the kinds of things that should go in your Internet business plan. You don't have to know anything about technology to know the value of decreasing the sales cycle, increasing orders, generating more leads and so on. The business plan always suggests the technologies, not the other way around. So create the business plan first, and then identify the technologies that will allow you to carry it out.

THE IMPLEMENTATION PLAN

Once you have determined your Internet business objectives, you can proceed with the process of designing and building the site. The implementation plan should have a much more operational focus because it involves identifying who does what by when. The plan can be as simple or as complex as you want to make it, but I recommend that it contain each of the following steps:

1. Restate the goals and objectives of the site.

The goals and objectives will come directly from the Internet business and marketing plans, but it's always a good idea to include them in the implementation plan so the project manager (even if that is you) and technical people don't lose sight of their destination. Keep the goals simple and straightforward, such as increasing/creating sales, reducing customer service costs, driving traffic to your retail stores or other outcomes that increase revenues, reduce costs or improve customer service.

2. Assign roles and responsibilities.

Building a successful Web site requires a project manager. That's usually someone who understands the vision and mission of the company, but also can work with the technical people. Some companies designate a senior manager, others outsource to a vendor who reports directly to the owner. Whatever you decide, make sure to choose someone who can commit the time and attention to get the job done right.

Never assign the project to a sales manager or IT manager on top of everything else they have to do. The person in charge has to be able to focus his or her undivided attention on building the site and must be willing to break the rules.

I also recommend giving the project manager full Profit & Loss (P&L) responsibility for the site. Let the IT people focus on the technology, but make your project manager responsible for the dollars.

If you are a single owner or a small business and you decide to outsource, select the vendor at this stage because they will be involved in every step the rest of the way. Also, be very clear about who will manage and hold the vendor accountable for delivering on time and within budget.

3. Conduct a design and site analysis.

This step answers critical questions such as:

- What do you want the site to accomplish?

Strategy is a commodity—
Implementation is an art.

PETER DRUCKER, Ph.D.
(b. 1909)
Professor, author

- How do you want the site to look and feel?

- How do you want to interact with visitors on the site?

- What kind of "bells and whistles" do you need? For example, How will you capture visitors e-mail addresses, on-line credit card purchases, shopping carts, pop-ups, auto responders, password security, etc.

- How many pages do you want on the site?

- What other types of information do you need to capture from visitors?

- Will this design work to achieve my objectives?

In particular, pay attention to what you want people to do once they come to the site. Many individuals and companies get so caught up in creating beautiful graphics and adding the bells and whistles that they lose sight of this critical component. What happens is the customer gets frustrated because the site is too cluttered and they can't find what they want, or it's too slow, so they leave... never to return. Stay focused on your goals and objectives and design your site in such a way that people can easily take the action you want them to take. Make it easy for them to buy what you're selling them. That is the whole idea... remember?

4. Create the content.

Nothing will kill a Web site quicker than bad content. You can have graphics that dazzle and you can make it easy for visitors to get around your site, but if you don't offer meaningful content, people won't come back.

Content flows directly from the goals and objectives of the site. For example, if you intend to educate consumers about your products and services in order to help their buying decisions, you will need benefit-oriented content that clearly differentiates your products and services from the competition. If you want to attract job applicants, you need information about the jobs available, your benefits program and other aspects that might lead people to see your company as a good place to work.

When creating your content, focus on providing real value to the visitor. That means providing the information they want and making it quickly and easily accessible. Focus on WIIFM—What's In It For Me from your customers' point of view.

5. How to market and promote your site.

Surprisingly, most companies actually overlook this step. It's like throwing a party and nobody comes, because *nobody got the invitation*. You have to invite them, give them a reason to come, provide an address with step-by-step directions, remind them of the good time they will have when they get there, and then reconfirm they are coming. The more you can do, the better off you are.

If you don't commit the resources needed to make people aware of your site, all your efforts will go for naught. To effectively market your site, I recommend a three-pronged approach that includes:

1. The proper use of search engines and Pay Per Click.

2. Various online marketing tools. (E-mail, E-zines, JVs, Affiliates, etc.)

3. Traditional (offline) promotional tools. (Direct mail, ads in print media, ads in radio and TV.)

Some people dream of succes while others wake up and work hard at it.

ANONYMOUS

More important, don't skimp when it comes to budgeting for your marketing efforts. For "brochure" Web sites that do little more than educate customers about your products and services, I recommend an 80/20-budget split, with 80 percent going to marketing and 20 percent going to building the site. For more sophisticated e-commerce sites that cost more to develop, I recommend a 70/30 split. Remember, you can always add technology once your site is profitable.

6. Develop a timeline.

Strive to get your site up and running as soon as possible. Create an aggressive timeline, but build in a certain amount of flexibility. Establish deadlines and hold people accountable for them. Again, even if that person is you.

7. Develop a direct response website.

Developing a direct response selling website—or landing page (a mini-site) should take approximately 30–35 days. (There are models to follow and lots of information about landing sites and how to design them in the *Roadmap To Riches* workbook.) Developing a professional corporate Web site should take approximately 60 to 120 days. You can't get it perfect the first time, so don't even try. Continually monitor the site to tweak it to optimum potential—which always seems to be just out of reach.

Start small, launch your site and get your customers involved. They will tell you what changes and enhancements need to be made. We send an automated email after a customer orders from our website, first of all thanking them for their order of course, then asking if the found the website easy to navigate, the order process easy to follow, and if they had any problems or suggestions we should know about. We have had a lot of very good feedback from our customers that we have acted on.

8. Measure your results.

The old cliché that "you can't manage it unless you measure it" holds true for Web sites as well. To determine the effectiveness of your Web site, measure three specific areas:

- Site usage (i.e., unique visitors, which pages get the most hits, time of day when most people visit the site, sales, stickiness, etc.)
- Actual performance versus goals and objectives
- Return on investment

Ultimately, your Web site should produce a meaningful result that adds to your profits, reduces your expenses or does both. If it doesn't do either, your site probably isn't working for you or for your target market. If that's true for your site—it's time to call in the direct response professionals we list in the workbook.

PLANNING TIPS

To facilitate the planning process I suggest:

- Keep your action plan simple. The Internet changes so rapidly that any complex research or lengthy plan will become obsolete by the time you finish. Be careful of "analysis to the point of paralysis."
- Share your plan with others in the company and get their support and buy-in. If you don't get buy-in from everyone, someone will find a way to make it fail.

A goal is a dream with a deadline.

HARVEY MACKAY
Businessman, author, motivational speaker

Cash ain't cash, unless it's cash.

RED SCOTT
Chairman TEC Florida

- Start small, move quickly and build on your success as you go. Expect to revise the plan often as you raise your websites targets.

- Manage by objective. If the project's goals are being met, you can justify the ongoing investment. If not, it will be easy to shut it down.

Demand success but tolerate small failures. Don't be afraid to break the rules and push the envelope.

The harder I work the luckier I get.

SAMUEL GOLDWYN
Movie executive

Now turn to Step # 48 "Planning for On-Line Success"
in your *Roadmap to Riches* workbook.

CHAPTER
49

An Effective Web Site—by Design

Building a great Web site requires flawless execution of two key elements: design and content. The following tips on how to design an effective Web site and fill it with world-class content, will start you off on the right foot. If you already have a site, I suggest you use this as a check list against it to see if your site needs some revision, updating, and redesign.

KEY DESIGN ELEMENTS

Web site design requires a lot more than deciding how many pages to have, where to put your logo, and what graphics to use. It involves decisions that affect what visitors will do on your site, how they will do it, and, most importantly, how they will buy whatever you are trying to sell them. Finally, how all of those things will create and sustain your relationship with them. All prominent and effective Web sites contain certain essential design elements. Here are some of the most important, there are more in the *Roadmap to Riches* workbook.

Customer Convenience

A good Web site is first of all, fast loading so they don't have to sit there and wait for fancy graphics to load (by the way, most people *won't* sit and wait). More importantly, it's easy to navigate, which means the site works quickly and well, with as few clicks as possible to get to the desired information. As a rule of thumb, don't make visitors click more than three times to find what they're looking for, especially on a retail site. In addition, make sure your guests know where they are at all times. Make sure they can order in only two steps. It takes a great shopping cart to do that.

This may seem hard to believe, but I've seen retail Web sites that don't even have order forms. Others don't accept credit cards. Don't drive them away by making it hard for them to get what they want. Build in as many ordering, payment, and delivery options as possible.

Look at your site from the visitor's point of view. Think about where they might go next and make it easy for them to get there. Ask someone who has never visited your site to find something and see how long it takes them to locate it. Don't assume others can easily get around on the site just because you can. Do the "Mom" test. If your mom can navigate it easily...your site works. If your mom can't...get back to work.

The best test is to go to your own website *as a customer* and try to order everything on your site. See if you can get it to perfectly process your order—and then proceed to immediately fix anything that doesn't work perfectly, completely and clearly. I am amazed at how many business owners never try this approach. I

Don't spend your time on anything your customers don't perceive to be of value.

JOE KARBO

personally do it on a continual basis to make sure everything is consistently running the way it is supposed to, and I continually find things I can tweak to make the process run smoother.

One Stop Shopping

Techies call it Transaction Transparency. What it boils down to is…"one stop shopping." Letting the online visitor experience the entire process of interacting with your company without leaving the Web site. For example, if you have a retail site, transparency allows the customer to complete the entire transaction—from researching product information all the way through ordering, payment and delivery—without having to leave your site.

The automaker BMW demonstrates how transparency can change the entire buying experience. Its Web site allows you to "build" your own car online by selecting make, model, options, colors, etc. When you click on the button to schedule a test drive, the site automatically runs a credit check to see if you can afford the car.

It then prints a glossy brochure about the car you selected and automatically mails it to you. The BMW dealer brings the car to your home or office, gives you the keys and lets you test drive it by yourself. When you return, the dealer has the lease or purchase papers ready to sign. In this manner, BMW takes you through the entire process without having to leave the Web.

In contrast, some online banks, insurance companies and discount stock brokers allow you to fill out all the paperwork online, but then require you to print the paperwork and send it to them via the postal service. Some antiquated government regulations still mandate the use of printed forms, so the online brokers have no choice (at least until the government catches up with the Internet and changes the policy). Nevertheless, having to go offline to complete the transaction annoys most Internet users to the point where they click out and cancel the transaction.

Order Fulfillment

On the Internet, people care more about fulfillment than price. Internet buyers want things now. If you don't fulfill an order when you promise, you will lose the customer. If they pay for a product on your website—no matter if it is a digital product or an item to be shipped—instantly send them an auto responder generated "thank you for your order" acknowledgment receipt showing that you received their order. If it is a digital product, you can send them the link to their product download in this acknowledgement receipt. If it is a product that is actually being mailed to them, you can give them the tracking number and the link to the appropriate website to track the product. This can all be done through autoresponders. A good shopping cart will have autoresponders available to you.

I can't stress enough the importance of timeliness of fulfillment and acknowledgment of an order. Even though the average person is getting more comfortable shopping online, there is always the thought in the back of our minds, that we are entering our credit card information out in "cyberspace." It immediately puts their mind at ease and builds trust, knowing their information went to the desired location. You have already started to establish a "relationship" with that customer. They already feel they can trust you.

Real communication happens when people feel safe.

KEN BLANCHARD
Author, businessman, speaker

If you sell retail, customer expectations will determine whether or not to show out-of-stock or back orders items on your site. If you don't show an out-of-stock item, some customers might think that you don't carry it. On the other hand, some customers might get annoyed at coming to your site to order a product only to find they can't get it right away. In this situation, it pays to know what your customers expect and will put up with.

Internet buyers love information products (e-books, special reports, etc.) that allow for instant download. It solves the problems of shipping and saves the overseas customer not only expense, but time. When a customer orders a CD based product, I ship the product, but also allow them to download it immediately so they get immediate gratification. They can be using the product right now while the mailed CD on the way to them. Also, when a customer orders a product that must be shipped I always send a "bonus" of a downloadable gift so they also benefit from immediate gratification.

Stress Site Security

The Internet was originally built to share information, not protect it. As a result, any good hacker with the right equipment can crack the codes and steal information. Not surprisingly, people need to feel that their transactions on your site are safe from prying eyes. To give customers a feeling of security, I include a statement that explains the steps we have taken to make our site as secure as possible, and include an email and a toll free phone number so if they decide they are not comfortable doing business online, I haven't lost the sale. In addition, I suggest you include an "About Us" section that describes who you are, what you do, how long you have been in business, etc., to quell any doubts about your standing as a legitimate enterprise. When possible, offer testimonials from satisfied customers.

Be Proactive

Another remarkable feature of the Internet is that as you capture information about your site visitors, you can use that information to proactively sell and service them rather than merely responding to the actions they take. For example, Amazon.com recommends books, music and other products based on its customers' previous purchases. By proactively servicing your customers, you will make them feel cared for, and they will want to use your site on a regular basis.

Timeliness

This has two components—timely delivery of product (delivering when you say you will or before) and timely delivery of content (keeping your content updated and fresh).

Avoid statements on your home page that say "last modified a month ago" or "content updated on the first of each month." Those kinds of statements turn your page into yesterday's news. Instead, let people find out for themselves that nothing has changed. Better still; change your content on a regular basis. Have a "What's New" section on your home page and update it frequently.

Choice

For Internet users, having choices rates a very close second to convenience. Give your customers as many choices as possible in how they interact with you, what types

> The main thing is to keep the main thing the main thing.
> STEPHEN COVEY

> Vision without action is a daydream. Action without vision is a nightmare.
> JAPANESE PROVERB

of information they give you, how they pay, how they have the product delivered and so on. The choices should make sense for the person using the site first, and your business second, not the other way around.

In particular, don't overlook language choices. Many sites do business only in English; yet try to reach other countries. To better serve international customers, offer an appropriate number of language options on your site. Remember the World is now available to you.

Site Interaction

Let your visitors interact with your site. Ask if they like it. Ask if they have any complaints. Remember that a good Web site constantly changes and evolves. To make the right changes, ask your visitors what products, features and options they would like to see that your site doesn't currently offer.

As I mentioned previously, we send an auto responder generated follow up email asking these questions. We provide a direct link to a customer service email so they can respond easily and immediately. You would be surprised how many people take the time to not only answer the basic questions, but actually write out in some detail suggestions on how to make the website better. We love that.

They almost always start off with thanking us for caring enough to send a follow up email. We read all of them and have implemented many of the customers' suggestions. This was especially helpful when we were first starting and had much to learn. We still welcome customer comments as that's where we get most of our best ideas, and you will too.

Focus on content

Design your site for your target market, not for the casual surfer. Provide well-written, meaningful content that delivers real value to your intended audience. Keep in mind that although you want an attractive design, graphics do not make a Web site. Having to wait for a long loading graphic to see your ego-stroking logo sure is not going to win my business. I'll click out so fast you will never know I was there. You know I'm right because I bet you do the same thing. Getting people to the content they want as quickly as possible will earn the appreciation of your customers and prospects.

Now, I realize that logos are important, but there is a time and a place for them. You can either have graphics back-loading, or you could put the graphics on the bottom of the home page. Of course all of this is discussed in more detail in Step 49 of the *Roadmap to Riches* workbook.

Not all sites necessarily contain all of these elements. The trick is to pick and choose the ones that will best serve your audience and incorporate them into your site.

CREATING GREAT WEB CONTENT

The quality of your content plays a significant role in the success of your site. Too often web sites provide basic information about the company and nothing more. People don't want a heavy sales pitch, but they do want more than just an online brochure. Here are eight principles for creating effective Web content:

If you listen enough, your customers will explain your business to you.

PETER SCHUTZ
(b. 1930)
Former President and CEO of Porsche

Web users want to get data quickly and easily. They don't care as much about attractive sites and pretty designs.

SIR TIM BERNERS LEE
Inventor of the World Wide Web

(sorry AL GORE)

Establish your corporate USP (Unique Selling Proposition)

Clearly and quickly articulate two key points; what separates your company from all the competitors, and how visitors will benefit from doing business with you.

Answer the question that every online visitor asks: "What's in it for me?" This is where you use your Unique Selling Proposition (USP) to differentiate yourself from your competitors and stress your benefits. Customers and prospects want to know what you can do for them, that your competitors can't or don't do. That's true whether you do business online or off, but it happens a lot quicker online. If your site doesn't immediately tell people why they should do business with you, most people will never go beyond the first page before clicking off.

Use the three "Cs"s of online copywriting

Create Clear, Concise and Compelling online copy that supplies your visitors with useful, educational, benefit-oriented information. Good copywriting:

- Tells a story about your product or service
- Focuses on the benefits of using your product or service
- Asks for and entices customers to take action now
- Tells customers what's in it for them if they act right away
- Closes the sale by answering objections before they are asked

Use attention-grabbing headlines and subheads

Powerful headlines on each page entice the reader to continue on to the body of your text. Use subheads to break up large bodies of text. Keep your content interesting and easy to read. Effective headlines and subheads provide new information, reveal secrets or promise answers to problems your target audience wants to solve. For example:

- "New report identifies 12 strategies to increase your web sales."
- "Free report reveals the truth about outsourcing"
- "Ten steps to improve your web site"
- "What your competitor doesn't want you to know about…"

Give them "Low Hanging Fruit"

Give your visitors what I call "low hanging fruit" for free. Offer high value articles, reports, white papers—offer them something so you at least get their name and e-mail address. Then you both get something of value.

Allow for plenty of white space

The Internet has taught people to "skim" read. On a computer screen, huge blocks of text strain the eye and turn off the reader. Instead, use short sentences and paragraphs (broken up by subheads and plenty of blank space) to lead the reader's eye quickly down the page. Bullet points work especially well when describing a list of features or benefits.

Romance the reader

When describing your products and services, tell a story. Colorful, descriptive language captures the imagination of your online guests. Avoid exaggeration

> Be distinct—or be extinct.
>
> TOM PETERS
> Author, speaker

> God is watching—give him a good show.
>
> REV. DAVID TYLER SCOATES
> (1934–2000)
> Minister, author, counselor

and obvious sales hype. If online customers even think you are lying, they will never trust you again.

Use Testimonials

Nothing sells products and services like good comments from your customers. Prospects believe the word of a customer long before they'll buy into even the best written ad or most lavish TV commercial.

Include an 800 Number

I've found that customers like to call and talk to a human being when they order. I don't know why, but testing tells me that my orders increase by up to 45 percent when I include our toll free number with our hours. If I'm running a hot new product or offer, I'll direct the customers to an inbound telemarketer to take the orders 24/7/365.

OTHER DESIGN CONSIDERATIONS

A complete list of design considerations could fill an entire book. Following are some of the more important ones:

Contact information. Make it easy for site visitors to reach you by having a "Contact Us" link on every page. Even if they don't contact you, it's comforting to them to know that they can. Include your real street address, phone, fax and e-mail on your contact page. By the way, people often do not trust a P.O. Box; so always use your real street address. We have had some really great "drop in" visitors through the years that have become friends and loyal customers.

Screen size. The current computer industry standard is a 17-inch screen, but many users will likely have a smaller size. Don't try to squeeze too much information onto the screen or some viewers may not be able to see everything. Test your site on various screen sizes and different resolutions to make sure it works to the lowest common denominator.

Multiple browsers. Test your site on a variety of browsers, especially America Online, Internet Explorer and Netscape. Also, make sure it works on all versions of each browser, not just the most current version. Remember, some of your rural or International visitors may not have the latest, newest or fastest technology, and many Internet users are afraid of new technology and wait until the "bugs" are worked out. You will be surprised at how different your website will look on different platforms and different browsers.

Connection speed. More and more people are switching to high-speed connections (i.e., cable and DSL), but they still represent a small percentage of online users. Believe it or not, most people still connect at speeds slower than the old standard of 56K. Keep that in mind when designing your pages. People typically won't wait longer than 10 seconds for a page to load.

Some of your customers will be in both second and third world countries where the access to modern hardware, software and connectivity are just not available. They are among our best customers, so we made our page loading as time efficient as possible.

Professional look. Don't let some 19-year-old college whiz kid who dabbles in computers lay out your Web pages. Use an experienced design professional who

What would you attempt to do, if you knew you could not fail.

ROBERT SCHULLER

can incorporate a nice mix of text and graphics. Remember—Business first—Technology second.

Relevant graphics. Graphics add color and excitement to a Web site. They also cause the pages to take longer to load, so use them appropriately and sparingly. More important, use graphics that have meaning to your audience. A teenage boy will wait several minutes to download a picture of Pamela Lee, but how long will a customer wait for a picture of your building?

Avoid clutter. Great Web sites include only the text and graphics that help visitors get what they want. They leave out everything else. Avoid clutter on your Web site at all costs.

Scalability. Plan for growth. Start small, but build your site with room to grow.

Suppose your site attracts far more visitors than expected, and you're server can't handle the volume. If you have the wrong software and hardware architecture, you have to start over again from ground zero. With the right technology, you merely add another server and increase your capacity without having to redo the site. The last thing you want is to have to tear down a site and start over because you didn't build in scalability.

Offer links to other Web sites. People appreciate the additional information. Plus, search engines use the number of links to your site in their ranking criteria. Do not link from your content. Instead, have a separate "links" tab that takes the visitor to a listing of all your links. Also, don't send people off your site. Instead, have the links button open a new window on your site.

Check for on-line and off-line systems integration. If you intend to sell products on your Web site, for example, make sure your accounting and inventory tracking systems can import the information every time you make a sale. Otherwise you have to re-enter the data by hand. Automate everything that can be automated so you can get away from the business and not have to be tied down to your website.

> More is not better. Better is better.
>
> HOWARD HYDEN
> Businessman, TEC speaker

Now turn to Step #49 "An Effective Web Site—by Design"
in your *Roadmap to Riches* workbook.

50
Marketing Your Web Site
(Not Your Product)

Think of your website like the Indian gambling casinos that are built on tribal lands far away from the cities where their customers live. The casinos have to market and do things the Las Vegas casinos never had to do to attract patrons. They market themselves in innovative and creative ways to bring the traffic they need to prosper.

The same principle applies to your Web site. You can build the greatest site on the planet, but if no one knows about it, they won't visit. Attracting visitors to your Web site requires spreading the word in as many ways as possible. You have to market you website before you can market your products.

• MARKETING ONLINE

One of the best ways to reach Internet users is . . . through the use of the Internet. I recommend a number of online marketing tools:

SEARCH ENGINES

The first thing someone who is looking for a product on the web will do, is search for it using one of the many search engines available.

Search engines are the software programs that sort and index the Web and identify Web pages according to pre-selected criteria. For example, if you select "restaurants" as your search criteria, a search engine will create a list of every site that contains that word. People typically use search engines when they want to find multiple sources of information about a particular topic, or when they need to find a specific Web site but don't have the URL (Uniform Resource Locator) address (www.companyname.com) or any other information directing them to the sites they need.

Search engines often turn up thousands or even millions of sites in response to search requests. However, most people only scan the first 10, 20 or 30 sites listed on a search. If you want people to find your site, it has to rank near the top of the search engine's list. **You want your product to come up in the top 3–5 search listings on all of the major search engines.**

Getting the top search engine placement requires two things; designing your Web pages in a way that "optimizes" each page to improve its ranking on the search results. And then registering your site with the current top ranked search engines. I recommend you list with the top search engines manually rather than through an

Success isn't a result of spontaneous combustion. You must set yourself on fire.

ARNOLD H. GLASKOW
Author

We find that advertising works the way the grass grows. You can never see it, but every week you have to mow the lawn.

ANDY TARSHIS

automated system. An interesting exercise is to try an exact same search on the top 10 search engines to see how different they all are.

To help optimize your Web pages for search engines, I recommend the following:

Identify search words that relate to your company/product/service. Unless you happen to have a "tip-of-the-tongue" brand identity, people probably won't search for your Web site with your company name. Instead, they will use "keywords" they associate with your product or service.

For example, suppose you run the Gold Coast Real Estate agency. Rather than using your name, people are more likely to search with keywords like *real estate, realtor, real estate broker, real estate agent,* and *real estate salesperson.* Also consider words like *three-bedroom home* and *new construction.* If these kinds of words don't show up on your site, your site won't show up on the search engines.

In the case of *The Lazy Man's Way to Riches* they might search for the title, the author, or a "keyword" or phrase such as; *self-help,* or *direct response business, Internet marketing, direct mail.*

Consider all possible keywords and permutations of searches your target market might use and include them on your site. You need to be aware of how your product will be used by the buyers and how they will search for it. The more frequently your website is the subject of a search; in other words, the more popular it is... the higher it will rank. That is the goal.

Establish strategic page titles. Every page on a website needs a page title that is readable by the search engines. All page titles should include your key search words. That gives search engines the information they need to rank your site higher on the list.

Use hidden search words. Search engines scan all the words on a Web page, not just those visible to the public. Hide key search words behind your graphics. Your visitors won't see them, but the search engines will. Be careful here as the search engines are smart enough to recognize when you are "Packing" a site just to get higher ratings and they will penalize you for flagrant abuses.

Use search word density. Search engines also look for the frequency of key words. If a particular search word isn't mentioned frequently on your site, it won't show up high on the list. Use your key search words as often as possible.

Plan for misspellings. People often misspell words during their Web searches. Seed your site with deliberately misspelled key words hidden behind graphics. If people frequently misspell your company name, reserve domain names for all the common misspellings and have those sites point to your main site.

Consider multiple entry pages. If your site has multiple objectives, such as generating leads, selling products and attracting employees, you need separate entry pages (the page where someone first enters your site) for each objective. Each entry page should have its own set of key search words. Optimize each entry page and submit them separately to the search engines.

Monitor your ranking. Search engines often shuffle the deck or change their search criteria. Plus, new sites can come online and bump you down the list. For those reasons, check the search engines once a month to see where you come up. If your site has slipped in the rankings, you may want to resubmit it to the search engine with reconfigured keywords.

Many companies mistakenly believe that all they have to do is register with the right search engines and the world will beat a path to their virtual doors. Not so, search engines can help lead people to your Web site, but an effective Web marketing campaign comprises many different elements, search engines being one of the most important.

So, don't ignore the search engines, but don't rely on them as the only means to drive people to your site. Even the best ones only index 15–20 percent of all the pages on the Web, so there's no guarantee they will find you. Plus, if you don't show up near the top, you might as well not be on the list at all. That's why I recommend being in the top three to five listings for your keywords.

Four to eight times a year, submit your site to the appropriate search engines. And then don't spend any more time or money trying to improve your standing with them. Instead, focus your attention on other ways to market your site.

PAY PER CLICK SEARCH ENGINES

Do you want your website to achieve a "top 3" ranking on a major search engine? Of course you do. Imagine how nice it will be to have your website number one on Google, Yahoo, or AOL for a while, drawing millions of eager buyers to your site.

No Problem!

"Pay Per Click" search engines offer anyone with a website and lots of cash the opportunity to get and keep a top spot in the search engine ranking—no programming required. Unlike traditional search engines which base their rankings on the websites content and "code", "Pay Per Click" search engines sell their rankings to the highest bidder. So when visitors search for a certain keyword or phrase, the website owner who paid the most, comes up first and gets the premium rankings and the lion's share of the traffic. It's a pretty slick program that seems all the more evil because the average visitor doesn't know the rankings are rigged.

Buy a Top Ranking?

When I first found out about "Pay Per Click" search engines I was appalled and shocked that there were search engines that encouraged web merchants to buy their way to the top of the search engine rankings. Dirty Pool I say. Un-sportsman-like, despicable, not honest or honorable, and certainly un-American. I'm sure it must be against the laws of both God and nature.

But wait—maybe it's OK *if it works* for me—or you. Well, it does work, **but** you have to be careful of the "Pay Per Click" game or they will quickly own your house, car, and your first born child. I say game, because it's basically gambling…and like gambling you can win big if you've got huge profit margins to work with (that's

I have enough money to last me the rest of my life, unless I buy something.

JACKIE MASON (b. 1934)
Comedian

Money was never a big motivation for me, except as a way to keep score. The real excitement is playing the game.

DONALD TRUMP (b. 1946)
American entrepreneur, TV celebrity

The man who wants to lead the orchestra must turn his back on the crowd.

JAMES CROOK

another reason to own your own product) or you could lose your shirt if you don't know the rules and aren't keeping a close eye on what you're doing.

To give you the "Readers Digest version" of how pay per click works...you make a list of key words people might use to search for your site on a search engine. You then bid on those words to buy rank in the search engine. Then each and every time a visitor clicks through to your site through a sponsored search engine, you pay whether they buy anything on your website or not.

When setting up your account, you have the ability to set a spending limit where you will be notified by email if your funds have run out and need replenished. On your account page, you are able to monitor which key words drive more traffic to the site and which don't. This is something you **need** to do. You also have the ability to change your bid if you find certain words are not bringing in any traffic, or worse; the wrong kind of traffic. For instance, you may be getting a lot of visitors, but no sales, which indicates you are using the wrong keywords.

There is nothing more depressing then seeing you paid for XXX XXX number of click throughs, and only had X sales. So, when you sit down to make your list in the first place, think about which words seem most likely to be used for searching for your product or site. Having said that, when you find the right key words...it works magic.

Getting a top ranking on search engines the traditional way can take months of hard work and there is no guarantee of a good ranking. Using the "Pay Per Click" model short cuts this time and labor intensive process. Even though it is a shortcut to the traditional method, it can still take a lot of time to maintain it. We eventually designated one employee to being responsible for monitoring our Overture account.

"Sponsored Search?"

The 800-pound gorilla in "Pay Per Click" is Overture.com. Overture.com started it's "Sponsored Search" in 1998. Overture came on strong after the Dot.Com implosion of the late 90s. The resulting decline in banner ad effectiveness, the pop-up blocker, and the general decline of advertising dollars cost the traditional search engines lots of money and the "Pay Per Click" model was born of necessity to earn back lost revenue. Overtures search listings appear in the search results of some of the webs traditional search engine giants such as; Yahoo, MSN, CNN.Com, WSJ.Com, Lycos Europe, Lycos Japan, and others.

Anyone who buys "Premium Listing" (a top three spot) for a particular keyword phrase on Overture also appears as a top three on the first page of the other search engines as well. Overture pays these other search engines a commission for any of their links that get searched by surfers. These commissions are now a significant revenue source for the other search engines and have greatly expanded Overture's importance and reach across the Internet.

Based on Overture's success, the "Sponsored Search" model search engines are sprouting up to cash in on the cash cow that is "Pay Per Click." You'll probably receive more traffic from Overture than from all the other pay per click engines combined. However, because the others are less popular, buying highly targeted traffic is much cheaper than at Overture. To find out all about "Pay Per Click" just go to your *Roadmap to Riches* workbook.

E-MAIL

I never forget that people the world over open their "snail "mail over the wastebasket, and they read their e-mail with one hand on the mouse ready to click "Delete." Sure e-mail is the "Killer App" and who doesn't check their e-mail first thing when you go on-line? We all do. That's why it is high on my list.

E-mail gives you the opportunity to compete in the Internet market for next to nothing cost wise and everyone who has a connected computer uses e-mail in some way.

Here are some ways you can use e-mail;

- Instant local and global communication.
- You can communicate with words, sounds (even voice), and video.
- You can send letters, e-books, contracts, drawings, photographs, anything digital for next to nothing.
- You can market and sell via e-mail.
- You can accept orders via e-mail.
- You can build relationships via e-mail.
- You can make huge amounts of money by creating your own opt-in e-mail lists.

E-mail always offers new ways to generate and retain customers but they all rely on knowing who those people are that make up your list. So the game is to harvest as much pertinent and relevant information as they will give you. And they will give you a lot of information if you ask properly and give a good reason.

Think about your list and the people on it as having rungs on a ladder. The lowest rung is an untargeted offer sent to a list of unknown recipients. The highest is the most targeted offer, sent to the recipient most likely to respond.

The lowest rung nearly always has the lowest response rate, lowest effective <u>CPM</u> (Cost per thousand), highest unsubscribe rate, and most complaints. The highest rung is the opposite; it boasts the highest response rate, highest CPM, and lowest unsubscribe rate.

The goal is to push the people in your database up the e-mail relevancy ladder. Move recipients up a notch or two. Suppose my site sells SCUBA Trips. With 100,000 people in my database, how can I mail smarter? The first step is to build an e-mail relevancy ladder, starting from the bottom:

1. I don't know anything about this person in my database. He's a blind subscriber.

2. This person is interested in the outdoors. I know this because he downloaded an article I wrote about outdoors sports.

   Because he answered a survey on my site when he downloaded an e-book on underwater photography, I know...

3. This person is interested in SCUBA

4. This person's a man.

5. His first name is Hal.

> Communication leads to community, that is to understanding, intimacy and mutual valuing.
> ROLLO MAY
> (1909–1994)
> American psychologist

> The most basic and powerful way to connect to another person is to listen.
>
> JOE KARBO

6. Hal likes warm water diving.

7. Hal likes underwater photography.

8. Hal takes two trips a year.

9. Hal usually takes those trips with three of his buddies who share the same interests.

10. Hal takes his trips in May and September

11. Hal wants help planning his May trip.

12. Hal and his buddies want to go diving in Belize.

13. Hal is ready to choose a charter company.

E-mail is a great way to push people up that ladder. The message for each rung can look the same but convey different information. Here are examples for rungs 1 and 10.

The Bottom Rung of the Ladder

> *Dear Friend,*
>
> *Somehow, you're on my e-mail list. I don't want to waste your time or clutter your inbox with spam. Please take a moment to respond to this message so I can either continue to communicate with relevant messages, or take you off my list. Simply click one of these links:*
>
> *I enjoy SCUBA*
>
> *I do not snorkel or dive*
>
> *Thank you!*

A click on the top link adds a piece of information to the database and, in this case, pushes that person up two rungs. A click on the bottom link unsubscribes that person from the list.

The Top Rung of the Ladder

Through surveys and e-mail messages, I know Hal takes two trips a year, brings three buddies, and travels in May and September. People plan vacations several months in advance, so it's safe to assume in January, Hal is planning his May SCUBA expedition. Here is an example of what I might send to him then:

> *Hal:*
>
> *I'll bet as you wait for this cold, snowy winter to end, you're dreaming of your SCUBA trip. Based on what you've told me in the past, you may be thinking of going in May. Have you and your buddies talked about where you might go? I've done some preliminary research. Are you planning to do some diving this May? One of the best places for May diving is Belize. If you're ready to plan your May trip, I'd love to whip together something exciting for you and your friends.*
>
> *Yes*
>
> *No*

Thanks again!

P.S. If you no longer have an interest in SCUBA, click <u>here</u>, and I'll remove you from our database.

If Hal clicks "yes," he'll move up one rung and I'll send an auto responder immediately with some details of potential trips.

If he clicks "no," I'll send him an immediate auto responder, asking when he's planning trips for the balance of the year.

Automated e-mail allows you to have a series of discussions with potential customers. As each person is qualified and travels up the ladder, he becomes a hotter prospect for your offer.

All you have to do is develop a ladder based on what you market, and then create a message for each rung. I offer free reports and articles that will tell me what my list wants more of. I also do surveys to find out what requests they have, and I monitor the forum on the website to keep in touch with what they are talking about.

BANNER ADVERTISING

Banner advertising involves paying a fee to list a banner ad about your company on other sites. Some companies charge per impression (how many times your banner shows up on the screen), others charge per "click-through"—the number of times someone actually clicks on the ad. Using banner advertising effectively requires knowing the sites your target audience visits on a regular basis. If you have a high-traffic site, you may also want to consider selling advertising on your site. When using banner advertising use an active hyperlink with the magic words "click here" to increase the effectiveness of your ad by up to 300 percent.

Use motion, such as a blinking sign that says "free." Motion out-pulls static banner ads.

Use bright colors. Red, blue and yellow typically out-pull duller colors.

Test your banner ads in three locations: search engines, niche sites (sites your target market visits) and high-traffic, general interest sites.

Banner advertising no longer works like it once did, so I don't use it, but there are still places, products and audiences for which it is useful. If you want to use banner ads test carefully and as always . . . track the results.

ONLINE MICRO-MARKETS

Online micro-markets include news groups, which offer a very effective method for reaching highly targeted audiences. Most news groups won't allow you to advertise your company or your Web site on the posting but they will allow you to have a signature file, which consists of two to five lines at the end of the posting to provide your contact information.

In addition to your name and e-mail address, your signature file also can include a tagline, such as "come to our site for a free report on subject XYZ."

With a signature file, you can announce a new product or service, a price reduction, a two-for-one deal or anything else that might interest your target market. When you launch your Web site, every e-mail that comes from your company should have a signature file that lists the URL and some sort of pull component (a compelling reason to visit the site).

> Half of my advertising is wasted—I just don't know which half.
>
> SAM WANAMAKER
> Merchant

Get linked or
get lost.

RECIPROCAL LINKS

Contact other sites that appeal to your target market and offer to establish reciprocal links. After putting their link on your site, you must follow up to make sure they link back to you. It is the link back to you that brings business to you, so check to see that it works properly.

NEWSLETTERS/E-ZINES

An E-Zine is one of the best tools you can have to do effective on line marketing. It is so important that I devote an entire chapter to it.

• OFFLINE MARKETING

Marketing your Web site offline involves all the traditional marketing tools. Instead of promoting your products or services, however, your primary goal is to attract people to your Web site.

Start with your current customers and contacts and then move on to the rest of your target market, give them a compelling reason to come your site, such as a free report, new product information, a two-for-one deal, 10 percent off their first online order or something compelling. Regardless of which media you use, your "pull component" represents the critical factor that will draw people to the site.

Do or do not,
there is no try.
YODA

Offline methods for promoting your site include:

- Put your website address on all of your corporate paper. There is no need to include the http:// any more, just use the www.yourcompanyname.com on your letterhead, business cards, invoices, memos, catalogues, Fax cover sheets and everything you have printed for your company.

- Place your website address in all your advertising: newspapers, magazine, direct mail, billboards, taxi, radio and TV.

- Printed flyer or brochure detailing the benefits of your Web site as an insert in you outgoing correspondence such as letters, bills, invoices, etc.

- Postcards.

- Offering a free report or white paper on the site.

- Messages about your site on your telephone on-hold recording.

- Radio, billboards and trade magazine print ads.

- Public relations.

- Advertising specialties such as: Pen, coffee cups, refrigerator magnets, and other trade show give-aways.

- Media reviews, where you submit your site to be reviewed by magazines, newsletters, radio talk shows, etc. This works especially well if you have a strong and compelling pull component that has value to the general public.

Effective Web site marketing and promotion incorporates the proper use of search engines with online *and* offline promotions. However, the key to a successful marketing campaign lies in your commitment to spreading the word about your site.

Without a coherent marketing plan and—more important—the budget to make it happen, you won't get many people to your site.

A mistake I see companies make is focusing too much on building the site—and not *enough* on promoting it. If you don't spend the time and money to drive people to your site, you won't achieve your online objectives.

Over time, people may get in the habit of using your site, but you have to start the ball rolling, and that takes time and money.

Lead, follow, or get out of the way.

THOMAS PAINE
(1737–1809)
Journalist, patriot

Now turn to Step # 50 "Marketing Your Web Site (Not Your Product)" in your *Roadmap to Riches* workbook.

Marketing Your Product On-Line—the Direct Response Way

MONEY IN YOUR "INBOX"

"You've Got Money!" There is nothing like money in your mailbox unless its money pouring into your on-line merchant accounts 24/7/365. And then having it directly deposited into your bank account. It sure makes working at the computer all day a lot more enjoyable when you receive constant e-mail receipts of new orders, and a big credit card settlement batch report via email at the end of each day.

One of the reasons that so many on-line businesses failed during the "Dot-Bomb" era is because they refused to accept the fact that—**"nothing happens until somebody sells something."** The idea that one could make a fortune on the Internet without selling something, was stupid and short sighted at best. To make any business successful, large or small, you need cash flow. To get cash flow you need customers. To get customers, you must first market and sell your product or your service.

You might be a great author, attorney, chiropractor, retailer or wholesaler, but so what? The Yellow Pages are full of great attorneys, chiropractors, retailers and wholesalers. So, no matter how great your technical skills are or how innovative your product is, your business will die a horrible death if you cannot sell your product or service to the visitors on your site.

NOTHING HAPPENS UNTIL SOMEBODY SELLS SOMETHING

An old advertising quote says, "Any fool can make a bar of soap, it takes a clever man to sell it." This is as true today as it was when it was said many years ago. Anyone can make a bar of soap. In fact, it is now possible to make soap so advanced that it is even self-rinsing. But even if it's the most advanced soap on the planet it won't matter if *no one buys it.*

Now, I hate to think of this wonderful "Lazy Man" program as just another bar of soap, but that's essentially what it is, metaphorically speaking. There are hundreds of thousands of great books out there that no one has ever heard of and no one will ever buy because they haven't been marketed properly. Even a great book like the "Lazy Man" does not sell itself. Therefore, it takes a smart marketer to sell millions of copies of a book and keep it "top of mind" for 30 years—So pay close attention and I'll show you exactly how to find your "Riches" on the Internet— just like I have.

A large income is the best recipe for happiness I ever heard of.

JANE AUSTEN
(1775–1817)
English novelist

The best and fastest way to learn a sport is to watch and imitate a champion.

JEAN CLAUDE KILLY
(b. 1943)

There are many elements to a campaign. Leadership is number one. Everything else is number two.

BERTOLT BRECHT
(1898–1956)
German playwright

THE OWNER IS THE CHIEF SELLING OFFICER

Because the selling of your product or service is so vitally important, it really needs to be your number one business objective or your number one goal at all times.

With that thought in mind, think about your role as Owner/CEO in the company and your role as marketer and chief salesperson. How does thinking of yourself as the chief marketer and sales person change the way you look at the following?

1. Your "to-do" list—list the important Marketing/Selling (M/S) steps you must do.

2. The way you allocate your time—when will you do the M/S stuff?

3. Your hiring process—how will you now look at your staff's M/S responsibilities?

4. Employee training—What additional M/S training do they need?

5. What is your skill level at Marketing/Selling? Are you personally skilled at and focused on, Marketing/Selling? If not, then refocus. Get additional education and coaching in M/S before you need it.

ADDING HIGH VALUE

As a business consultant, I constantly ask myself the following question... "Am I adding value right now, that's equal to—or greater than, the fee that my client is paying me." That question helps me to prioritize my activities, and consider the value that I am adding to my client. I recommend that you make a habit of asking yourself that same question every day.

The following is a list of a few of the activities that I—and you, should consider of *high value*.

- Create or develop something unique and special in your product or service.

- Create a marketing plan that will force you to achieve your sales objectives.

- Study the marketing strategies of your competitors, and other successful businesses outside of your industry.

- Attend direct response marketing conferences, seminars, workshops and boot camps.

- Study the recommended copywriting, advertising and marketing books. They are all listed in your *Roadmap to Riches* workbook.

- Network with owners and representatives of businesses that target your same market, or share your customers.

- Meet with a mastermind-marketing group on a regular basis. If you do not know of one, form one—you will be surprised at how easy it is.

- Build your personal marketing "swipe" file. That's nothing more than a "Good Idea" list culled from articles, ads, competitors, recommendations, etc.

- Write articles for local newspapers, magazines trade journals, and your own newsletter or E-Zine. This is actually easy and it stimulates your creative juices.

- Train all employees who have client contact about the current product offers and up-selling techniques. They need to be "salespeople" too.

- Train your telephone-answering people how to properly present your product or services. They should only work from a professionally prepared script. It is much better to suffer through a poorly read script for a while, than it is to have your calling customer given incorrect information by a poorly trained or untrained employee.

- Write the sales letters and manage the direct mail marketing campaign personally. You can then hire professionals to help you "polish" the letters you write. (Your *Roadmap to Riches* workbook lists several pros—but do it yourself first)

MARKETING DIRECTOR?

There are more similar activities but I think you get the idea. Normally, this is all done by a Director of Marketing, but I assume you do not have a Director of Marketing. Moreover, even if you do, you as a business owner really must get involved personally in these activities. You must become the Director of Marketing for your own company, products, and website. That is near the top of your most important roles as a business owner. You dare not leave this most critical part of your business to someone else.

I can almost hear you saying right now, "but I'm already doing all of those things." And my response to you is, "how much time, are you devoting to these **high value** activities?"

Do you need to hire a manager or assistant to relieve you of all the *other* duties so that you can focus exclusively on the activities that have the most impact on your business?

WORK <u>ON</u> YOUR BUSINESS—LET OTHERS
WORK <u>IN</u> YOUR BUSINESS

In CEO training sessions at TEC International, we teach CEO's that to be successful, you have to stop working in your business and start working on your business. In other words, do not do any activity that would not pay you what you are worth.

For example, if you want to be worth $300 an hour, why would you be doing work that you could hire someone else to do for $8–$10 an hour?

If you ask me, "Richard, I have only $2000 to market my product. Where should I spend this money to get the highest return on my investment?" My response would be to invest in your own personal education.

Nothing will bring you a greater return on your marketing dollar than your personal investment in becoming a master direct response marketer on the Internet.

I regularly spend thousands of dollars every year, investing in books, tapes, CDs, workshops, seminars, conferences, and every other form of educational medium that will enhance my skill at being a direct marketer.

In my experience as a trainer and coach to CEO's, I have noticed that the successful ones all have a passion and an insatiable desire to learn, and they invest heavily in their own personal education. They know that school is never over for the true professional.

> You don't get paid for the hour. You get paid for the value you bring to the hour.
>
> JIM ROHN
> Entrepreneur, author, speaker

Do not be fooled into thinking that you are in the business of *producing* and *delivering* a product or service. That's as wrong as whiskey for breakfast!

WHAT BUSINESS ARE YOU IN?

You are in the business of *marketing* those products and services. The faster you realize this, the faster the cash will flow into your business.

Neither McDonald's nor Microsoft became the leader in their industry because they were number one in quality of products or services.

Frankly, I think both of them make mediocre products at best. However, they are both excellent at marketing and selling their products.

Marketing is your business, not just a part of it. This is especially true on the Internet.

There are many different ways of marketing on the web. I'm going to share with you seven that I consider to be web marketing necessities.

MARKETING NECESSITIES

1. YOUR OWN OPT-IN MAILING LIST

E-mail is free to send out. Even if you have to buy a listserver or some other type of application to do your email, you are only talking about a couple of hundred dollars a year to send out unlimited two way communication to your prospects and customers.

Not only is it virtually free, e-mail marketing is effective. That is what so many people are using it as "spam." It can produce sales constantly and at virtually no expense.

Because of the power of e-mail marketing, opt-in e-mail is the future online. It prevents you from being accused of spamming.

An opt-in list is a list of people that have granted you permission to contact them. A double opt-in list means they simply confirm that yes, it was they who really signed up, and they *do* want to be on your list. That avoids someone simply forgetting later that they did sign up. It protects your business, which is alway good business.

Don't even try to build a business online without developing your own opt-in list. It's just not worth it to jeopardize what will become a great income producing business for you by not doing it right.

You build your own opt-in list by offering something of value, for which a suspect or prospect would trade his name, e-mail address and other pertinent or relevant information for.

You should start building your own opt-in mailing list today! (Of course all of your customers belong on your opt-in list.) You can build your own opt-in list by just asking people to voluntarily subscribe to your email list, or you can offer them a free report, or an e-book. Other ways to build a list could be by offering a tip of the day or quote of the day, or offering free audio programs and streaming video. A resource list is also a great way to get sign ups.

They say a marketer's and consumer's dream is the World Wide Web. It's the best of mass advertising and the best of target marketing.

DAVID KING
DDB Needham Ad Agency

There are innumerable ways to build your own opt-in list. Let your imagination run wild. But if your imagination is overwhelmed, we list a lot of resources in the *Roadmap to Riches*.

One more note about opt-in. It is critical to point out that you always need to have an opt-*out* or unsubscribe link on e-mails sent out too. For whatever reason they have decided to opt-out, you need to honor that request, and immediately unsubscribe them. Anything you send to them from that point forward, is unwelcome and unethical "spam."

2. E-ZINES

As I mentioned in the previous chapter, I feel this is so important I have devoted an entire chapter to it, but a few notes to wet your appetite are appropriate here.

All of the Internet heavy hitters publish an E-Zine.

On the Internet, content is king . . . and it better be fresh and relevant to today's consumers. All of the **successful** web business owners publish E-Zines that provide high quality, useful content. They share information that is of great benefit and value to their readers. They give honest evaluations and reviews of products and services, never endorsing something just to earn a buck. And they gain incredible trust and loyalty among their subscribers. Once you establish that, the selling part is easy.

3. YOUR OWN AFFILIATE PROGRAM

An affiliate program is a great way to earn money online. I'm not talking about promoting other people's affiliate program; I'm referring to having other people promote your affiliate program and sell your products.

I don't know of any successful web business that doesn't have an affiliate program. Whatever you do as far as marketing your web business, imagine hundred's and even thousands of other people marketing your web business in a similar manner worldwide. We have affiliates all over the world. Do you see the huge potential here?

It is not difficult to start your own affiliate, program but it is even easier if you follow the instructions in the *Roadmap to Riches*.

4. ENDORSED E-ZINE SOLO MAILINGS

The quickest of all web-marketing options to produce results, is placing endorsed solo mailings in other people's e-mail newsletters/E-Zines. An endorsed solo mailing is an exclusive advertisement, usually much longer in length than a regular classified ad that is sent to the entire database of subscribers by itself.

These take the form of a letter from the owner of the E-Zine to his subscribers. This means more exclusive exposure for you, because there are no other advertisements to compete with yours. Plus, it is a third party endorsement of your fine product from someone else the subscribers know and trust. I always offer a generous revenue split to the E-Zine owner so he will try his hardest to sell my product to his subscribers—its extra money for him and extra sales for me.

In addition to the sales this generates, it also creates lots of subscriptions to my opt-in list. Because in the endorsed letter I also offer something of high-perceived

> The human mind is the worst possible place to store business information.
>
> KONICHI OHM AE
> Consultant

value for free—that they can instantly download. By offering them something free, they now become subscribers to my opt-in list, which you now know is like gold.

The great thing about endorsed solo mailings is the fact that you can have your mailing sent in the morning and literally be pulling in results by the same afternoon.

5. SELF SPONSORED SOLO ADS

Like the endorsed solo ad, but you or a professional copywriter write the copy, structure the offer, price it and keep all the money, except for what you pay for the ad.

If you know where to find the "deals"—the E-Zines with the best prices and the ones that pull in the best results—you can use them repeatedly with a new product and just repeat the cycle. Advertise in each one and then next time, advertise a new product in each one. Repeat the cycle as long as it is profitable. If you have a nice offer, you will see profits from this advertising week after week.

You can find out who accepts solo mailings by doing a bit of research at your favorite search engine. Type in "solo mailings" "exclusive mailings" or "E-Zine ads" and you will find quite a list.

6. VIRAL MARKETING TOOLS

How many e-books have you seen online lately? A lot. I have not counted, but I know I would need more than my hands and toes to count them all. What about articles? Same thing, there are a lot of them. And, have you noticed that at the bottom of almost every article and somewhere in almost every e-book is a line of text that reads something like this . . .

"... You have permission to give this article (or e-book) away at your website..."

Can you guess why?

Of course, you can. When you give the article or e-book away, the next person is going to see the same line. And they will give it away. More and more people read it and more and more pass it on down the line. Within just a few short weeks, thousands of copies of the article or e-book have been broadcast across the World Wide Web.

And every single one of them serves as a sales letter, all directing readers back to a website where a sale is waiting to be made.

Every heavy hitter uses "viral marketing." Whether they offer free software demos, or articles, or e-books, they all offer something they have permission to give away.

And it spreads like a virus.

Wouldn't you like to catch that one?

There is good news, you can! Viral marketing—it is all in your *Roadmap to Riches* workbook.

7. JOINT VENTURE PARTNERSHIPS

Don't kid yourself. Not one of the top Internet people got to where they are by themselves. They had help on the way up.

I have never worked a day in my life without selling. If I believe in something, I sell it, and I sell it hard.

ESTEE LAUDER
(1908–2004)
American businesswoman, cosmetics pioneer

If you build a great experience, customers tell each other about that. Word of mouth is very powerful.

JEFF BEZOS
(b. 1964)
Co-Founder of Amazon.com

One of the keys to successful business on the web is to participate regularly in joint ventures. A joint venture is a project whereby you combine your assets (customers, advertising, products, services, knowledge, skills, traffic, or endorsement) with those of one or more non-competing individuals with a similar customer base.

For example, your strength might be that you can produce high quality e-books for sale online. However, you only have a small customer base. On the other side of the coin, we have a person who has established a large mailing list for her weekly E-Zine. She needs products to sell, but does not have the time to create her own. This is a joint venture waiting to happen. You combine your asset (products) with her asset (customers) and you both can come out winners. (Endorsed solo ads are like that)

You provide the products, she sells them, and you both earn a negotiated percentage of the profits that neither of you would have had without the other.

There are literally thousands of joint venture ideas out there, so it would be impossible to cover even a portion of them here. The heavy hitters regularly involve themselves in joint ventures. JVs with competitors are quite common on the Internet.

JVs are popular with firms who share the same customer, but are not direct competitors such as: cosmetic companies and women's shoe companies. Tire sellers and brake shops, personal injury attorneys and chiropractors, computer training and software sellers, sports magazines and a seller of vitamins and food supplements. There is no end to the combinations you can put together to make money on JVs. This is where you can make your mark if you are creative.

> The old adage "people are your most important asset" turns out to be wrong. People are not your most important asset. The right people are.
>
> JIM COLLINS
> Author

Now turn to Step #51 "Marketing Your Product On-Line—the Direct Response Way" in your *Roadmap to Riches* workbook.

52

Outsourcing—Working with Outside Vendors

THE BENEFITS OF OUTSOURCING

Political correctness aside, outsourcing can also be a good thing. Outsourcing the technology (but definitely not the strategy) side of e-commerce offers considerable advantages over building a site internally. I recommend outsourcing because:

- Practically all entrepreneurs and even most companies, lack the in-house resources. They simply don't have the knowledge, skills or manpower to build an effective **Selling** Web site.

- It's difficult and costly to hire and keep in-house Web superstars.

- The Internet changes swiftly and constantly. Companies that don't build Websites frequently as a business, find it almost impossible to keep up with effective new trends and emerging technologies.

- Independent vendors provide faster time to market. A good vendor working under deadlines will get a Web site up and running much faster than a business that is trying to service its existing customers and create an online presence at the same time. Generally, their number one priority is your project.

- Independent Vendors can help you avoid costly mistakes. Experienced Web designers know how to avoid the pitfalls that can delay or completely derail an Internet project.

- An outside vendor lends an objective viewpoint to the project.

When you try to build your site internally, you tend to be more tactical. Plus, other projects and day-to-day responsibilities get in the way or get shuffled aside. Unless you have a sophisticated in-house IT department that can dedicate the time and manpower to building the site, it's much more efficient and cost-effective to outsource.

Outsourcing allows you to maintain a certain distance from the project and take a much more strategic approach. You can focus on the strategy and business objectives while the vendor worries about making the technology work and meeting your objectives and deadlines.

In order to have a first-class Web site, you need a capable server, high-speed access to the Internet, highly skilled technical people who are on call 24 hours a day and machines that don't break down. You can get all that from a reliable vendor for a few

> Hierarchy is an organization with its face toward the CEO and it's ass toward the customer.
>
> JACK WELCH
> Former CEO of
> General Electric

> Work on your business—not in your business.
>
> RICHARD G. NIXON
> (b. 1940)

hundred dollars a month. The only economic decision that makes any sense is to outsource. In my opinion, it's always the better decision.

SELECTING A VENDOR(S)

Okay, you've decided to outsource. How do you select the right vendor?

Don't hire a vendor/consultant you wouldn't hire as an employee

You will work closely with this person/team for several weeks or months, so make sure the vendor has the values, and attitude that fit your culture, style, and your business objectives. Make sure they understand your company and your customers.

A critical thing to consider is does that person have the same communication style as you. It can be costly and incredibly frustrating if you want to communicate by phone, but the other person will only communicate by e-mail. A lot of valuable time is wasted waiting for e-mails to be retrieved if one of you is not at the computer at any given time. We've learned this the hard way. Trust us on this one!

Location, Location, Location

Take in to consideration where the vendor is based. If you are in different time zones, a lot of communication time, whether it is by e-mail or phone, is lost because of the time difference. And if you have to ship things back and forth, that can cause problems as well. When time is of the essence, as it almost always is in business, this time difference can be a nightmare of a problem. This is another lesson we have learned the hard way.

Check references carefully

Before you even get to the stage of checking the vendors references see if the person "applying" actually read your job or project description. We have found so many people respond to a project posting that appear to never actually have read the details of the posting. They are not even close to being able to accomplish what we need. They just appear to be randomly responding to every posting. If they can't or don't read your ad, then they can't or won't read your instructions.

Once you have weeded through those time wasters, then it's time to check references for the qualified candidates. In addition to checking out Web sites the vendor has built, you really need to talk to his clients to get a broader perspective.

Was the vendor easy to work with? Could they communicate easily with the vendor *when they wanted to?* Did its employees deliver what they promised on time and within budget? How did they resolve problems? Above all, look for someone who understands your business goals and objectives and how the site needs to support them.

Know the vendor's capabilities

Web design companies are springing up all over the place. Some do the marketing piece well, while others offer better technical expertise. Look for a vendor that excels in both areas. If you have to make a choice between several vendors go with the one who has the best grasp on marketing and customer service.

They are out there if you look hard enough. Keep in mind that many of the best people in the business "moonlight" in their spare time, working from their home. I've been pleasantly surprised at the high quality and low price of most of the independent contractors we've worked with.

Demand transfer of knowledge

When the vendor completes the project, he or she should train at least two people on your staff to update and maintain the site. You don't want to have to run to the vendor every time you need to make a minor change. That will drive you nuts and cost you a lot of unnecessary money.

It doesn't take an experienced IT person to maintain a Web site anymore. Anyone proficient with above average computer skills can make updates and minor changes. If you need to add new capabilities or functionalities, then call the vendor. But once the site is up and running, someone in-house should maintain it.

VENDOR BIDS

Typically, Web design vendors/consultants offer two types of bids—time and materials or fixed bid. Each has its advantages and disadvantages.

A time and materials contract offers more flexibility, but once the vendor goes on the clock, costs can escalate dramatically. I strongly advise against time and materials bids.

A fixed bid keeps your costs from getting out of hand, but makes it harder to shift directions mid stream. Making changes to the plan usually requires a written change request order and the payment of additional fees.

I recommend a fixed bid because it will get you to market quicker and it just makes better business sense to limit your expenditures. If you agree to a fixed bid, give the vendor very clear specifications, such as X number of pages, with Y functionality at Z cost.

Remember, too, that time to market is important. If you decide to go with a time and materials bid, don't spend too much time trying to fine-tune the site and make it perfect or you will never get online. Instead, get the basic site up and running and make enhancements as you get feedback from your customers. Make sure your vendor gives you "De-Bugging" time once the site is up and running.

> Every new project goes through three stages:
> It won't work,
> it will cost too much,
> I thought it was a good idea all along.
>
> ANONYMOUS

Now turn to Step #52 "Outsourcing—Working with Outside Vendors" in your *Roadmap To Riches* workbook.

E-Zine, the On-Line Silver Bullet

If there is a Silver Bullet for on-line success the E-Zine is it. There is just no better to way to generate on-line cash than to have your own E-Zine cash cow.

Just follow my simple instructions and you can generate Riches up to $20,000 every month—and more. These numbers are proven sales achievements from average folks just like you who have used the right E-Zine production and marketing information. And, you can be the next to join the growing band of successful on-line entrepreneurs.

Whether it is Michael Angier's "Success Net Strategies," Dr. Kevin Nunley's "Marketing Tips" or Dr. Ralph Wilson's "Web Marketing Tips," all of the heavy hitters publish an E-Zine. For most, it is a weekly E-Zine. My E-Zine has generated tens of thousands of dollars in sales and is growing mightily. Some of the "heavy hitters" I know personally—and some of them are just e-mail friends. I'll introduce you to all of them in the *Roadmap to Riches*.

WHAT IS E-ZINE PUBLISHING?

So, you've heard about this great Internet phenomenon of E-Zine publishing but you're not sure where to start? This chapter serves as an introduction to the wonderful world of E-Zine publishing.

First off—What is an E-Zine? Is it the same as a newsletter? Basically yes.

The word "E-Zine" is a shortened version of "electronic zine." The word "zine" is actually a shortened version of "fanzine," which is a word used to describe short self-published magazines usually published for passion rather than profit. Typical fanzines are devoted to a certain movie or recording star, a band, movie genre, political cause, or a celebrity of some sort.

E-Zines can be e-mail-based, Web-based, or presented in some other electronic format. However, for the most part, when publishers speak of their "E-Zines," they're usually referring to an e-mail publication of some kind. So, if we wanted to be as clear as possible, we could say "e-mail publication" at every opportunity. But that gets pretty cumbersome, and "E-Zine" sounds a lot better.

Keep in mind that the evolution of these words has all primarily taken place in the past ten years, so the definitions are far from static. For the purposes of this chapter, the word "E-Zine" should be interpreted as meaning "e-mail publication." "E-mail newsletter" is also often used synonymously with these other terms. And in case you were wondering, "E-Zine" is pronounced EE-zeen.

Strike while the iron is hot.
PROVERB

E-Zines are just an e-mail letter that's become more sophisticated. The Electronic Magazine is a publication sent by e-mail to an Opt-In list of subscribers who have asked to receive it. Notice I said Opt-In, meaning that it is not spam. The people who read the newsletter actually asked to receive it and look forward to reading it.

And E-Zine usually consists of several good articles based on the primary subject or theme of the E-Zine, maybe a couple of advertisements, a freebie or two, a pull factor (Free E-mail, quote of the day, joke of the day, etc.) and maybe some information about the site that publishes the E-Zine.

CONTENT IS KING

If you want to launch your own E-Zine, then you need two important things . . . your newsletter must be a useful, and it must be a selling machine. The two key words here are "useful" and "selling." You will not find any better combination for a successful E-Zine. Period.

On the Internet content is king and it better be good—and it better be fresh. We all want value and we feel cheated when we don't get it. Even if yours is a free e-zine, waste people's time and your list will melt away with each "Unsubscribe." Subscriptions and Un-subscribes are the public's way of voting—make sure you earn their vote with each issue. Good content and value wins customers.

Some E-Zines are nothing more than glorified sales letters. Their only existence is to pitch ad copy to you. They don't last long. Then, there are those E-Zines that aren't as blatantly trying to pitch their "Miracle program of the Month" to you, but their articles and tips are nothing fresh or relevant, but are just re-runs from something published over and over again. No value there either—hit the "Unsubscribe" Button quick.

All of the **successful** web business owners publish E-Zines that provide high quality, useful content. They provide information that is of great benefit and value to their readers. They give honest evaluations and reviews of products and services. They never endorse something just to earn a commission. And they have earned incredible loyalty among their subscribers.

Once you establish that, the selling part is easy. It is easier to sell to those who see value in your material. Michael Angier has 80,000+ subscribers on his list. If Michael so much as hints about a good product or service, several thousand people reach for their credit cards. Why? Because they trust a winner. They know he provides only the best. They have read his content and are happy with it—they trust him, and so do I.

HAVING AN E-ZINE MAKES IT EASIER TO SELL ON THE WEB.

It is easier to sell to those who regularly hear from you. Statistics show that the average person needs up to eight exposures to a particular offer before they will make a purchase. By regularly publishing an E-Zine you increase the exposure of your offers to those on your list. Because it can take up to ten ad impressions to make a sale, the serial effect of your E-Zine being read every week vastly improves your sales over time. And, of course, the more your readers hear from you, the stronger your relationship grows.

You can have everything in life you want, if you'll just help enough other people get what they want.

ZIG ZIGLAR
Author, motivational speaker

It is easier to sell when you have an established reputation. The more quality newsletter issues you get under in your archives, the more established your reputation becomes. And reputation sells. One of the quickest ways to build credibility is to consistently provide a high-quality, content rich e-mail newsletter.

By building strong and lasting relationships with those on your list, your subscribers will pay attention when you make a recommendation. And, attention as the advertising "gurus" know, is the first step towards a good sale to a happy customer who will become a valuable client.

It is easier to sell to your existing customers. One of the basics of any kind of marketing is the fact that it is much easier, and less expensive to sell to those who have already made a purchase from you than it is to seek out new customers. With an E-Zine you will be able to continually place offers before the eyes of those who have previously done business with you and dramatically improve your odds of a another sale.

There is no doubt that people purchase from those they know and feel comfortable with. When an E-Zine I have subscribed to for a while e-mails me an offer, I immediately take a look at it. Why? Because throughout the years that I have known them, we have developed a trusting relationship. And I know from experience that they always recommend things of value. Once your reputation is established, the selling part is easy.

MAKING MONEY WITH E-ZINE PUBLISHING.

This part looks at the various sources of E-Zine revenue. Whether your financial goal is simply to make a little extra money with your E-Zine, or if you're after an entire new career for yourself as an E-Zine publisher, the following overview of E-Zine revenue will help get you understand the incredible value of your E-Zine as a money maker.

E-Zine revenue can come from a number of sources. Your own E-Zine may derive its revenue from a single "profit pillar" or a combination of several. The following are various sources of E-Zine revenue. Each can be another pillar supporting your E-Zine.

- **Sales of your product**—The sale of your product or service is the main source of revenue. Because you own the product there are no royalties, commissions, fees, and you get to keep all the profits. If you are lucky enough to have your own proprietary information product (or something else that can be down loaded—such as music) the profit margins are among the best you can find on this planet.

  Example: I sell the original version of the great book *"Financial Success Through Creative Thought"* by Wallace D. Wattles as an e-book. The price is US$15.00 and it is instantly downloadable by anyone—anywhere on earth. There are no shipping charges, taxes, or anything for the buyer to pay and the buyer gets a classic high value book that is out of print.

  I get US$15.00. My total costs for the rights to the book, producing it as an e-book, marketing it, selling it, shipping it on-line, and overhead came to

Good ideas are not adopted automatically. They must be driven into practice with courageous patience.

HYMAN RICKOVER
(1900–1986)
US Navy Admiral

If not us, who?
If not now, when?

ANONYMOUS

US$963. Figure another US$100. per month for recurring on-line charges and my costs for the first year are US$1200. plus US$963. for a total of US$2,163. The first year I sold only 586 copies for US$8,790. leaving me a net profit of US$6,627. Now the total production costs of the book are paid in full and I own it outright. This year I project minimum sales of 5,000 copies—you do the math. I love this business!

- **Affiliate Programs**—Affiliate programs work two ways—you can have affiliates who sell your products and services and you pay them a commission on what they sell. Or... you become an affiliate for others whose products and services you sell and you earn a commission for selling to your list. Commissions from affiliate or revenue-sharing programs are a popular alternative, or supplement, to paid advertising. A large collection of <u>affiliate program resources</u> is available in the *Roadmap to Riches* to help get you started.

- **Advertising**—The sale of E-Zine advertising is a far distant second to product sales—but still a lucrative source of E-Zine revenue. Ad sales are the only source of revenue for many E-zines. You can either sell your own advertising or have your ad inventory brokered by one or more E-Zine ad networks. I generally use the advertising space in my E-Zine to sell my own products—it makes me more revenue than selling the ad space would. The ads you see in my E-Zines are mostly ads for my JV partners. I also run ads for products I use and have found to be exceptional.

- **Subscription Fees**—While the great majority of E-Zines are free, there are some very successful paid-subscription e-mail publications. The free model works so well that I haven't tried the paid model yet—but it is on the plan for next year. There is more on free versus paid below.

- **Content-Based Revenue**—Some of your revenue may come directly from the content you produce. Potential sources of content-based revenue include syndication, sold access to your E-Zine archives, or even the sale of books/e-books and other information products that are derived from your E-Zine's content.

- **Joint Ventures**—Doing a JV with another E-Zine publisher who will write an endorsed letter of my product to his list is nirvana (publishers' heaven). You pay him a commission (make him a special affiliate) for each sale he makes to his list. If his letter is compelling and his list is made up of people who are legitimate prospects for your product the percentage of visitors will be staggeringly high. You will collect most of their names by offering them something of value in exchange for their name and e-mail address so you build your list. And... the sales will be high as well.

- **Selling Your E-Zine**—While this was rare, it is now a booming business. Several publishers have had success with creating and growing an e-mail publication and then selling it to a larger company. I recommend you create your E-Zine with the sole purpose of selling it somewhere down the road, it is a business asset that you can live off of now, and harvest the business value later by selling it.

When determining the sources of revenue for your own E-Zine, I recommend that you integrate as many as possible without losing your focus. A revenue

---

Advertising is selling Twinkies to adults.

DONALD R. VANCE
Author

model based on multiple "profit pillars" will be much more stable, especially if one source of revenue should dry up due to market conditions or something else beyond your control.

FREE OR PAID E-ZINE?

There is a great debate going on about free versus paid newsletters/E-Zines. Should I offer a free E-Zine or a paid E-Zine? It really depends upon what the focus of your E-Zine is going to be. Do you want to produce income through sales of your products or services in your E-Zine—and maybe some nice ad revenue. Or do you want to produce income from the subscription to the E-Zine itself?

So, why don't more E-Zine publishers charge a subscription fee for their publication? This question is usually asked by folks new to the E-Zine publishing business, who are used to print publications that always charge an annual or monthly subscription fee.

But it's definitely a valid question. Why is it that the great majority of e-mail publications are available for free?

The primary reason is that E-Zine publishers are usually able to make a decent amount of money selling products and advertising in their publications. By charging a subscription fee, they would be severely limiting their audience, as a lot less people would subscribe.

If you're considering a paid-subscription e-mail publication, make sure you do some projections first:

Say you think you could generate 1000 paying subscribers in your publication's first year of existence, each of whom would pay you US$20 for your E-Zine. Will the US$20,000 you generate cover all of your expenses and give you the profit you want, and will it be more beneficial than publishing a free, ad-supported E-Zine?.

For the same publishing effort, you might be able to generate 50,000 subscribers to a free E-Zine. If that E-Zine was published weekly, and you sold only a single ad spot at an average of a US$30. CPM (cost per thousand impressions), you would already be looking at US$78,000 per year in ad revenue. You would additionally benefit from more referred Web site traffic, increased exposure for yourself, greater potential secondary revenue (affiliate program sales, etc.), and an abundance of helpful reader feedback.

A factor of 50 in number of subscribers to a free E-Zine compared to an E-Zine selling for US$20 is not at all far-fetched. People on the Net are easily that many times more inclined to take something similar for free instead of paying for it.

If you publish a paid-subscription E-Zine, and your competition comes along and offers a free E-Zine with equal quality information, which one will potential subscribers choose?

Yet despite the argument above, paid subscription E-Zines can be successful, and I'm not at all against the practice of publishing them, in the right context.

There are quite a few successful paid-subscription e-mail newsletters on the topics of stocks, IPOs, unclaimed domains, and search engine news. But these are

> You only get out what you put in.
>
> ANONYMOUS

Entrepreneurship is the last refuge for the trouble-making individual.

JAMES K. GLASSMAN
Columnist

in addition to the 1000s of free e-mail publications, on the same topics as the paid versions. These free E-Zines are quite clearly fundamental in driving subscriptions to the paid versions.

And that's the approach that stands the best chance of success: Offer a paid version only after you have a successful free E-Zine or two under your belt. Learn the craft with a free E-Zine first and built it up. Then try converting your free subscribers to a paid subscriptions. Just be prepared to lose 80 percent of your subscriber base when you do.

By starting with a paid-subscription E-Zine, you'll miss out on the incredible traffic-building potential of a free E-Zine. You'll also miss out on many word-of-mouth referrals, affiliate program sales, and wonderful abundance of educational reader feedback on your E-Zine.

The bottom line reason why you need to publish your own E-Zine—whether it is a free or paid E-Zine—is that it is one of the easiest ways to see continued profits on-line or off-line. They are virtually the perfect on-line selling machines! There is no question in my mind that this is an absolute necessity if you want to earn **substantial** monthly income on the web.

Now turn to Step #53 "E-Zine, the On-Line Silver Bullet"
in your *Roadmap to Riches* workbook.

Building Your E-Zine as an Asset

Your E-Zine will serve as an outstanding platform for joint venture deals. These two breakthroughs (E-Zine marketing and joint venture marketing) give just about anybody the opportunity to gain total financial independence, regardless of your formal education (or lack of) and other superficial barriers to institutionalized advancements. In other words, what I am trying to say is . . . you (and I don't care who you are) can make a very nice income by starting your own E-Zine.

This section give you 10 powerful ideas for growing your E-Zine. Here are some ways to rapidly build your E-Zine . . .

1. Create a private membership site

Another great way to use your articles is to create your own private membership site. There are two methods of doing this; both offer a unique method of generating more profits.

Free. If you use this as a free membership site, you can generate profits in several ways. You can include links and banners on each page of your website. You can require the visitor to purchase a product of yours in order to gain access to the free site. You can require the visitor to subscribe to your E-Zine before they obtain access (subscribers = future customers!). If you aren't planning to do any "polishing" to your articles, then I recommend you go this route.

Paid. The other method is to have people pay to join the membership site. In this scenario you would charge a fee, either monthly or annually. The fee based on how much information you are including. You will definitely want to "polish" your articles. You may consider purchasing reprint rights to several high-quality information products to add to the membership site to create more perceived value. Your RTR workbook is a good place to find out how and where to get other products.

2. Survey Your Readers

Ask them, how can I provide better service? What am I doing right? How can I improve? What would you like to see me do? Ask your subscribers what your strengths and weaknesses are. Find out their opinions on what would make your E-Zine better.

And not only your E-Zine, ask them about your business—what would make it better? Ask them to critique your website or sales letter. Get them to offer their opinion on what you are doing on-line and off-line as well. Using their feedback to improve your service will make it easier to attract new subscribers.

> When people talk listen completely. Most people never listen.
>
> ERNEST HEMINGWAY
> American novelist

> Quit telling your clients what they need. Ask them what they want.
>
> SAM BOWERS
> TEC Speaker

An essential aspect of creativity is not being afraid to fail.

DR. EDWIN LAID

3. Write for Other E-Zines

This is one of my favorites. Many E-Zine owners are too timid or unwilling to try to write any of their own articles, so they publish other people's articles in their E-Zine. Other E-Zine owners publish their own content but also like to feature articles from other authors as well. So there is a big demand for E-Zine articles out there—and it is quite easy to get your article published in a number of E-Zines. Each article you write, that is used in someone else's E-Zine, has your resource box at the end directing them to your website. That's a great traffic builder.

I recommend you subscribe to as many E-Zines related to your field as possible. And as you receive the various issues, mark the E-Zines that you feel might accept an article from you—and list the contact information of the publishers of those E-Zines. E-mail them and tell them why you enjoy being a subscriber to their E-Zine. Give them a little positive feedback, massage their egos a bit.

Then when you have an article ready that is appropriate for their audience, write to them and say that you have included this new article. Tell them that they are free to publish it in their E-Zine so long as the article and the resource box remain unchanged. In my experience, this technique helps to bring in exactly the new subscribers I want.

Benefits of Submitting Articles to Other E-Zines

- You can help brand your web site, business and yourself by submitting articles to other E-Zines. You can include your name, business name, your USP, web site address and e-mail address in your resource box.
- You will become known as an expert on the topics you write about. This will give you and your business extra credibility which will help your product sales.
- Your article might also be placed on the publisher's home page. If they publish each issue on their home page this gives you great extra exposure.
- You might get extra exposure if the E-Zine publisher archives your E-Zine on their site. People might want to read the back issues before they make the decision to subscribe to your E-Zine.
- You get free advertising to their entire subscriber base.
- You could get extra income from people wanting to hire you to write other articles, books, or be asked to speak at seminars. This is a great way to multiply your exposure and income.
- You could allow other E-Zine publishers to publish your articles in their free e-books. Since people give them away, your advertising could multiply all over the internet like a virus.
- You will get your article published all over the web when you submit it to an E-Zine publisher that has a free content directory on their web site. They'll allow their visitors to republish your article.
- You'll gain people's trust. If they read your article and like it, they won't be as hesitant to buy your product or service.
- You could get your article guaranteed to run in another E-Zine. You agree to run one of their articles in your E-Zine if, in exchange, they run yours in their E-Zine. It's a win/win situation.

The skill of writing is to create a context in which other people can think.

EDWIN SCHLOSSBERG

In the RTR are a dozen resources where you can find E-Zines related to your subject or theme.

4. Create an Auto Responder Course

If you have a pool of 1000 suspects/prospects, statistics show that on average, it takes 10 contacts with that pool of suspects/prospects before everyone who will ever buy will make a purchase.

You will get some the first time, more the second time, and even more the third and fourth time you run an ad. Then the response drops off and by the 10th ad anyone who was going to buy has now done so. I don't know why this is true but as a marketer who tests everything, I know it to be true from my experience.

The National Sales Association provided these statistics:

> 2% of sales are made on the 1st contact
>
> 3% of sales are made on the 2nd contact
>
> 5% of sales are made on the 3rd contact
>
> 10% of sales are made on the 4th contact
>
> 80% of sales are made on the 5th–12th contact

Bottom line: The key marketing success strategy is to follow-up, then follow-up again and again on a regular basis with your existing contacts.

A great way to do this is to create an auto responder course. (For more information on auto responders, visit your RTR) My recommendation is to setup an 8 to 12 message course. For each day's message, use one of your existing articles. If you have a long article you might break it into 8 to 9 pieces and use each piece as a separate part of the course.

Throughout the entire course, with each day's message, provide a brief opening and closing—before and after the main article. In the opening and closing paragraphs, mention your main product. You will also want to include the website link so people will be able to easily find their way to your product. See exactly how to do it in your RTR workbook.

5. Promote Your E-Zine on Your Website

This seems so obvious but some don't do it. Every page of my website includes a form which allows my visitors to subscribe to my E-Zine. Do the same thing on your website—or at least make your E-Zine prevalent on your website. This isn't so much a technique for building your E-Zine, as it is a foundation for the other techniques. Also, many of the websites, where you can list your E-Zine, require or request the URL of a web page that includes subscription information for your E-Zine—so it is important to include information about your E-Zine, in your website. Let's face it, after you finally got someone to visit your website, it's vital to get their contact information so you can pull them back to become a customer.

6. Create a viral marketing tool with your back issues

Viral marketing is a popular item on-line because it works. The idea of passing your marketing on to someone else, and they pass it on to someone else, and they pass it on to someone else is an exciting one. You may have spread the advertising to

---

As CEO's, we tend to be pathologically positive.

DAN WERTENBERG
TEC Speaker

Ask and it shall be given unto you.

GOD

only ten people, but if each of those did the same and so on, in a short time the marketing can be passed on to thousands of people as it takes on a life of its own.

The easiest way to produce the viral marketing effect is by publishing a free e-Book. Offer the free e-Book to others and they in turn offer it to others and so forth down the line. Soon, the e-Book (if it's a high quality one) will be downloaded into the hands of thousands of readers.

I've heard that Mark Joyner created an e-Book that was downloaded over one million times—I hope that's true but even if you discount it by 75 percent that's still a quarter of a million copies. Wow! It's easy to take your archived issues and compile them into an e-Book. Include links to your products and other affiliate programs, as well as banners at the top and bottom of each page which are also linked to websites you earn profits from. And you begin giving it away as a freebie by promoting it, and allow others to do the same.

Note. Get permission. If you are going to publish your back issues in a free e-Book and you have published someone else's articles in your newsletters, then make sure you get their permission to include the article in your e-Book. Most will gladly accept the free advertising, but don't take this for granted. Ask first.

An e-book will work best if you use your own original articles. In fact, it will work best if you don't include the entire back issue, but just the articles themselves. If each of the articles is targeted towards one audience, you can develop a great free e-Book.

If you are going to publish your entire back issue, then consider seeing if your advertisers will be interested in paying a small fee to be included. Instead of the one-time mailing of your issue which they paid for, they now have the opportunity to get their advertisement published in thousands of copies of the e-Book.

Some will be interested in the small fee for inclusion. If you don't feel comfortable doing it this way, then raise your advertising prices slightly and explain that the back issues will be developed into an e-Book so that their advertising will continue to gain exposure. Even if you don't want to charge extra, at least mention it—that way they'll know they are getting a bonus when they advertise with your E-Zine. To learn all about creating your own e-book just turn to your RTR workbook.

7. Cross-Marketing

Cross-marketing reduces the need for spending money in marketing, and pushes "buttons" that allow you to pull far higher ad responses than traditional marketing methods. Once you have over a thousand subscribers you may want to build your E-Zine with cross-marketing.

There are basically three forms of cross-marketing; endorsement, simple ad exchange, and content contribution.

1. Endorsement cross-marketing is when Publisher A endorses Publisher B, and then Publisher B endorses Publisher A. If you enter into such a marketing relationship, there are certain conditions to follow. First, only endorse a product worthy of endorsement.

2. The basic ad exchange, if you're only endorsing each other's E-Zines, no exchange of money is needed. You each write and ad for your own

E-Zine and run it in the other's publication. But, if you endorse each other's products, then you need to operate on a per-sale commission basis. Sign up as each others affiliate and the affiliate software handles all the details, and gives each of you a report on the sales, and automatically cuts you each a check.

3. Content contribution cross-marketing has been used by many E-Zine owners to gain large subscription bases. This process takes places when Publisher A agrees to publish the work of Publisher B, and Publisher B does the same for Publisher A. If you have an E-Zine, you might form an alliance with another E-Zine owner wherein he supplies you with a guest article to publish in addition to your own articles, and you do the same for him. The growth comes in when you write a compelling article and include a resource box at the end of the article.

My experience tells me that when you develop these relationships, you'll find it to be more profitable than anything else. Most other E-Zine owners know this. There are forums devoted to getting publishers together to arrange just such relationships and make these win–win deals. The RTR lists the forums you should visit.

Unfortunately, it would be beyond the scope of this chapter to touch on all the ways to make money with cross-marketing in coordination with publishing your E-Zine. New methods are being tried every week so watch your RTR for the latest developments.

8. Per-Subscriber Advertising

How much is one subscriber worth to you?

For every 1,000 subscribers you have, you can charge about US$30. for an ad in your E-Zine. If you have 1,000 subscribers and charge $30 for each ad, and sell 5 ads per issue, you make US$150. per issue. If you publish weekly, that's 52 weeks times US$150. = US$7,800. divided by 12 months = US$0.65 a month from advertising revenue. Therefore, each subscriber is worth US$0.65 per month to you—US$7.80 per year on advertising alone. When you have 20,000 subscribers times US$7.80 annual value of 1 subscriber = US$156,000. per year in ad revenue. This is serious money and it is entirely possible for you to accomplish this within a year or two.

9. Point Of Subscription "Joint-Offers"

Here's an easy way to double, triple or explode your subscription rate from your website.

As you'll notice, when you submit your address into my "Free Subscription" form, you're taken to a page where you're offered subscriptions to other E-Zines you might be interested in also. There is a brief description of each one and a check box. Check as many as you want and you are automatically subscribed to all that you want. "Feel free to try them all—unsubscribe at any time." This is nothing more than a twist on the basic Joint Venture concept and it works for all the JV partners who use it. Each JV partner offers the same multiple subscription form on his site. As you acquire more and more subscriptions you will be able to approach publishers with larger lists and the program works even better—and grows your list even larger. See your RTR for complete instructions.

> With money, you are wise, you are handsome, and you sing well too.
>
> YIDDISH PROVERB

10. Reformat Your Content For Extra Sales

Too many people miss out on more profits because they think inside the box. Simply by reformatting your present content you can make many additional sales at high profit.

What kind of reformatting am I talking about? Think about these... **A printed manual.** Simply print out your great articles, a table of contents, head out to your favorite copy shop and print up some manuals. It should cost you about three cents a page. A 100-page manual, with binding can be duplicated for around $4.00. Sell it for $19.95 (or more) and you've got a nice profit maker. In higher print volumes you can get the cost down to under a half dollar.

Audio Cassettes. Read the articles and record onto a cassette. Many people purchase cassettes at seminars and don't mind paying $7–$20 a copy, depending upon length and content. Considering you can have them produced for less than fifty cents a piece, that's another nice profit stream. Now that cassettes are losing favor record in MP3 format or just put them on a CD you can mail.

Compact Discs. Burn the articles onto a CD. Of course, you'll need the equipment to do this one. You can purchase an external writable CD drive for about $150 at your favorite computer store, which usually also includes labeling software. Blank CDs can be purchased for about twenty cents each. See the profit here?

DVDs. It is now easy to produce your own DVD versions of your material and include video clips, audio, motion, special effects and other wow factors. The perceived value of a DVD is quite high in relation to other technologies. Video Tapes. Turn your articles into an actual presentation as if you were speaking live to a seminar audience. Have someone video your presentation. You've got another nice product from the same information! Videos can go from $10-$50 a piece, depending upon length and content. These can also be put on to DVDs for and sold for a premium price.

Combination package. Of course, you can really see some significant profits when you combine several of these together into a package. A cassette, printed manual, a CD, a video tape/DVD combination can command hundreds of dollars per package. I also have my website, E-Zine, and books translated for sale and download in numerous other languages. There are always foreign entrepreneurs looking for good material and they are willing to license fees to have great content. I recommend you look into this as an additional source of income as well.

Now turn to Step #54 "Building Your E-Zine as an Asset" in your *Roadmap to Riches* workbook.